T0270710

Capital Flows Without Crisis?

The last decade has seen a massive increase in international capital flows to emerging markets. This development has offered opportunities to those countries that have opened themselves up to overseas capital, but it has also created risks. These risks have been powerfully demonstrated by a series of financial crises in many different parts of the world. The result has been a much greater focus on the challenges of delivering domestic economic stability in a world where large and rapid movements of financial capital are now possible, particularly for developing countries.

In this volume a team of policymakers and academics from fourteen different countries, as well as representatives of the international financial institutions primarily responsible for responding to the crises, examines the challenges and options facing policymakers today. The book includes both detailed analysis of individual economies from around the world to understand how they have coped with the dilemmas raised by increased capital mobility and in-depth analysis of the broad systemic issues of why crises occur and how we can prevent them.

By analysing economies from many different parts of the world, the book provides a broad and comprehensive look at the similarities and differences in recent financial crises. The aim is to answer a central question: can policies be designed that allow countries to reap the gains from international capital without compromising domestic economic stability?

Dipak Dasgupta is Sector Manager, Economic Policy in the Middle East and North Africa region of the World Bank, and a member of its Economic Policy Board. **Marc Uzan** is the Executive Director and the Founder of the Reinventing Bretton Woods Committee. **Dominic Wilson** is an International Economist at Goldman Sachs, Hong Kong.

Routledge studies in the modern world economy

Capital Flows Without Crisis?
Reconciling capital mobility and economic stability

Edited by Dipak Dasgupta, Marc Uzan
and Dominic Wilson

Routledge
Taylor & Francis Group

LONDON AND NEW YORK

First published 2001 by Routledge
2 Park Square, Milton Park, Abingdon, Oxon, OX14 4RN

Simultaneously published in the USA and Canada
by Routledge
270 Madison Ave, New York NY 10016

Routledge is an imprint of the Taylor & Francis Group

Transferred to Digital Printing 2005

Typeset in Garamond by Asia Pacific Press at The Australian National University

British Library Cataloguing in Publication Data
A catalogue record for this book is available from the British Library

Library of Congress Cataloging in Publication Data
Dasgupta, Dipak.
   Capital flows without crisis?: reconciling capital mobility and economic stability/
Dipak Dasgupta, Marc Uzan & Dominic Wilson.
   p. cm. -- (Routledge studies in the modern world economy ; 31)
Includes bibliographical references and index.

   1. Capital movements. 2. International finance. 3. Financial crises. 4. Economic
stabilization. I. Uzan, Marc. II. Wilson, Dominic. III. Title. IV. Series.

HG3891 .D373 2001
332'.042--dc21

                                                                        00-065305

ISBN 0-415-25479-5
Publisher's Note
This book has been prepared from electronic files provided by the editors.

Contents

Figures

Tables

Contributors

István Ábel, Division Head, Monetary Policy Department, National Bank of Hungary

Prema-Chandra Athukorala, Senior Fellow, Economics Division, RSPAS, Asia Pacific School of Economics and Management, The Australian National University

Matthieu Bussière, Senior Economist, International Monetary Fund

Eliana Cardoso, Lead Economist, World Bank

Zsolt Darvas, Senior Researcher, Economics and Research Department, National Bank of Hungary

Dipak Dasgupta, Task Manager, *Global Development Finance*, World Bank, Development Prospects Group

J. Soedradjad Djiwandono, Visiting Professor, Harvard Institute for Development

Uri Dadush, Director, Development Prospects Group, World Bank

Ross Garnaut, Professor, RSPAS, Asia Pacific School of Economics and Management, The Australian National University

Stephen Grenville, Deputy Governor, Reserve Bank of Australia

Ann Helwege, Professor of Economics, Tufts University

Yiping Huang, Economics Division, RSPAS, Asia Pacific School of Economics and Management, The Australian National University

Gregor Irwin, Fellow in Economics, Lady Margaret Hall, University of Oxford

Grzegorz W. Kolodko, Visiting Scholar, IMF, Warsaw School of Economics and Former Deputy Premier and Finance Minister of Poland

Ross H. McLeod, Fellow, Indonesia Project, RSPAS, Asia Pacific School of Economics and Management, The Australian National University and Editor of *Bulletin of Indonesian Economic Studies*

Marcus Miller, Professor of Economics, University of Warwick

Christian Mulder, Senior Economist, International Monetary Fund

Vladimir Popov, Professor of Economics, Moscow Academy of National Economy

Hak K. Pyo, Professor of Economics, Seoul National University and University of Tokyo

Rogelio Ramirez de la O, Director General, Ecanal SA

Ligang Song, Fellow and Director, China Economy and Business Program, RSPAS, Asia Pacific School of Economics and Management, The Australian National University

Marc Uzan, Executive Director, Reinventing Bretton Woods Committee

David Vines, Director, Global Economic Institutions Research Program, ESRC

George Vojta, Vice Chairman, Bankers Trust Corporation

Nancy Wagner, Senior Economist, International Monetary Fund

Peter G. Warr, John Crawford Professor of Agricultural Economics, RSPAS, Asia Pacific School of Economics and Management, The Australian National University

Dominic Wilson, International Economist, Goldman Sachs

Lei Zhang, Professor of Economics, University of Warwick

Abbreviations

ASEAN	Association of South East Asian Nations
CEFTA	Central European Free Trade Agreement
CIS	Commonwealth of Independent States
CPI	consumer price index
FDI	foreign direct investment
GDP	gross domestic product
GNI	gross national income
GNP	gross national product
IMF	International Monetary Fund
LIBOR	London Inter-Bank Offered Rate
NAFTA	North American Free Trade Agreement
OECD	Organisation for Economic Cooperation and Development
OPEC	Organisation of the Petroleum Exporting Countries
PPI	producer price index
PRI	Partido Revolucionario Institucional
RPI	retail price index
WTO	World Trade Organisation

Editors' Introduction

THE CONTEXT

Rapid economic liberalisation in emerging markets, which gathered pace in the late 1980s and early 1990s, coupled with ongoing technological progress in transport and communications, has resulted in sharply increasing trade and financial integration of developing countries with global markets in recent years. The number of developing countries considered as 'emerging' markets (or significant investment targets for international investors) has increased from a handful in 1986 to 31 in 1998, covering virtually all the large developing countries, including China, India, Russia, Indonesia and Brazil. There has been a massive increase in international private capital flows to these countries (Table 1). Net long-term annual private flows increased from about US$43 billion in 1990 to a peak of about US$304 billion in 1997 (World Bank 2000). In the process, these flows have far surpassed net official flows of about US$30–60 billion annually.

These developments have yielded significant benefits to developing countries, increasing investment opportunities and bringing financial and productive innovation. But they have also created new risks, especially with regard to private capital flows and vulnerability to sudden external shocks. In particular, the combination of domestic political instability, policy and institutional weaknesses, and global capital market imperfections, has led to several recent episodes of sudden, large and rapid capital outflows, precipitating deep economic and financial crises—especially in countries with weak domestic banking sectors.

Recent crises have also been accompanied by marked evidence of contagion as crises in one country have spilled over to other countries in the same region and elsewhere because of increased trade and financial integration.

There are two main implications of this increased volatility. The first is the increased probability of financial crises in developing countries that have become more reliant on volatile capital flows. The number of financial crises increased throughout the 1980s and especially the 1990s (World Bank 1999). Virtually all 31 countries identified as emerging markets in the 1990s have experienced at least one incident of loss of external liquidity as a consequence of financial crises. The second implication is that a crisis in any one country is now known to increase the probability of a crisis in other countries in the same region or elsewhere, because of contagion and rising covariance in asset markets.

The recent financial crises that began in East Asia in July 1997, and spread to Russia and Latin America in 1998 and 1999, have dramatically revealed the extent of these risks. This set of crises is only one of a longer sequence of similar events that include the Mexican crisis of 1994, the debt crises of the 1980s and indeed a string of financial crises stretching back to the nineteenth century during various periods of international capital mobility. Country after country has found that sudden reversals in international capital flows create huge policy dilemmas and frequently result in economic crisis, with large losses in output, jobs and social welfare that are often very costly and which themselves may engender much wider social and political upheaval.

THE AIM OF THE BOOK

The experience of the last two years—and of earlier episodes of crisis—demonstrates that the integration of emerging economies into the global financial system poses much larger policy challenges than had previously been anticipated. The early 1990s will be remembered for the euphoria that emerged about the benefits of financial liberalisation, private capital flows and emerging markets. It is now clear that the benefits and risks can be quite finely balanced, particularly for developing countries, and that for countries to exploit the potential gains from access to foreign capital requires a more complex set of preconditions than has typically been acknowledged in the past.

Given recent experience, it is unsurprising that the challenge of reconciling international capital mobility with domestic economic stability has now emerged as the most pressing and controversial topic in international economics and policymaking. The turbulence in international financial markets has prompted a wide range of efforts to improve the international financial system. In their struggle to find solutions to a rapidly changing environment, policymakers are considering a wide range of options from minor tinkering to a radical overhaul of the international financial architecture.

Table 1 Net long-term flows to developing countries, 1990–8 (US$billion)

	1990	1991	1992	1993	1994	1995	1996	1997	1998[a]
Net long-term resource flows	100.8	123.1	152.3	220.2	223.6	254.9	308.1	338.0	275.0
Official flows	56.9	62.6	54.0	53.3	45.5	53.4	32.2	39.1	47.9
Private flows	43.9	60.5	98.3	167.0	178.1	201.5	275.9	299.0	227.1
Private debt flows	15.7	18.6	38.1	49.0	54.4	60.0	100.3	105.3	58.0
Commercial banks	3.2	4.8	16.3	3.3	13.9	32.4	43.7	60.1	25.1
Bonds	1.2	10.8	11.1	37.0	36.7	26.6	53.5	42.6	30.2
Other	11.4	3.0	10.7	8.6	3.7	1.0	3.0	2.6	2.7
Portfolio equity flows	3.7	7.6	14.1	51.0	35.2	36.1	49.2	30.2	14.1
Foreign direct investment	24.5	34.4	46.1	67.0	88.5	105.4	126.4	163.4	155.0

Notes: [a]Preliminary.
Source: World Bank, Debtor Reporting System.

In this volume, a team of policymakers and academics from 14 countries and authors from international financial institutions examine the challenges and the options for reconciling international capital mobility with domestic economic stability. Thirteen papers analyse the broad systemic issues of why crises occur and the ways to manage and prevent them. Another eleven papers provide detailed analysis of the experience of individual economies from around the world to understand how they have coped with policy dilemmas raised by increased capital mobility.

The key feature of the volume is the breadth of its coverage. Despite the common elements that run through many recent financial crises, it is clear that there have been substantial differences in experience across countries. Since the effects of and responses to financial crisis varied greatly from country to country, comparison of individual experiences can provide valuable insights into the most appropriate ways to manage future challenges. The country experiences draw on those as recent as the crisis in Brazil in early 1999. These experiences are used to answer some key questions about the difficulties of accommodating international capital flows without compromising domestic economic stability.

The central question that the book addresses is whether policies can be designed that allow economies to reap the gains from greater access to international capital while minimising the risk that international capital flows will compromise domestic economic stability. Achieving this balance involves tackling systemic issues as well as maintaining suitable domestic policy settings.

SYSTEMIC ISSUES

Understanding vulnerability

We are still some way from a complete understanding of the sources of volatility in capital flows to emerging markets and of the systemic causes of vulnerability. Identifying the causes of volatility for the various types of capital flows and understanding the risks they pose is essential to informed policymaking. For example, if it can be shown that the volatility of capital flows is especially acute for short-term capital flows, then greater focus on these flows is justified. If volatility is related to intrinsic imperfections in global capital markets such as information asymmetries and the absence of complete risk markets, then more systemic international intervention may be needed. Risks may also vary according to domestic circumstances. Where volatility is found to be related to domestic financial market failure, the appropriate sequencing of financial sector reform and capital account opening must be reexamined.

Part 1 of the book addresses these kinds of issues. Dipak Dasgupta and Uri Dadush discuss the evidence for and reasons behind the higher degree of volatility in capital flows to developing countries. They also examine the tendency for flows to operate procyclically, heightening booms and deepening busts. Stephen Grenville discusses issues of international capital market failure, the role of highly leveraged institutions, and the need for improvement in the international financial architecture. Marcus Miller and Lei Zhang examine the theoretical case for capital account liberalisation in the presence of financial sector weakness and deposit guarantees. They emphasise the need to proceed cautiously and to condition the degree of capital account liberalisation on the quality of banking regulation.

Crisis management

A second set of systemic issues relates to the role of national and international authorities in crisis management. The role of central banks is often at the heart of managing national financial crises since a run by international creditors is often coincident with or caused by a run on the assets of the domestic banking system. Their management of national liquidity needs is also central to preventing and managing crises. Because domestic resources may not be sufficient, these resources may need to be supplemented in a crisis by recourse to an international lender of last resort or liquidity from international financial institutions.

Despite the need for international assistance in a number of crisis economies, the role and prescriptions of international financial institutions has come under criticism. The conventional remedy to currency crises was to advocate tight monetary and fiscal policy to restore investor confidence and improve the external balance. Although tightening policies may help to signal to markets that policy 'slippage' will not occur, there are risks that investor confidence may be more severely damaged by the fall in economic activity brought about by austerity programs. In the Asian economies, tight policies were gradually reversed as the depth of the recessions became apparent. At the same time, faster than anticipated recovery in some crisis economies in Asia and elsewhere may have restored some credibility to these conventional remedies in some circumstances.

Part 2 of the book looks at these issues of crisis prevention and management. Soedradjad Djiwandono discusses the problems of central bank independence in managing national financial crises, in the context of Indonesia. In crises, the independence of central banks is deeply impaired and they may find themselves without the resources to act effectively as a lender of last resort. Matthieu Bussière and Chris Mulder discuss the effectiveness of maintaining a high degree of national liquidity, albeit at considerable costs, as a way to offset weaknesses in fundamentals and the effects of contagion. David Vines and Gregor Irwin discuss the inherent pitfalls and problems of international policy advice and conditionality that accompany the provision of supplementary international liquidity. They also examine the risk that forced fiscal and financial contractions to exacerbate domestic economic downturns while failing to stem the loss of investor confidence.

DOMESTIC POLICY SETTINGS

Having addressed these general systemic issues, the rest of the volume then turns to the varied set of country experiences that form the core of the book. Despite some superficial similarities, there are also striking differences in the causes and responses to financial crisis. In some cases, crises had their roots in unsustainable government policies or simple exchange rate overvaluation. In others, the behaviour of private investors and weaknesses in financial systems were more important.

In each of the country studies, the purpose is to focus on addressing a number of important questions. How can countries best reconcile the scale and volatility of private capital movements with domestic goals, particularly with respect to exchange rate settings? What macroeconomic policies are best suited to support and sustain an open capital account while maintaining domestic stability? What is the appropriate sequencing of capital account opening in developing economies? And what are the institutional preconditions for developing economies to pursue financial openness successfully?

Managing the exchange rate

An important set of issues surround the question of appropriate exchange rate policies (including exit strategies from a particular choice that may have become inappropriate). Do fixed exchange rate policies and defenses of such fixed exchange rates, make the problem of domestic economic instability worse? Would a shift to a floating exchange rate system reduce the problems of preventing or managing financial crises on the capital account? Fixed exchange rates can be useful as a nominal anchor for inflation control and to ensure stability in international economic transactions. But exchange-rate based stabilisation often leaves the exchange rate overvalued and adhering to a fixed exchange rate with an open capital account in the face of speculative attacks can be very difficult. Without massive and usually unsustainable intervention in foreign exchange markets, countries may be faced with either large devaluation or a painful tightening of monetary policy, or both. In addition, fixed exchange rates can, in conjunction with other market failures, encourage firms to gamble on exchange rate stability and take on large currency exposures. The ability to defend exchange rates may also be compromised by banking sector weakness. Where the banking system is fragile, authorities may be reluctant to increase interest rates in defense of the currency.

Vladimir Popov's discussion of Russia's crisis in 1998 and Eliana Cardoso's description of the Brazilian crisis of January 1999 give prominence to the difficulties induced by fixed or pegged exchange rates as a reason for subsequent crises—in both cases following exchange-rate based stabilisation programs. Peter Warr's treatment of the Thai case and Ross McLeod's analysis of Indonesia's crisis also suggest that greater exchange rate flexibility might have reduced the chances of crisis. Rogelio Ramirez de la O's paper on Mexico, Istvan Abel's discussion of Hungary's experience and Nancy Wagner's study of Poland all argue that floating exchange rates were at least one reason why these latter countries avoided financial crisis in the most recent episode. Indeed, the Polish case provides an example of a country that has gradually introduced greater flexibility to its exchange rate system without precipitating a crisis.

Monetary and fiscal policies

The second key macroeconomic question concerns the appropriate settings for fiscal and monetary policies both before and during financial crises. The adjustment of domestic policy in the face of large capital inflows is particularly important. Under fixed exchange rates, monetary policy may prove relatively ineffective. Several of the papers dealing with the East Asian crisis countries indicate that efforts to sterilise short-term capital flows under conditions of high capital account openness will push domestic interest rates higher, encourage further flows and exacerbate booms and domestic asset price bubbles. Raising policy interest rates may thus be a very direct and damaging means by which international volatility may be transferred to domestic conditions, amplifying booms and busts.

A possible alternative—given the problems of using monetary policy—would be for fiscal policy to be more flexible, and accommodate or adjust to the volatility of international capital flows. Eliana Cardoso's paper on Brazil and some of the other country papers show that fiscal policy adjustments may be difficult in practice. Fiscal policy is a much more slowly moving target variable than capital flows—which are highly volatile—and fiscal policy is also at least in part endogenous and typically tends to be pro-cyclical.

The appropriate monetary response to a crisis also presents difficult choices. Ross McLeod discusses the problems of monetary policy incoherence in Indonesia's crisis management. Other papers also question the wisdom of a sharp tightening of monetary policy in a crisis. Brazil's experience offers an example of a country where interest rate hikes have been relatively successful. In Brazil's case, the currency stabilised, and inflation fell, allowing interest rates to be lowered and, while the economy did fall into recession, the length and size of the downturn were not nearly as large as predicted.

The openness of the capital account

The last two years have seen renewed attention given to the problems of open capital accounts for developing economies. Indeed, since the crisis in Thailand began, many prominent policymakers and economists have advocated some forms of capital control as tools for reducing the volatility and negative effects of capital movements. Related to this are issues of the design of capital control measures, including their efficacy and their value as a temporary measure during a sudden crisis. At one level, it is always possible for national policies to limit the extent of the impact of international capital flow volatility through *dirigiste* capital controls that effectively insulate an economy altogether from significant influence of international capital flows. But for most countries this is unlikely to be an efficient response. The more useful or interesting question is whether market-oriented or indirect instruments can be employed that achieve both the gains from wider access to international capital flows, while minimising the effect of volatility in international capital flows on domestic economic stability.

A number of country studies tackle these issues directly. The Malaysian experience, which saw controls on capital outflows imposed after the onset of crisis, receives generally favourable reviews in Prema-Chandra Athukorala's paper. Limits on certain forms of capital inflows are also relevant to the experience of Poland and other Central European economies. The evidence from Latin American experience, however, is more mixed.

The institutional preconditions for successful liberalisation

Beyond the narrow question of macroeconomic and capital account policies are deeper questions about fundamental institutional weaknesses in developing countries. Are excessive corruption, financial collusion, lack of transparency, close government-business ties, and lack of adequate accounting and legal frameworks important contributors to vulnerability? Are there some preconditions here that would reduce the vulnerability of developing countries to external loss-of-confidence shocks? Or are international capital markets much more capricious in the way they 'discipline' developing economies? In many cases, crises have been followed by comprehensive institutional reforms. Hak Pyo's paper on Korea provides a good discussion of post-crisis institution building issues.

Greater emphasis is also being placed on issues of sequencing. There is wide acceptance that effective prudential regulation must precede substantial opening of the capital account. The papers on the East Asian crisis economies stress the problems of rapid moves to capital account liberalisation with insufficient attention to the strength of the financial sector. Yiping Huang and Ligang Song discuss the contribution of China's heavily controlled capital account in mitigating the fall-out from crises elsewhere in the region. They argue that without considerable financial sector reform, further capital account liberalisation is a dangerous option.

Country experiences also illustrate that establishing a track record of institutional credibility may increase the available policy options in a crisis. In the wake of the Russian crisis, the National Bank of Poland did not increase interest rates to stem capital outflow and in fact went ahead with a scheduled cut in their benchmark rate. By doing this, they signalled to the market that they had confidence in the currency and the zloty strengthened after the rate decrease, precisely because the markets supported the authorities' judgement. In Brazil, by contrast, the recent history of inflation implied that lowering interest rates in the face of downward pressure on the currency was not an option. The savage market reaction in East Asia despite the authorities' long history of sensible management illustrates the difficulties that developing economies face in establishing institutional credibility.

LOOKING TO THE FUTURE

The volume ends with a set of forward-looking papers. National governments and international institutions are considering—and in some cases committing to—a wide variety of changes to policies and institutions. George Vojta discusses the role of the private sector in building a better and more stable framework for private capital flows. Grzegorz Kolozdko addresses the need to modify the policy advice given to developing economies in the light of recent experiences.

Finally, Ross Garnaut reflects on key themes from the earlier papers. He concludes that despite the many variants of financial crisis, important lessons can be drawn about how best to reconcile capital mobility and domestic economic stability in the future.

Part 1

Crises in a world of mobile capital

1 The benefits and risks of capital account opening in developing countries

Uri Dadush and Dipak Dasgupta[*]

Capital account opening and integration with global financial markets can enable countries to raise investment above levels that can be financed by domestic savings. Countries can also gain access to a broader range of financing options, including longer-term and equity finance, improve the allocation of their assets and diversify risks and smooth expenditures in the face of temporary shocks. Financial integration may also increase discipline of governments to correct policy weaknesses and benefit the economy in general due to the technological, management and labour productivity improvements associated with foreign investment.

But not all of these benefits may be realised by developing countries. For example, capital markets will not facilitate expenditure smoothing if access to global capital flows becomes suddenly limited in the face of adverse shocks, and may even have the opposite effect. Similarly, the disciplining role of capital flows may be capricious if contagion in international markets leads to capital flow reversals far beyond that which appears warranted by fundamentals (for example, in 1996–8 changes in net external finance forced a shift in the current account by almost 9 per cent of GDP in Korea and 19 per cent of GDP in Thailand). Capital inflows will not increase investment or productivity if the country receives mainly short-term capital flows (as distinct from foreign direct investment, for example) and must hold large stocks of reserves to protect against the risk of sudden outflows of short-term capital.

This chapter argues that the risks associated with capital account liberalisation in developing countries are much higher than in high income countries for four distinct reasons

- developing countries are marginally creditworthy borrowers, and can be shown to face much greater volatility in inflows

- capital flows to developing countries tend to behave pro-cyclically in times of strain, exacerbating rather than mitigating shocks originating in the real economy

- weaknesses in the financial sector and public finances of developing countries tend to amplify shocks originating in the capital account

- developing countries lack social safety nets, thus making the poor more vulnerable to such shocks.

The policy implication is that developing countries need to ensure that these risks are carefully managed so that capital account liberalisation can proceed safely. Managing the risks during the transition towards full capital account liberalisation implies that certain forms of capital inflow, because of their resilience, maturity and risk-sharing characteristics, are preferable to others during the transition period.

SPECIAL SOURCES OF RISK AFFECTING DEVELOPING COUNTRIES

The creditworthiness of developing countries is deemed (in global financial markets) to be much more marginal than that of industrial countries. There is a close relationship between income and credit rating, and more than three-quarters of fifty-one developing countries are rated below minimum investment grade (or junk-bond category), whereas most mature industrial countries are rated in the safest category (Moody's Investor Service 1998) (Figure 1.1). There appears to be a minimum income level (about US$10,000 per capita income in 1995 dollars) above which countries are assumed to have traversed into a solid investment grade credit rating. Under the World Bank definition, a country is developing if its income per capita is below US$9,655 (in 1997 dollars, World Bank 1999b). Some countries, oil exporters in the Middle East, Israel, Hong Kong-China, Greece and Argentina (classified as a developing country), appear to have special characteristics that raise their risk profile in the market despite their high incomes.

Figure 1.1 Creditworthiness of developing countries

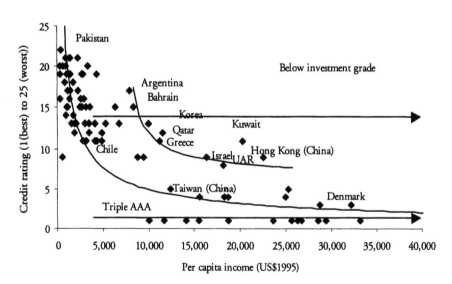

Per capita income (US$1995)

Notes: Ratings provided by Moody's Investor Service. Alphabetical ratings converted to numerical ratings by authors.
Source: Moody's Investor Service, 1998. Ratings and Rating Actions, Sovereign Ceilings for Foreign-Currency Ratings, 18 February. Online. Available HTTP: http://www.moodys.com. World Bank, 1999. *World Development Indicators*, World Bank, Washington, DC.

Reflecting their marginal creditworthiness in international financial markets and institutional weaknesses inherent in their underdevelopment, developing countries appear to face four main sources of risk from capital account liberalisation and financial market integration.

GREATER VOLATILITY IN CAPITAL FLOWS

Small open developing countries (such as Indonesia or Argentina), which are marginally creditworthy, face a very different set of risks from global financial markets than mature industrial countries (such as Canada or Sweden). The volatility of flows to developing countries is potentially larger (Figure 1.2). Observed capital flows provide only an indirect indication of the volatility of autonomous capital flows, since they also reflect shifts originating in the current account, such as terms of trade shocks.

The volatility of capital flows can, however, also be measured indirectly through price variables, such as exchange rates, spreads on sovereign bonds and stockmarket prices. There is a dramatically greater volatility in spreads on sovereign bonds for a large number of developing countries than for industrial countries (Figure 1.3). Further, there is close relationship between such greater volatility and poorer credit ratings, after controlling for the level of per capita income which proxies for other sources of volatility such as terms of trade and commodity dependence. Omitting the four countries in recent deep crisis (Romania, Ukraine, Russia and Pakistan), which are also outliers in the sample, improves the significance of the regression.

Similarly, real exchange rates are two–three times more volatile on average in developing than industrial countries, and the large capital movements associated with capital account openness may amplify this volatility, as during the Southern Cone crises of the 1980s and the East Asian crisis of 1997 (Figure 1.4; World Bank 1996). Volatility in capital flows increases the volatility of real exchange rates and associated

Figure 1.2 Volatility of capital flows to developing economies, 1975–97

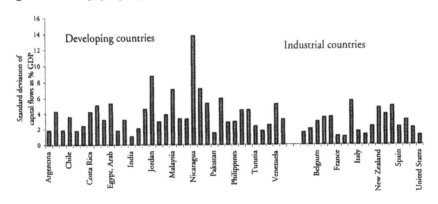

Note: Capital flows are defined as the current account plus the change in reserves.
Source: International Monetary Fund (IMF), various years. *International Financial Statistics*, IMF, Washington, DC.

Figure 1.3 Volatility increases in crises

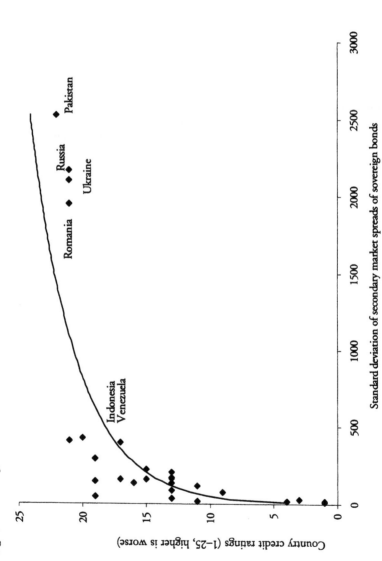

Standard deviation of secondary market spreads of sovereign bonds

Note: The regression run was log(Volatility)=5.71*+1.10log(Rating)-0.42(Per capita income), with adjusted R²=0.54; *** = significant at 1 per cent;
** = significant at 5 per cent;* = significant at 10 per cent.
Source: Euromoney Bondware; Moody's Investor Service, 1998.

real interest rates (McKinnon and Pill 1997; Corbo and Hernandez 1996). Large unpredictable shifts in the real exchange rate impose substantial adjustment costs and may reduce the long-term level of investment and growth, especially in sectors dependent on foreign markets and exposed to international competition.

There is considerable evidence to suggest that capital flows to developing countries are more volatile because of inadequate information and the presence of information asymmetries which contribute to herd behaviour in international financial markets (Eichengreen and Wyplosz 1996; Calvo *et al.* 1996; World Bank 1999). Not only are these information inadequacies more prevalent in the case of developing countries (this is just one aspect of their marginal creditworthiness), but herd movements in international markets also have a disproportionate effect on them because of the small size of their financial markets. Changes in flows in international capital markets originate in large part from changes in stock adjustment behaviour, and such stock adjustments can have disproportionately large effects in small, recently liberalised, emerging country markets. For example, the total market capitalisation of all major emerging markets is only about 5 per cent of the market capitalisation in G7 countries, and an increase of United States pension fund holdings in emerging markets from about 1 per cent to 2 per cent would represent about 1 per cent of GDP of all emerging markets and 10 per cent of their total market capitalisation.

Figure 1.4 Variability of real exchange rates, industrial versus developing economies, 1975–97

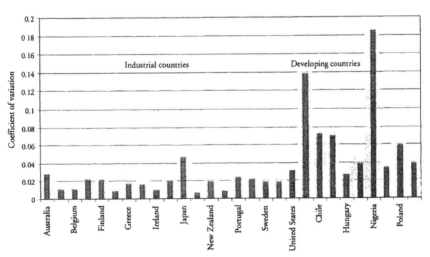

Source: International Monetary Fund (IMF), various years. *International Financial Statistics*, IMF, Washington, DC.

PRO-CYCLICAL CAPITAL FLOWS

Developing countries are more prone to external shocks than industrial countries, reflecting their narrower economic bases and greater dependence on primary commodity exports. Although the median size of external shocks during 1973–91 was about the same, the occurrence of large external shocks was twice as great in developing countries than in industrial countries (Figure 1.5) (Dadush and Dhareshwar 1993; World Bank 1993).

Often credit rationing to the marginally creditworthy becomes tighter under adverse shocks and looser under favourable shocks. Any adverse shocks arising from country-specific economic situations (such as terms of trade deterioration, macroeconomic policy mistakes or an unexpected bank failure) can expose marginally creditworthy developing countries to sudden and greater credit rationing in international markets. Such changes worsen rather than smooth adjustment. Independent shocks arising from global capital markets also tend to have a bigger pro-cyclical impact in terms of access to credit for marginally creditworthy borrowers than in mature industrial countries and are a strong predictor of financial crises (Frankel and Rose 1996; Kaminsky and Reinhart 1997). A flight to safety in global capital markets may lead to much greater reduction of access to international capital flows to developing country borrowers than for mature industrial

Figure 1.5 Developing economies' susceptibility to external shocks

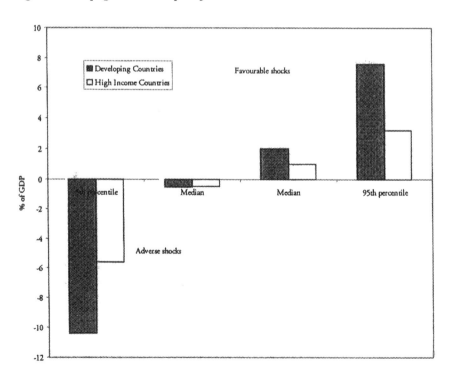

Source: World Bank, 1993. *Global Economic Prospects and Developing Countries,* World Bank, Washington, DC.

country borrowers, whose credit standing is only likely to deteriorate in extreme circumstances. The pro-cyclical response of capital flows is also evident in responses to domestic demand conditions, as in Korea, again exacerbating rather than stabilising volatility in output (Figure 1.6).

Even when capital flows to developing countries do not behave pro-cyclically, research has shown that developing countries generally find it harder to finance shocks than industrial countries. In one study, industrial countries were able to finance about one-half the size of adverse shocks by running a larger current account deficit or a lower surplus, whereas, on average, over the period 1971–93, developing countries were unable to rely on significant amounts of external financing to weather external shocks (Dadush and Dhareshwar 1993; World Bank 1993 and 1994). In times of global financial strain, capital flows tend to become strongly pro-cyclical. Thus, the pro-cyclicality problems are more evident when broken down by sub-periods—in the years before the debt crisis (1973–8), developing countries were able to finance about one-third of adverse shocks; during 1979–85 (the start of the debt crisis), this proportion fell to 17 per cent; after 1985 (the worst years of the debt crisis), lower and middle income countries were forced to overadjust to unfavourable external shocks by actually running a much smaller current account deficit or a larger surplus, as capital flows reversed. Independent shocks originating in global capital markets, such as higher interest rates, have the same effects. Furthermore, the current account adjustment was typically achieved more by contraction of domestic demand and import compression than by export expansion in developing countries as compared to industrial countries (Figure 1.7).

WEAKNESSES IN THE BANKING SYSTEM AND IN PUBLIC FINANCE

Sharp changes in capital flows can exacerbate the difficulties facing the weaker financial systems in developing countries, as in the Southern Cone crisis in the early 1980s, the 1995 peso crisis and more recently in the East Asian financial crisis (Figure 1.8). Financial intermediaries tend to be less well regulated—accounting and financial disclosure practices

Figure 1.6 Korea: capital flows and excess demand pressures move in tandem

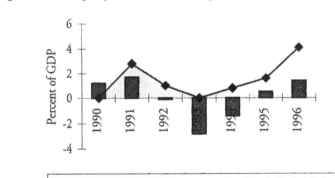

Source: Asian Development Bank and World Bank, 1998. *Managing Global Financial Integration: Emerging Lessons and Prospective Challenges,* Manila, mimeo.

Figure 1.7 Import reduction and export expansion in the wake of external shocks

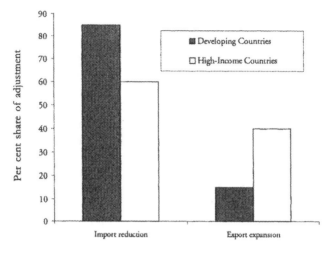

Source: World Bank, 1993. *Global Economic Prospects and the Developing Countries,* World Bank, Washington, DC.

Figure 1.8 Banking crises and volatility, 1980–94

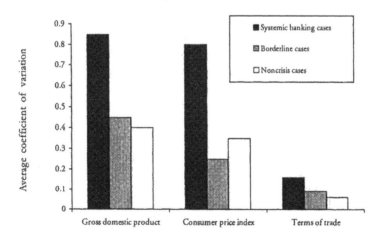

Source: Caprio, D. and Klingebiel, D., 1996. *Bank Insolvencies: Cross-country experience,* Policy Research Working Paper 1620, World Bank, Washington DC.

are less transparent; principal-agent, asymmetric information, moral hazard and governance problems are more pervasive; and central banks have less ability to prevent systemic crises (World Bank 1999). Several developing countries that liberalised their financial systems in the 1990s lack the institutions and regulatory system required to bear the risks of sudden capital flow reversals which can massively tighten liquidity. Even in the safer and more highly developed financial systems in industrial countries, financial liberalisation with open capital accounts has come at some cost and significant risk (see Chapple 1991 on New Zealand's experience).

Nor can most developing countries use counter-cyclical fiscal policy to dampen the impact of large swings in capital flows on aggregate demand due to low revenue levels (taxes average about 15 percentage points of GDP lower in developing countries), larger budget deficits (on average twice as large as in industrial countries), absence of automatic fiscal stabilisers (unemployment insurance and social security expenditures) and less flexible tax policies (Schadler *et al.* 1993; World Bank 1996). Indeed, Gavin (1998) finds that fiscal policy in Latin America is sharply pro-cyclical (in contrast to that in the OECD countries), with fiscal balances sharply tightened when the domestic economy is contracting, thus amplifying changes in demand induced by changes in external finance (Figure 1.9).

THE ABSENCE OF SOCIAL SAFETY NETS

Even though developing countries are seemingly able to adjust to volatility in capital flows and other external shocks with large forced turnarounds in current account balances (as in East Asia), the adjustment carries enormous costs. Changes in output and employment expose households in developing countries to larger risks, since low real incomes and savings and limited access to credit markets mean that recessions can be extremely painful. In some countries, the poorest have suffered the most as a result of currency crises (World Bank 1999). Hausmann and Gavin (1995) find that, during the 1980s, greater economic volatility in Latin America (compared to OECD countries) worsened income distribution significantly, and, after controlling for lower economic growth and educational attainments, raised the percentage of the region's total population in poverty by about 7 percentage points (Figure 1.10). In sharp contrast to industrial countries, few if any developing countries have effective social security and unemployment insurance programs to mitigate the effects of recessions.

CHARACTERISTICS OF DIFFERENT TYPES OF CAPITAL INFLOWS

The preceding discussion has tended to lump together all forms of capital inflows. But different forms of flows vary greatly in terms of their resilience in time of crisis and risk-sharing attributes. For example, in 1998, the first full year of the crisis in emerging markets, foreign direct investment flows to developing countries declined only marginally, from US$163 billion in 1997 to US$155 billion, and actually rose in Thailand and South Korea, two of the crisis countries. In contrast, all forms of inflows from international capital markets—bonds, portfolio equities and bank lending—collapsed, each being cut approximately in half. Whereas holders of both bonds and equities suffered large capital losses, some bank lenders (especially those engaged in bank-to-bank lending) benefited from rescue packages and associated restructuring operations which effectively socialised the losses. In the immediate crisis period, by far the largest sources of capital flow reversals were short-term bank loans and capital flight by domestic residents, rather than a reduction in new sources of long-term capital (Global Development Finance 1999). A detailed analysis of the benefits and risks associated with each source of capital inflow is beyond the scope of this chapter, but these examples illustrate the advantages for developing countries associated with sources of capital such as foreign direct investment which are resilient in crisis, take a longer-term strategic view, share in the risks and can bring benefits other than the narrowly financial.

Figure 1.9 Pro-cyclical fiscal policy in developing versus OECD economies

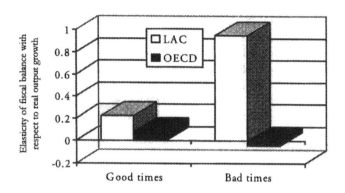

Source: Gavin, M., 1998. Fiscal policy in emerging market economies, paper presented at the Capital Flows seminar, College Park, Economic Development Institute (World Bank) and University of Maryland, May; World Bank, 1993. *Global Economic Prospects and the Developing Countries,* World Bank, Washington, DC.

CAPITAL OUTFLOWS

Estimates derived from the errors and omissions in the balance of payments suggest that capital outflows by domestic residents in developing countries are large. They amount to an equivalent of between one-third and one-half of capital inflows to developing countries in recent years, even in times of relative calm in the international financial markets, such as 1996. The size of outflows from developing countries illustrates the importance of the portfolio diversification motive in international investment (by the relatively affluent residents of developing countries).

Thus, both inflows and outflows are motivated in part by the diversification opportunities afforded by the low correlation between developing and industrial country assets. A more telling interpretation is that this reflects a trading of risks, as investors from industrial countries seek higher returns in developing countries (but with greater risks), while investors in developing countries seek lower risks (with lower returns) by investing abroad. This interpretation also helps explain the rationale for developing countries borrowing from abroad at significant spreads above international reference rates (LIBOR + a spread) and then redepositing sums abroad to earn returns below such rates.

The analysis of the benefits and risks associated with capital account liberalisation cannot abstract from the welfare implications of such behaviour. First, there are important externalities involved in foreign borrowing, which tend to raise the social cost and risk above the private costs and risks, and this wedge is likely to be greater for

Figure 1.10 Latin America: volatility increases poverty

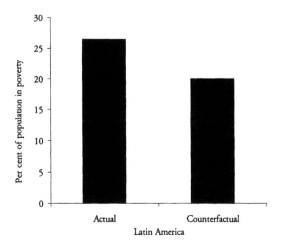

Source: Gavin, M. and Hausmann, R. 1995. *Overcoming Volatility in Latin America*, Inter-American Development Bank, Washington, DC.

less creditworthy countries. Second, those that derive the benefit from portfolio diversification through capital outflows are the relatively wealthy few and the mechanisms for offsetting these transfers may not exist. In the event of a crisis, there is a long history in developing countries of socialising the losses associated with foreign borrowing—these transfer mechanisms may thus be working in reverse during crises, accentuating welfare losses for the poor while protecting the better-off international investors and relatively wealthy residents.

POLICY OPTIONS TO REDUCE RISKS IN DEVELOPING COUNTRIES

Policy options to reduce the greater risks of financial crises in developing countries associated with open capital accounts and the volatility of global capital flows can be considered at four levels

- at the policymaking level in the developing countries themselves
- in terms of altering the behaviour of private market intermediaries in global financial markets
- at the level of regulatory and policy decisions in source industrial countries
- at the level of changes in international financial policies and arrangements.

Policymakers in developing countries are the most directly concerned about the risks of open capital accounts. There is no single set of domestic policies that is likely to be sufficient to insulate economies from the risks of external crises caused or amplified by volatile international capital flows. Prudent macroeconomic policies (low fiscal deficits, flexible exchange rates, low inflation and supporting monetary policies) are an often suggested first line of defense. But these may not be sufficient to prevent excessive volatility in external capital flows and resulting crises—even though virtually all the East

Asian countries pursued generally stable macroeconomic policies prior to their recent crises, they were not able to avert a crisis because their underlying problems arose from excessive private (not public) external borrowing in fragile financial settings. Consequently, sound macroeconomic policies need to be combined with improvements in financial regulation that prevent excessive and imprudent risk taking by the private sector. Such improvements in prudential regulation (and associated private corporate behaviour) may take years, if not decades, of deep-seated institutional changes. Consequently, in order to reduce the risks of crisis, improved macroeconomic policies and prudential regulation of financial sectors may need to be combined with an orderly pacing and sequencing of capital account liberalisation. Discrimination between certain forms of capital flows may be called for in this transition. The benefits of openness to foreign direct investment and other similar types of longer-term capital flows are likely to outweigh their risks—these types of flows have proven to be much more resilient, have better risk-sharing characteristics and contribute more effectively to long-term growth. The same is not true for short-term capital flows such as commercial debt portfolios or interbank credit lines that seek quick returns, have few risk-sharing characteristics and are highly volatile (see World Bank 2000). In developing countries with fragile financial sectors, restrictions on such volatile short-term flows may be essential to reduce the risks of financial crisis. Such restrictions were common in many industrial countries in the 1960s and 1970s in their transition to better private risk management, and have been applied with some effectiveness in Chile and Colombia in more recent times. The design of such restrictions should seek to minimise distortions and be as market-oriented as possible (through differential taxes by type of flow, for instance).

Alteration of the behaviour of market intermediaries in source countries may also be a desirable goal. Periods of (pro-cyclical) excessive risk taking (euphoria) or excessive risk aversion (panic) by such international lending intermediaries gives rise to excessive volatility in capital flows. They arise fundamentally from two different sources. The first is a lack of adequate information about circumstances and risks in emerging countries, more acute in cross-border capital flows to emerging markets with weaker institutions. Second is the presence of significant moral hazard in the actions of international public agencies that affect their risk-taking behaviour. The former can be addressed by policies that improve the timely disclosure and greater transparency of information in developing countries. This important aspect of improvements in country policies is now being promoted by international financial agencies. But this, by itself, is unlikely to resolve the problem unless the incentives for market intermediaries to gather better information and adequately assess the risks of lending to emerging markets change. This requires, most importantly, a change in the perception that private capital flows, especially short-term international banking flows, will be bailed out from the risks of default, either by host country governments or by international financial rescue packages. Private market participants need to be exposed to a greater share of the burden or losses in the event of external payments crises in developing countries. This, over time, should reduce excessive risk taking and volatility in private market behaviour.

Regulatory authorities in source countries can also play a role in reducing excessive risk taking by their financial institutions in lending to emerging markets. For example, when interest rates fall in industrial countries and intermediation margins or opportunities for profitable investments at home are temporarily reduced, there is tendency by international banks to take on greater risks by expanding their lending to emerging markets (until another crisis occurs). Given such behaviour, there may be a need for more prudent regulatory policies in source countries. One proposal that is being advocated currently is a higher risk weight (than the 20 per cent under the Basle rules) on lending by international banks to emerging markets, based on an assessment of the health of an individual recipient country's financial system. This would raise the cost of borrowing by developing countries but improve the pricing of risk, and thereby reduce the incidence of crises and volatility of flows and spreads over time.

A number of policies to improve the international financial architecture to help prevent or reduce financial crises in developing countries have been proposed. They range, in addition to policies discussed above, to those that involve: expanding an international lender-of-last-resort function; improving the process of orderly restructuring of international debts; and taxation of global capital flows and/or setting entirely new institutional rules for international capital flows. The proposal for expanding an international lender of last resort (from international public funds) has received a battering on the grounds that it encourages moral hazard, reduces burden sharing by the private sector, requires difficult direct supervision of policies in crisis-affected countries and may impose an excessively harsh burden on the poor in crisis-affected countries. Similarly, proposals for setting taxes on cross-border short-term capital flows (the Tobin tax) and other suggested large-scale institutional changes in international capital flow arrangements have met with some scepticism because of inherent difficulties with implementation. However, the proposal for a more orderly process of debtor–creditor negotiation in the event of a crisis, including the possibility of the declaration of international debt standstills in crisis-affected countries, merits greater attention. It may have significant advantages by involving private market participants more directly, imposing substantial costs on both borrowers and lenders, avoiding moral hazards associated with international public bail outs and involving debtor and creditor country governments in improving coordination arrangements.

CONCLUSION

Given their low endowments in capital and the narrowness and shallowness of their financial markets, developing countries can potentially derive great benefits from integration in world financial markets. But they are also exposed to great risks. While improvements in international policies to prevent such crises may be important, these will take time and are likely to be difficult to implement. Therefore, policymakers in developing countries need to be able to deal more effectively with these risks themselves. In the light of the special risks to which they are exposed, the preconditions for prudent capital account liberalisation in these countries are stringent (Williamson 1993). They include solid creditworthiness history, sustainable fiscal and current account positions, an appropriate exchange rate level, credible anti-inflation policies implemented by an independent central bank, adequate prudential regulation of banking and corporate sectors and effective social safety nets. The East Asian crisis illustrates that considerable time may be required before such preconditions are adequately satisfied in even some of the more advanced developing countries. Consequently, a more discriminating approach to the pace and sequencing of the opening of capital accounts to different types of capital flow is needed.

NOTE

* Views expressed in this chapter are those of the authors alone and do not necessarily represent those of the organisation with which they are associated.

2 Financial crises and globalisation

Stephen Grenville

As part of the debate on the East Asian crisis, two separate views emerged to explain the crisis—one which blamed deficiencies in the crisis countries themselves (such as cronyism, corruption and misguided policies) and one which found intrinsic flaws in the international capital markets.

Time has brought some perspective to these issues and a consensus is emerging that a variety of problems contributed. Not surprisingly, with complex and multiple causation, many things must be fixed. The domestic/international dichotomy is useful because it allows us to focus exclusively on the international issues, without implying that the domestic deficiencies were unimportant.

The focus of this chapter is on Australia, but within a wider context, to draw out lessons for Australia and others. This chapter addresses two main questions

- why was Australia not subject to the same degree of contagion as its near neighbours?
- as participants in the debate on reforming the international economic architecture, what elements of reform should Australia be promoting?

WHY AUSTRALIA ESCAPED

There were certainly serious concerns that the East Asian crisis would do significant damage to Australia—not due to fear of contagion but in that the international environment would be unfavourable, with stunted growth in export markets, particularly in the region which had provided Australia with such stimulus over recent decades. However, domestic demand has remained strong (with very few adverse confidence effects from East Asia), and the lower exchange rate has effectively buffered Australia from the worst expectations. No one expected Australia to be sucked down into the same financial maelstrom—adverse impacts were expected to be from secondary effects. It was always clear that Australia would avoid the direct contagion, because it was not subject to the fatal combination that had infected East Asia—the interaction of large and volatile capital flows, with a fragile domestic financial sector. Capital flows to Australia have not been as volatile or as large, but more importantly, Australia did not have a fragile domestic financial sector.

Australia is very dependent on international capital inflows, with an average current account deficit of around 4.5 per cent of GDP over the last decades. These flows are large, but nothing like the flows experienced in East Asia—in 1996, for example, Thailand received capital flows equal to 13 per cent of its GDP. Just as important, the capital inflows that funded the Australian deficit were quite stable. Even in the mid 1980s Banana Republic crisis, which saw a large change in the value of the Australian dollar, the most that the current account adjusted in any one year was a little under 2 per cent of GDP (in 1986–7). Compared with changes in current account balances in some countries in East Asia in 1998 of up to 15 per cent of GDP in a single year, fluctuations in Australia were manageable. One-third or more of Australia's capital inflow is in the form of foreign direct investment, which, even in the crisis countries, has tended to be quite stable. A minor part is in the form of the elements which turned out to be extraordinarily volatile and flighty in East Asia—bank-to-bank flows. The three crisis countries had been receiving bank-to-bank flows at an annual rate of around US$50 billion in the years leading up to the crisis, and were subject to outflows of nearly US$75 billion in the first nine months of the crisis. Nor, incidentally, was Australia vulnerable as a creditor: Australian banks had not lent extensively to East Asia.

Australia has had plenty of experience of changing sentiment—flavour of the month at one moment and poor cousin the next—but has not had the kind of total *volte face* experienced in East Asia, where 'euphoria turned to panic without missing a beat' (Sachs, 'The wrong medicine for Asia', *The New York Times*, 3 November 1997). One reason why Australia has not been subject to these sorts of dramatic reversals is the depth and maturity of its financial markets. The institutions and instruments that foreigners have invested in have tended to be longstanding and stable, with quite well defined prices and behaviour, so there was no basis for the kind of blind-panic flight that occurred in East Asia. Surprises occur in Australian financial markets, but not to the extent that occurred in East Asia.

More importantly, Australia's financial sector (centred on the banks) is particularly strong. The strength of the Australian financial sector is in large part because it has already had its learning-by-doing crisis, nearly a decade ago. Almost every episode of financial deregulation has been accompanied by a period of crisis and turmoil. In Latin America in the 1980s, the nub of the issue was captured in the title of the definitive analysis of the period— 'Goodbye financial repression, hello financial crash' (Diaz-Alejandro 1985). Even the United States, less than a decade ago, experienced the Saving-and-Loans crisis, the direct result of lop-sided deregulation and market-distorting official guarantees. The United Kingdom and Japan had credit-induced asset booms and busts only a decade ago. Sweden experienced a meltdown of its financial sector in the early 1990s. Australia was not an exception to this generalisation, but had its crisis in the 1980s. It is hardly surprising that a cosy, protected financial sector, when newly exposed to the chill winds of international competition and hard-edged, sharp-pencil tactics, is at its most vulnerable. Perhaps the most dangerous aspect is that the additional competition lowers credit standards—the new competitors look for customers to lend to, and the old institutions preserve their markets by being readier to lend to customers who previously would not have been regarded as creditworthy. Deregulation gave borrowers a new-found freedom, and for some it was a case of giving them more rope with which to hang themselves.

Failure gives rise to a corrective process that makes a repeat less likely. Australia's financial failure during the 1980s was the main reason why the financial sector was in such good condition when the East Asian crisis hit in the 1990s. The corporate sector had learnt the dangers of currency speculation and had become much more cautious. Australia has had bad foreign currency-denominated borrowing experiences (with Swiss franc loans), but fortunately they were, at least in macro terms, insignificant. Australia's foreign exchange crisis (which occurred in the mid 1980s, associated with the Banana Republic debate) occurred separately from the prudential problems in the banking system, associated with the boom and bust of the asset price bubble of the late 1980s. East Asia had its foreign exchange crisis superimposed on its prudential crisis.

Most of the players in the Australian market have a good understanding of how the foreign exchange rate would normally behave—the exchange rate is reasonably well anchored in the fundamentals. Even so, some puzzling things still happen. One such puzzle is the Australian dollar's tendency to move more than might be expected over the course of the commodity cycle. Even when terms of trade changes are temporary, some change in the exchange rate might be expected. But, quite persistently since the float, the movement in the exchange rate has been around 25 or 30 per cent between peak and trough, much more than can be explained simply in terms of the textbook reaction to cyclical terms of trade changes (Gruen and Kortian 1996).

Australia has, over time, learnt to adapt to this world. With low inflation well established, there is less danger that these cyclical fluctuations in the exchange rate will damage inflationary expectations—they seem to be absorbed, to a large degree, in margins. The Reserve Bank of Australia's response is to be ready to intervene in the more extreme swings of the exchange rate, principally because there is always some danger that extreme swings may damage confidence in the domestic economy (particularly downward swings). In the process, the central bank makes a profit through the rather old-fashioned form of trading under which it buys cheap and sells dear (Andrew and Broadbent 1994). This experience puts in doubt the Friedmanite idea that speculators always buy cheap and sell dear, and if they do not, they quickly go out of business. Why have the processes of natural selection not weeded out the central bank's counterparties from this zero-sum game?[1]

With this experience in mind, it was not surprising that the East Asian currencies, once unhooked from their semi-fixed pegs, moved excessively, each overshooting by far more than any conceivable initial overvaluation. For all the virtues of exchange rate flexibility, it is dangerously naïve to sell the idea that floating the exchange rate will be a painless solution to international financial integration.

Having made the case that Australia was never vulnerable to the sort of catastrophic capital reversal experienced by some East Asian countries, the question remains as to why Australia is so interested in the issues of the new financial architecture. The short answer is that international capital markets are not working as well as they should. Even if Australia can survive in the current world, developed and emerging markets alike would benefit from changes in the international architecture.

A REFORM AGENDA

Since the crisis broke, there have been five issues on which Australia has spoken out in international fora

- representational issues
- hedge funds
- bailing in the private sector
- capital controls
- transparency.

International representation

Well before the East Asian crisis, it was obvious that the international institutions formed shortly after World War II no longer represented the current world economy. As a small country, Australia accepts that many important international decisions will be made in a small subset of the largest countries, such as the G3. It is harder to accept that important decisions (such as the development of global prudential rules) should be made in a group as unrepresentative as the G10, which contains four smallish European countries of which only one is as large as Australia. With only one Asian and no Latin American representation, the exclusion of emerging markets is just as obvious. The IMF has the formal representation of all members, but only the United States has enough votes to veto issues. Constituencies represent hugely different population sizes and degree of interest in international issues. This is why the idea of G22, formed in the aftermath of the East Asian crisis, is so attractive. In this form, it has been vetoed by European countries not yet ready to give up their overrepresentation on international economic issues. One beneficial result of the East Asian crisis was to bring this issue to the fore, and while G22 no longer exists, a wider representation on the working groups discussing some of the important issues (such as highly leveraged institutions, offshore markets and short-term capital flows) has been achieved.[2]

Hedge funds

Australia had searing experiences with volatile exchange rates in the mid 1980s, but has now come to terms with its floating exchange rate. The float has been enormously beneficial for Australia. Some overshooting is accepted as a puzzling but tolerable quirk of the market.

In the most recent episode (coinciding with the East Asian crisis), however, a variant on this theme emerged—speculators who believe that they can make money by attacking an exchange rate which has already overshot, so that it overshoots even further. The tactic is straight-forward enough—quietly take a short position in the currency which is already undervalued, and then, by a mixture of highly public additional short selling and vigorous orchestration of market and press opinion, force the exchange rate to fall further. As it falls, a bandwagon forms, with market players anxious to sell the currency as it becomes cheaper, in the belief that it will become cheaper still. As the herd moves in, the original speculators can square up their position, at a profit.

This was the situation in East Asia in mid 1998. We have referred to these attacks as being driven by hedge funds, but this terminology is more specific than needed to make the point. It was useful that the Australian dollar weakened somewhat in 1998, reflecting the fundamentals of a much less benign external environment. This softening of the exchange rate was an important factor in buffering Australia from the external crisis. But too much of a good thing is a bad thing. The gathering downward momentum, one-sided sentiment and thin market were certainly matters of considerable concern, reflected in central bank actions to support the exchange rate.

The most disturbing element is that it was part of a concerted effort at market destabilisation. Players' objective was to push down the yen to the stage where the renminbi was under irresistible pressure to devalue, which would have broken the Hong Kong dollar peg. The Australian dollar was a minor secondary target. This episode only came to an end because of the combined effects of the Long Term Capital Management near-meltdown and the financial crisis in Russia—the region was saved by crises elsewhere. So while Australia survived quite well and has the resilience to weather similar episodes, it carries from this experience a strong viewpoint into the debate on international financial architecture concerning hedge funds (or as they are known in that context, highly leveraged institutions). There are those who deny, even now, that hedge funds played any significant role. The hedge funds themselves do not deny their actions. (George Soros (1998) has written a best-selling book about it!) The movement of exchange rates over the period, even large currencies such as the yen, provides more evidence. As the hedge funds cut their short positions in yen to cover their disasters in the ruble, the yen rose 15 per cent in a little over a day, driven by events unrelated to any Japanese fundamentals. Is this a well functioning market?

When Australia first talked about its experience with hedge funds in mid 1998, this was derided as the Australian anecdote. But you may recall the old quip about the plural of anecdote being data. Hong Kong, South Africa, Malaysia and Thailand all pointed to their anecdotes. Then came the near-collapse of Long Term Capital Management and the tenor of the debate changed. But as the Long Term Capital Management crisis recedes, international concerns have become more muted, even stifled. The G7 authorities are prepared to concede that there were prudential issues involved in the high leverage of these funds—they threatened those who had lent to them. But there is less recognition of the market integrity issues involved—the damage done by inducing more volatility (and otherwise unnecessary interest rate increases) into exchange markets (RBA 1999a and 1999b).

Bailing in the private sector

There should be a greater readiness, in the event of crisis, to bail in private sector creditors—to require a standfast on repayments and the working out of orderly arrangements for repayment, which may well involve delay in repayment and, possibly, creditors taking a 'haircut'.

Some private sector participants in this debate have articulated a sort of bewildered resentment at the idea of compulsory bailing in in the course of an orderly debt arrangement—they talk in terms of consenting adults, who have freely made a contract which no one should rend asunder. It does, however, seem a bit more complicated than this. First, private creditors accept, within all domestic jurisdictions, the possibility of bankruptcy procedures *in extremis*, which involve two elements—the declaration of inability to pay in full and some kind of standfast in which the available assets are assembled and decisions made on an equitable distribution. This procedure overrides individual deals done either before or after the event. The justification is that an orderly arrangement is better for everyone than an unseemly rush to seize available assets. This rationale carries over into the international forum in principle, although finding legal jurisdiction is another matter. This was well illustrated in late 1997, when Korea was within days of defaulting on government-guaranteed bank debt owed to foreign banks. Under the detailed orchestration of the United States and IMF authorities, a deal was struck whereby US$24 billion of bank-to-bank debt was rolled over, at an attractive interest rate for creditors. This deal changed sentiment towards Korea dramatically, and it would be hard for any creditor to claim that the outcome was anything other than greatly beneficial to them.

The case for bailing in the private sector goes beyond this, at least in cases where the official sector (often through the IMF) has taken part in something analogous to a lender of last resort, in which additional funds are made available to shore up creditor confidence. The rationale for such a facility goes beyond the normal bankruptcy arrangements, to the further argument that where the problem is one of liquidity rather than insolvency, a lender of last resort will avoid runs on debtors. Given that it is taxpayers' money (usually via the IMF) which is being put at risk to bail out private sector creditors, taxpayers are entitled to expect some contribution from the creditors. The relevant lessons come from Mexico in 1994–5. Prior to the crisis, investors had received higher returns for the risk. When confidence evaporated and creditors refused to roll over their loans at the end of 1994, default loomed. The IMF and the United States government acted as lender of last resort, repaying all creditors in full and without delay. This was, in almost all aspects, extremely successful. The run was contained, and Mexico experienced a 'V-shaped' recovery. But it did highlight the moral hazard that goes with bail outs—it left the impression that lenders would be protected when things went wrong (Dooley 1997).

The contrast to this is bailing in the private sector—enforcing a standfast and haircut. This not only addresses the source of the immediate problem, but is also equitable, and directly addresses the moral hazard problem.

In making this case, Australia has argued that such arrangements should focus exclusively on sovereign or quasi-sovereign debt, in particular the bank-to-bank flows— the bulk of the capital reversal in East Asia was taking place between banks, who were using their access to government guarantees in order to finance the capital outflow. This makes an important distinction between those who can easily take the money and run (on the basis of government guarantees) and those who lent to non-banks, who will have to work through the domestic bankruptcy system to gain repayment.

Much self-righteous indignation has been expressed by private sector creditors at the idea that the authorities might impose standfasts and haircuts. This would sound less disingenuous if it were not coming from the same voices who were so astounded by the Russian default of August 1998—astounded not by the patently parlous creditworthiness of the country they had lent to, but by the absence of any official rescue package to save them from default.

Controls on capital flows

Two important lessons from the crisis are

- that short-term flows were particularly vulnerable to reversals
- that the transition from financial regulation to deregulation is a particularly vulnerable time.

There is now a wide acceptance that, instead of a blanket presumption in favour of quick and complete financial deregulation, deregulation should be orderly, keeping pace with the build up of the necessary institutional infrastructure, particularly capacity for prudential supervision. While this is now generally accepted, the operational corollary is not. If the problem was the huge capital inflow, what will prevent a recurrence when the next wave of euphoria arrives, and later evaporates?

One aspect is clear enough—far-reaching prudential rules should be put in place, such as restrictions on banks' short-term borrowing and on foreign currency-denominated borrowing. In putting these prudential rules in place, it is important not to simply shift risk out of the formal financial sector and leave it with those who are even more vulnerable—this would encourage problems later.

The other issue is whether Chilean-style controls on short-term capital inflow may also be useful. Such restrictions on short-term borrowers may not be perfect, but they make more sense than some of the alternative solutions put forward. One suggestion is that countries should hold foreign exchange reserves equal to all the short-term debt which is going to fall due over the next year (quoted by Greenspan 1999). This raises the issue of why this short-term debt was useful in the first place, if the proceeds must be stored in reserves (at a lower rate of return than the cost of borrowing).

One lesson is that countries should resist the blandishments to set up arrangements like the Bangkok International Banking Facility, and should be wary of fly-by-night, foot-in-the-door financial entrepreneurs whose aim is to sell sophisticated (hard to understand) financial products to unsophisticated (gullible) customers, under the guise of market broadening.

Transparency

Great emphasis has been placed on transparency. But the transparency which is being advocated in the debate is a very partial concept. Whereas a case could be made that markets work better if all participants have full information, the emphasis so far has been confined to getting the official sector to provide detailed and frequent information. Hedge funds and other major players are under no such obligation (even the investors in Long Term Capital Management were not given details of the portfolio). If markets truly work better when better informed, this principle should apply to all players who are big enough to move markets. This view is gradually being accepted in the international arena.

THE CONTEXT OF THE DEBATE: GLOBALISATION

Given the complexity of the issues, it has been disappointing that much of the debate has been driven by ideology. Ideology adds a special piquancy to the debate on capital flows. The argument here is reminiscent of similar debates on free floating for the exchange rate. Free in this context has the same connotation as in the free world or free speech—indisputably a good thing. Absence of any rules seems to be a particular virtue. A theologian picked up the flavour of the debate, likening the arguments in *The Wall Street Journal* to his own specialisation.

> Behind descriptions of market reforms, monetary policy and the convolutions of the Dow, I gradually made out the pieces of a grand narrative about the inner meaning of human history, why things had gone wrong, and how to put them right. Theologians call these myths of origin, legends of the fall, and doctrines of sin and redemption (Cox 1999).[3]

Some commentators took this vantage point because they wanted to view the issues as part of a wider debate on the inevitable global triumph of the free market paradigm (see, for example, Zuckerman 1998). It was, in many ways, a curious prism through which to view the issues, because it was pretty clear that, whatever the deficiencies of alternative systems, this was hardly a triumph of market forces. Whatever the advantages of more open capital markets, the collateral damage from the excessive inflows and the subsequent massive capital reversals has been great, and could hardly be justified in terms of some market-clearing or *tâtonnement* process. Whereas it seems hard to deny that for every foolish borrower there had been a foolish lender, the response was to argue that there had been a shortage of liquidity (people could not get out of their positions quickly enough!) or deficient transparency (investors, by some extraordinary oversight, were unaware of cronyism, corruption or lack of effective bankruptcy procedures).

For some, this response was part of the commercial imperative for maximising the return on investments—if investors were seen to have been foolish, then this would reduce the chance of official assistance in repayment. The strongest advocates were the representatives of financial markets, who not only saw commercial advantage in continuing to open new markets, but for whom the experience of Mexico in 1994–5 was quite satisfactory—they achieved good returns (including a risk premium) in good times and were bailed out, to a greater or lesser degree, in bad times.

The free market triumphalists found allies elsewhere. In academic circles, over the years, considerable intellectual endeavour had gone into showing that markets are efficient—whatever the convoluted and volatile path of financial prices over time, this is not only rational but indeed optimal (Garber 1990). The rationale for any one participant in pushing the price further away from its fundamental equilibrium was often along the lines of the greater fool presumption—however artificially high the price, someone would pay more for it later.

The first stage of the debate following the crisis had an almost surreal air about it, with the IMF pressing at its Annual Meeting in Hong Kong at the end of 1997 to add capital account deregulation to its mandate, at the very moment when the excessive inflows and reversals had been shown to be so damaging.

The wider debate on globalisation is very relevant. One contribution (Friedman 1999) provides useful terminology. He talks of the Electronic Herd—the anonymous fund managers behind their screens—and sees the proper response for emerging markets as being to don the Golden Straitjacket, whose specifications are a predominantly private sector economy, balanced budgets, low tariffs and open capital markets, including unrestricted foreign investment. This sounds very much like the Washington consensus, and as a framework of reference it makes good sense, particularly if it accepts the feasibility (and indeed the desirability) of some adaptation to the local environment and acknowledges that there is more to a successful society than an identikit market economy. Friedman acknowledges complexities and subtleties—indeed, his title (*The Lexus and the Olive Tree*) emphasises the need to balance technology with tradition. Furthermore, he does not confuse inevitability with desirability, as the triumphalists do.

Two aspects—the inevitability of the process and whether the endpoint is the pure free market model—require further comment. Some powerful forces clearly do encompass the globe in an irresistible way, reflecting superior technology, the need for a common standard and the greater world integration through the communications revolution. There are plenty of examples of dominant players and technology. But there are just as many examples of persistent national characteristics and behaviours. To imply that the whole package of essentially United States systems and values has to be accepted in its entirety oversimplifies the forces at work.

Just as importantly, it would be a mistake to see these forces of globalisation attaching themselves uniquely to a textbook competitive free market model.[4] Many aspects of globalisation are, in fact, the opposite—a dominant technology, a winner-takes-all player or a set of market behaviour rules such as the Basle capital adequacy rules are hardly the atomistic competition of the textbooks. This is not to suggest that the endpoint should be the nineteenth century brand of capitalism foreseen by some of the global triumphalists. 'On the brink of the 21st century, the United States is at a point reminiscent of its entry into the twentieth...Today, of course, the new frontier is the global economy' (Zuckerman 1998:20). Not everyone feels so warmly sentimental towards the age of robber baron capitalism, and some feel uncomfortable with the idea that 'unimpeded access to that burgeoning marketplace was the one indispensable condition for the flowering of American enterprise' (Zuckerman 1998:20).[5]

A necessary question is whether the allocation decisions of the Electronic Herd make sense from an economic viewpoint—are they shifting capital (and the real resources it represents) to the highest global usage? On recent performance, the answer would have to be no. Leaving aside the extraordinary *volte face* from optimism to pessimism in East Asia (and the misallocated investment that preceded the crisis), did the reassessment of United States equity prices in 1987 (in the deepest market with the fullest information) make sense? Or the gyration of the yen/US dollar rate, from 80 in April 1995 to 147 a couple of years later? Are markets, with their constant quest to respond to the latest data, factoid or rumour, the best allocators of capital and reliable guardians on the gateway to investment? Have the umpires—the credit-rating agencies—been forward-looking and insightful in their judgments? What should economies which did wear the Golden Straitjacket but were still subject to speculative attack (for example, Hong Kong) have done? Should we be spending more analytical time examining the behaviour of the herd, rather than simply noting its inevitability?

If we accept that not all the outcomes of globalisation are good, and that countries are not simply pawns on the global chessboard, then what needs to be worked out, on a case-by-case basis, is what modifications to the cut of the Golden Straitjacket can feasibly be achieved. Is it feasible to discourage the more volatile elements of the herd?[6] Some have resisted extra rules (collective action clauses and explicit efforts to limit moral hazard) on the grounds that these will reduce the flow of capital to emerging countries. If absence of moral hazard and full pricing of risk meant that capital flows would be smaller, then this has to be viewed as an improvement. If little short-term capital flowed to emerging markets, then it would be hard to argue that there would be any great loss.[7] The harder question is how to achieve effective restraint. Just as anomalies in the Basle capital adequacy requirements artificially encouraged bank-to-bank short-term inflows, feasible rules can influence outcomes in the opposite direction. Countries can, at least, avoid the frictionless conduit represented, for example, by the Bangkok International Banking Facility.

Far from demonstrating Adam Smith's invisible hand, globalisation is occurring within a complex set of rules, technical standards and regulations—some imposed by governments, but others by technological imperatives or by the private players in markets. What is required to reap maximum benefits from globalisation is a set of rules that recognise market sensitivities and are clear and transparent. Markets can and do accept differences between regulatory regimes, and the view that all capital flows to the country which prostrates itself lowest before the demands of the market seems nonsensical. After all, each of the crisis countries attracted excessive inflows into regimes which departed substantially from the Golden Straitjacket. More recently, Malaysia tapped international capital markets at a time when its anti-market rhetoric was still fresh in the minds of investors.

The starting point should accept the benefits of capital flows and the power of markets in allocating resources, but should also recognise that in every domestic market there are (often extensive) rules of the game and market infrastructure—what is needed now is a similar set of rules of the game for international flows. There should be no presumption that the Electronic Herd should, alone, set the specifications of the Golden Straitjacket. Many issues require careful thought—for example, the handling of intellectual property rights will determine how the benefits are shared between creator and user. These are not issues which the free market determines well, and a framework of rules is needed to achieve both efficiency and equity.[8, 9]

Capital will follow risk-adjusted profit opportunities, and within this constraint, countries have opportunities to protect their societal interests. It would be nonsensical for a country to insist on reinventing, *ab initio*, technology or rules (for example, Basle capital rules for prudential supervision or accounting rules), but it seems entirely feasible for countries to put their own supplements on rules, without becoming pariahs in the eyes of international financial markets. Globalisation is an opportunity for countries to improve their living standards. Individual countries must decide how deeply they will avail themselves of this opportunity. It is not an all-or-nothing choice.[10] They may pay a price for this in terms of GDP, but this is a choice countries can (and will) make. Total failure does not await those who modify the rules, sensibly, to fit their views of society and who recognise that production and distribution issues cannot be separated.[11] Sovereignty may have been modified by the Internet, but it has not been abolished.

The early analogy put forward (by Larry Summers, 'Go with the flow', *Financial Times*, 11 March 1998) was with airline travel—bigger planes have brought the benefits of cheap travel to a wider group, and if this involves the occasional dramatic large accident, this should not be seen as a reason for banning international plane travel. But where does this analogy lead? Surely to the dual acceptance of the benefits to be derived from the new technology and the need to make travel safer, even if this involves rules and regulations.

Seen in this light, the obvious position in contemplating the transition from regulation to liberalisation is to acknowledge the desirability of moving along the path as quickly as possible, but to also acknowledge that it is a bumpy path. There has been, since 1997, some progress. The core rhetoric no longer simply extols the importance of immediate and total deregulation, but now includes words like orderly to describe the process. To acknowledge this is one thing; to practice it is another. In trying to put some practical content into the idea of orderly deregulation, there may be reminders of the old Irish joke about asking the way to Limerick: 'I wouldn't go there from here'. There is fairly unanimous agreement that we do want to go there from here. But deregulation has some of the characteristics of a rolling snowball, whose momentum is self-generated and uncontrollable. While there is a longstanding and extensive literature on sequencing, it is rather unsatisfactory. Countries often take the reform/deregulation opportunities in whatever order they arise. The necessary infrastructure is not something which can be created instantly,[12] or even in advance of the requirement. Rather, it is put in place by trial-and-error and learning-by-doing, and some luck is required to get this safety net firmly in place before it is needed. What is pretty clear is that the process of reform-through-crisis is a very painful one.

CONCLUSION

When the East Asian crisis first broke, it was seen by some as an opportunity for reform— there would be some pain, but the forces of beneficial change would be given impetus. As the crisis developed, it became clear that for some countries (like Indonesia) the downside of the crisis was far outweighing the opportunities for seizing the moment to reform.

For all of these countries, the ideas embodied in the Golden Straitjacket, or the Washington consensus, have much to be said for them. Many of their recommendations these countries had been striving (however imperfectly) to put in place. The danger, now, is that the idea will be oversimplified and oversold. The basic elements of the Golden Straitjacket are desirable and, over time, feasible. But it should be possible to adapt it, to some extent, to the local environment and, more importantly, modify it so that the Electronic Herd is not so damaging.

Each of the elements Australia has advocated are aimed at building on the exisiting framework—bailing in the private sector, restraining short-term capital and increased disclosure by major participants, including hedge funds. Greater transparency is something which all market participants (not just the official sector) should observe. And, finally, wider representation in the economic councils of the world—if the Golden Straitjacket is to be the current international fashion, its design should be a more democratic process, not confined to groups representing the (very different) international world of half a century ago, egged on by those who want to use globalisation as a battering ram for their narrow commercial advantage. Some of the discussion of globalisation is in terms of a kind of breathless proselytising for a meta-trend whose time has come—coming ready-or-not globalism. Rather, it should be an opportunity to reap the rewards which come from sensible international integration.

NOTES

[1] At a recent conference on exchange rates run by one of the big players, they predicted dramatic further strengthening from the then prevailing level of US66 cents. This was on the basis that the fifty-five-day moving average had moved above the 200-day moving average, and that they were experiencing strong customer demand. I asked them why they had not recommended buying the Australian dollar six months earlier at US55 cents. If moving-average and market-momentum rules are the guide, it is hardly surprising that overshooting occurs-there simply are not enough market players looking at the fundamentals, and prepared to back their assessment.

[2] We note with some satisfaction that the Financial Stability Forum has recently been enlarged to include some non-G7 economies, including Australia.

[3] The same tone had been picked up much earlier: 'Economic liberalism was the organizing principle of a society engaged in creating a market system. Born as a mere penchant for non-bureaucratic methods, it evolved into a veritable faith in man's secular salvation through a self-regulating market.' (Polanyi 1944:135).

[4] Friedman (1999:85–6) comes close to putting this pure free market view: 'those people who are unhappy with the Darwinian brutality of free-market capitalism don't have any ready ideological alternative now. When it comes to the question of which system today is the most effective at generating rising standards of living, the historical debate is over. The answer is free-market capitalism...Today there is only free-market vanilla and North Korea'.

[5] The markets were seen, even in the age of unbridled capitalism, as being especially volatile: 'While the productive labors of a society, the functioning of its ships and railroads, its mills and factories, give the effect of a beautiful order and discipline, of the rhythmic regularity of the days and seasons, its markets, by a strange contrast, seem to be in a continual state of anarchy' (Josephson 1934:192).

[6] In Friedman's terminology, the short-horn cattle.

[7] This argument has particular force in relation to East Asia, where national saving rates have been so high.

[8] Similar variation may be possible in other rules. Bankruptcy rules, for example, have to fit societies' views on balancing creditor and debtor rights. Competition rules, patent rules and legal decisions all find their basis in individual societies, with views on property rights and equity which are not ruled solely by the market.

[9] As more international trade takes place in weightless technological services and products whose marginal cost is small compared with the average cost, the copyright and patent rules become more important. Countries which are large producers of high technology products and intellectual property will be interested in incorporating into the Golden Straitjacket rules which protect their citizens' commercial position.

[10] Singapore and Taiwan provide successful examples—they restrict their banks from lending domestic currency offshore, making it difficult for foreign speculators to short the currency.

[11] As implied by Friedman's matrix (1999).

[12] Dennis de Tray ('World Bank's lessons from Indonesian economic crisis', Jakarta Post, 14 April 1999) describes it this way: 'globalization operates at light speed along fiber optic cables, while institutional development takes decades.'

3 Sequencing of capital account liberalisation

A challenge to the Washington consensus?

Marcus Miller and Lei Zhang

Ever since the Basle accords of 1988, progressively harmonised prudential regulation has been required of banks participating in the global economy; since the early 1990s, policies towards emerging market economies have been dominated by the Washington consensus (Williamson 1994:26–8), which looked to financial (and trade) liberalisation as the way to growth and prosperity. But the need to sequence these steps was not emphasised, and emerging market economies were, in effect, encouraged to liberalise markets as quickly as possible. In April 1997, for example, the Interim Committee of the IMF came out in favour of amending the IMF articles to make the capital account liberalisation one of the purposes of the Fund (Eichengreen 1999:116).

It is, however, a lot easier to abolish capital inflow controls than it is to ensure that the local financial system is in good regulatory order to handle the resulting inflows: so in practice freedom of capital movements will precede effective regulation. The financial crises of the 1990s have demonstrated that the combination of massive inflows with distorted incentives is a recipe for disaster; and, for the Washington consensus, this has proved an expensive lesson in economics of the second best (that is, the need to relax some first order conditions for optimality when others are not satisfied).

This chapter examines the challenge to the Washington consensus posed by recent events, and how it should be modified as a consequence. We begin by considering just why the combination of market liberalism and poor regulation should be so potentially dangerous. The reason lies in the interaction between government guarantees given to bank deposits and the limited liability enjoyed by shareholders, which poses potentially serious problems of moral hazard (Krugman 1998). Massive short-term capital flows from global capital markets can enormously magnify these problems, leading to financial and economic crises with major economic costs.

Evidently not all steps of market liberalisation lead to faster growth (Rodrik 1998)—they may even, as in 1997–8, lead to disaster. At the very least, this is a significant qualification to the prior Washington consensus, with obvious implications for emerging market economies with inadequate prudential regulations. More specifically, the extent of capital account liberalisation should be conditional on the quality of prudential regulation and supervision—a dramatic example of the logic of second best. Countries like China and India, for example, would not be well advised to follow the quick fix of the earlier consensus; the lesson of the East Asian crisis is that improving domestic regulation and corporate governance is a necessary precondition for enjoying the benefits of financial liberalisation.

DEPOSIT INSURANCE, LIMITED LIABILITY AND BANKING

In emerging market economies where capital markets are underdeveloped, most domestic firms rely on banks for investment finance; banks, of course, finance the bulk of this lending by taking deposits from the public. While this may seem straightforward enough, it is in fact problematic. For, with balance sheets on which illiquid assets are matched by liquid liabilities, banks cannot collectively honour all the claims for cash for which they may be liable, and the banking system is thus exposed to liquidity crises in the form of bank runs.

In one of the most widely cited theoretical papers on this subject, Diamond and Dybvig (1983) interpret these runs as shifts of equilibrium. They show that the banking system has multiple equilibria, and a failure of depositor confidence can precipitate a shift from good to bad. The history of banking crises in Britain and America demonstrates that bank runs are no mere theoretical curiosa. To protect their banking systems against the risk of self-fulfilling crises of confidence, the central bank can act as lender of last resort in favour of solvent but illiquid banks, as the Bank of England began to do towards the end of nineteenth century. Alternatively the state can provide deposit insurance, as the Federal Deposit Insurance Corporation has done in the United States since 1934. Because 'the consensus in favor of deposit insurance is quite broad among regulators' (Dewatripont and Tirole 1994:111), we focus on this method.

Insured depositors need not withdraw their funds just because they fear others may do so; and this can avert liquidity crises. But the combination of deposit insurance with limited liability poses a serious risk, namely that of solvency crises due to moral hazard—the distorted incentives that face those who own and manage banks. Unless bank shareholders have a substantial amount of equity at risk, those owning and managing these highly levered companies, whose borrowing is guaranteed by the state, have an incentive to take on risky projects—with limited liability, the benefits accrue to shareholders but the losses are borne by the insurer. For shareholders, limited liability is like having a put on the cash flows from the business; and, by increasing the volatility of these flows, they can increase the value of the put.

Prudential regulation of banks is designed to handle this problem. In practice, since the Basle accords of 1988, Western economies have imposed capital adequacy ratios on banks as a means for achieving prudential control. The principle is simple—if the combination of deposit insurance and limited liability gives rise to moral hazard, take away limited liability. Since they require shareholders to have a minimum percentage of their own funds at risk, the capital adequacy ratios endorsed by the Basle accords should ensure that the put option conferred by limited liability will never be exercised. (How the capital adequacy ratios are to be enforced is not specified in the Basle accords, which leaves key issues of implementation to national authorities.)

The basic logic of the situation is illustrated in Figure 3.1. The circle on the left indicates the illiquid assets available in the economy, while the circle on the right shows the amount of liquid liabilities. The intersection of the two circles, labelled B, illustrates the liquidity transformation achieved by the banking system. Because of the risk of bank runs, these bank deposits have to be insured. The moral hazard that arises when deposit insurance is combined with limited liability is shown below the line in the lower part of B. The solution to this taken under the Basle accords, effectively removing the privileges of limited liability by bank regulation, is shown as the upper part of B. (Another solution, not discussed above, is to leave banks with limited liability but to take away their deposit insurance. This is indicated as the narrow banking approach shown in the lower half of C. These banks can meet their depositors demands and may not gamble, but do little for the financing of investment.)

In what follows, we first use a profit maximising approach to show how distorted incentives can lead banks to gamble for resurrection, and then illustrate various regulatory measures to offset this.

IMPRUDENT BANKS AND REGULATORY RESPONSES

Imprudent banks

To analyse moral hazard arising from unregulated banking, we use a simple model of asset valuation, where the privilege of limited liability is represented as a put option (Merton 1977; Fries *et al.* 1997). We then show how prudential regulation effectively removes this put value.

Assume the total deposits, D, are invested in domestic interest-earning assets with returns X. The bank can choose two mutually exclusive portfolios, either with safe returns (with no uncertainty) or with risky returns (with a negative trend and substantial

Figure 3.1 Limited liability, moral hazard and the Basle accord

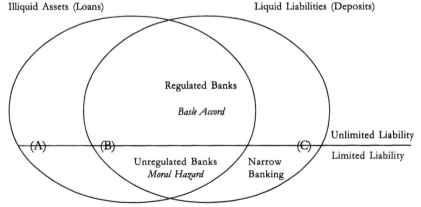

volatility). Let the equity value of the bank, that is, the value of assets less deposits, be given by V_N. To simplify the analysis we scale both the returns and the equity value of the bank by total deposits, so x = X/D indicates the returns per unit of deposit and v_N = V_N/D, the equity value per unit of deposit.

Equity values of the bank for safe and risky investments are represented by v^S_N and v^R_N respectively (Figure 3.2). These are increasing linear functions of loan returns, x, plotted along horizontal axis. Both schedules start from -1 (indicating net liability per unit of deposit when asset values fall to zero) with v^S_N having a slope of 1/r (where r is market rate of interest) and with v^R_N having a slope of 1=(r + μ) (where μ is the negative trend for the risky asset).

For returns close to x_B, the net equity (if choosing a safe asset) of the bank is close to zero. Observers predict that loan managers will gamble for resurrection by switching to more risky assets. In the presence of limited liability, banks can increase their net equity values by increasing the variance of returns. This is because high returns will enhance bank profits but low or negative returns will be written off through bankruptcy.

It might appear that risky assets are always dominated by safe assets as v^R_N lies everywhere below v^S_N. But this would be to ignore the limited liability of the bank shareholders and how, as a consequence, expected profits depend on the variability of returns. These imply that the net equity of the bank is given by the schedule GG when deposits are invested in risky assets. So risky investment is more profitable than safe investment when bank capital is low (that is, to the left of S where GG crosses v^S_N).

Figure 3.2 Moral hazard in banking: gambling for resurrection

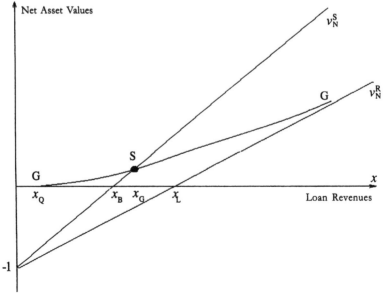

Given the possibility of switching from safe to lower-yielding, high-risk assets, loan managers will be tempted to gamble when net returns of the safe portfolio are at x_G or below. Without deposit insurance, it would in principle have to be depositors who prevent loan managers from behaving in this way by monitoring the portfolio manager when x is close to x_G and promptly punishing any sign of gambling (by firing the manager, for example). But as Dewatripont and Tirole (1994) point out, the risk of bank runs leads governments to guarantee deposits. Consequently, it is the government that usually takes upon itself the task of monitoring portfolio allocation decisions and punishing mismanagement.

If the state provides the guarantee but fails to check moral hazard, the consequence will be costly banking crises. Eichengreen and Rose (1999) estimated that an emerging market banking crisis could cost about one-year's normal economic growth. Using the samples of those banking crises that occurred during 1970s, they show that bank losses and public sector resolution costs could exceed 10 per cent of GDP.

Regulatory responses

Here we look at two particular regulatory responses that can be used to prevent banks switching to inefficient portfolios when their net asset values are low—early closure and the Basle accords.

Early closure rule. The early closure rule would be consistent with the 'prompt regulatory action' incorporated in the FDIC Improvement Act of the United States passed in 1991 designed to 'ameliorate bank moral hazard behavior and protect depositors from loss' (Mazumdar 1997:284). Suppose the regulatory agency would close down the bank when its equity falls to zero. This means that the put option offered by limited liability has no value—the freedom to walk away from losses is only of value if banks are allowed to run at a loss! Consequently, safe assets dominate risky assets, and the incentive to gamble disappears (Figure 3.3).

Basle accords. Since the Basle accords of common minimum capital requirements were adopted by the G10 in 1988, about 100 countries have now implemented them. The accords require the banks to maintain levels of their own capital above a certain percentage of risk-weighted assets. The minimum capital ratio requirements are 4 per cent of tier one capital and 8 per cent of total (tier one plus tier two) capital in relation to risk-weighted assets (where weights can range from 0 to 100 per cent) (BIS 1997:38).

How does implementation of the accords mitigate the moral hazard problem? If the bank chooses the safe assets, whose risk weight is zero, then observing the Basle ratios means that the bank needs to inject capital only when its equity falls to zero. Hence, the value of equity given the choice of safe assets is the portion of v^S_N above zero (Figure 3.3).

What happens if the risky assets are chosen? In this case the Basle accords require that $v^R_N/[\omega(\sigma)(v^R_N + 1)] \geq R_B$, where the numerator is the bank's capital and the denominator the risk-weighted total assets (with $\omega(\sigma)$ being the risk weight), and R_B is the capital adequacy ratio. This means capital injection would occur when the equity value falls to $R_B\omega(\sigma)/(1 - R_B\omega(\sigma))$, indicated by the horizontal line BB (Figure 3.3). Using the same argument as above, at the point of capital injection, the slope of the equity value for choosing the risky assets is simply $1/(r + \mu)$. So the net asset value to the bank when

Figure 3.3 Effects of the early closure rule and Basle accords

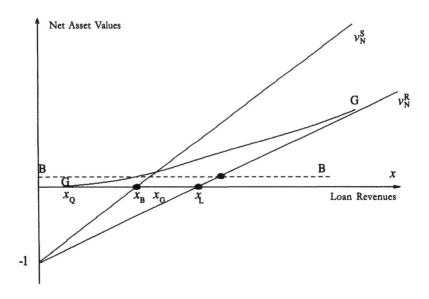

investing in risky assets is given by the portion of v^R_N above the BB line. This implies that the introduction of Basle accords (if credibly implemented) would destroy the option value associated with the risky portfolio.

The reason for this is that the Basle accords require banks themselves to finance the recapitalisation. This effective bail in makes banks internalise costs and reduces the net equity value from line GG to v^R_N. (The option value exists because banks are subsidised when making losses under limited liability through deposit insurance. This value is simply a transfer from taxpayers to banks. The net social losses if banks choose their own closure points are shown by the value of v^R_N at point x_Q, which can be substantial.) So under the Basle accords, the risky investment would not have been chosen and this eliminates the moral hazard problem.

EFFECTS OF CAPITAL ACCOUNT LIBERALISATION

A fully liberalised capital account can exacerbate the moral hazard problem faced by the domestic banking system (Figure 3.4). Assume initially there is a capital shortage, only the high return and high quality projects are financed by banks. Let us represent the net asset values for banks by v^S_N, that is, as if banks only invest in safe assets. A sudden surge of short-term capital inflows channelled through the domestic banking system may mean that the country is running into diminishing marginal returns for some projects. Average returns would be lower. If lower return projects also have high uncertainty then this will rotate equity value downward to v^R_N. Under limited liability and no banking regulation, banks will gamble for resurrection so to increase the equity value to line GG.

If the initial equity value for the bank is at point A, the large inflow of short-term capital may increase its value to point B. (Here point B is vertically above A, assuming the additional deposits financing the same quality projects. If the quality of the assets is lower, then B will shift to the left along line GG. This may increase the adverse incentives for the bank if A initially lies to the right of intersection of GG and v^s_N.) Such portfolio shifts generate larger social losses, indicated by point C. This suggests that if the domestic banking sector is not well regulated, fully liberalised capital account transactions will exacerbate the moral hazard problem.

In the above case, foreign depositors are assumed to be protected by deposit insurance. But this may not be true. If they see local banks mismanaging portfolios without any regulatory response, they can forecast bank insolvencies. They also know that, while the local central bank can print domestic currency, it can't print dollars! So, if foreign currency reserves are low (relative to foreign currency deposits), they have no assurance that there is an effective lender of last resort. This is a recipe for a bank run as foreign currency depositors head for safety. And the central bank, having lost all its reserves, will be forced to float the currency. This twin crisis can carry far larger costs than a domestic banking crisis (World Bank 1999). The increased occurrence of these twin crises in periods of financial liberalisation (Kaminsky and Reinhart 1997; Demirguc-Kunt and Detragiache 1997) demonstrates the severe consequences that capital account liberalisation can cause in the absence of domestic banking sector reform.

Figure 3.4 Effects of fully liberalised capital account transactions

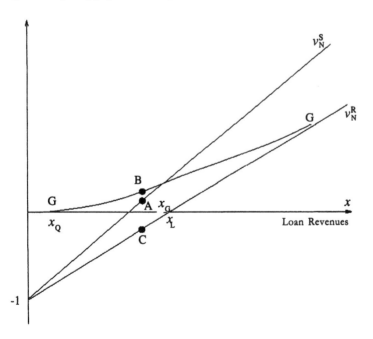

In short, if returns fall to the critical value, x_G, and this does not trigger an appropriate regulatory response, it can be the signal for the exit of foreign depositors and a full-blown financial crisis. The danger of allowing or encouraging substantial short-term capital inflows to pour into a weakly regulated banking system is only too apparent. Short-term foreign deposits may easily exceed foreign currency reserves and low bank returns trigger exit rather than regulation.

Note that for assets in fixed supply the combination of deposit guarantees and limited liability can also give rise to rapid asset price inflation. As Krugman (1998) observes, fixed assets may be priced on the basis of the best possible outcomes (at 'Pangloss values'), with the government covering losses in all other cases. In his assessment, the crisis was the bursting of an asset price bubble created by moral hazard in banking.

Lastly, we note that the willingness of the IMF to act as a lender of last resort in foreign currency terms is necessarily hampered if there is unchecked moral hazard in the local banking system. Unconditional lending in this situation will not avoid the problem, it may even lead to greater losses to local tax payers (as the American S&L experience confirms).

SEQUENCING OF CAPITAL ACCOUNT LIBERALISATION

In theory, capital account liberalisation can have substantial benefits—faster productivity growth, risk diversification and consumption smoothing. This may be true if capital inflows are mainly in the form of foreign direct investment, but is less the case for short-term inflows. Using a sample of about 100 countries from the mid 1970s to the end of the 1980s, Rodrik (1998) has shown that capital account convertibility has no significant effect on growth. This may partly reflect the role of highly volatile non-foreign direct investment and portfolio flows in precipitating crisis when the domestic banking sector lacks well functioning prudential regulation and supervision. Improving the conditions for the domestic financial sector may be essential in fully realising the benefits of a liberalised capital account.

Assume capital account liberalisation involves little cost while improving the regulatory framework for the domestic banking sector is costly. Figure 3.5 shows these relative costs where the horizontal axis indicates the degree of capital account liberalisation (higher to the right) and vertical axis the quality of bank regulation (higher when moving upwards). Point F illustrates the first-best solution with a fully liberalised capital account and high quality of bank regulation. The curves labelled I_i represent isoloss contours with losses increasing in the southwest direction.

Given the degree of capital account liberalisation, losses decrease when bank regulation improves (which reduces moral hazard). Given the quality of bank regulation, increasing capital account liberalisation would first improve welfare (as the benefits of liberalisation dominate) and then reduce it (as crises become more frequent and severe, so costs of liberalisation dominate). When the quality of bank regulation is very poor, a fully liberalised capital account is a recipe for disaster. This can entail huge output losses indicated by the black hole (Figure 3.5). The East Asian crisis provides a vivid example.

Figure 3.5 Sequencing of capital account liberalisation

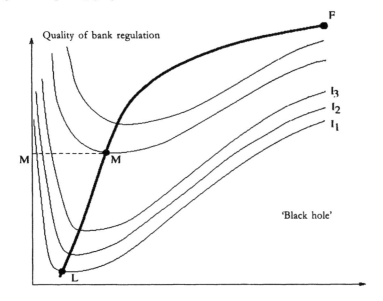

Since moving up the isoloss curves is costly, the best response would be to condition capital account liberalisation on the given quality of bank regulation. This is equivalent to locating a point on the isoloss contour which is tangent to the horizontal line. Joining these points together gives the time path for capital account liberalisation (LMF in Figure 3.5).

CONCLUSIONS

How should the Washington consensus be revised in the light of the East Asia crisis? Some highly relevant suggestions were contained in a recent World Bank (1999:124) report as follows

> Capital account liberalization should also proceed cautiously, in an orderly and progressive manner, given the large risks of financial crises—heightened by international capital market failures—in developing countries. Benefits of capital account liberalization and increased capital flows have to be weighed against the likelihood of crises and their costs. Clearly the benefits from foreign direct investment (FDI) and longer-term capital inflows outweigh the costs associated with the increased likelihood of financial crisis, and developing countries should pursue a policy of openness. But for more volatile debt portfolio and interbank short-term debt flows and the related policy of full capital account convertibility, there are higher associated risks of financial crisis and greater uncertainty about the benefits. Tighter prudential regulations on banks, and, where the domestic

regulatory and prudential safeguards are weak, restrictions on more volatile short-term inflows that minimize distortions and are as market-oriented as possible (through taxes, for instance), may reduce the risk of financial crisis.

The implications for China are clear: while foreign direct investment is fine, dollar deposits are dangerous.

Part 2

The management and prevention of crises

4   The muddling through of crisis management in Indonesia

A case for central bank independence

J. Soedradjad Djiwandono

The Indonesian crisis developed as a sequence of events, starting with an external shock as part of the contagious financial panic in the region that hit Jakarta's financial market in mid July 1997. The policy responses and market reactions that followed exposed the fragility of the national banking system. In the process a banking crisis developed. It seeped through the payment system, revealing structural weaknesses in the national economy, which was embedded with corruption and crony capitalism. The economy could not withstand the financial crisis and very soon an economic crisis developed. Before long the economic crisis had exposed institutional weaknesses in Indonesia's social and political system. Ultimately the Indonesian crisis involved practically all aspects of people's lives.

Among the many factors contributing to the Indonesian crisis, and to a certain degree the East Asian crisis as a whole, there are two closely related problems that most people agree to be the major problems facing the economy—the weak banking or financial system and unsustainable proportion of corporate debt in foreign currencies. Very close to the centre of these issues is the absence of a robust financial infrastructure, including an independent central bank.

The absence of an independent central bank is not the sole cause of the financial and banking crisis in Indonesia. The transformation of Bank Indonesia to an independent central bank would certainly not be a panacea. However, it is an important issue in its own right, and not just a reaction to the recent crisis. This chapter discusses issues of central bank independence and its relevance to macroeconomic management and economic welfare in Indonesia during the recent crisis and for the future.

A CALL FOR AN INDEPENDENT CENTRAL BANK

Indonesia adopted a system of independent central banking at the end of May 1998, when President Habibie announced his decision to put the governor of Bank Indonesia outside the cabinet—the governor of Bank Indonesia no longer has ministerial rank and no longer occupies a position of assistant to the president. In a sense this decision returned Bank Indonesia to its pre-1983 status. The legal basis for an independent Bank

Indonesia was made official with the enactment of a new bill a year later. It is explicitly mentioned in the new law that Bank Indonesia is an independent state institution, free from government or other party intervention, except on matters specifically mentioned in the law.

Discussions on the need for an independent central bank had been underway for some time before the May 1998 decision, but had been limited to seminars or parliamentary hearings with the governor and the board of directors of Bank Indonesia. The issue became more pressing when Indonesia faced financial and economic crisis in mid 1997. In fact, the issue was raised during the negotiation for an IMF stand-by loan in late October 1997. It became a requirement of the IMF-supported program, as mentioned in the second letter of intent to the IMF in January 1998.

Independent central banking is a new trend. It has been accepted practice by most countries since the end of the 1980s, when a number of economies adopted market economies after discarding economic planning. It was also mentioned as one of the requirements for joining the European Union in the Maastricht Treaty. However, as Alan Blinder (1998:53) has written, 'the term itself is somewhat vague and has occasionally been misused'. The term independence should be interpreted as meaning that the central bank has the freedom to decide on how to pursue its goals, and that its decisions are very hard for any other branch of the government to reverse—once central bank goals have been decided, the government cannot intervene on how the institution endeavours to achieve them. Stanley Fischer (1994) described this as the condition that the central bank should have instrument independence but not goal independence. In turn, the central bank has to exercise its independence in a transparent and accountable manner. Of course there are constraints that limit the authorities in making choices in policy objectives as well as instruments, as Krugman (1998e) reminds us with his eternal triangle.

At the outset it should be noted that even though there are a variety of modes of macroeconomic management, central bank responsibilities generally include monetary management, payment system and occasionally banking supervision. The central bank has the authority to supply base money and the responsibility for managing the money supply and credit and thus, interest rates determination. There are cases in which interest rates are determined by the government and, in that case, it is the responsibility of the central bank to maintain stability.

The central bank may have the sole responsibility or may work with other institutions to manage the exchange rate. In addition it may have the responsibility for managing international reserves. With respect to exchange rate determination the central bank may have the responsibility to determine which system of foreign exchange to adopt or may execute a foreign exchange system which is predetermined by the government. In economies that rely on exchange controls the central bank is usually responsible for their execution.

Central banks determine, and sometimes hold, the reserves of commercial banks, and usually oversee the national payments system. Central banks were also traditionally responsible for maintaining the stability of financial system through banking supervision and acting as lender of last resort. However, recent trends in many economies have been to entrust the supervision of banks and other financial institutions to a separate agency outside the central bank. After gaining greater independence, the Bank of Japan and Bank of England have both been released from conducting banking supervision. In fact, the United States Federal Reserve is one of the few major central banks that is still responsible for bank supervision.

The central bank may also function as the government bank. In fact, the original task of central banks was not to conduct monetary policy or support the banking system, but to finance government spending. This was the case for the Bank of Sweden, the world's oldest central bank, during its early development. Central banks may also manage government debt and provide economic and financial advice to the government.

In the early development of most emerging market economies the central bank is often the major source of financing government budget deficits. However, together with financial sector development, there has been a distinct transformation of central banking towards a more clearly defined function to include three core responsibilities—monetary management, the payments system and banking supervision. This development was influenced by a new approach to the role of the financial sector in development originating from seminal works by Shaw (1973) and McKinnon (1973). These works showed that most developing countries suffered from a condition of repressed finance whereby the financial sector, including the central bank, was put under government control in the name of economic development. As a result the banking sector was underdeveloped and ill equipped to serve the economy as financial intermediary. The economy was usually dominated by the government sector, which ran central bank-financed budget deficits.

Proponents argued that economic development would be better served by a liberalised financial sector (financial deepening), giving a theoretical basis for the financial liberalisation that followed. Some countries started a process of financial liberalisation in the early 1970s and 1980s and others joined them in the 1990s. Indonesia started financial deepening as early as in the late 1960s with deposit rate liberalisation and in the early 1970s through freeing foreign exchange control. But it was only in the 1980s that liberalisation really took its steady course.

Macroeconomic management is conducted through both fiscal and monetary policy. In the early stages of development in emerging market economies, when the state sector is still playing a dominant role, macroeconomic management is usually conducted to achieve growth and stability. With a tendency for the fiscal policy to be expansionary, monetary policy is aimed at supporting the achievement of economic growth while at the same time checking inflationary pressures.

Monetary policy in market economies is the major responsibility of the central bank. Some studies have shown that countries with independent central banks do indeed tend to have lower inflation rates and low inflation does not appear to come at the cost of slower growth. But correlation does not prove causation. *The Economist* ('Survey the world economy', 25 September 1999:4) reminds us that Germany's Reichsbank was statutorily independent when the country suffered hyperinflation in 1923. Despite some exceptions, it is generally agreed that the more independent the central bank the more effective is monetary policy in achieving monetary stability.

Monetary stability is more than just price stability. Notwithstanding the current record low rates of inflation in the industrial economies, the world is still experiencing financial crisis. With central bank independence in industrial countries, the financial system may be facing new challenges—asset inflation on the one hand and economic deflation on the other. Both seem to be developing at present in the United States and Japan respectively, at a time when inflation is very much under control. This development challenges the present day conventional wisdom that the monetary objective of a central bank is stable inflation measured in terms of the consumer price index. As Indonesia had been exposed to some economic bubbles in the past, asset inflation is certainly an issue that in the future should be addressed.

Problems facing macroeconomic management have recently become much more complicated, making central banks responsibilities more challenging. As *The Economist* ('Survey the world economy', 25 September 1999) states, 'the role of central banks has traditionally been defined in terms of banks, money and inflation. Thus at the pinnacle of their power it is disconcerting that they still have to ask three questions. What is a bank? What is money? And what is inflation?' With new innovations in financial instruments and new techniques of financial intermediation in global finance, the concept of independent central banking may need to be redefined. As if answering this issue, at least partly, the IMF in the recent interim committee meeting produced a document that specifically listed definitions of a central bank, financial agencies, financial policies and government.

INDEPENDENT CENTRAL BANKING IN PRACTICE

The central bank in a market economy is responsible for the development of a national payments system to facilitate consumption, production, investment and trade activities. In money supply creation through a fractional reserve banking system the central bank is commonly in charge of determining the reserve requirement policy, the development of payments system techniques and the regulation and infrastructure of the clearing system.

In the past it has been common to make the central bank responsible for banking supervision. However, as Fischer (1994) argues, this function is not one of the core functions of central banking. The recent tendency has been to put banking supervision together with supervision of other financial institutions under a separate autonomous body.

A crucial lesson arising from the Indonesian crisis is the necessity of placing the supervision of banks and other financial intermediaries, like finance companies and multi-finance institutions, under the same institution. In a world of global finance (compounded in Indonesia by the tendency for cross-ownership in different financial institutions), supervision of different but closely connected financial institutions is becoming ineffective and inefficient. Separate supervisory bodies would increase the chances of overlapping jurisdiction. These problems arise irrespective of whether the supervisory authority is a part of an independent central bank. It is crucial that the authority of the supervisory body cover these closely related financial institutions and that it is independent.

With the central bank both holding responsibility for banking supervision and acting as lender of last resort, monetary management was compromised during the crisis in Indonesia, as the monetary tightening required for stabilising the currency might have adversely affected the rescued banks. Against the Indonesian context of limited independence, central bank effectiveness in both functions was reduced even further

(Claessens *et al.* 1999). This strengthens the argument for a separate independent authority for the supervision of banks and other financial institutions. The argument for independent central banking is made in reference to its monetary management function.

The power to manage the money supply and bank credit gives huge leverage to the central bank, particularly in developing economies in which the banks are very dominant in the financial sector. For economies in which the central bank has the authority to control the interest rate, the policy objective is usually predetermined. The following are examples of policy goals in different countries listed by Fischer (1995).

- The German Bundesbank has been given the responsibility of maintaining the value of the currency. It is also required to support general government economic policy in so far as this is consistent with its first objective.
- From 1993, the Banque de France has been responsible for maintaining price stability within the framework of general economic policy of the government.
- The Reserve Bank of New Zealand is responsible for price stability.
- The United States Federal Reserve banks have a more general objective—to safeguard the long-term growth of money supply and credit in line with the long-run growth of production, maximum employment, price stability and a normal rate of interest.

The independence of the central bank refers to its independence in conducting monetary policy for price and/or exchange rate stability. The United States Federal Reserve is probably the only exception, with responsibilities in wide-ranging areas, and yet it is considered one of the most independent central banks. The legal status of independence has to be specifically determined in legislation. If independence is not considered important, it is not important to formulate the central bank's functions very specifically—a very detailed formulation would not make much difference. This was the case with the Bank of England before the adoption of the 1997 Act.

In a study of central banks in seventy-two developing countries, Cukierman *et al.* (1992) observed

- two countries whose central banks are responsible only for maintaining price stability, with the right to deviate from the policy of their respective governments
- seventeen countries whose central banks are responsible for maintaining price stability and other responsibilities in line with price stability
- twenty-two countries whose central banks are responsible for price stability and other responsibilities not necessarily in line with price stability
- ten countries whose central banks are not given specified responsibilities
- fifteen countries whose central banks are responsible for specific areas outside price stability.

BANK INDONESIA: LACK OF INDEPENDENCE AND THE CRISIS

At the start of the Habibie government in May 1998, by declaring Bank Indonesia's governor no longer a cabinet minister, the president gave Bank Indonesia the status of an independent central bank. But legally Bank Indonesia became independent only after the new law on Bank Indonesia was enacted in May 1999. A brief look at details of the law confirms that all the necessary requirements for an independent central bank are clearly stipulated in the law, including a clear specification of its objectives and functions, and definitions of independence, transparency and accountability. This is definitely most welcome for the development of Indonesia's banking system.

In contrast to the former law, which used a very broad definition of Bank Indonesia objectives, the new law very specifically states that the central bank has a single objective—to achieve and maintain the stability of the rupiah. Stability of the rupiah refers to both price and exchange rate stability.

Bank Indonesia's main functions encompass three areas—formulating and implementing monetary policies, managing the payments system and supervising banks. The explanatory notes of the law state that in order for the central bank to achieve effectively and efficiently the stability objective, these three functions should be integrated. It is not very clear as to what is actually meant by integrating these activities—it is somehow not in tune with the single objective of the central bank. Of the three major functions of Bank Indonesia, the most important as regards independence is that of monetary management. However, it was the intervention in Bank Indonesia's banking supervisory authority that was the trigger for the drastic loss of confidence in Indonesian banking sector in the wake of the recent crisis.

The monetary policy objective as specified in the 1968 law on Bank Indonesia was to safeguard the value of the rupiah, both in terms of prices of goods and services (price stability) and foreign currencies (exchange rate stability). Bank Indonesia was not legally independent prior to the new law. First, the responsibility for monetary policy was placed in a monetary board chaired by the Minister of Finance. The governor of Bank Indonesia was only one member, together with other economic ministers, even though he/she had the right to deviate from the board's views. Second, since 1983 the governor of the central bank was given the status of cabinet minister. The central bank became part of the government and as a consequence the governor was neither legally nor structurally independent from the government.

Bank licensing was the responsibility of the Minister of Finance. But the Ministry of Finance could only issue bank licenses on receiving a recommendation from the central bank. In other words, the central bank had the responsibility of reviewing new proposals for bank licenses to determine whether or not requirements had been fulfilled, but not to then issue bank licenses. Banking supervision was the responsibility of the central bank, while supervision for other financial institutions was in the hands of the Ministry of Finance.

With respect to the payments system there were no substantive problems that Indonesia had to face, with the exception that with rapid growth of economic activities the volume of transactions and thus fund flows had been growing tremendously. With new developments in global finance, the monetary authorities faced new challenges. The volume of daily transactions of US dollars in the money market increased from a little over US$2 billion at the beginning of the 1990s to more than US$8 billion just before the crisis. At the same time the daily volume of transactions in the capital market also increased tremendously. All of these resulted in large increases in the volume of daily payments for financing transactions. The volume of payments that the central bank clearing system had to clear increased from Rp5 trillion per day at the beginning of the 1990s to more than Rp20 trillion in 1996. These developments required the institutional development to serve payments for financing transactions efficiently and safely.

Although it is less crucial, a note on the task of managing the national payments system is in order here. Among the three functions of the central bank, one element of the system, the clearing of payments, does not conceptually have the characteristics of a public good. In future, the more advanced the private sector the more reason for the central bank to let this task be provided by the private sector instead of the central bank.

With respect to the central bank's role as the government bank, Indonesia developed a balanced budget policy concept which was controversial, but to a certain extent effective in containing the impact of fiscal policy on inflation.

The lack of central bank independence both in the determination of its goals and the choice of instruments constrained its effectiveness in the conduct of monetary management during the crisis. Prior to the crisis Bank Indonesia had great difficulty in convincing the monetary board to raise the compulsory reserve requirement for banks. It did not enjoy the freedom of determining exchange rate depreciation or appreciation since there was always some controversy between increasing the rate of depreciation for export purposes and limiting depreciation for inflation control. In August 1997 Bank Indonesia, under the instruction of the monetary board, reluctantly resorted to administrative intervention by instructing some state enterprises and semi-government foundations to transform their deposits with banks to central bank certificates to tighten liquidity. The reverse problem arose in October and November 1997 when the president gave instructions to loosen liquidity by allocating bank credit to small and medium-scale enterprises. During the crisis the president directly intervened by issuing instructions on monetary operation. These examples illustrate that Bank Indonesia did not enjoy independent status in the conduct of monetary management either conceptually or legally.

In the conduct of banking supervision Bank Indonesia faced problems that arose internally from the structural weaknesses of Indonesia's banking system, but also externally due to government intervention. The decision to close sixteen banks as the first step in the Indonesian banking restructuring on the eve of an IMF stand-by arrangement on 5 November 1997 attracted strong criticism. It was argued that the bank closures caused bank runs, which led to the banking crisis. It is ironic that the closing of these insolvent banks, which was aimed at boosting market confidence, completely eroded it amongst both clients and correspondents. Confidence was shaken even among banks as the interbank money market was compartmentalised. The argument is not against closing insolvent banks, an important part of banking restructuring, but against the timing and manner in which it was done (Djiwandono 2000).

The lack of Bank Indonesia's independence in its conduct as bank supervisory authority was clearly demonstrated in the problems related to the closing of the sixteen banks. Judging from the path of the rupiah, the market reaction was at first positive (within a couple of days the rupiah strengthened from Rp3900/US$1 to 3200), but very soon cooled. (The short-lived strengthening of the currency was helped by a joint intervention in the foreign exchange market by Bank Indonesia, the Monetary Authority of Singapore and the Bank of Japan.)

The fact that the sixteen closed banks included three banks that were partly owned by the president's family members was interpreted by foreign market players as indicating that the government was going to be even handed and serious in addressing bank problems. However, when one of the president's children and the former owner (even though actually just a minor owner) of one of the closed banks was known publicly to be allowed to take over a small bank almost immediately after the bank closure, the foreign market reaction turned negative and the pressure on the rupiah resumed. The domestic market reaction was completely different. For some time there had been concern about the weakness of some private banks, even though the public was never sure about the exact number of the weak banks nor exactly which were the problem banks. When the public learned that even banks known to be owned by president's family members were liquidated, many believed that other banks would follow. As a result depositors started to move their funds.

Lack of independence turned out to be costly. Government intervention in the process of bank closure and bank acquisition led to a negative reaction, offsetting the positive impact of a sound policy resolving problem banks within a framework of bank restructuring. The erosion of public confidence in the banking system was further enhanced by the reaction of some of the president's family members, who sued both the Minister of Finance and the governor of Bank Indonesia in court.

In addition, there seemed to be a conflict of interest in the central bank's operations as both manager of monetary policy and bank supervisor associated with the function of lender of last resort. This conflict of interest can easily emerge during periods of distress in the banking sector. In a crisis period, when a number of banks face liquidity problems that could in the short term turn into insolvency problems due to the general worsening of economic environment, monetary tightening for exchange rate stability can conflict with the implementation of policy for rescuing banks.

In a non-transparent environment with weak governance the problems became more complex. Government intervention in bank supervision constrained the central bank in pursuing its monetary policy objectives. Both banking supervision and monetary management became ineffective. The possible conflict of interest between monetary management for stability and banking supervision for financial sector stability strengthens the argument for establishing a supervision authority outside the central bank.

The recent East Asian crisis has served as a wake-up call for monetary authorities on the issue of the close relation between effective monetary policy and a sound banking system, including stringent and effective banking supervision. These two policy objectives, though both usually under central bank jurisdiction, were not recognised as closely interconnected. Issues of policy coordination between monetary policy and banking soundness has only received serious attention from monetary authorities as well as pundits and international institutions since the mid 1990s (Lindgren *et al.* 1996; Enoch and Green 1997). With the benefit of experience gained in the recent crisis, it is certainly now popular to say that effective monetary policy requires a robust banking system—a sound banking system is a *conditio sine qua non* for effective monetary policy. It is also current wisdom that financial liberalisation should be accompanied or even preceded by strengthening banking supervision.

Operating monetary policy for stability is basically a macroeconomic issue dealing with short-term variables. Tight or loose monetary policy and high or low interest rates are in general short-term issues. On the other hand, policies to produce a sound banking system, which deal with issues like banking efficiency, bank soundness as minimally measured in terms of capital, asset quality, management performance, earnings and liquidity are more micro. Likewise prudential regulation, banking supervision and the financial infrastructure are all micro and in general medium or long-term issues.

While it seems correct to say that a sound banking system is required for effective macroeconomic management, it is less certain that an economy can design a feasible program to strengthen the financial sector and ensure effective monetary policy at the same time. This would require a program that could produce a solution for micro, long-term problems in combination with macro, short-term problems. This is a daunting task facing monetary authorities of crisis-ridden economies like Indonesia, and a new challenge for both theory and policy. The results will provide a package of policies for a sustainable solution to the recent crisis.

Returning to the issue of central bank independence, the Indonesian experience would definitely attest to the argument for central bank independence for effective monetary management. There are new challenges facing the monetary and supervisory authority because of the close relationship between monetary management, which should be the sole responsibility of an independent central bank, and the soundness of banking system, which requires an independent and robust supervisory authority.

Conceptually there are some points that need clarification. It is stipulated that Bank Indonesia has been granted autonomous authority to supervise banks. But, by December 2002 Bank Indonesia is to hand over this authority to an independent financial supervisory body which will be created at a later date. As a matter of expediency it is well understood why Bank Indonesia is keeping this task now. However, retaining it for good while other financial institutions remain under a separate supervisory body would invite problems.

For Bank Indonesia to exercise its authority as an independent institution it is imperative that its functions as central bank be clearly specified and that its independent status be stipulated in law. In turn, Bank Indonesia should exercise its independence in a transparent and accountable manner. To ensure credibility Bank Indonesia must be regarded as an institution run by professionals with a high degree of integrity, from the governor to the lowest level of official. Adherence to good governance and transparency are the key words for Bank Indonesia to be an effective independent central bank.

The final point is to reiterate that no matter how important the legal base for central bank independence is, it does not guarantee to make the central bank an effective institution in achieving monetary stability and serving as a solid foundation for a robust banking system. Bank Indonesia still has to earn its reputation as an independent central bank. In the wake of rampant bank scandals this is a tough challenge to meet, and can only be done by solidifying the institution with professionalism and credibility. Good governance and transparency should be the iron rules guiding everyone from the governor down to the lowest level of Bank Indonesia personnel, or the new legal status will not mean much.

5   International policy advice in the East Asian crisis

A critical review of the debate

Gregor Irwin and David Vines

The East Asian financial crisis plunged a number of the most rapidly growing and successful economies in the world into financial chaos and a deep depression. This chapter discusses the international policy advice which was given both before and during the crisis, and outlines some of the questions that remain to be answered. This initial review is deliberately tentative. Our purpose is to point to areas needing further work rather than to provide definite conclusions.

The International Monetary Fund (IMF) published an assessment of Fund-supported programmes in Indonesia, Korea and Thailand at the beginning of last year (Lane *et al.* 1999). This is a useful resource document for the present chapter. The IMF paper concentrates on the cases of Thailand, Korea and Indonesia, and we will do the same.

We sketch a diagnosis of the crisis and briefly discuss the issues relating to crisis-prevention, and to early warning systems, which emerge from this diagnosis. We also discuss the criticism that the advice given by the IMF in the lead-up to the crisis did too little to warn the Asia-crisis countries about the danger that they were in. The claim that this confused long-term issues with what was required to solve the immediate crisis is examined, as are the reasons underlying the macroeconomic policy advice which the Fund gave as the crisis evolved, and the severe criticisms which have been made of that advice.

CAUSES OF THE CRISIS AND LESSONS OF CRISIS PREVENTION

In a series of earlier papers we present an interpretation of the causes of the crisis. This builds on the ideas of vulnerability to panic and collapse which were first put forward by Radelet and Sachs (1998) and elaborated on by Krugman (1999a and 1999b). Specifically we have argued that the Asian crisis was the result of the inter-relationship between financial and macroeconomic vulnerabilities.

We argue that vulnerability was created by capital liberalisation in the presence of a bank-based financial regime, which contained implicit promises of a government bail-out of the financial sector in the event of bad out-turns[1] (see Irwin and Vines 1999, 2000a, b). In a system underwritten by guarantees, financial liberalisation can lead to excessive investment, and the existence of multiple self-fulfilling equilibria, with the possibility of a sudden panic, a reversal of foreign capital flows, and collapse in investment.

This vulnerability was re-enforced by the maintenance of a fixed exchange rate peg into the era of capital liberalisation (Corbett and Vines 1999; Irwin and Vines 2000b). This led to an overhang of unhedged foreign currency borrowing, because of the implicit promise that the exchange rate would not be devalued. As a result, countries were exposed to the risk of a financial crisis whose key aspects were a large fall in investment, a collapse in the exchange rate, a large increase in the value of the overhang of unhedged foreign borrowing, and thus, through this additional route bail-out obligations for governments which they could not meet.

The first major lesson from the crisis is that allowing exposure to these vulnerabilities involves taking big risks. Policy advice by the IMF in the early to mid 1990s failed to draw attention to this vulnerability sufficiently strongly, and can be faulted.[2] There are lessons for crisis prevention to be learned in the field of financial regulation, particularly the need to have a healthy and well-regulated banking system.[3] Prior to the crisis banking regulation was lax[4] and the private sector maintained extremely high debt-to-equity ratios by international standards.[5] In Irwin and Vines (2000a) we show how financial sector regulation, which restricts the leverage of the private sector, can both reduce the over-investment problem and avoid vulnerability to this form of financial crisis.

There are also lessons to be learned in the design of macroeconomic policy, and in particular the exchange rate regime. In Irwin and Vines (2000b) we argue that financial liberalisation can mean that fixing the exchange rate is both undesirable—because of the loss of monetary policy as an effective policy tool—and potentially unsustainable—because it increases vulnerability to financial crises of the kind described above. Instead, we argue in favour of a move towards inflation targeting. But this itself raises significant problems in terms of sequencing. Clearly it now seems problematic to argue that one can liberalise the capital account before reforming the financial sector—and use capital account liberalisation as an agent of reform in the way in which trade liberalisation is used.[6] But what pieces of a newly reformed financial structure need to be in place before liberalisation is done? Is floating the exchange rate a precondition, to avoid the vulnerabilities associated with a fixed rate? Or does that instead create vulnerability by exposing the economy to the vagaries of an exchange rate determined in thin markets: must floating the exchange rate instead wait upon the construction of the deeper markets which come with liberalisation?

Can capital controls assist in the sequencing of this transition to inflation targeting and a floating rate? There is some—but not total—agreement that foreign direct investment (FDI) inflows are less vulnerable to reversal and outflow than portfolio and other short-term flows. There is also widespread agreement that inflow controls in the manner of Chile—which require that a proportion of short-term inflows be placed in a non-interest-bearing deposit—can influence the composition of capital inflows in the direction of FDI, and that this is less footloose in the event that a crisis leads to outflows[7]. But there is little agreement as to whether this will cause a country to be less vulnerable to capital withdrawal (because there is a smaller stock of liquid, footloose foreign funds) or whether such controls will make little difference (because the existence of a stock of liquid domestic funds may be sufficient to facilitate outflow in such circumstances).[8] Nevertheless, it does appear that such controls can give a country some breathing space along the path to liberalisation, perhaps even allowing it to temporarily dampen a boom in demand with interest rates higher than in the rest of the world without forcing it to abandon a pegged exchange rate regime.[9]

LESSONS FROM CONFUSING LONG-TERM ISSUES WITH A SOLUTION TO THE IMMEDIATE CRISIS

At the scene of a traffic accident we would be surprised to see the ambulance crew spending much time fixing the brakes of the cars that had crashed, rather than concentrating on trying to get the injured passengers onto life support systems.[10] According to one diagnosis (Feldstein 1998), the IMF did just this. An explanation by a Fund official of what the IMF thought itself to be doing, ran

> These...programs were not conventional IMF austerity programmes...these are close to programmes in transition economies. The Asian economies also have deficient policy and institutional structures...The Thai, Indonesian and Korean reforms seek to build the necessary institutional and policy structures consistent with their integration into global financial markets (Nellor 1999:249).

The defence offered in the Fund's own considered assessment (Lane *et al.* 1999) was that

> ...the strategy had to include two broad strands: the immediate crisis, triggered by the serious weaknesses in the balance sheets of financial institutions, had to be dealt with; and the systems had to be reformed to minimise the likelihood of a recurrence...The overriding question is whether it was right to place so much emphasis on structural measures in the financial and corporate sectors...The answer is clearly yes. Given the state of the financial system and the related difficulties in the corporate sector, which played a key role in the emergence of the crisis, the programs would have had little chance of success and little hope of gaining credibility in without beginning a set of decisive steps to address these problems. Macroeconomic policies would have been undermined by the continuing deterioration in financial sector conditions, which was bound to lead to a rapid liquidity expansion and a ballooning of quasi fiscal deficits. Moreover the ultimate goal of the programs—a quick return to sustainable growth—would not have been possible in an environment of protracted and deepening structural problems in the financial and corporate sectors.

The criticism of Feldstein (1998) is that the stance of the Fund led to a 'Christmas tree' approach to financial and structural reform, with all sorts of requirements for reform stuck together. Some of these might, he argues, have been desirable. But there were too many of them, and more importantly, they were stuck together with no clear framework connecting their relevance to the crisis at hand.

The key analytical point is that all can applaud a desire to promote policies which foster long-term economic progress. But for the Fund to become heavily involved in such policies may involve confusing both responsibilities and time-scales. Ever since the Keynesian revolution it has been understood that there is a distinction between—on the one hand—the short-run stabilisation of output, prices, and the external balance, and—on the other hand—structural polices which promote longer-term growth. We argued above that the crisis was the kind of coordination-failure problem which requires short-run, crisis-prevention macroeconomic policies. The IMF should focus on these.[11] This is a second major area in which lessons should be drawn from the crisis.

The remainder of the chapter is confined to macroeconomic adjustment policies with a shorter time horizon, and whether they were adequate. To do this we first discuss in more detail the onset and unfolding of the crisis, and present our interpretation of how it appeared to the IMF at the time.

THE INITIAL CRISIS AND INITIAL ADVICE

The Thai baht floated on 2 July 1997 after months of pressure. The short-term effect was a 20 per cent depreciation against the US dollar. Soon afterwards pressure mounted on the Indonesian rupiah; the intervention band on the rupiah was widened on 11 July, and the currency floated on 14 August. For some time the Korean won was relatively unaffected by the currency speculation elsewhere in the region, but by October 1997 it was under considerable pressure and by December that year it had depreciated by 20 per cent against the US dollar.[12]

The initial approach adopted by the IMF-supported programmes in dealing with the crisis had two elements. The first was an application of the Fund's 'financial programming' approach. This combined a monetary policy designed to be consistent with a modest depreciation of the exchange rate—so as to promote adjustment through the promotion of net exports—with some tightening of fiscal policy—so as to curb domestic absorption.[13] The second was the provision of large financing packages, from the Fund and with bilateral support. These were designed to help restore confidence and to help tide the economies over a period of adjustment.[14]

However, instead of the modest exchange rate adjustment envisaged, coupled with the expected restoration of confidence, currencies in the region went into free fall. By the end of January 1998, the Thai, Indonesian, and Korean currencies had fallen by approximately 50, 75, and 40 per cent, respectively, compared with their pre-crisis levels.

Understanding, and forming a judgement about, the policy advice which was given as the crisis developed depends on the view taken as to why this happened. In what follows we first attempt to give a sympathetic 'rational reconstruction' of the Fund's monetary policy response to its understanding of what was going wrong. Then we provide an alternative interpretation of what happened. This leads to a discussion of how monetary policy might have been better conducted.

MONETARY POLICY AND THE INTEREST RATE DEFENCE

Our view of the IMF's response: 'addressing the risk of a devaluation-inflation spiral'

In retrospect, it seems that the Fund both identified the cause of the exchange rate pressure as a widespread fear of a breakdown in monetary discipline, and were concerned to prevent further devaluations becoming self-fulfilling.

It is important to sympathise here with the difficulties faced by international advisors as the crisis developed. In all three countries there was what Lane *et al.* (1999) describe as a 'lack of resolution' in the application of appropriate monetary policies. The Indonesian authorities initially raised interest rates but then rolled the increase back; later, in November, the bank runs which followed the closure of a number of banks led to liquidity support whose effect was a very significant monetary expansion. The Korean authorities were reluctant to raise interest rates at the outset. In Thailand there was a tendency to lower interest rates at the first signs of exchange rate instability. More generally, the credibility of policies was impaired in all three countries by financial sector weaknesses which were seen by many to limit the authorities' scope to raise interest rates (Lane *et al.* 1999:39, 69).

A sketch of the problem as it might have appeared to the IMF, and the IMF's response, follow.

'Suppose', the Fund might have said, 'that markets do not know whether the authorities in a country are attempting to stabilise the exchange rate around a level consistent with the moderate depreciation envisaged in the initial Fund programmes—say by 10 per cent—or whether, instead, that the authorities are reconciled to letting the exchange rate go, say to fall by 50 per cent. If speculators believe that policymakers will follow the first course then the exchange rate would fall by only this amount, without any need to raise the interest rate differential between the country and the rest of the world at all. But suppose instead that speculators come to fear that policymakers will follow the second course. Then to achieve only a 10 per cent depreciation would require that the interest rate differential between the country and the rest of the world be raised by 40 percentage points. However that, in turn, might be so costly that the authorities would not do it. So the fear could be self-fulfilling.'

If this interpretation is correct then we could think of the Fund's interest rate policy as motivated by a response to the possibility of a self-fulfilling breakdown of monetary discipline. We interpret the Fund's concerns as being designed to prevent a cumulative collapse of the currency. That is, we take it the Fund was concerned to prevent a circumstance in which the currency falls because of fears of monetary expansion, fears that become justified because they provoke the very monetary expansion which was feared.

One representation of the Fund's response to this perceived possibility is just that it was designed to strengthen the resolve of the authorities, by encouraging them to do what was necessary to frustrate attempts by speculators to take the economy to the self-fulfilling crisis outcome. A representation of the Fund's response to this perceived possibility is told here as a story of a sequential process, in which markets were not initially sure of the resolve of the policy authorities.

Suppose that speculators initially believe that there is a 50 per cent probability that the policymakers are of a 'strong' type, who are prepared to pay a high price to prevent the currency from ultimately falling more than 10 per cent. Suppose that speculators also believe that there is a 50 per cent probability that the policymakers in the country under consideration are of a 'weak' type, who are only prepared to pay a low price—in terms of unemployment, for example—to prevent the currency from ultimately falling by more than the moderate depreciation of 10 per cent, and who might be prepared to allow the ultimate depreciation to be as much as 50 per cent. Then, if interest rates were not raised immediately, there would be immediate pressures on the currency to depreciate, and to a first approximation this depreciation might be one of around 30 per cent (= 0.5*[10 + 50]). Let us suppose that the consequence of this is inflation in the second period. Now imagine that the policymaker really is strong. In the second period the strong policymaker would face an incentive to raise interest rates, so as to bring the currency back to its modest depreciation of only 10 per cent before some third period, well into the future, when the economy had settled down. The inclination to do this would be much stronger than for a weak policymaker. However, it would be known that this would be costly, because the inflation which had occurred in the second period might be difficult to 'squeeze' out of the system, due to nominal rigidities. Such a strong policymaker might find it preferable to try to avoid such future costs by raising interest rates now. We can interpret the Fund's policy advice as an indication to policymakers of the advantages of doing this.

But we can push this story one stage further, and interpret the advice given by the IMF as advice to policymakers to attempt to signal that they were strong policymakers who would not let the currency collapse.[15] It might be that a strong policymaker could signal in this way at a relatively low cost. This would be the case if a weak policymaker was not prepared to make even a small initial rise in interest rates in the first period; in that case a strong policymaker would be able to convince speculators of the policymaker's strength, and thus that the currency would not ultimately fall by more than 10 per cent. In such a circumstance a strong policymaker could defend the currency by means of only a rather modest rise in interest rates.

If this story of rationalisation of the IMF's position has some validity then the following critical comment seems to be in order. We know that there are a number of possible outcomes of such a signalling game, not all of which would be so attractive for a strong policymaker. It might be that the difference between weak and strong policymakers is not as great as has been supposed. It may be that a policymaker who was only 'medium weak' would attempt to match the initial rise in interest rates which would be introduced by a strong policymaker; in that case a strong policymaker would not be able to convince speculators of the policymaker's strength, and thus the currency would ultimately fall by more than 10 per cent. To convince speculators, the strong policymaker must instead raise the interest rate to a much higher level—so high as to be too costly for a 'medium weak' policymaker to implement. It may be that such a signal might be too costly to send for a strong policymaker. This remark raises questions—possibly significant ones—about the viability of using the 'interest rate defence'. It may provide one reason why the Fund's interest-rate defence turned out to be so costly. It suggests that, because we know that signalling games are rather complicated, it would be useful, at the very least, to set out the whole idea more formally so as to see what reliance could really be placed on it.[16]

What happened—a spiral of devaluation and output collapse

A stronger criticism of the IMF's position, as we have interpreted it above, follows. Central to the reason for defending the currency in the above account is the objective of preventing inflation which would subsequently be difficult to remove. However, what actually happened is that, although the currencies collapsed, inflation did not take off. In Korea and Thailand the inflation of non-traded goods' prices was negligible, and in Indonesia it was low. This is most simply demonstrated by comparing the extent of exchange rate depreciation with the extent of CPI inflation. Normally one would expect consumer price index (CPI) inflation, after lags had washed out, to be roughly equal to the exchange rate depreciation times the import content of output and expenditures, plus any domestic demand effects. In all of these countries CPI inflation was significantly less than this.[17] Thus, what was observed was rapidly rising import costs, much less rapidly rising prices in the consumption basket, and a low or negative increase in the price of the domestic content of the consumption basket.[18]

Although the currencies did collapse, instead of the devaluation-inflation spiral which it had been the Fund's purpose to prevent, there was—by contrast—a collapse in output. It was this which became entangled in the currency collapse, so that there was an output-devaluation spiral. In its initial programme projections for Thailand, Korea and Indonesia, the IMF estimated that in 1998, GDP growth rates would be 4, 2, and 3 per cent, respectively. But by October 1998 these projections had been revised downwards to -8, -7, and -15 per cent, respectively.[19] The mistake was not understanding early enough that output would collapse, and not having a clear understanding of the spiral involved.

The proximate reason that this massive downturn occurred was that investment collapsed; gross fixed investment fell by more than one quarter in Korea and Thailand and by more than half in Indonesia. There were several initial reasons for this. Some of the investment which had been undertaken in the previous boom came to seem unsound. Part of the previous boom had been in unsatisfactory projects whose return was buoyed both by optimism about market growth which the downturn then suggested was unsustainable (McKibbin and Martin 1998). In addition, some of the investment had been in projects for which the expected returns were buoyed by implicit promises of government guarantees. With the onset of the crisis, it began to seem unlikely that these would be sustained. Both of these reasons created a desire to reduce investment in the region. Furthermore, the developing recession created excess capacity and made formerly good investment turn bad in the non-traded sector. The fall in investment magnified the downturn caused by the export collapse.

But worse was to follow. The falls in the exchange rate became entangled in the collapse. As Krugman (1999) has argued, a falling exchange rate increased the indebtedness of firms, leading to a reduction of collateral available to finance investment, leading to a further fall in investment, and thus to a need for a further fall in the exchange rate to restore macroeconomic equilibrium. Furthermore, as argued by Corbett, Irwin and Vines (1999), since a falling exchange rate increased the indebtedness of firms, the likelihood of government guarantees of losses being honoured fell, because the losses became so large. This was a further reason for falling investment, leading to a yet further fall in the exchange rate.

Thus the fall in the exchange rate was associated not as, according to our interpretation, the Fund had feared, with a spiral of exchange rate falls, inflation, and further exchange rate falls. Instead it was associated with a spiral of exchange rate falls, increases in indebtedness, output falls, and further exchange rate falls.

The debate about the interest rate defence

In light of the above, it is now argued by many that the Asian crises rapidly and radically worsened because macroeconomic policymakers—in the light of IMF advice—failed to treat the right problem: at the scene of the traffic accident they did not have quite the right life-support systems with them. They applied medicines, it is said, appropriate for the IMF's perception of the problem, which was that there was a risk of an inflation-devaluation spiral, instead of policies which would have been appropriate for the cumulative collapse in output discussed above. This is in fact a complex debate which needs some disentangling.

A justification of the Fund's approach

We can put this view in terms of a trade-off between the problems caused by higher interest rates and those caused by a more depreciated exchange rate.

It was the essence of the Fund view that any further move along the trade-off towards lower interest rates was likely to be welfare-reducing, because there might have been further falls in the exchange rate which might well have ignited the devaluation-inflation spiral which the Fund feared.

This view was put in a blunt way by Nellor (1998:251): 'the possibility of operating with lower interest rates and a larger devaluation is not a useful option'. Lane *et al.* (1999:85–6, 121) put this view in a more measured way.

> The basic objective of monetary policy in these programs was to avoid an inflation devaluation spiral…Monetary policy, albeit only after some period, achieved its basic objective of avoiding a depreciation inflation spiral in both Korea and Thailand—without necessitating persistent and egregiously high real interest rates…Monetary policy in Indonesia, until the stabilisation of recent months, is quite a different story: a virtually complete loss of monetary control in the face of the banking collapse and political turmoil…This experience illustrates the danger that even in a previously stable economy, a vicious circle of inflation and depreciation can emerge.

But as the adverse effects of falls in the exchange rate on the health of the financial and corporate sectors became apparent, the Fund view was modified, and acquired a second component. This was that letting the exchange rate fall any further than it had was likely to have a greater negative effect on the financial and corporate sectors than the adverse effect of the interest rate defence required to prevent it (Lane *et al.* 1999:70–5).

Criticism of the Fund's position

The problem of output collapse identified above—in which a falling exchange rate increased the indebtedness of firms, leading to a reduction of collateral available to finance investment, a further fall in investment, and a further fall in the exchange rate to restore macroeconomic equilibrium—was clearly exacerbated by the higher interest rates resulting from the Fund-supported interest rate defence. Furman and Stiglitz (1998) argue that interest rates were pushed to a level at which the benefit which they caused through defending the exchange was less than the cost of the higher interest rates in weakening the balance sheets of firms, and further that their effect on the exchange effect may have actually been perverse, due to their impact on balance sheets that were already crippled by currency depreciations.

In partial support of this argument we note that non-traded goods' price inflation was either low or negligible. This—at the least—calls into question the claim by Lane *et al.* (1999:67–83) that interest rates were 'consistently negative from late 1997 through August 1998' in Indonesia, and that in Korea and Thailand, real interest became low or negative in the months immediately following the onset of the exchange rate crisis. The authors justify this claim by comparing nominal interest rates and CPI inflation.[20] However, from a different perspective based on non-traded goods' price inflation, real interest rates were very high indeed. This highlights the problem that the measurement of real interest rates is difficult in periods of rapid changes in relative prices. What the figures for non-traded goods' price inflation quoted above do suggest is that—at least from one point of view—there was a highly restrictive monetary environment, in that the rapid increases in consumer prices were hardly passed on at all.

This argument effectively asserts that the interest rate increases adopted were so large as to have gone into the region of negative returns, in effect asserting that not only did they contribute to the output fall but they actually worsened the exchange rate collapse (Stiglitz 1998a and 1998b; Furman and Stiglitz 1998). Although these increases raised the yields on holding assets in the crisis countries, they also—so the argument goes—contributed to the collapse described above by adding to the default risk and thus not necessarily assisting with the stabilisation of the currency. Indeed, they may even have had the opposite effect.

This is clearly a difficult debate. There is a review of the evidence on this problem in Lane *et al.* (1999:70–5) but it is inconclusive. Thus, these authors ask

> whether the authorities should have pushed interest rates to much higher levels in order to stabilise the exchange rate. In addition to concerns over the likely effects of such a policy on the real economy, it is not clear that this approach would have been successful in stabilising exchange rates under the conditions prevailing in early 1998. For one thing, real interest rates far higher than those that actually prevailed might have had little favourable impact on international capital flows, or may even have had a perverse effect, due to their impact on balance sheets that were already crippled by currency depreciations.

This passage co-opts the arguments of the IMF's critics, who believed that interest rates did actually reach levels at which such perverse effects became important, in order to claim that interest rates should have been raised as far as they were but no further. But no evidence is given in support of this judgement.

AN ALTERNATIVE APPROACH

The unsatisfactory nature of the above debate suggests another perspective. Here we want to reframe the question for monetary policy not so much as whether the currencies should have been defended more or less, but whether there might have been ways of achieving a given degree of stabilisation at lower interest rate cost, that is, whether lower interest rate increases than those which occurred could have been consistent with no-worse outcomes for the exchange rates, which were, after all, very large falls. This takes us back to the signalling issue raised by our interpretation of the Fund's position. We wish to ask whether the Fund could have acted to prevent an inflation-devaluation spiral in some way other than attempting to signal a commitment to defend the exchange rate.

A comparison with the United Kingdom is salutary. After its exit from the ERM, UK policy quickly gravitated to a new form of nominal anchor, namely an inflation target. This was presented to the public very soon after the exchange rate collapse, and provided a trajectory for prices which it was the intention of monetary policy to follow. It was made clear that the interest rate would be manipulated in order to steer prices onto this trajectory. The important thing about such an inflation target strategy is that it effectively operates in two dimensions. The instrument of monetary control remains the interest rate. But there is also an announced target for prices towards which the interest rate is aiming to steer the economy. This second aspect is a critical part of this strategy. It is useful for domestic price and wage setters. But it is also crucially important for the foreign exchange market by providing a partial anchor for the long-run nominal exchange rate.[21]

The sooner something like this second element of the strategy is in place, the more quickly interest rates can be cut to low levels without endangering the exchange rate. The government has less need to signal its intention not to inflate by means of high interest rates.

Economists in the IMF have examined the conditions necessary for the introduction of such a strategy in a useful paper (Eichengreen *et al.* 1999). Institutional conditions include the creation of an independent, or quasi-independent, central bank with the remit to pursue price stability as its central objective. There must be good data for a chosen measure of inflation, and also there must be the analytical capacity to make forecasts of this, and to project the difference that interest rate changes would make to out-turns for it. There must be operational capacity to manipulate the discount rate in a financial system which has been structured—through the terms of access of commercial banks to the discount window—so that this manipulation sets the base of the structure of market interest rates. Finally, the central bank must be widely believed to be accountable for achieving the inflation target, and the way in which it makes its decisions—feeding back from gaps between the inflation forecast and the inflation target to changes in the discount rate—must be transparent and must be considered to be so. Of course all of this takes time to achieve. The idea that it could have been quickly available as a strategy for the crisis countries is unrealistic.

Nevertheless, the question remains as to whether the interest rate defence could have been achieved at lower cost by some reorientation involving elements of an inflation target strategy. As it was, in the absence of the preconditions just described, the authorities—with Fund advice—cast their strategy in terms of defending the exchange rate, rather than in terms of stabilising the price level, on the key grounds that the former involved responding to a day-by-day observable variable whereas the latter would have involved responding to developments in a variable which policy could not manipulate in a well-understood way (Lane *et al.* 1999). Nevertheless, they did not wish to give any precise hostages to fortune about the exchange rate, and as a result were unwilling to commit themselves to any more than 'achieving exchange market stability'. This gave market participants very little to base their forecasts on. In the absence of this, as the example discussed above shows, the attainment of exchange stability can occur at many different exchange rates. The one chosen depends upon the market's perception of the authorities' intentions. During the crisis months, it seems that there was a process of repeated testing of the authorities' position at lower and lower exchange rates. Crucially, it seems that this very testing drove the authorities into partial retreat, perhaps helping to create the vicious circle which it was the intention of the authorities to avoid. In this context, the task of signalling which—according to our interpretation—the authorities were hoping to perform was severely complicated.

We believe that there might have been a gain in instead revealing the authorities' intentions to achieve low and stable inflation after the crisis and in describing—in broad terms—how interest rate policy would be constructed so as to achieve this objective. This would have avoided giving the markets the alternative hostage to fortune of trying to defend the current rate in the market. It would have given market participants freedom to take the spot rate lower as they chose. At the same time market participants would have been given the rough expectation that lower exchange rates would be associated with higher (nominal) interest rates and also with capital gain as the currency returned towards levels more consistent with the illustrative inflation strategy.

LESSONS FROM THE FISCAL POLICY EXPERIENCE

We have already set out the rationale for the original fiscal stance of the IMF programs. The relevant figures appear in Lane *et al.* (1999:87–93). The initial programs sought fiscal consolidation of 2.1 per cent of GDP in Thailand (or 3.2 per cent excluding the costs of bank restructuring). In Indonesia the programmed adjustment was smaller (1.1 per cent and 1.6 per cent of GDP, respectively), and even smaller in Korea (0.8 per cent and 1.6 per cent of GDP, respectively). In Korea and Indonesia the current account deficit was modest and so the fiscal consolidation sought was relatively small. In Thailand the large current account deficit suggested to the IMF the need for a larger fiscal adjustment to make room for additional external correction.

All of the reasoning underlying these calculations is effectively based on the assumption that these economies would be operating at close to full utilisation of resources. Fiscal consolidation was required to 'make room'—so the argument went—for the resources which would be diverted into the trade balance by the modest currency depreciations which the programs envisaged, and also to 'make room' for amortised costs of financial restructuring. Such fiscal stringency was required 'in support of' the interest rate defence required to prevent the inflation-devaluation spiral which was feared. One can see how fiscal stringency could also have been thought to be a signalling device, helping to confirm the message that the policymakers were not the type who would 'let prices go'.

Unfortunately, the full-utilisation assumption and the resulting policy turned out to be entirely inappropriate. It was eventually abandoned, and by mid-1998 the fiscal position had swung round to helping to moderate the collapse in output; '…program revisions accommodated a substantial part of changing economic conditions on the fiscal position from the start of 1998. Later in the programs, revisions went beyond accommodation to incorporate some additional stimulus' (Lane *et al.* 1999:97).

However the critical issue is timing. The case of Indonesia makes the point most strongly. In the last two months of 1997 the Fund had accepted that there would not be a budget surplus of 1.1 per cent of GDP as projected above, but was still seeking to ensure—along standard lines—that fiscal deficits should not rise during an adjustment program. Indeed because of the costs of the bank restructuring the Fund was still seeking to achieve a surplus of 1 per cent of GDP (Fischer 1998). It has been claimed that, in November and December 1997, after the dust settled from the bank closure fiasco,[22] a genuine effort was made to stabilise the fiscal situation. But it became clear that, because of the collapse of output, the budget due at the very beginning of 1998 would only achieve a surplus of minus 1.5 per cent or minus 2 per cent of GDP. One might have argued then in the face of collapsing output that allowing the fiscal deficit to rise would help cushion the output fall, rather than helping to ignite the feared inflation-devaluation spiral.

The Fund chose not to accept the deficit along these lines, and were strongly critical. The result was in fact a signal, not that more would be done, but instead that policy was out of control. Until that point the rupiah had gone from 2.5k to the dollar to 4k to the dollar; that is, despite Indonesia's travails, its currency had hardly fared any worse than that of Korea or Thailand. But in the aftermath of the public renunciation in Washington of what was happening in Jakarta, the markets turned on Indonesia. By the end of January the rupiah had reached over 17k to the dollar. Although it subsequently recovered, this was the moment at which the gravity of the Indonesian outcome diverged from that of the other crisis countries. There is thus a plausible line that the attempt to seek excessively tight fiscal policy led to the currency collapse which it was the very purpose of policy to avoid. The prevalent view is that the meltdown was inevitable because the crisis coincided with the endgame of the Suharto regime. But this view may provide too much cover for those who committed policy mistakes. It does seem that there could have been a less dreadful outcome than the one which emerged as 1998 wore on.

The fiscal errors in Indonesia were by far the worst. But elsewhere the same kinds of mistakes were made. There was an initial move towards fiscal tightening, so as to build up a 'war chest' to pay for the costs of bailing out and restructuring the financial sector. This was coupled with a refusal to let the automatic stabilisers operate as output plummeted.[23] One can thus certainly argue that elsewhere too, fiscal austerity worsened the depressions. But, more than this, one can argue that the (predictable) failure to meet the fiscal targets added to the air of crisis, making adjustment harder. Fiscal positions were eventually greatly relaxed, but too late.

LESSONS FROM FINANCIAL RESTRUCTURING

As we have noted, the IMF was initially overly concerned with long-term institutional reform. But certain immediate measures are necessary to facilitate the return to functioning of the troubled financial and corporate sector. 'Financial and corporate sector restructuring tends to be a protracted process even under favourable circumstances. During this process, uncertainty about the state of the financial system and the corporate sector is likely to persist for some time and to influence market perceptions of private sector creditworthiness' (Lane *et al.* 1999). Many experiences—from the US in the mid 1930s, and the Scandinavian experience of the early 1990s, to the Japanese failure to act in the mid 1990s—have shown that decisive reconstruction facilitates the early resumption of growth.

In the three countries being discussed, actions were taken to suspend or close a number of clearly insolvent institutions at the beginning of the programs in all three countries, but further progress proved to be a long and drawn out affair, inhibiting the recovery process. In Thailand it took a year for a comprehensive strategy to emerge. In Korea and Indonesia the initial process was slower still.

What all of these processes have demonstrated is that it is unrealistic to rely on private schemes for recapitalisation, as had been initially hoped by the IMF; public coordination and public money is needed. The *quid pro quo* for this must be decisive changes in ownership and management, which are likely to be resisted: this is part of the reason for the difficulty in effecting speedy and decisive action. Ensuring rapid progress in the face of this coordination problem may require external state-managed intervention.[24]

Reconstruction can involve—indeed require—decisive action to be taken against the interest of foreign creditors of the private sector. It is important that the IMF not seem too beholden to the interests of these creditors.

There are two additional questions which we do not address in detail here. The first concerns to what extent (if at all) changes in the 'international architecture' are needed in order to facilitate the restructuring of sovereign debts, and the writing down of these debts in some circumstances. The Korean experience illustrated the need for the IMF, where necessary in conjunction with national Treasuries, to be able to 'cajole' private sector creditors into rolling over sovereign debt. At the time it looked to outsiders as if the Banks to which Korea owed money were extracting too high a price for this rollover; but at the same time it seemed to insider Banks that this was not so, which is why coercion was necessary. More than this, at times actual write-downs, rather than mere cajoling may be needed. Despite the potential moral hazard problems involved, and despite the potential threats that this would pose to the system of international capital flows, it seems that the IMF needs to be able to develop the legitimacy and powers for such action in extreme circumstances.

The second concerns the extent to which economy-wide action on private sector debts is necessary. In the absence of decisive economy-wide reconstruction, the Korean experience is now suggesting that rapid growth can nevertheless be resumed; recovery in Korea has actually overtaken the process of restructuring. A sufficient sustained depreciation of the real exchange rate can lay the basis for an export-led recovery, which effectively recapitalises the industrial sector through an inflow of profits, thereby improving the loan book of the financial sector. This process enables balance sheets to be rebuilt rather than written down. (But this is by no means costless for taxpayers, since the counterpart of a heavily depreciated real exchange rate is a reduction in real incomes.) At the other end of the spectrum, Indonesia suggests that when the overhang is too large this is just not possible. With between one-half and three-quarters of the financial and corporate sector bankrupt, an interlocking structure of unresolved claims hangs over the whole private sector. The prospect of resolving this logjam by individual bankruptcy proceedings through the bankruptcy courts seems slim. Some economy-wide bankruptcy proceedings seem essential. But very little work has been done on how they might be designed or implemented.

LESSONS FOR THE RAPID RESUMPTION OF GROWTH

This paper has reviewed the lessons to be learned from the failures of the policy advice given in the run-up to and during the East Asian crisis. The early part of the paper reviewed prevention measures. Crucial, we have argued, is a reconstruction of financial systems and of the parts of the corporate industrial sector damaged by the crisis, and we briefly reviewed the issues involved in the final section of the paper. But the central concern of the paper has been to review how macroeconomic policy might better avoid exacerbating a crisis in the short-term and how macroeconomic policy might help create the preconditions necessary for the resumption of growth after the onset of a crisis. Central to this is the creation of a framework during a crisis, where the interest rate defence does not need to be so heavily relied on for the defence of the currency. We suggested a move as rapidly as possible towards a floating exchange rate with an inflation-targeting framework as the nominal anchor. The more rapidly some such framework can be put in place the sooner will it be safe to ease both monetary and fiscal policy, thus aiding recovery.

When the short-term recovery is achieved, one important long-term question remains. How much work on prevention is necessary to remove future vulnerability? And how can we ensure that the economies do enough structural reform to avoid being at risk of a repeat crisis?

NOTES

* This is a revised version of a paper presented at a conference on *International Capital Mobility and Domestic Economic Stability* held in Canberra, Australia, 13–16 July 1999 and hosted by the Reinventing Bretton Woods Committee, The World Bank and The Australian National University. We are grateful to participants at the conference, and particularly grateful to Ross Garnaut, for helpful comments. We would also like to acknowledge valuable conversations on these issues with Charles Adams, Stan Fischer, Timothy Lane and Paul Masson (IMF), Joe Stiglitz (World Bank), and Caroline Atkinson (US Treasury).

1 See Irwin and Vines (1999, 2000a and 2000b).

2 See the passages on pp. 52, 66 and 67 which say precisely this in the report by John Crow, Richard Arriazu, and Niels Thygesen (IMF 1999) which was commissioned by the IMF. The views expressed are contested on pp. 106–11 of IMF (1999) in the Comments by the Fund's Research Department on the report, which are published alongside the report itself.

3 It is important not to overemphasise the extent to which problems will be solved by improved transparency alone.

4 Smith (1998) discusses weaknesses in the regulation of the financial sector in South Korea in the period before the crisis.

5 According to Lane *et al.* (1999), average ratios of corporate debt-to-equity were 395 per cent and 450 per cent in Korea and Thailand, respectively, compared with 144 per cent in Germany and just 106 per cent in the United States.

6 'Although country circumstances differ, the general advice on international financial sector liberalisation is first to open to longer-term investment, particularly foreign direct investment, and only to open at the short end when the necessary preconditions, in the form of macroeconomic stability and a strong banking and financial system are in place' (Fischer 1998).

7 This view is, however, contested by Claessens *et al.* (1995).

8 This lack of agreement is reflected in the ambiguity in studies like that by Athukorala and Warr (1999) as to whether the ratio of M2 to reserves, or the ratio of the stock of short-term capital inflow to reserves, is a measure of vulnerability.

9 See Williamson (2000).

10 We owe this metaphor to Stephen Grenville.

11 This view is in accord with the view presented by US Treasury Secretary Larry Summers in a speech at the London Business School on 14 December 1999, reported in the *Economist*, 18–30 December 1999:153.

12 Lane *et al.* (1999) provide a very clear and detailed description of these events.

13 For Korea and Indonesia, the current account deficit was modest and so the required reduction suggested by this approach would be small (as indeed it was in the initial programme—see Lane *et al.* 1999). In Thailand the export fall was superimposed upon a large current account deficit suggesting the need for a larger fiscal adjustment to make room for additional external correction (see Lane *et al.* 1999).

14 The sufficiency of financing is the key to the viability of a Fund-supported program. The size of short-term liabilities was such that it was essential that creditors roll over at least a good part of their positions. Inducing them to do so required: persuading them that the programmes would work, showing them that there was enough official money available to make them work, and suggesting that pulling money out would not be in their long-term interests—a particularly difficult task when dealing with short-term, fixed-value credits.

15 This argument has been developed formally by Hwee Loo Tan in an MPhil thesis submitted to Oxford University in April 1999.

16 In particular it would be useful to formalise the role of the IMF in this game.

17 1998 CPI inflation outcomes were 80 per cent, 8 per cent and 10 per cent in Indonesia, Korea and Thailand, respectively.

18 See Lane *et al.* (1999) for details of what happened to CPI inflation.

19 See Lane *et al.* (1999) for more detail.

20 The relevant summary figures are: maximum nominal interest rates of 60 per cent and above in Indonesia, over 30 per cent in Korea, and over 25 per cent in Thailand; and 1998 CPI inflation outcomes of 80 per cent, 8 per cent and 10 per cent, respectively.

[21] Such a target cannot entirely remove uncertainty about the long-run nominal exchange rate. This is because it does not remove uncertainty about the long-run real exchange rate, but only about the price level at which this real exchange rate will be reached.

[22] In dealing with the Indonesian crisis the IMF was forced to take rapid action, and closed sixteen banks. But it took this action without being able to say whether those banks which remained open were candidates for closure in the longer-term reform process, and the result was widespread panic.

[23] This statement is deliberate. It is not adequate to argue, as in Lane *et al.* (1999) that there was gradual adjustment of the programs as the severity of the downturn became apparent.

[24] See Pyo (1999) for a description of the difficult conflicts of interest which also face the state when it attempts such intervention.

6 Which short-term debt over reserve ratio works best?

Operationalising the Greenspan Guidotti rule

Matthieu Bussière and Christian Mulder[*]

The East Asia crisis has highlighted the critical role of reserves. Countries at the core of the crisis—Thailand, Korea and Indonesia—had very limited reserves in relation to short-term debt. So did Russia a year later. Against the background of widespread emerging economy crises, and the role therein of reserves, Alan Greenspan, chair of the United States Federal Reserve, has advocated the use of reserves over short-term debt as a key indicator for assessing reserve adequacy (Greenspan 1999a and 1999b). In this he follows earlier ideas by Guidotti, then-deputy Finance Minister for Argentina, that countries should be able to go without foreign borrowing for at least a year. More specifically, Greenspan proposed that reserves should exceed scheduled amortisation of debt for the following year (that is, short-term debt by remaining maturity).

Bussière and Mulder (1999) found broad support for the notion that holding reserves that exceed short-term debt by remaining maturity would help avert deep crises. Other authors have found similarly important effects for short-term debt in relation to reserves in predicting external crises (Borensztein *et al.* 1999; Rodrick and Velasco 1999).

However, important questions have been raised by users regarding the specification of these indicators. Should other financing needs, such as a current account deficit, be covered as well, by reserves? Should corporate short-term debt be covered by reserves too? Should foreign assets of the banking system and other non-reserve assets be taken into account instead of only reserve assets? Should foreign assets be augmented when variability of flows is high? This paper seeks to answer these four questions. They are operationally of great significance as it implies large changes in the reserves required. Based on the approach by Sachs, Tornell and Velasco (1996) and Bussière and Mulder (1999), we analyse these issues, estimating for a sample of twenty-two emerging markets the factors that contributed to the depth of crises during crisis periods (Table 6.1).

AUGMENTING SHORT-TERM DEBT WITH FINANCING NEEDS

Should short-term debt be augmented by an estimate of financing needs other than debt repayment? These other financing needs are primarily driven by the current account deficit. They can be met by borrowing but also by equity inflows, both in the form of

Table 6.1 Name and definition of variables used

Variables	Definition	Source
Dependent variables		
Crisis index	The crisis index is a weighted average of the nominal exchange rate depreciation and the loss of reserves during the crisis periods	
Periods considered	November 1994–April 1995 July–December 1997 July–October 1998	
Countries considered	22 emerging market economies: Argentina, Brazil, Chile, Colombia, Hungary, India, Indonesia, Jordan, Korea, Malaysia, Mexico, Pakistan, Peru, Philippines, Poland, Russia, South Africa, Sri Lanka, Thailand, Turkey, Venezuela, Zimbabwe	
Independent variables		
Res	Official reserves (including gold at market prices)	IFS
STDEV4	Standard deviation of reserves	Derived
CAGDP	Current account (CA) over GDP (+ is deficit) in the preceding 12 months	IFS
RERINS	Real effective exchange rate change in the preceding 48 months	IFS/INS
STD	Short-term debt (by remaining maturity)	BIS consolidated statistics
STDR	STD/Res	Derived
STDP	STD of the public sector	Based on BIS consolidated statistics (see text)
STDB	STD of the banking sector	
STDC	STD of the corporate sector	
STDNC	STD of the non-corporate sector (STDP+STDB)	Derived
Foreign direct investment	Foreign direct investment	IFS
B assets	Banking sector foreign assets	IFS
C assets	Corporate sector assets held with foreign banks	BIS locational statistics
B&C assets	B assets + C assets	Derived

Notes: For additional details see the data appendix in Bussière and Mulder (1999). BIS is Bank for International Settlements.

foreign direct investment and portfolio equity inflows, with foreign direct investment inflows generally by far the larger category. We therefore present tests augmenting short-term debt (in the short-term debt over reserves ratio, which captures reserve adequacy) with the current account deficit both before and after foreign direct investment.

Equation 1 in Table 6.2 is the benchmark equation from Bussière and Mulder (1999), which includes as explanatory variables short-term debt by remaining maturity over reserves (STD/Res), the current account deficit (CA/GDP) and the real effective exchange rate (RERINS). All three variables are significant (at the 1 per cent level) and the adjusted R^2 shows that the equation explains about half of the crisis index during Tequila, Asian and Russian crisis episodes.

When short-term debt is augmented by the current account deficit (Equation 2, Table 6.2), the ratio of short-term debt to reserves is also significant, but less so than in the benchmark equation, while the R^2 is significantly reduced. The same result is obtained if we adjust only for the non-foreign direct investment-financed current account deficit. Thus, empirically, a simple adjustment of the short-term debt-to-reserves ratio with prospective financing needs does not work as well in helping to predict the depth of crises in crisis periods as an unadjusted short-term debt-to-reserves ratio taking into account the current account deficit. Nonetheless, as Equation 1 shows, a higher current account deficit (scaled by GDP) does suggest a need for a higher reserves-to-short-term debt ratio. This equation implies, as detailed in Bussière and Mulder (1999), that for a short-term debt-to-reserves ratio of 1, an additional current account deficit of 1 per cent requires an increase of about 5 per cent in the level of reserves to keep the exposure to crises unchanged.

SECTORAL COMPOSITION OF SHORT-TERM DEBT: DOES CORPORATE SECTOR DEBT MATTER?

A second key question that has been raised is whether all short-term foreign debt should be covered by reserves—in particular, whether corporate sector debt should be included. Given the size of debt of the corporate (and banking) sectors this can significantly increase reserves that central banks would need to maintain. To test the proper composition of debt we first approximate the share of the various sectors, as the Bank for International Settlements does not collect a breakdown by sector of its series on short-term debt. To approximate the share of each sector in short-term debt, it is assumed that its share in short-term debt is equal to its share in total short-term debt.

Table 6.2 Augmenting the short-term debt ratio with the current account deficit

	(1)	(2)	(3)	(4)
RERINS	-0.38	-0.35	-0.38	-0.34
	(-3.95)	(-3.39)	(-3.71)	(-3.40)
CA/GDP	1.67		0.29	0.34
	(2.67)	(0.40)	(0.48)	
STD/Res	0.28			
	(6.66)			
(STD+CA)/Res		0.17		0.18
		(5.75)		(6.62)
(STD+CA-FDI)/Res		0.19		
		(5.86)		
C	-20.48	-12.79	-11.05	-12.46
	(-4.46)	(-3.06)	(-2.79)	(-3.06)
R^2	0.50	0.44	0.45	0.44
Adjusted R^2	0.48	0.42	0.42	0.42

Notes: The dependent variable is the crisis index. The bracketed terms are t-statistics.

The most noticeable result, detailed in Equation 3 (Table 6.3), is that short-term debt of the non-corporate sector (the banking and public sectors) has a coefficient which is about twice the size of the coefficient of the corporate sector short-term debt ratio. The coefficients of the public and bank sector debts are about the same size (Equation 4). These results suggest that corporate sector debt should not be overlooked when analysing the vulnerability of emerging markets, but it may not on average have the same weight as the short-term debt of other sectors.

THE ROLE OF BANKS' FOREIGN ASSETS AND CORPORATE SECTOR FOREIGN DEPOSITS

A third key question is whether non-reserve assets play a role in protecting countries against crises. Non-reserve assets would seem to help for various reasons, especially the associated positive wealth effects in the case of a depreciating real exchange rate, but also the possibility that assets can be used by individual parties to offset liabilities. To test the effect of non-reserve assets, we use Bank for International Settlements data on assets of the non-financial sector and IFS data on the foreign assets of the deposit-taking banks and other banking institutions. We conduct two tests. First, we add these assets to the reserve assets to form a new ratio of short-term debt to 'amplified assets', and second, we deduct the assets from short-term debt, to test the argument that non-reserve assets offset the impact of short-term debt. The latter specifications were always less significant than the former, indicating that, if anything, assets amplify reserve assets rather than offset debt. We therefore focus on the former results (Table 6.4).

The first equations (Equations 1–3) show the impact of the non-financial sector assets, the second (Equations 4 and 5), the effect of bank assets and the third (Equations 6 and 7), the impact of both sectors foreign assets (Table 6.4). When reserves are

Table 6.3 The role of bank, corporate and public sector debt

	(1)	(2)	(3)	(4)
RERINS	-0.38	-0.34	-0.37	-0.37
	(-3.95)	(-3.43)	(-3.77)	(-3.74)
CA/GDP	1.67	1.87	1.73	1.72
	(2.67)	(2.95)	(2.76)	(2.70)
STD/Res	0.28			
	(6.66)			
STDNC/Res		0.44	0.36	
		(6.42)	(4.30)	
STDPS/Res				0.33
				(1.50)
STDB/Res				0.36
				(3.84)
STDC/Res			0.18	0.18
			(1.74)	(1.72)
C	-20.48	-17.00	-20.04	-19.89
	(-4.46)	(-3.92)	(-4.35)	(-4.11)
R^2	0.50	0.49	0.51	0.51
Adjusted R^2	0.48	0.46	0.48	0.47

Notes: The dependent variable is the crisis index. Bracketed terms are t-statistics.

augmented by either corporate or both corporate and bank sector assets they perform almost as well as just reserve assets. Adding just banking sector assets performs worse. One explanation for this counter-intuitive result could be that the short-term debt data of the Bank for International Settlements do not include foreign currency deposits held with domestic banks. Domestic banks often hold foreign assets (claims on non-residents) to offset such foreign currency deposits. It could be that the foreign assets of banks do not enter as a risk-offsetting argument because the foreign currency deposits do not enter the estimations as a risk-augmenting variable.

When non-reserve assets are added as separate ratios in relation to short-term debt, only the ratio of short-term debt to bank plus corporate assets comes close to being significant at the 95 per cent level. Moreover the combined effect of short-term debt-to-reserves and non-reserves is not diminished but rather strengthened. Thus there is no strong indication that these non-reserve assets significantly reduce external vulnerability, except possibly to offset the vulnerabilities associated with foreign currency deposits in the domestic system.

The impact of including South Africa in the sample is also assessed. The ratio of interest was adjusted in the baseline equation in an *ad hoc* manner by taking the average debt-to-reserves ratio. This adjustment was necessary as South Africa is an extreme outlier in the sample with a very high debt-to-reserves ratio, and because the absence of

Table 6.4 The impact of non-reserve assets

	(1)	(1')	(2)	(3)	(3')	(4)	(5)	(5')	(6)	(7)	(7')	(8)
RERINS	-0.38	-0.38	-0.42	-0.39	-0.39	-0.35	-0.37	-0.36	-0.38	-0.39	-0.38	-0.28
	(-3.95)	(-3.78)	(-4.05)	(-4.03)	(-3.85)	(-3.23)	(-3.75)	(-3.52)	(-3.69)	(-4.02)	(-3.81)	(-2.37)
CA/GDP	1.67	1.66	2.12	1.67	1.66	1.92	1.62	1.58	1.85	1.52	1.48	1.38
	(2.67)	(2.56)	(3.27)	(2.66)	(2.55)	(2.75)	(2.59)	(2.43)	(2.81)	(2.42)	(2.26)	(1.69)
STD/Res	0.28	0.28		0.26	0.26		0.28	0.28		0.25	0.25	
	(6.66)	(6.52)		(5.65)	(5.53)		(6.62)	(6.48)		(5.60)	(5.45)	
STD/(Res+C assets)			0.34									
			(6.01)									
STD/(C assets)				0.00	0.00							
				(0.89)	(0.85)							
STD/(Res+BAssets)						0.28						
						(4.83)						
STD/Bassets							0.00	0.00				
							(1.05)	(1.04)				
STD/(Res+B&C assets)									0.47			
									(5.79)			
STD/B&Cassets										0.04	0.04	
										(1.47)	(1.46)	
STDNC/(Res+B assets)												2.11
												(2.77)
C	-20.5	-20.3	-20.1	-20.9	-20.8	-15.7	-22.5	-22.2	-20.3	-23.0	-22.7	2.2
	(-4.46)	(-4.23)	(-4.09)	(-4.52)	(-4.30)	(-3.11)	(-4.52)	(-4.33)	(-4.00)	(-4.73)	(-4.52)	(0.58)
R²	0.50	0.50	0.46	0.51	0.51	0.38	0.51	0.51	0.45	0.52	0.52	0.24
Adjusted R²	0.48	0.47	0.43	0.48	0.47	0.35	0.48	0.47	0.42	0.49	0.48	0.20

Notes: The dependent variable is the crisis index. Bracketed terms are t-statistics. Equations with an accent exclude South Africa.

an impact of South Africa's high short-term debt over reserves might be explained by the high level of its other assets. When South Africa is excluded, there is barely any difference in the ratios—the equations that exclude South Africa (marked with an accent), have exactly the same coefficients as those that include it (without accent) (Table 6.4). When the *ad hoc* adjustment for South Africa is dropped the ratio of short-term debt to bank and commercial assets becomes slightly more significant. The limited effect may be due to the fact that many of South Africa's assets consist of foreign direct investment. Other reasons include its well run banking system and its potential to mine additional gold reserves. South Africa is clearly an outlier, but whether this is because of its relatively high non-reserve asset position is not clear. Yet, this adjustment does not affect the results.

Finally the issue of whether short-term debt of the non-corporate sector over reserve assets augmented by banks' foreign assets would perform well was assessed. They do not (Equation 8, Table 6.4). In other words, a selective treatment on the debt side and an inclusive treatment of assets does not work well. Instead the results point to comprehensive treatment on the debt side and a selective, official reserve asset-focused treatment on the asset side.

THE VARIANCE OF RESERVES

It has also been suggested (Greenspan 1999a) that reserves should be augmented in such a way that countries would be able to avoid new borrowing with a probability of 95 per cent. This has been dubbed the liquidity-at-risk approach. It is not easy to operationalise. It is extremely difficult to construct a probability distribution for the balance of payments. Unlike some other financial variables, most balance of payments series do not follow random walks. Most attention is therefore devoted to explaining and predicting the relations that dominate the behaviour of these variables rather than to the statistical properties of the unexplained factors.

As an approximation, the variation in the balance of payments could be measured by the standard deviation of reserves. This measure summarises how changes in the current and capital account, driven by both exogenous events and policy actions, are reflected in fluctuations in reserves. To provide some indication of the need to augment reserves with a measure of uncertainty, we include the standard deviation of reserves as measured over the past four years. This measure is barely significant (Equation 1, Table 6.5). In addition we test the standard short-term debt-to-reserves ratio adjusted for the standard deviation of reserves. We deduct twice the standard deviation, in analogy to the value-at-risk approach, where a two standard deviation interval corresponds to a 95 per cent confidence interval under a normal distribution. This measure does not work at all. A smaller adjustment of the reserve level does work, but is not as significant as the standard measure.

This result suggests that while it may be worthwhile, for some particular countries, to augment the reserve targets with a measure of uncertainty, such as the impact of the variation of oil prices on export earnings, an adjustment based on the overall degree of uncertainty in the balance of payments does not appear to be empirically supported in the context of the models that explain this class of crisis-depth models.

Table 6.5 Testing liquidity-at-risk

	(1)	*(2)*	*(3)*	*(4)*
RERINS	-0.37	-0.25	-0.26	-0.35
	(-3.77)	(-2.01)	(-2.10)	(-3.07)
CA/GDP	1.74	2.21	1.98	2.07
	(2.77)	(2.75)	(2.38)	(2.82)
STD/Res	0.27			
	(6.45)			
STDEV4	0.00	0.00		
	(1.15)	(1.60)		
STD/(RES-2*STDEV4)*100			0.00	
			(-0.90)	
STD/(RES-STDEV4)*100				0.09
				(3.87)
C	-22.96	-3.30	3.04	-9.47
	(-4.53)	(-0.63)	(0.72)	(-2.01)
R^2	0.51	0.17	0.15	0.31
Adjusted R^2	0.48	0.13	0.11	0.28

Notes: The dependent variable is the crisis index. Bracketed terms are t-statistics.

CONCLUSIONS

This chapter addresses several questions that are very important from an operational perspective in interpreting the adequacy of reserves in relation to short-term debt. This relation has been emphasised by policymakers and supported by empirical research. In an operational context, much more data tend to be available than for systematic cross-country analysis. Inevitably questions arise as to the exact specification of any benchmark. Here we try to bridge the gap between such demands and systematic analysis by exploiting several data sources to study the impact of non-reserve assets, the sectoral composition of debt, the impact of the current account deficit and the need for some bandwidth or liquidity-at-risk type of augmentation.

The results point to a need to be comprehensive on the side of liabilities that are to be covered by reserve assets, and more exclusive on the asset side; short-term corporate sector debt matters, and needs to be covered by reserves. Reserves need not be augmented by the current account deficit. However, the current account deficit scaled by GDP should, just as an over-appreciated exchange rate, be taken into account in setting reserve targets. A simple rule of thumb is that the reserve target, set in terms of short-term debt, should be augmented by 5 per cent for each per cent of current account deficit, and by 1 per cent for each per cent the exchange rate is overvalued. A simple augmentation of reserves by the standard deviation of reserves is not supported by the test results.

Non-reserves assets have only a limited impact in offsetting external vulnerabilities. This is puzzling. After all, many industrialised countries have extensive short-term external debt, but this does not seem to make them particularly vulnerable. This could be due to two reasons

- their short-term debt is overwhelmingly covered by overall assets (most assets tend to be liquid and to be a multiple of short-term liabilities)
- the foreign currency risk embedded in foreign debt is closely monitored at a micro level to be offset by foreign currency assets or cash flow. Thus few industrialised country governments borrow in foreign currency, and few corporations borrow foreign currency unless for projects that generate foreign currency cash flows or are covered by foreign assets. Where countries do borrow in foreign currency and do not set sufficiently high micro standards this might contribute to crises (as, for example, in Finland in 1991–2).

In any case, in the sample of 21 emerging market economies used in the present sample, no evidence is found that non-reserve assets play an important role. The bottom line resulting from this test is to be inclusive on the liabilities side and exclusive on the asset side in setting reserve targets.

Finally we would like to highlight another important policy question—does it make a difference whether countries target a short-term debt ratio through the imposition of capital controls or through reserves? A number of practical and theoretical considerations bear on this question. Higher reserves, while reducing interest costs, are likely to increase the overall interest burden. Controls of short-term debt may not be effective and result in underestimations of the stock of short-term debt. These issues remain to be studied in detail.

NOTE

* Views expressed are those of the author and not necessarily of the International Monetary Fund.

Part 3

European experiences

7 Poland's experience with capital flows in the 1990s

Nancy Wagner

In recent years, Poland has been central and eastern Europe's most dynamic economic performer, posting an annual average growth rate of 6 per cent over the past five years. Annual inflation has been on a steady downward path and reached the single digits, for the first time since transition, in the fourth quarter of 1998. Moreover, Poland's sound policy fundamentals have supported market-oriented reforms. Over the past few years, these strong fundamentals have attracted substantial capital inflows, particularly in the form of foreign direct investment, which have played an increasingly important role in Poland's growth and development. These inflows accelerated during 1998 and remained remarkably stable even in the wake of the Russian crisis. This chapter describes developments in the financial account of Poland's balance of payments since 1991, examines some of the macroeconomic consequences of these flows and compares Poland's foreign direct investment developments with other transition and emerging market economies.

CAPITAL FLOWS AND THE IMPACT ON MONETARY AND EXCHANGE RATE POLICY

A striking feature of the Polish economy since 1995 has been the strength of capital inflows. Since its debt restructuring in October 1994, Poland has been particularly successful in attracting foreign direct investment and has now surpassed Hungary as the largest cumulative recipient of foreign direct investment among the European transition economies. This is in sharp contrast to the early years of transition, when Poland experienced a net outflow of capital.

The early years of transition

Poland began its transition with a high level of external debt, much of it the result of heavy borrowing during the early 1980s to support high government expenditures. When the stabilisation program began in 1990, Poland's external debt stood at about 83 per cent of GDP. As ties to the Soviet Union unravelled, Poland suffered a rapid loss of access to credit, which was exacerbated by the fact that Poland had not been fully servicing its debt to official creditors since the 1980s and had partially suspended the servicing of its debt to private creditors in 1990. Thus, during the initial stage of transition, official flows and exceptional financing (debt relief and accumulation of arrears) played the dominant role in Poland's external financing, while private capital flows were negative on a net basis.

The Paris Club debt reduction agreement, signed in April 1991, lowered Poland's external debt to 63 per cent of GDP by the end of the year. Poland's debt ratio declined further to 56 per cent of GDP by the end of 1993, although the country continued to incur external arrears during 1992 and 1993. For the most part, Poland remained cut off from the international capital markets during this period, as the debt problem remained at the fore. Nevertheless, Poland began the structural reforms

Figure 7.1 Poland: financial and current account developments, 1990–8 (US$million)

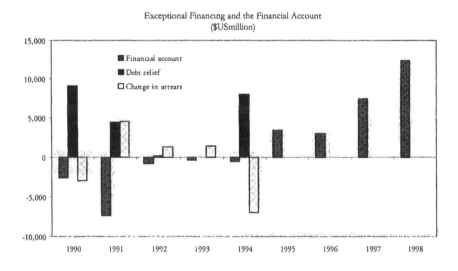

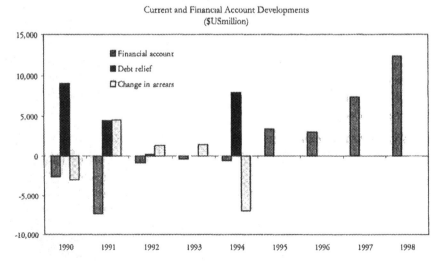

Source: National Bank of Poland, staff estimates.

needed to attract capital flows. Foreign direct investment and portfolio equity investment were liberalised in 1991, although portfolio inflows to debt securities were not liberalised until 1993.

Access to private capital markets

The turning point from the perspective of the international financial markets occurred in October 1994, with the conclusion of the London Club agreement (the Brady debt reduction plan). Debt relief was in the order of US$8 billion, and arrears declined by almost US$7 billion (Figure 7.1). By the end of 1994, Poland's external debt stood at 45 per cent of GDP. Thus, between 1990 and 1994, Poland shifted from being a heavily to a moderately indebted country, which finally allowed the country access to the global private capital markets. Poland's international creditworthiness was also underpinned by growing political and social stability.

By 1995, private capital inflows began to play an important role in the balance of payments, as exceptional financing was replaced by voluntary flows of a long-term nature. Although foreigners had been permitted to invest in treasury bills and securities on the Warsaw stock exchange as early as 1992, portfolio investment picked up only after the agreement with the London Club. Foreign direct investment inflows also surged following the agreement. Foreign direct investment, on a net basis, more than doubled in 1995 compared with 1994. The growing current account surplus and the sharp reversal in Poland's financial account position led the National Bank of Poland to conduct large-scale sterilisation operations, further stimulating interest-sensitive inflows. Official reserves soared in 1995, increasing by almost US$9 billion. To introduce some exchange rate risk, a crawling band, with a fluctuation margin of ±7 per cent, replaced the zloty's crawling peg in May 1995.

The transition process in central and eastern Europe has typically been characterised by widening current account deficits associated with a sharp increase in consumption, owing to pent-up demand from the previous suppression of consumption, and in investment to replace largely obsolete capital stock. Poland was no exception, although the deterioration in the current account began quite late into the transition period.

Real exchange rate appreciation has also been a normal part of the transition process, as structural reform, privatisation and foreign investment have lead to greater productivity, particularly in the tradables sector. The delay of Poland's access to international capital markets in the early 1990s and the postponement of privatisation reduced upward pressure on the real exchange rate. This could have been one of the contributing factors underpinning the export-led growth during this period, which resulted in current account surpluses. However, after Poland gained access to the capital markets, current account deterioration began—after registering a surplus of more than 3 per cent of GDP in 1995, the current account went into deficit in 1996, and the deficit has steadily widened each year since then. Over the same period, the real effective exchange rate (CPI-based) appreciated by 18 per cent.

The decline in foreign interest rates in 1996 encouraged strong foreign demand for Polish securities. The surge in inflows aroused concerns about exchange rate appreciation, potential loss of export competitiveness and the inflationary impact. With the shift in the exchange rate regime in mid 1995, the central bank had scope to introduce greater flexibility in its interest rate policy. To this end, it lowered its base lending rates twice in 1996 to reduce the interest rate differential between Polish and foreign securities. The more volatile exchange rate and lower, more flexible domestic interest rates slowed the pace of capital inflows in 1996.

In reaction to signs of overheating by 1997, the central bank raised nominal interest rates (with real interest rates climbing to nearly double-digit levels) and boosted reserve requirements in an attempt to stem the rapid expansion of domestic credit. Capital inflows picked up again. In mid 1997, following the Czech and Thai currency crises, Polish stock and currency markets tumbled, then rebounded smartly as investors refocused on the country's rapid economic growth and declining inflation. This pattern was repeated after the events in Korea in the fall of 1997. Thus, Poland weathered a series of external shocks and, indeed, became one of the favoured destinations for emerging market investors.

With high yields on Polish treasury securities, continued strong macroeconomic fundamentals and a decline in Poland's credit risk, capital inflows accelerated further in early 1998. Sterilisation of the inflows contributed to the persistence of high interest rates, which further stimulated capital inflows. Moreover, with inflation falling faster than nominal interest rates, real interest rates edged upward, which contributed to a slowdown in economic activity in the latter part of the year. With reserve requirements at high levels, the National Bank of Poland could not consider another hike in obligatory reserves to assist in sterilising the impact of the inflows.

In February 1998, as the zloty pushed toward its upper limit, the newly created Monetary Policy Council widened the fluctuation band from ±7 per cent to ±10 per cent. Nevertheless, the zloty continued to experience strong appreciation pressures, moving toward its new upper limit. In an effort to stem the upward pressure, the Monetary Policy Council cut its key intervention interest rate by 850 basis points during the period from April 1998 to the end of the year. The Monetary Policy Council also slowed the crawling peg's monthly rate of depreciation progressively from 1 per cent to 0.5 per cent. The interest rate and crawl rate cuts partially offset one another in terms of the impact on the attractiveness of the zloty.

Strong inflows continued in mid 1998, with the zloty reaching successive record highs in August, breaking through the 9 per cent 'psychological barrier' above parity. However, profit taking and nervousness in the face of escalating turbulence in Russian financial markets knocked the zloty off its perch near the top of its ±10 per cent trading band.

The Russian crisis

In contrast to the financial crisis in East Asia, Poland's geographical proximity placed it at greater risk of contagion from the Russian financial crisis, which began mid 1998. With respect to the three primary transmission mechanisms of contagion—trade exposure, financial market and corporate sector exposure and increased cost of financing—Poland was on fairly firm ground. Regarding trade exposure, the share of trade with Russia and the other countries of the former Soviet Union amounted to less than 20 per cent. Direct banking sector exposure to Russia was relatively small. While the crisis initially triggered a jump in the spread on US dollar-

Figure 7.2 Interest rate spread between Polish and US two-year treasury bonds, 1997–9 (basis points)

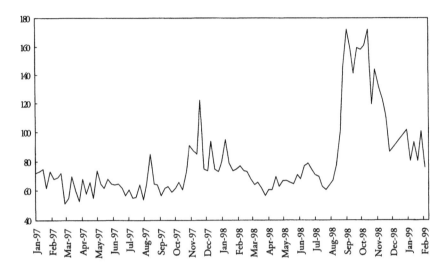

Sources: Polish authorities and staff estimates.

denominated Polish treasury paper, the spread has since declined to almost pre-crisis levels (Figure 7.2).

In the wake of the Russian devaluation and de facto debt default in mid August 1998, a massive withdrawal of foreign investors from Polish securities briefly pushed the zloty down to below parity. Of the US$4–5 billion in foreign investor holdings of government securities, it is estimated that approximately US$1 billion exited the country. Substantial sums also departed from the equity markets, with the main index on the Warsaw stock exchange declining by more than 30 per cent from the end of July until it started to recover toward the end of the year. It was apparent that the withdrawals also reflected redemptions from the more liquid emerging markets to meet investors' needs to cover positions as a result of the Russian crisis—the relatively high liquidity of the Polish markets and the high share of Poland in emerging market investors' portfolios made it an attractive market to tap. Indeed, the fairly quick rebound in Poland's financial markets suggested that the sell off was primarily liquidity-driven rather than based on fundamentals.

In early September, the Monetary Policy Council cut the floor of its benchmark interest rate, a move that surprised most market participants, who had expected that the central bank's stance would remain unchanged in the midst of the ongoing turmoil in emerging markets. This action was intended to differentiate Poland from Russia and to send a signal that Poland should be judged on its own strong fundamentals. In the event, the markets reacted favourably to the cut, with the zloty strengthening in the aftermath. In late October, the Monetary Policy Council widened the exchange rate band again, to ±12.5 per cent.

Notwithstanding the more flexible exchange rate, foreign exchange reserves increased rapidly in 1998, rising from US$20.7 billion at the end of 1997 to US$27.4 billion by the end of 1998. This development was attributed largely to the functioning of the central bank fixing, rather than to deliberate intervention. In fact, exchange market intervention was sharply curtailed after February 1998, and by the time of the Russian crisis, the central bank had, for all practical purposes, ceased intervening actively on the market. However, the fixing had tied the central bank's hands in controlling official reserves, and the strong inflows were translated immediately into growth in reserves.

Figure 7.3 Poland: size and composition of net capital flows, 1995–8 (US$million, per cent)

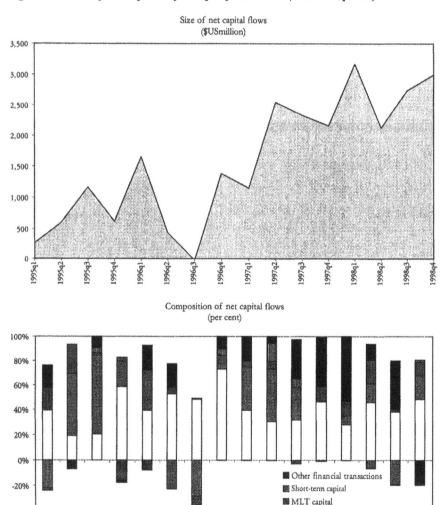

Note: Excludes net errors and omissions and valuation adjustments.
Source: National Bank of Poland.

Following the crisis in Brazil in January 1999, Poland's financial markets again shuddered, but the recovery was far more rapid than in the aftermath of the Russia upheaval. The zloty rebounded within days to around 7 per cent above parity. Amid signs of slowing economic activity and concerns about deteriorating competitiveness, the Monetary Policy Council cut its key interest rates by 200–300 basis points on 20 January 1999. This removed the upward pressure on the zloty, and by February, the currency was trading in a range of only 1–3 per cent above parity.

Figure 7.4 Poland: four periods of capital flows (cumulative net inflows during the period (US$million))

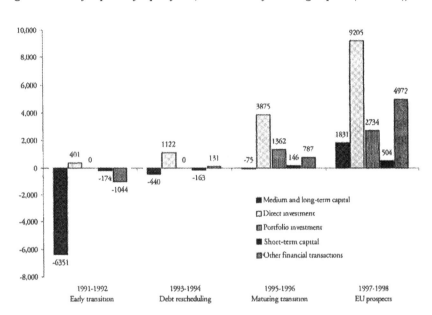

Source: National Bank of Poland.

Current issues

Sterilisation through open market operations has been very costly for the central bank, as it has involved a portfolio reallocation in which the central bank's domestic currency debt (National Bank of Poland bills with a relatively high yield) has been issued in exchange for international reserve assets at a much lower yield. The quasi-fiscal costs of sterilisation have led to a significant deterioration in the central bank's profit position and have contributed to the difficulties of reducing the high reserve requirements currently imposed on banks. With the opening of the banking system to greater foreign competition in the run up to European Union membership, such reserve requirements may lead to substantial disintermediation. The National Bank of Poland is currently in negotiations with the government to convert a large stock of non-marketable government debt on its balance sheet into a form that can be used in open market operations. This would relieve the central bank of the quasi-fiscal burden of sterilisation and might allow it to lower its reserve requirements to a level compatible with a more competitive banking environment.

A new foreign exchange law took effect in January 1999. Although some restrictions remain in place, particularly as regards short-term capital flows, the law is a step in the direction of a more liberalised capital account and formally makes the zloty an externally convertible currency. The law also makes it possible to impose special restrictions in emergency situations such as those caused by excessive capital movements. The law is intended only as the first step to liberalising the capital account since Poland's commitment to the OECD requires that it fully liberalise the capital account by 1 January 2000.

THE COMPOSITION OF CAPITAL FLOWS TO POLAND

The major components of Poland's financial account are foreign direct investment, portfolio investment, medium and long-term credits, short-term credits and other financial transactions (Figure 7.3). This last category includes transactions in foreign currency held in bank vaults, current accounts, deposits placed abroad and deposits accepted from abroad (including repurchase agreements).

Four distinct periods

Since 1991, there have been four distinct periods for capital flows to Poland (Figure 7.4). The first period—early transition—occurred during 1991–2 when amortisation due for medium and long-term loans was the overriding feature of the financial account. During this period, Poland was running up large arrears. The next period—debt rescheduling on the horizon—was 1993–4, when the financial account was almost in balance and there was a minor amount of foreign direct investment entering the country.

The London Club agreement in October 1994 appeared to be the catalyst for a major acceleration in capital inflows in the third period—maturing transition—of 1995–6, when foreign direct investment inflows became the dominant feature in capital flow developments. In the most recent period of 1997–8, with European Union membership now in sight, foreign direct investment inflows accelerated further, as Poland became one of the favoured destinations for emerging market investors. Also notable was a sharp rise in the category of other financial transactions. In particular, there was a large drawdown of Polish residents' assets abroad at the same time that there was a pick up in non-residents' acquisition of currency and deposits in Poland, perhaps in response to the high interest rates offered on domestic currency deposits.

Non-foreign direct investment capital inflows

Over the entire period 1991–8, net cumulative flows of medium and long-term credit were negative (with a net outflow over this eight-year period of about US$5 billion) if amortisation due is used for the computation of net flows. However, if actual repayments are used to compute net flows, then there was a cumulative net inflow of US$3 billion over this period. Cumulative disbursements reached approximately US$8.5 billion by the end of 1998. During the early years of transition, the government was the primary borrower, but by 1995–6 the banking and enterprise sectors began to

Figure 7.5 Non-residents' portfolio investment in Poland, 1997–8 (US$million)

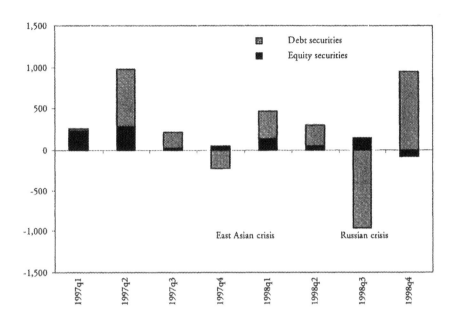

Source: National Bank of Poland.

account for the majority of longer-term borrowing abroad. Reflecting this shift in type of borrower was a similar shift in type of creditor. In the early years, the majority of these loans were provided by international financial institutions, but their share has declined significantly since 1995.

The Polish government issued some US$400 million in bonds on the international markets in 1998, and the 1999 budget authorises up to US$700 million in foreign borrowing. Shortly after its initial public offering in November 1998, Telekomunikacja Polska SA successfully accessed external financing via a US$1 billion Eurobond issue, the largest corporate debt issuance ever from the region. Also in November 1998, Krakow, Poland's third largest city, debuted in the municipal bond market with a two-year DM66 million note, and the issue was also regarded as a success.

Short-term credits have played a very small role in Poland's capital flow developments throughout the entire period examined in this chapter. As of the end of 1998, the ratio of the stock of short-term external debt to official reserves was less than 13 per cent, significantly lower than in most of the other European transition and emerging markets.

Portfolio investment was negligible until the conclusion of the Brady bond deal in late 1994 and the assignment of investment grade ratings to Poland. In 1995 there was a surge in portfolio inflows, which continued into the first quarter of 1996. This raised concerns about the vulnerability of Poland to a sudden reversal, with the central

Figure 7.6 Poland: foreign direct investment financing of the current account deficit, 1996–8 (US$million)

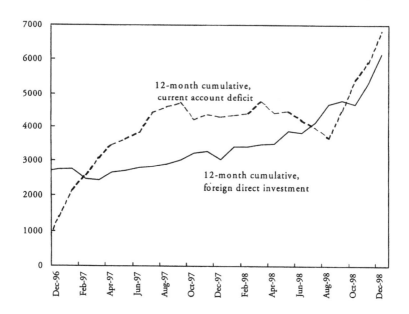

Source: National Bank of Poland.

Figure 7.7 Poland: share of foreign investment by country of origin, as of December 1998 (per cent)

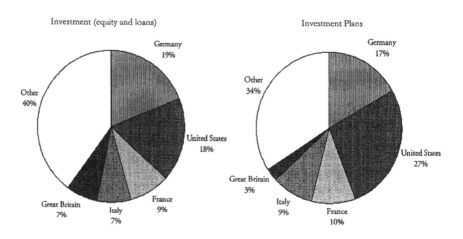

Source: Polish Agency for Foreign Investment.

Table 7.1 Poland: stock of foreign direct investment by country of origin, as of December 1998 (US$million)

Rank	Country	Equity and loans	Investment plans	Number of companies
1	Germany	5,117.3	2,231.0	163
2	United States	4,911.2	3,654.4	112
3	France	2,398.9	1,294.3	60
4	Italy	2,037.6	1,224.3	64
5	Great Britain	1,929.5	366.6	28
6	Netherlands	1,878.9	410.8	42
7	International[a]	1,813.1	815.3	18
8	Korea	1,412.4	496.3	4
9	Russia	958.0	616.0	1
10	Austria	758.3	155.1	31
11	Sweden	691.5	336.8	37
12	Switzerland	666.2	235.9	13
13	Denmark	558.4	43.4	28
14	Norway	455.8	439.0	12
15	Canada	235.6	57.1	21
16	Ireland	226.1	n.a.	3
17	Japan	198.3	188.4	11
18	Finland	191.2	59.0	16
19	Belgium	156.8	100.1	19
20	Portugal	147.2	63.0	3
21	Croatia	138.0	70.0	1
22	Australia	98.1	90.0	4
23	Czech Republic	68.4	n.a.	4
24	Spain	62.3	n.a.	3
25	Turkey	48.0	58.0	2
26	Liechtenstein	29.5	12.0	3
27	China	25.0	25.0	1
28	South Africa	25.0	40.0	1
29	Hong Kong	20.0	20.0	1
30	Slovenia	6.0	1.0	1
31	Taiwan	5.7	200.0	1
32	Israel	5.4	20.0	3
33	Greece	3.6	4.0	2
34	Luxembourg	2.3	n.a.	1
	Total[b]	27,279.6	13,326.8	714

Notes: [a] Includes international organisations and multi-country investment concerns.
[b] Includes only foreign direct investment projects over US$1 million.
Source: Polish Agency for Foreign Investment.

bank lowering interest rates to stem the inflows of interest-sensitive capital. In the event, portfolio flows tapered off later in the year.

However, by 1997, as the central bank moved to tighten monetary policy to prevent overheating, these inflows resumed, reaching a peak during the second quarter of 1997 (Figure 7.5). Portfolio inflows to the equity market were relatively stable. Although foreign interest in equity securities was strong, the inflow into Polish treasury securities was even greater and more volatile. In the fourth quarter of 1997, at the peak of the East Asian crisis, there was a sharp reversal of flows in debt securities. During the first half of 1998, foreign investors returned to the treasury markets, but the Russian crisis sparked an even greater outflow in the third quarter than that associated with the East Asian crisis. In October 1998, inflows into debt securities just edged into positive territory again, and remained at a low level in November. However, in December 1998, almost US$1 billion flooded back into the debt market, the largest monthly inflow ever into Polish securities. Note that inflows to the equity market remained positive on a net quarterly basis, even at the peak of the crises in East Asia and Russia, until the fourth quarter of 1998.

Despite the obvious foreign interest in Polish debt and equity markets, portfolio flows have not been one of the major components of foreign financing for Poland. This may reflect, in part, the relatively low level of financial development. As a proxy for financial development, consider the ratio of broad money to GDP in Poland. At the end of 1998, the ratio was about 40 per cent. By comparison, the figure for the Czech Republic, which has been the recipient of large portfolio flows, was about 70 per cent.

Developments in foreign direct investment

The bulk of Poland's financing of its rising current account deficits has come in the form of foreign direct investment. In fact, over the past two years, cumulative net foreign direct investment inflows (based on data from the National Bank of Poland) have almost fully financed the cumulative current account deficit (Figure 7.6). For a more detailed examination of developments with respect to foreign direct investment, data from the Polish Agency for Foreign Investment must be used. These data differ significantly from those prepared by the National Bank of Poland for the balance of payments statistics, showing US$5.2 billion was invested by non-residents in Poland during 1996, the largest amount in the transition economies in central and eastern Europe. This increased to US$6.6 billion in 1997, bringing the stock of foreign direct investment to US$20.6 billion by the end of 1997, which exceeded the stock in Hungary (previously the recipient of the largest cumulative inflows of foreign direct investment).

At the end of 1998, the total stock of foreign direct investment in Poland was US$30.7 billion, of which projects with investment exceeding US$1 million represented US$27.3 billion. There were 714 investors (from thirty-four countries), up from 585 and 492 at the end of 1997 and the end of 1996. Germany was the largest investor in terms of value (with 19 per cent of the foreign direct investment stock in Poland), followed by the United States (18 per cent), France, Italy, Great Britain and the Netherlands (Table 7.1 and Figure 7.7). European Union countries had invested US$16.1 billion or 59 per cent of the total stock. Asian investors, on the other hand, had invested only US$1.6 billion, or less than 7 per cent. Korea was by far the largest

Table 7.2 Poland: stock of foreign direct investment by sector, as of December 1998 (US$million)

Branch	Equity and loans	Percentage of total	Investment plans	Percentage of total
Manufacturing	15,912.1	58.3	6,970.6	52.3
Food, beverages & tobacco products	4,460.7	16.4	1,471.0	11.0
Transport equipment	3,627.9	13.3	2,083.3	15.6
Other non-metallic products	2,576.8	9.4	1,249.8	9.4
Pulp, paper, paper products, publishing, printing	1,353.9	5.0	325.3	2.4
Chemicals & chemical products	1,272.4	4.7	470.0	3.5
Electrical machinery	1,016.3	3.7	372.7	2.8
Other machinery & apparatus	584.8	2.1	343.1	2.6
Rubber & plastics	422.7	1.5	228.1	1.7
Basic metals & metal products	354.2	1.3	252.6	1.9
Other goods	242.4	0.9	174.7	1.3
Financial intermediation	4,802.9	17.6	1,140.4	8.6
Wholesale & retail trade, repairs	2,942.7	10.8	2,193.7	16.5
Construction	1,685.3	6.2	1,133.8	8.5
Transport & communication	719.3	2.6	159.2	1.2
Hotels & restaurants	429.8	1.6	207.1	1.6
Community, social & personal services	397.8	1.5	386.1	2.9
Electricity, gas & water supply	241.8	0.9	1,000.0	7.5
Real estate, renting & business activities	112.0	0.4	123.5	0.9
Agriculture	24.1	0.1	8.0	0.1
Quarrying & mining	11.8	0.0	4.4	0.0
Total foreign direct investment over US$1 million	27,279.6	100.0	13,326.8	100.0

Source: Polish Agency for Foreign Investment.

Asian investor, accounting for US$1.4 billion, while Japan had invested less than US$200 million and ranked seventeenth among the investing countries.

Plans as of December 1998 call for additional investment of US$13.3 billion, or almost 50 per cent of the current stock. The largest value of planned investments is attributed to the United States (27 per cent). In terms of number of investors, Germany again takes the lead with 163 investors, followed by the United States with 112.

Despite the advent of the Russian crisis in August 1998, foreign direct investors continued to make transfers into the Polish economy in the second half of 1998. The total amount of foreign direct investment inflows to Poland in 1998 reached a record US$10.1 billion, of which US$5.1 billion occurred in the latter half of the year. Inflows in 1998 were up by more than 50 per cent compared with the previous year. The stock of foreign direct investment by the end of 1998 (accumulated since 1989) stood at US$30.7 billion.

Manufacturing was the destination for 58 per cent of all cumulative foreign direct investment in Poland at the end of 1998 (Table 7.2 and Figure 7.8). Within the

Table 7.3 Poland: top thirty foreign investors[a], as of December 1998

Investor	Equity and loans (US$million)	Plans	Origin	Branch
Fiat	1357.4	708.8	Italy	manufacture of cars
Daewoo	1348.4	471.1	Korea	car production, electronic equipment, construction, insurance
Gazprom	958.0	616.0	Russia	construction
Bayerische Hypo- und Vereinsbank AG	724.0	n.a.	Germany	banking
EBRD	653.5	216.0	International[b]	banking, capital participation in enterprises
Metro AG	598.0	650.0	Germany	wholesale & retail trade
Polish American Enterprise Fund	505.0	n.a.	USA	capital funding of private firms and participation in privatisation
IPC	440.0	35.0	USA	paper industry
ING Group	420.0	n.a.	Netherlands	banking
Commerzbank AG	389.0	7.2	Germany	banking
Philip Morris	372.0	80.0	USA	tobacco industry
Reemtsma Cigaretten-fabriken GmbH	368.1	202.1	Germany	tobacco industry
Adam Opel AG	360.0	260.0	Germany	automotive industry
Coca-Cola Beverages	360.0	n.a.	Great Britain	soft drinks production food processing
Harbin BV	325.9	n.a.	Netherlands	brewing
ABB Ltd.	310.2	216.9	International[b]	power supply systems, turbines, electric engines
Nestlé	309.0	43.0	Switzerland	food processing
Saint Gobain	296.0	150.0	France	glass, insulating material production, construction
Pilkington	295.0	50.0	Great Britain	glass plant
IFC	284.2	n.a.	International[b]	investment in private sector projects across all industry sectors
PepsiCo	283.0	380.0	USA	sweets, soft drinks, crisps
Thomson Multi Media	264.0	93.5	France	TV tubes and sets
BP Amoco Plc	250.0	n.a.	Great Britain	gas production, distribution of oil products
Citibank	235.2	290.0	USA	banking
Kronospan	234.0	40.0	Switzerland	paper products, furniture products
France Telecom	232.0	n.a.	France	telecommunications
Glaxo Wellcome	230.4	n.a.	Great Britain	pharmaceuticals
Lafarge	209.0	141.0	France	cement production
Epstein	200.0	n.a.	USA	construction, meat processing, development
Statoil	200.0	400.0	Norway	distribution of petroleum products, retail trade

Notes: [a]Ranked by book value of capital.
[b]Includes international organisations and multi-country investment concerns.
Source: Polish Agency for Foreign Investment.

Figure 7.8 Poland: share of foreign investment by sector, as of December 1998 (per cent)

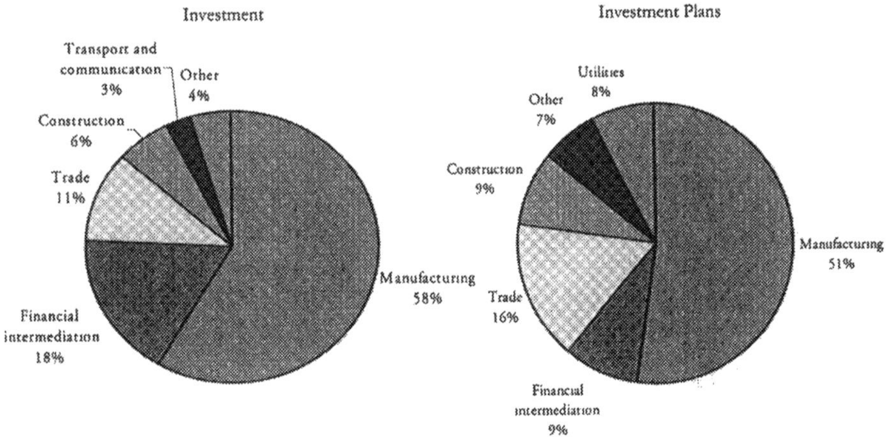

Source: Polish Agency for Foreign Investment.

manufacturing category, the food products sector was the major recipient, followed closely by transport equipment. The next largest sectoral destination for investment, after manufacturing, was financial intermediation, which received 18 per cent of total cumulative foreign direct investment. Using survey data on plans for future investment, manufacturing is expected to continue to receive the lion's share (52 per cent) but wholesale and retail trade moves into second place, accounting for 16 per cent of planned investment, up from only 10 per cent of investment to date.

The largest foreign investors in the Polish economy have been car manufacturers, particularly Fiat and Daewoo (Table 7.3). The car industry has been attracted by Poland's low labour costs, prospects of admission to the European Union and good geographical location. Car manufacturers currently plan to produce one million or more cars in Poland in the near future. The demand in Poland, on the other hand, was estimated at about 700,000 cars by 2000, including significant numbers of imported vehicles. Thus, the car manufacturers appear to be focusing on both the domestic and export markets. Currently, only Fiat and Daewoo produce cars with a Polish content of at least 65 per cent, as much of the car manufacturing in Poland involves assembly plants using semi-knocked down imported kits. This approach to car manufacture has created relatively few new jobs and is low value added. Poland is now trying to encourage the development of car manufacturing with a larger Polish content and is proposing to raise tariffs on components used to assemble cars. The third largest investor in Poland, after Fiat and Daewoo, is the Russian gas company, Gazprom. In June 1998, Gazprom had plans to invest almost as much again as it had already invested in Poland, and these plans were only marginally scaled back in the aftermath of the Russian financial crisis.

By 1997, about 13 per cent of all Polish companies had foreign strategic investment. Such companies have played an increasingly important role in total expenditure on investment and in foreign trade (*Polish News Bulletin*, 31 July 1998, based on *Prawo i Gospodarka*, 28 July 1998). In 1994, these companies accounted for only 12 per cent of total investment spending, but this share rose steadily, to 16 per cent in 1995, 20 per cent in 1996 and about 25 per cent in 1997 (in manufacturing, the share in 1997 was greater than 45 per cent). Companies with foreign participation also contributed heavily to foreign trade, with share in exports rising from 25 per cent in 1994 to 43 per cent in 1997, while share in imports increased from 33 per cent to 50 per cent during the same period.

While the export-to-sales ratio, at 14 per cent in 1996, was significantly higher than the 9 per cent for domestically owned firms, this ratio had declined from 16 per cent in 1994 and 15 per cent in 1995, reflecting a shift in foreign investment oriented toward the domestic market. Thus, foreign direct investment has been increasingly oriented toward the services sector, particularly financial intermediation, retail and wholesale trade, transport and communications, and construction. Nevertheless, manufacturing still accounts for the largest share of foreign investment and contributes most substantially to export growth.

Motivation for foreign direct investment

The sectoral destinations give some indication of the reasons for foreign direct investment in Poland, which can be roughly characterised as market-seeking, cost-seeking, efficiency-seeking and natural resource-seeking. The cost-seeking motive is most obviously present in investments like car assembly with imported kits, where the major purpose would be to employ low-cost, low-skill labour and exploit Poland's advantageous location for exporting to the other regional economies. However, it appears that a growing percentage of foreign direct investment is of a market-seeking nature, particularly for investments in the non-tradable sector (financial intermediation, wholesale and retail trade and other services). Moreover, the export-to-sales ratio has been declining, again signifying a shift toward the market-seeking motive. It is difficult to assess how much investment is based on the efficiency-seeking motive, but Poland does have an attractive combination of a well educated labour force and low relative wages. For Poland, unlike a number of the former Soviet Union transition economies, the natural resource-seeking motive would be relatively negligible, particularly since the mining industry, for the most part, has not yet been privatised and will require massive restructuring.

The role of privatisation

In Hungary and the Czech Republic, privatisation was one of the major factors that attracted strong capital inflows. Poland, on the other hand, was a latecomer to privatisation relative to the other advanced transition economies. Privatisation-induced foreign direct investment has been estimated at only about 20 per cent of all foreign direct investment inflows, and many enterprises remain in state hands, ranging from steel and petrochemical giants to small vodka producers and Arabian horse farms.

The environment for privatisation has been unsettled by the global financial turmoil, but the Polish government went ahead with plans in late 1998 to launch an initial public offering for Telekomunikacja Polska SA. Orders were oversubscribed; demand from foreign investors, in particular, was two-and-a-half times the supply. As a result of the Telekomunikacja Polska SA initial public offering and the sale of a significant stake in Bank Przemyslowo-Handlowy, inward foreign direct investment flows in

November 1998—at US$952 million—were the largest in any month since transition, and December's inward foreign direct investment flows set a new record again—at almost US$1.2 billion.

Volatility of capital flows

The volatility of capital flows is an important vulnerability factor. High volatility can contribute to an unstable economic environment, which is not conducive to steady development. For most countries, the volatility of foreign direct investment is usually lower than that for portfolio flows. Some of the reasons underlying the greater stability of foreign direct investment include a longer-term investment perspective as well as greater difficulty in selling or dissolving a strategic shareholding. Portfolio flows, on the other hand, are more likely to respond quickly to changes in sentiment, arbitrage opportunities or other short-term fluctuations in financial markets. Moreover, portfolio flows are the component of capital flows most likely to suffer from contagion in other markets, as portfolio investors are more inclined toward herding behaviour.

For Poland, during the period 1995–8, the coefficient of variation for net capital flows overall was 0.7 (Table 7.4). In line with the discussion above, the different components vary significantly with respect to their coefficients of variation. Thus, the volatility of net foreign direct investment flows is the lowest, followed by that for other financial transactions. The heavy weight of foreign direct investment accounts for the relatively low volatility overall of capital flows to Poland. The remaining components of the financial account are more volatile, with volatility rising in order from medium and long-term credit, portfolio flows and short-term credit.

In using balance of payments data for foreign direct investment, it is important to recognise that these data, according to the IMF definition, include three categories—equity capital (which corresponds roughly to new investment), reinvested earnings (earnings of an overseas affiliate are regarded as exports of a service by the home country, and that which is retained by the host country is treated as a capital inflow), and intracompany debt flows. Thus, foreign direct investment data may well overstate the amount of stable equity investment. Data are not usually available on the maturity of intracompany loans, and in Poland there are no restrictions on short-term loans of this nature. These other foreign direct investment-related flows may make measured foreign direct investment somewhat less stable in a crisis situation.

Table 7.4 Poland: volatility of capital flow components, 1995–8

	Coefficient of variation	*Weight in total net flows*
Foreign direct investment	0.7	49.9
Portfolio flows	1.9	15.6
Medium/long-term credit	1.9	6.7
Short-term credit	2.7	2.5
Other financial transactions	1.8	22.0
Financial account	0.7	100.0

Note: Weights do not add to 100 because the financial account includes errors and omissions.

Table 7.5 Poland: gross foreign direct investment inflows, 1991–7 (US$million)

	1991	1992	1993	1994	1995	1996	1997
Inward foreign direct investment	359	678	1,715	1,875	3,659	4,498	4,908
Equity capital	268	433	1,109	1,096	2,105	3,159	3,116
In kind	91	135	217	212	298	314	453
Reinvested earnings	66	154	199	382	888	244	25
Loans	25	91	407	397	666	1,098	1,767
Foreign direct investment stock	425	1,370	2,307	3,789	7,843	11,463	14,587
Equity	n.a.	1,135	1,661	2,840	6,130	8,697	10,125
Other capital	n.a.	235	646	949	1,713	2,766	4,462

Source: National Bank of Poland.

For Poland, the breakdown of foreign direct investment flows into the components above reveals that capital loans have been increasing as a share of total foreign direct investment (Table 7.5). In 1995, when the initial surge in foreign direct investment began, loans accounted for only 18 per cent of all inflows. The share of loans rose to 24 per cent by 1996 and to 36 per cent in 1997. This rising trend continued into 1998, with data for the first half indicating that loans constituted about 43 per cent of all foreign direct investment inflows. Retained earnings, on the other hand, were almost negligible in both 1997 and 1998.

Poland's total external debt stock would be higher by more than 10 per cent if the stock of foreign direct investment-associated credits were included. The external debt in 1997 and as of June 1998 was US$38.5 billion and US$39.0 billion respectively if credits associated with direct investment and trade credits are excluded. With foreign direct investment-associated credits included, the debt figures are US$42.8 billion and US$44.2 billion for 1997 and June 1998 respectively.

Prospects

Poland has planned an ambitious program of privatisation in the three years from 1999. The government's target for proceeds from privatisation in 1999, at Zl15 billion, was more than twice the amount received in 1998. The government has expressed no preference for either domestic or international investors, noting only that the national treatment rule is applied to the conduct of privatisations. If carried out as planned, this should strongly support continued healthy foreign direct investment inflows.

In 1999 the government planned to sell majority stakes in a wide variety of enterprises, including LOT (the Polish airline), Bank Pekao SA, two coal mines, six central heating plants, three power plants, two pharmaceutical plants and Nafta Polska oil company. Furthermore, sale of 25–35 per cent of Telekomunikacja Polska SA to a strategic investor was planned in 1999 (following the 15 per cent share sold in the initial public offering). The first stage of privatisation of PZU SA, the national insurance company, was also planned for 1999. The three functions of the energy sector—production, distribution and transmission—will be separated prior to privatisation.

Privatisation of the production and distribution subsectors will occur first; the transmission subsector will not be privatised until 2000 or 2001. A much more difficult issue is the privatisation and restructuring of the steel sector. For the two largest steel mills (Huta Katowice and Huta Sendzimira), work is already underway to prepare for the privatisation of their subsidiaries. The European Bank for Reconstruction and Development, which invested a record Zl1.4 billion in Poland in 1998, said that it planned to participate in the privatisation offers in 1999, including in such sectors as steel, petrochemicals, aviation and agriculture.

With respect to portfolio flows, as global markets began to settle down after the Russian crisis, emerging market investors started to turn increasingly to central and eastern Europe. Between the beginning of October 1998 and January 1999, the rise in Morgan Stanley Capital International's eastern Europe index exceeded the rise in the index for all emerging markets by more than 20 per cent. Poland and Hungary have been the primary countries contributing to this performance.

Many emerging market fund managers have recently been taking larger positions in central and eastern Europe, with Poland being one of the foremost recipients of investor interest. Within funds which specialise in the transition economies, Poland and Hungary receive the lion's share of investment today. The transition economies are being viewed increasingly as a two-tier market, with the European Union prospective countries clearly favoured as strategic opportunities.

The periodical *Central European* (1998b) conducted a survey of central and eastern European regional fund managers after the Russian crisis to see how their asset allocations were being changed. According to this survey (taken at the end of October), Poland benefited the most from the retreat from Russia. Of the thirteen regional funds surveyed, eleven were increasing their weightings for Poland. In contrast, seven were decreasing their weightings for Hungary. The average asset allocation weight given to Poland by these thirteen funds was 32 per cent, compared with a regional benchmark weight for Poland of 24.5 per cent. By comparison, Hungary's benchmark weight—32 per cent—was the highest among the regional economies, but the average asset allocation weighting for the thirteen funds was 25.2 per cent. Further boosting Poland's reputation in international markets, Fitch IBCA decided in November 1998 to upgrade its rating of Poland's foreign debt from triple-B to triple-B-plus, the same rating enjoyed by the Czech Republic. Although the Brazil turmoil temporarily buffeted Polish markets, their quick recovery suggested that emerging market investors continue to view Poland as a steady ship in stormy seas. Moreover, many market analysts believe that the trend toward Poland will be further supported by the Brazilian crisis and the introduction of the euro.

The reform of the pension system, beginning in 1999, should have a number of positive impacts over the longer term on the Polish economy. First, it is expected to favourably influence both private and public saving rates, and the new pension funds should promote capital market development. This is likely to lead to greater foreign interest in Poland's capital markets. The pension reform is now explicitly dealing with the intergenerational debt issue and may allow for some future reductions in the high rate of social contributions, which could enhance interest in the forthcoming privatisations as well as other foreign investment projects.

COMPARATIVE DEVELOPMENTS IN FOREIGN DIRECT INVESTMENT

This section compares developments in foreign direct investment into selected transition countries and some other emerging markets. In addition to Poland, the set of transition countries includes Bulgaria, the Czech Republic, Estonia, Hungary, Romania, the Slovak Republic and Slovenia. The section also looks at a wider comparison of emerging markets, including, in addition to the above transition economies, several emerging markets in Asia, Latin America and Africa.

Foreign direct investment flows to this group of central and eastern European countries declined in 1996 relative to 1995, but then resumed an upward trend in 1997. Russia, Romania, Poland and Bulgaria were the beneficiaries of the largest increases in inward foreign direct investment in absolute terms, while inflows to the Czech Republic declined for the second consecutive year. Poland was the largest

Figure 7.9 Annual foreign direct investment inflows to selected transition economies, 1995–8 (US$million)

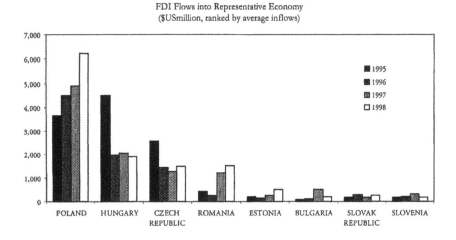

FDI Flows into Representative Economy
($USmillion, ranked by average inflows)

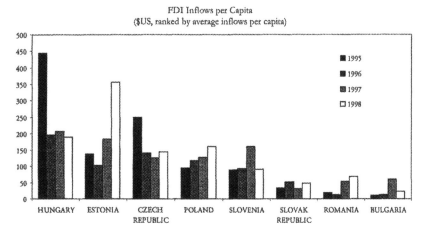

FDI Inflows per Capita
($US, ranked by average inflows per capita)

Source: IMF *International Financial Statistics,* staff estimates.

recipient of inward foreign direct investment flows, and 1998 further consolidated this trend (Figure 7.9). Poland is also notable for its much more stable year-to-year pattern of inflows and was the only country to receive steadily increasing amounts of foreign direct investment during this period.

However, when foreign direct investment flows are measured on a per capita basis, Poland drops to fourth place (Figure 7.9). Hungary moves into first place for the period 1995–8, with the spikes in the earlier years an indication of Hungary's quick move to privatise state-owned enterprises and to specifically attract foreign strategic investors. Estonia's second place per capita ranking is due to a major privatisation sale in 1998. Using either flows normalised by GDP or gross fixed investment puts Poland in third place when ranked by average inflows over the period, while Estonia and Hungary take the first two places again (Figure 7.10).

Figure 7.10 Annual scaled foreign direct investment inflows to selected transition economies, 1995–8 (US$million)

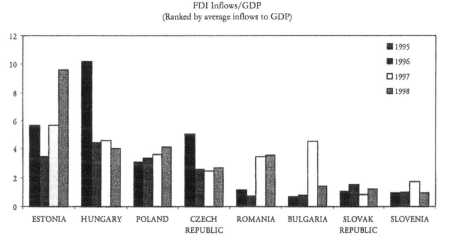

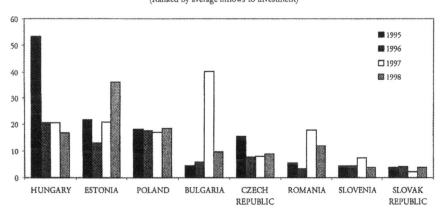

Source: IMF *International Financial Statistics,* staff estimates.

By 1998, Poland also led the other countries of the region in terms of total book value of foreign direct investment in the country, whereas on a per capita basis, it ranked fifth (Figure 7.11). Hungary and the Czech Republic, two of the first four countries, benefited from their much earlier efforts at privatisation.

In 1993–5, Poland ranked ninth out of the twenty-eight emerging markets with respect to average per capita annual inward foreign direct investment flows (Figure 7.12). In 1996–8, inward foreign direct investment flows rose substantially for all countries, and Poland edged up into eighth place. Over the same period, Poland ranked fourth in terms of average annual inward foreign direct investment flows and ranked seventh in terms of average annual inward foreign direct investment flows to GDP (Figure 7.13).

Figure 7.11 Foreign direct investment stock in selected transition economies, 1998 (US$million)

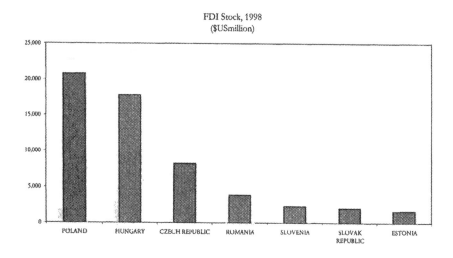

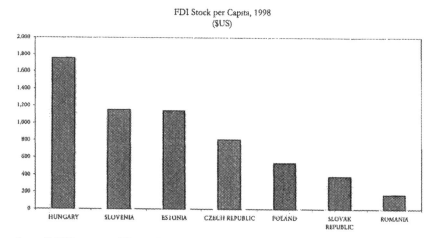

Source: IMF *International Financial Statistics,* staff estimates.

What accounts for these differences in normalised foreign direct investment inflows? There are a variety of variables that determine investor interest, including unit labour costs, relative wages (*vis-à-vis* investing countries), size of domestic market, quality of labour force, infrastructure, political stability and other macroeconomic and microeconomic factors. It would be useful to find an aggregate variable that captured many of these likely determinants. One such type of variable might be a country risk indicator, such as those published by, among others, *Euromoney*, the Economist Intelligence Unit and *Institutional Investor*. Country risk indicators are developed by using investors' and analysts' views on countries' future prospects based on many of the fundamentals listed above, often with a forward-looking orientation. Furthermore, analogous to efficient markets theory, in which a financial asset price should incorporate

Figure 7.12 Foreign direct investment inflows per capita to selected emerging markets, 1993–5 and 1996–8 (US$)

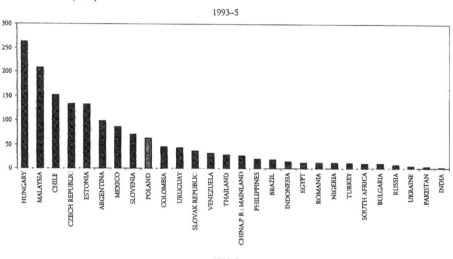

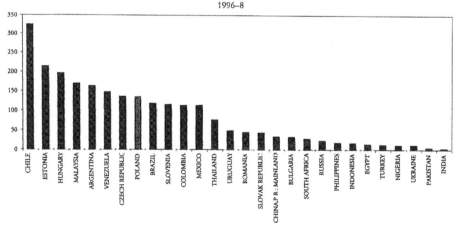

Source: IMF *International Financial Statistics, World Economic Outlook*; staff estimates.

Table 7.6 Country risk comparisons, 1995–8

Country	September 1998		March 1995		Increase in rank from 1995–8
	Rank	Score	Rank	Score	
Chile	30	76.6	34	75.9	4
Poland	**38**	**71.1**	**71**	**47.9**	**33**
Hungary	39	71.1	50	60.2	11
Czech Republic	40	71.0	35	73.9	-5
China	41	67.3	42	66.1	1
Uruguay	44	62.9	61	52.2	17
Colombia	45	62.9	48	60.9	3
Mexico	47	61.8	52	58.6	5
Argentina	48	61.3	56	55.5	8
Egypt	49	61.2	73	47.4	24
South Africa	50	61.1	45	62.9	-5
Estonia	51	61.1	66	49.4	15
Malaysia	53	59.7	28	78.6	-25
Thailand	54	59.2	30	77.9	-24
Philippines	55	58.4	60	52.7	5
Slovak Republic	58	57.4	53	57.9	-5
India	59	57.1	51	59.1	-8
Turkey	61	56.2	57	55.0	-4
Brazil	70	52.6	58	54.6	-12
Venezuela	76	47.3	67	49.4	-9
Romania	82	46.3	68	48.7	-14
Indonesia	88	43.6	40	69.7	-48
Bulgaria	93	42.3	90	40.7	-3
Ukraine	118	36.4	145	26.4	27
Pakistan	123	35.9	75	47.0	-48
Russia	127	35.3	141	27.8	14
Nigeria	132	33.6	112	33.4	-20

Note: Country risk ranks are based on *Euromoney* rankings for 181 countries. March 1995 figures are from *Euromoney:146–51*. September 1998 figures are from *Euromoney:202–7*.
Source: Euromoney, 1996. *'Asia's economies start to slip',* (September).

all available information, the country risk measures might operate somewhat like a price in incorporating all currently available information in assessing countries' prospects, including expected changes in policy, institutional factors, the changing political climate, as well as projections for the usual fundamental economic indicators.

For this purpose, the *Euromoney* country risk scores and rankings are used to provide a quantification of risk perceptions for each of the countries for March 1995 and September 1998 (Table 7.6). The total scores can range from zero to 100, with 100 being the most creditworthy or least risky country in which to invest; the ranks are the inverse, with the most creditworthy country receiving a rank of one. After its debt restructuring, Poland began to move up the ranks and was at number seventy-one in March 1995. By December 1997, in the wake of the East Asian crisis, Poland had risen to forty-eight, and the country risk ranking for September 1998 placed it at thirty-eighth.

In terms of both the country risk indicator (averaged over 1995–8) and purchasing power parity-adjusted GDP per capita at the start of the sample period (used as a crude proxy for productivity), Poland's inward foreign direct investment flows per capita are almost exactly on the trendline (Figure 7.14). This implies Poland's position as a recipient of foreign direct investment is quite well explained by investors' views on country risk and a rough measure of initial productivity, rather than on country-specific special factors.

Figure 7.13 Foreign direct investment developments in selected emerging markets, 1996–8 (US$million, per cent)

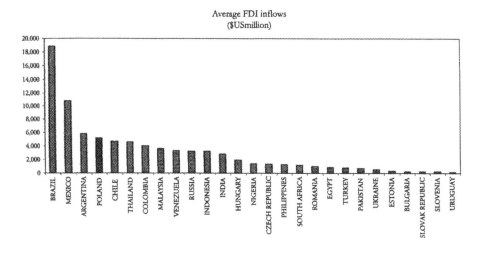

Average FDI inflows
($USmillion)

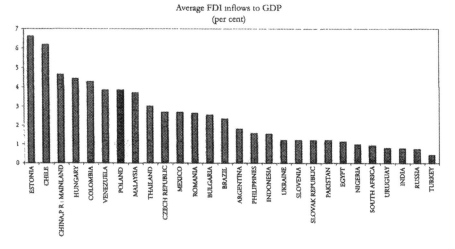

Average FDI inflows to GDP
(per cent)

Source: IMF *International Financial Statistics; World Economic Outlook;* staff estimates.

Figure 7.14 Average foreign direct investment inflows per capita versus country risk and purchasing power parity, 1995–8 (US$)

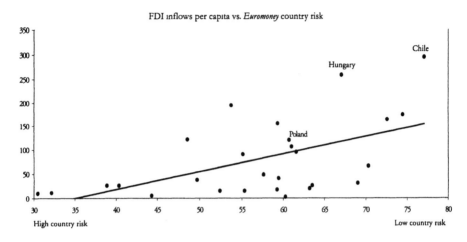

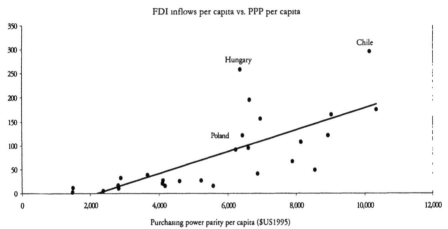

Source: IMF *International Financial Statistics, World Economic Outlook*; staff estimates.

CONCLUSIONS

Over the course of its transition to a market economy, Poland has developed a reputation for sound macroeconomic policies and openness both to trade and financial flows. This reputation has attracted significant capital inflows in recent years. Poland's prospects as a candidate for early European Union enlargement, its favourable geographic location and its impressive progress in market-oriented reforms have also made the country one of the favoured destinations for foreign investment. The forthcoming program for privatisation, the launching of pension reform and the interest expressed by investors in European Union convergence plays with Poland's debt suggests that foreign inflows could be even greater in the coming years.

Since the surge in capital inflows to Poland began in 1995, foreign direct investment has been the most significant component. Foreign direct investment is likely to continue to maintain its dominance in Poland's capital inflows, particularly if the privatisation program is carried out as planned. Moreover, this composition of capital inflows indicates that the probability of a sudden reversal of flows is low. Nevertheless, the share of credit in foreign direct investment has been increasing, and although there is little likelihood of default on such intracompany lending, these loans could dry up if the differential cost of borrowing domestically were to fall significantly.

Although portfolio inflows have played only a modest role in Poland's external financing, the share of such inflows may well increase in the medium term as the financial markets in Poland deepen and become more liquid. Market capitalisation in Poland is still quite low, but its expansion will be bolstered by the extensive privatisation program. Perhaps even more important will be the newly created pension funds, which should increase domestic savings and channel these savings into the financial market.

The crises in emerging markets from East Asia to Latin America, and in particular, the Russian crisis, have served to highlight the distinctions among the transition economies, with the fast-track market reformers, such as Poland, suffering temporary and relatively minor financial disruptions. Indeed, notwithstanding the initial negative impact on Poland's financial markets, the crises may well intensify inflows to Poland in the near term as investors seeking diversification find the number of safe candidates for investment shrinking. Poland appears to be particularly well positioned to sustain strong investor interest and maintain its access to international financing.

APPENDIX

Limitations and deficiencies of data on capital flows

In attempting to quantify capital flow developments in Poland, there are a number of data limitations that make analysis problematic. First, the category unclassified transactions was included in the balance of payments as a short-term capital account item until 1996. At that time, the National Bank of Poland decided to record this item as a special category in the current account since it was determined that most of these inflows were associated with unregistered cross-border trade with Germany, Russia, Ukraine and Belarus. Nevertheless, some proportion of these unclassified transactions are probably pseudo-financial account items and, thus, are incorrectly included in the current account. The capital flow data in this chapter adjust the balance of payments prior to 1996 to reflect the new methodology.

Another limitation is that detailed data on portfolio flows are available beginning only in 1995, although portfolio investment was negligible in the earlier years of transition. More worrisome, though, is the fact that unexplained net flows, in the form of errors and omissions, grew substantially in the period 1996–8, and the problem became particularly acute in 1998. According to Durjasz and Kokoszczynski (1998), companies may have borrowed more abroad than has been reported through the banking system.

For foreign direct investment, there are three sources of data—the balance of payments data prepared by the National Bank of Poland; *International Financial Statistics* data which are based on the National Bank of Poland balance of payments data but also include results from a survey of enterprises conducted annually; and registration and survey data from the Polish Agency for Foreign Investment. The discrepancies between the three sets of data are large. The balance of payments data are based on financial flows and, therefore, do not include investment transactions in kind (for example, investment in the form of imported equipment and materials). The *International Financial Statistics* data differ from the balance of payments data because they include reinvested profits (on a net basis), a reclassification of transactions that have been misreported in the balance of payments statistics, valuation differences (the survey is based on book value) and foreign direct investment outside the banking system.

The estimates of foreign direct investment based on the balance of payments and *International Financial Statistics* series are substantially below that provided by the Polish Agency for Foreign Investment. The major differences are that the Polish Agency for Foreign Investment statistics include gross reinvested profits, rather than net profits (with losses deducted), and bank credits may, in some cases, be included. In addition, there are no penalties imposed on enterprises for misreporting data to the Polish Agency for Foreign Investment, and there could, therefore, be some cases in which enterprises present an overly optimistic picture of their situation.

For example, in 1997, foreign direct investment inflows to Poland, based on National Bank of Poland cash flow data, were US$3.1 billion. The data reported in the *International Financial Statistics* show inflows of US$4.9 billion. The Polish Agency for Foreign Investment data, however, show inflows of US$6.6 billion, considerably higher than either of the other two estimates. Nevertheless, each of the three data series tells the same general story with respect to foreign direct investment trend developments.

In attempting comparisons with other countries, data limitations are exaggerated relative to those discussed above for Poland. In general, there are considerable difficulties in ensuring consistency of data for emerging market economies, but these difficulties are much more severe with data on capital flows. There remain significant gaps in data series, capital flow data are especially subject to country-specific approaches, and classification of such flows is innately difficult in the best of circumstances. For example, there are problems with different national treatment of foreign direct investment data (for example, inclusion of in kind versus strictly cash transactions, inclusion of loans and retained earnings versus strictly equity). In addition, foreign direct investment data are often based on surveys, the quality and coverage of which may vary significantly from country to country. Most analyses of foreign direct investment developments rely on *International Financial Statistics* data. However, the data provided for the *International Financial Statistics* should also be treated with caution in cross-country comparisons. Thus, any analysis should be viewed with the appropriate caveats in view of the data limitations.

8 Relative resistance to currency crisis

The case of Hungary, comparisons with the Czech Republic and Poland

István Ábel and Zsolt Darvas

The financial crisis that rocked emerging market economies in 1997 and 1998 has sounded alarms for transition economies like the Czech Republic, Hungary and Poland. Crises characterised by capital flight, currency depreciation, banking crises and economic recession began in East Asia in July 1997. Before the crisis hit East Asia, the Czech Republic experienced crisis in May 1997 (Figure 8.1), which Hungary survived relatively well, though the Hungarian forint temporarily moved towards the middle of its exchange rate band from a previously stable strong position. The Slovakian currency was also under attack a few days after the Czech crisis, but as Slovak capital markets are much less open, regulation is stricter, the banking system is more closely attached to the government, and also because the National Bank of Slovakia had been well prepared for the attack, they could defend their currency effectively. Poland's situation was similar to that of Hungary. This lack of contagion must be explained, as, contrary to this experience, both the Mexican crisis and the Thai crisis were followed by similar events intraregionally.

The Russian crisis of August 1998 had a more dramatic effect, not only on neighbouring economies but on markets all over the world. Despite its narrow band of plus or minus 2.25 per cent, Hungary survived the crisis within this band (Figure 8.2). In contrast, between 3 August and 24 August, Poland and the Czech Republic, with greater exchange rate flexibility, experienced exchange rate depreciation about twice as large (Poland 9.3 per cent, Czech Republic 7.7 per cent) (Begg and Wyplosz 1999) (Figures 8.3 and 8.4).

CAUSES OF THE EAST ASIAN VIRUS

Three main underlying elements are cited as the basic causes of the East Asian financial crisis (Hoenig 1998). First, to finance growth these economies relied on a large amount of short-term debt relative to equity. As investors can quickly move capital out of an economy short-term debt is an unstable source of funding.

Second, these countries maintained fixed exchange rates in the face of large deficits. This misled banks and enterprises who, underestimating the exchange rate risk, accumulated too high dollar-denominated short-term debt. This made them vulnerable to sudden exchange rate depreciation.

Figure 8.1 Czech Republic: exchange rate, 1997–9

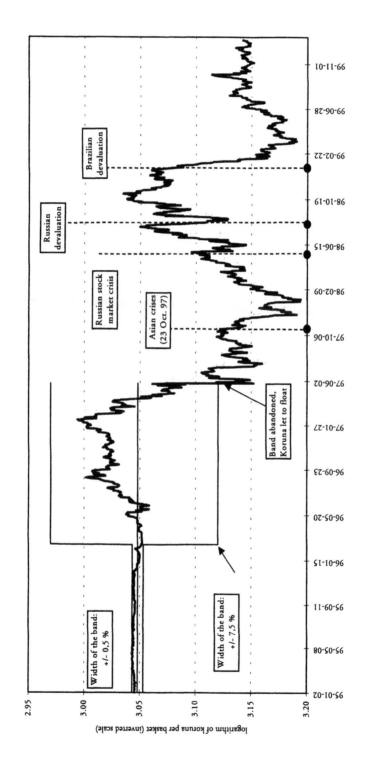

Note: Basket used prior to May 1997: 65% DEM, 35% $US. We used the same basket for the floating period for comparision purposes.
Source: Szapáry, G. and Darvas, Z., 2000. 'Financial Contagion in Five Small Open Economies: does the exchange rate regime really matter?', *International Finance*, 3(1):25–51; authors' calculation based on data from the Czech National Bank and Reuters.

Figure 8.2 Hungary: exchange rate, 1997–9

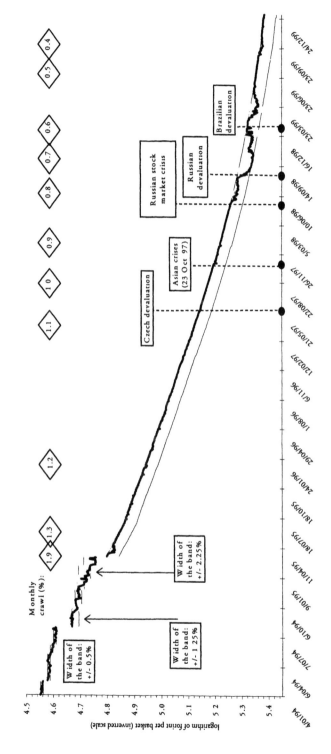

Note: Composition of the basket: 50% DM+50% USD for August 1993–May 1994; 70% ECU+30% USD for January 1997–December 1996; 70% DEM+30% USD for May 1994–December 1996; 70% DEM+30% USD for January 1997–December 1998; 70% EUR+30% USD since January–December 1999, 100% EUR since 2000.

Source: Szapáry, G. and Darvas, Z., 2000. 'Financial Contagion in Five Small Open Economies: does the exchange rate regime really matter?', *International Finance,* 3(1):25–51; National Bank of Hungary.

Figure 8.3   Poland: exchange rate, 1997–9

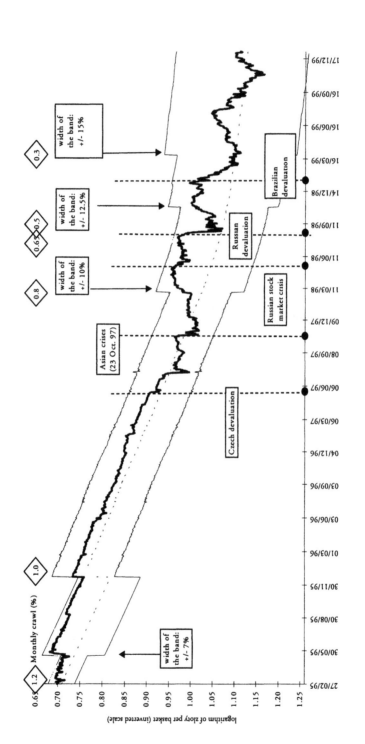

Note: NBH calculation based on different sources. Composition of the basket prior to 1999: 45% USD, 35% DM, 10% GBP, 5% FRF, 5% CHF; since 1999: 55% EUR, 45% US$.

Source: Szapáry, G. and Darvas, Z., 2000. 'Financial Contagion in Five Small Open Economies: does the exchange rate regime really matter?', *International Finance*, 3(1):25–51; Economics and Research Department, National Bank of Hungary

Figure 8.4 Hungary, Poland and Czech Republic: exchange rates, 1997–9

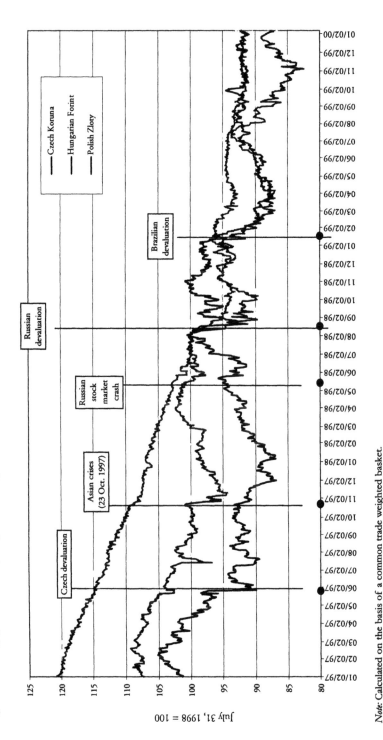

Note: Calculated on the basis of a common trade weighted basket.
Source: Authors' own calculations based on data from Reuters (exchange rates) and the National Bank of Hungary; IMF, *Direction of Trade Statistics*, IMF, Washington, DC.

Third, the banking system was flooded with foreign funds and credit was available for domestic clients too easily for questionable investment projects.

High debt, pegged exchange rates and, to a lesser extent, a weak financial system were common in transition economies. International organisations like the IMF and the OECD attempted to correct economic policies applied during the transition to make these economies less vulnerable. Namely, to help maintain investor confidence, they insisted on fiscal reforms to establish the foundation for sustainable growth and sound policies.

An important macroeconomic stabilisation program was implemented in Hungary in 1995 and major advances in the privatisation of banking, insurance and public utilities were achieved in subsequent years.

The most important reforms have been those to place financial systems on a sound footing—cleaning up insolvent practices and institutions, recapitalising weak but solvent banks, strengthening regulations and supervision and opening the markets to increase foreign and domestic competition. In the banking industry, Hungary followed the best strategy, selling struggling state-owned banks to foreign strategic partners. The same strategy is currently unfolding in Poland and the Czech Republic.

Sound financial systems have several characteristics. They institutionalise the savings and investment process by providing channels for the flow of funds from net savers to net investors. In so doing, they need to adjust to changes in the economic and social environment. They also need to be stable and resistant to shocks.

Current structural change and financial reform may or may not result in more liberalised financial systems (Cargill and Parker 1999). Financial reforms during the great depression in many countries restricted market forces to limit risk taking and enhance systemic stability. In contrast, the transition toward a market economy has been designed to increase the role of competition in the allocation of funds; this process is referred to as financial liberalisation.

Given the impact of the recent shocks on transition economies and the role liberalised capital movements played, there has been a great deal of discussion about the dangers of liberalisation. Borio, Kennedy and Prowse (1994), based on the experience of thirteen industrialised countries during the second half of the 1980s, conclude that liberalisation and financial crises are causally related.

Although the process of liberalisation may have been faulty, the need for further restructuring and supporting steady capital inflows is as strong as ever. The problems are mostly consequences of government failure in macro stabilisation or institutional modernisation. The market response to this failure may be greatly undesirable but the proper response is not to halt liberalisation, but instead to eliminate these distortions.

Resistance to contagion in transition economies

In a recent paper Árvai and Vincze (1999) address the following four factors which may shed some light on relative resistance to contagion

- business cycle characteristics (macro fundamentals)
- underdeveloped financial infrastructure
- exchange rate regime
- regulations and constraints on capital flows.

Macroeconomic fundamentals and contagion

The Czech and Hungarian economies are at very different stages of the business cycle. At the time of the crisis growth in Hungary was accelerating, while in the Czech Republic, growth had almost come to a halt. The Hungarian real exchange rate was stable after 1995, whereas the Czech koruna gradually appreciated as a result of fixing the exchange rate while domestic inflation ran at approximately 10 per cent. Current account and foreign direct investment developments were rather favourable in Hungary, while the situation deteriorated in the Czech Republic and Slovakia. The Polish case is more mixed. Evidently investors differentiated between the countries of central and eastern Europe. This seems to be in contrast to South East Asia, where contagion may be explained by the more similar export structure, and the fact that the profits that could be achieved by speculation were much higher than in central Europe. The case of Latin America offers another lesson—that positive contagion is also possible and relatively strong countries may even profit from the woes of others.

Based on macro indicators it is easy for investors to conclude that Hungary and the Czech Republic follow a different pattern. A risk-averse investor would conclude that assets originating in both countries should be held in the portfolio. Speculators who believe they are smarter than others can react with discrete jumps, and reallocate assets suddenly in response to change.

Banking and financial sectors

It is an advantage of transition economies that listed companies are not concentrated in the real estate and financial intermediation sectors of the economy, as they were in East Asia, and thus asset price bubbles are less likely to emerge.

Delayed restructuring of the enterprise sector can cause banking problems, especially if the enterprise sector has borrowed in foreign currency and production is marked for the domestic market. Privatisation and export orientation is an important factor in resistance to currency crises.

The natural way to defend a currency in case of attack is to raise interest rates. Large maturity mismatch could lead to large losses, but this does not seem to be a problem in transition economies like Hungary. The credit crunch in the 1990s reduced enterprise and household leverage, making the banking sector less vulnerable to interest rate hikes. The sort of problems that were influential in Britain at the time of the exchange rate mechanism crisis do not exist in Hungary, since mortgages are insignificant in bank portfolios.

Real rates are still quite volatile and, as a whole, very high, especially immediately following the crisis (Figure 8.5). Maintaining high rates not only contributes to restrictive policies and provides some protection against leveraged speculators but is also required for maintaining a relatively stable inflow of capital. For this reason, the interest premium has generally been high, especially following the Russian crisis to counterbalance higher country risk (Figure 8.6).

Nominal rates are still following a more or less steady decline in line with inflation, which is falling as transition progresses (Figure 8.7). Given the current volatility in world financial markets, the difference between the one-year rate and the compounded three-month rate is considerably unstable but dominantly negative, indicating that the market expects a continuous decline in rates (Figure 8.8).

Figure 8.5   Hungary, Poland and Czech Republic: real three-month interest rates, 1995–9

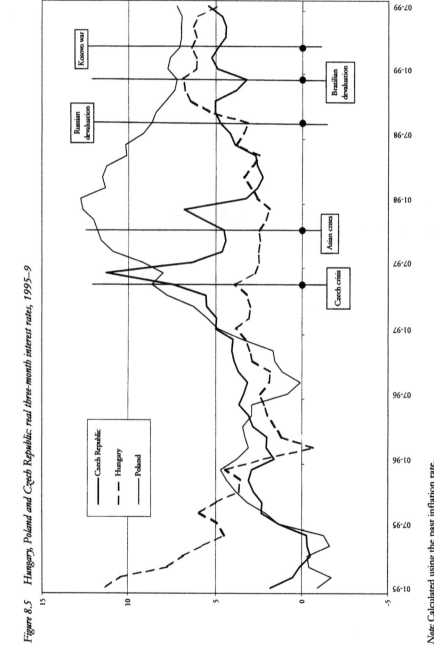

Note: Calculated using the past inflation rate.

Source: Authors' calculations based on data provided by the National Bank of Hungary and IMF, *International Financial Statistics*, IMF, Washington, DC.

Figure 8.6 Hungary, Poland and Czech Republic: interest rate premia, 1995–9

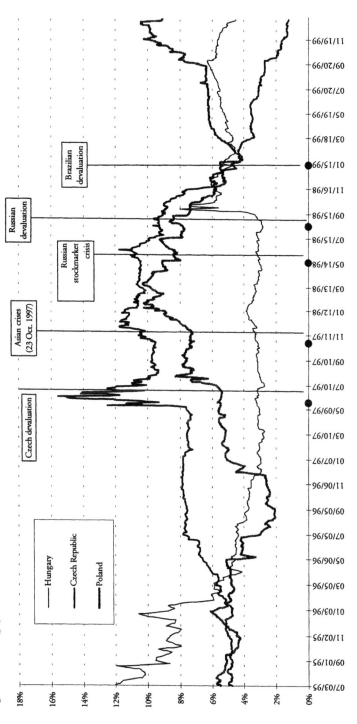

Note: The interest premium is calculated on the basis of domestic three-month interbank rates and the three-month forward-looking preannounced crawling depreciation (zero in the Czech Republic) minus the foreign interest rates.
Source: Szapáry, G. and Darvas, Z., 2000. 'Financial Contagion in Five Small Open Economies: does the exchange rate regime really matter?', *International Finance*, 3(1):25–51; authors calculations based on data from Reuters.

Figure 8.7 *Hungary, Poland and Czech Republic: three-month interest rates, 1995–9*

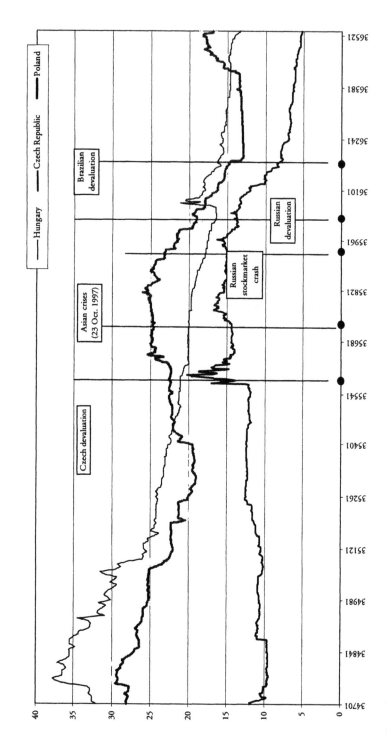

Source: Szapáry, G. and Darvas, Z., 2000. 'Financial Contagion in Five Small Open Economies: does the exchange rate regime really matter?', *International Finance*, 3(1):25–51.

On the other hand, it is an important countervailing force that in Hungary the banking sector is mostly privatised, and in addition, owned by foreign banks. Thus, there is lesser need to exercise the implicit option provided by the central bank as lender of last resort, and thus the inherent moral hazard problem is less serious.

THE EXCHANGE RATE REGIME

Probably the factor most responsible for vulnerability is excessive trust followed by excessive mistrust in a particular exchange rate regime. Defending a currency via intervention and reserve losses makes participation in an attack practically costless, whereas non-panicking can be extremely dangerous for an individual investor.

Early in transition, disinflation was a key policy concern. Most shocks arose from the domestic economy. Choosing to use the exchange rate as a nominal anchor for these countries used to be a simple and transparent way to demonstrate commitment to conduct monetary policy independently. Tight and narrow exchange rate bands, however, are always a risk (Eichengreen 1999).

After its initial narrow exchange rate band, with periodic realignments of the central parity, Poland has gradually widened its exchange rate band, eventually by a substantial amount (Figure 8.3). The Czech koruna was pegged in January 1991 at 28 koruna/ US$, with a narrow band of plus or minus 0.5 per cent. In May 1993 the peg was redefined against a basket comprised of 65 per cent deutschemarks and 35 per cent US dollars. In February 1996 the band was widened to plus or minus 4 per cent. In May 1997, however, speculative pressure forced the Czech Republic abruptly off its exchange rate peg and the Czech Republic has subsequently pursued a managed float underpinned by a domestic inflation target (Figure 8.1). Hungary has continued to defend a narrow exchange rate band around a central parity whose preannounced rate of crawl has steadily been reduced (Figure 8.2). Currently the crawl is 0.5 per cent monthly. Thus, all three countries have modified their original exchange rate regime during the years of transition, sometimes in response to shocks but sometimes in the hope of preventing tensions emerging.

Although rigid exchange rate regimes increase the probability that the currency becomes overvalued and consequently the probability of an attack, switching to a flexible exchange rate regime is not a safe way to prevent crises. Frankel and Rose (1996) found that 50 per cent of exchange rate crises occur under a floating exchange rate system. Perhaps this reveals that it is equally impossible to stick to non-intervention as it is to maintain commitment to an announced value of a currency. A reasonable mixture of floating and managing seems to be the only viable long-run exchange rate policy for developing countries.

Capital control and interest rates

When a currency crisis is developing, central banks normally raise interest rates. However, in many cases, a sudden increase in rates can make a banking system with large maturity mismatch unprofitable. To avoid this problem the Banque de France tried to segment money markets during the exchange rate mechanism crisis. It separated bona fide banks from speculators, and while the former could get central bank credit at normal rates, the latter could get loans only at penal rates. General interest rates

Figure 8.8   *Hungary, Poland and Czech Republic: yield curves, 1996–9*

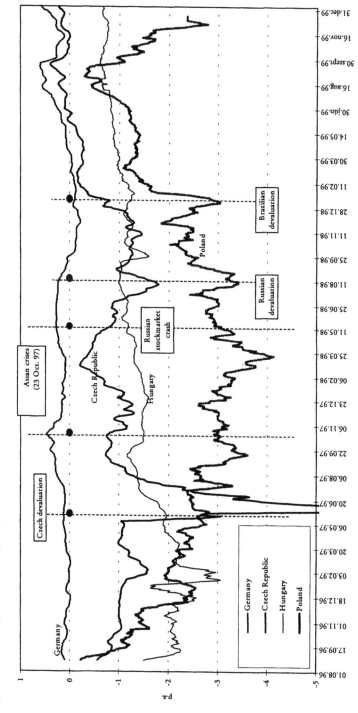

Note: The yield curve is the difference between the one-year and compounded three-month interest rates. Seven-day centered moving average.
Source: Authors' own calculations based on data provided by the National Bank of Hungary and Reuters.

increased, but the effect was not so damaging. Obviously, such an approach requires substantial confidence and is difficult to implement. Also the central bank can easily become a target of accusations of partiality.

Other types of segmentation can occur between domestic and offshore markets— the central bank may practice moral suasion to prevent domestic banks from lending to foreigners (as the Czech National Bank did in 1997), it can increase the reserve requirement depending on foreign lending (as the Bank of Spain did in 1992), or it can explicitly forbid lending to foreigners (like the Bank of Thailand in 1997). Segmentation may lead to further outflows if it is taken as a signal of further restrictions. Segmentation can be only a short-term expediency—circumvention will eventually happen.

Maintaining strict capital controls (as in Slovakia) or retarding the development of financial markets can create a situation where speculative capital has no avenue through which to flow. In this case the country can avoid crises for some time, even with unsustainable macro indicators. The costs of capital controls are manifold, including directly determinable costs as well as more intangible welfare losses. Poorly developed financial markets are thought to hinder the efficient working of monetary policy, resulting in prohibitively large transaction costs for many agents, and can narrow the range of available investment opportunities. By and large risk management will suffer. A concomitant problem with capital market restrictions is related to international competition. If some countries in the region liberalise, those that do not may suffer by losing business and having less access to international sources of investment. Domestic banks may be at very serious disadvantages *vis-à-vis* foreign banks working in a more liberalised environment. Furthermore, as rating agencies regard liberalisation as a positive indicator, restrictions can directly increase the funding costs of the whole country.

CAPITAL INFLOWS, THE STOCKMARKET AND THE EXCHANGE RATE

Volatile capital flows have a major impact on stockmarket prices. Exchange rate movements may reduce part of the volatility (Begg and Wyplosz 1999). If the room for manoeuvring is more limited stockmarket price swings may become larger. Exchange rate crises caused larger price changes on the Budapest than on the Warsaw or Prague stock exchanges (Figures 8.9 and 8.10). Evidently the major cause of these changes was the changes in the stock of foreign investment. Investment in government securities was heavily hit by regional crises (Figure 8.11).

Foreign investors have no direct access to short-term treasury bills and normally operate in the market for longer-term securities in Hungary. When they increase their investments the difference between the three-month and five-year benchmark increases. The rates are lower on longer-term securities. These investments also generate demand for local currency and consequently contribute to any appreciation of the local currency. There is a remarkable correlation between these factors (Figures 8.12 and 8.13). Since April 1999, however, this relationship has loosened, indicating that the main component is no longer related to foreign investment in government papers but rather comes from other sources like foreign direct investment, increasing corporate foreign debt or investment based on current account improvements.

Figure 8.9   Budapest, Warsaw and Prague stock exchanges: recent movements in stock prices, 1997–9

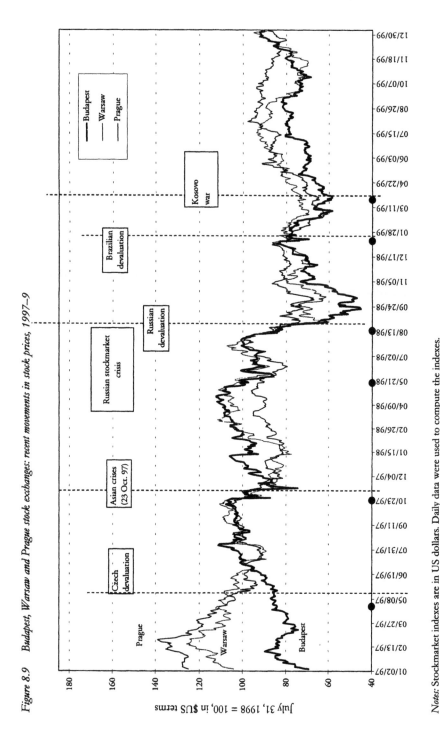

Notes: Stockmarket indexes are in US dollars. Daily data were used to compute the indexes.
Source: Szapáry, G. and Darvas, Z., 2000. 'Financial Contagion in Five Small Open Economies: does the exchange rate regime really matter?', *International Finance*, 3(1):25–51; authors' calculations based on data from Reuters.

Figure 8.10 The Budapest stock exchange index and DAX *(in US$ terms), 1997–9*

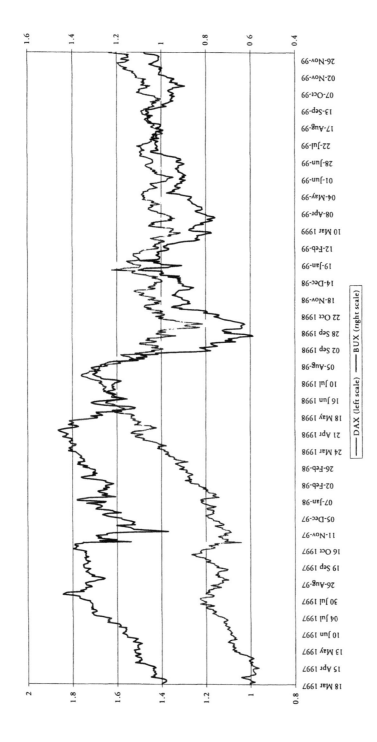

Source: Authors' own calculations based on data provided by the National Bank of Hungary.

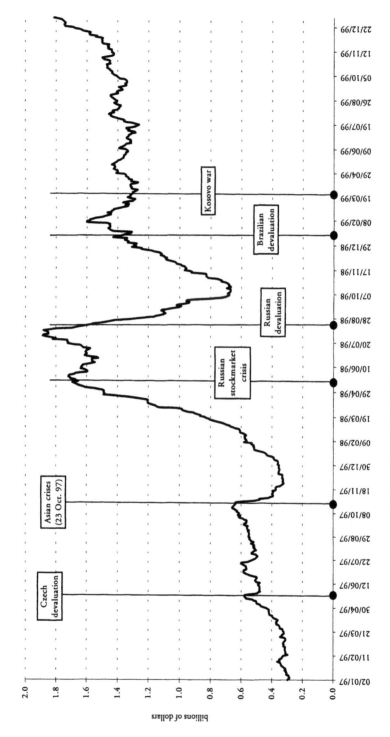

Figure 8.11 Hungary: non-resident holdings of government securities, 1997–9

Source: Authors' own calculations based on data provided by the National Bank of Hungary.

Figure 8.12 The forint within the 4.5 per cent intervention band and the yield spread between the three-month and five-year treasury benchmark, 1998–9

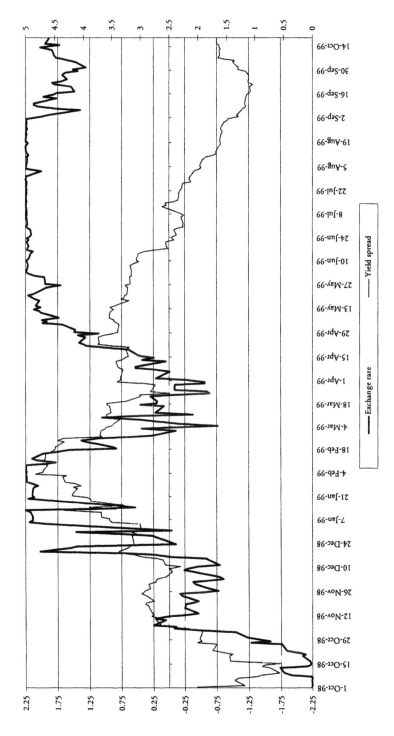

Source: Authors' own calculations based on data provided by the National Bank of Hungary.

CONCLUSIONS

Prudent macroeconomic policy and stable fundamentals are necessary but not sufficient conditions for a country to avoid speculative attacks. There are no universal rules or signals for forecasting currency crises. Therefore, it does not seem sensible to determine artificial rules to indicate vulnerability.

Contagion has played an important role in the waves of currency crises of the 1990s. The risk of contagion may be correlated with several factors like similarity of export structure. A country with well diversified international trade is less vulnerable to demand, price and exchange rate shocks. Theory suggests that if an economy is significantly exposed to international shocks, it should choose a less rigid exchange rate regime (Begg and Wyplosz 1999).

Experiences of the 1990s indicate that regional currency crises (such as the exchange rate mechanism, Latin American and East Asian crises) were more frequent than isolated crises, hence the danger of contagion must be taken seriously, even by countries whose economic fundamentals would not justify an attack. It can also be observed, however, that during regional or global crises there are countries which may experience positive contagion, that is, capital fleeing countries attacked flows to safe havens. Chile may serve as an example in the follow up of the 1994 Mexican crisis.

During calm periods, unsustainable fundamentals are longer tolerated. The May 1998 attack on the Czech koruna is an obvious example—the high current account deficit and overvalued currency had been tolerated for a substantial period of time.

In cases when currency crises have been coupled with banking crises, the implicit commitment of monetary authorities to bail out troubled banks and the inherent moral hazard has been a common cause of the problem. This implicit commitment is stronger if the banking system is not privatised. National banking systems (like those in East Asia) are more exposed to the problem of moral hazard than those in which the share of foreign capital is higher.

The main sources of currency crises are budget deficits and public debt. Debt raises the chance of a crisis if the financing is monetary or from bond issues, either domestically or abroad. Not only existing debt matters, but also the prospect of growth in debt. For instance, the probability of an increase in public debt increases if the monetary authorities implicitly commit themselves to bail out the financial intermediary system. Modern financial markets increase the vulnerability of countries with substantial debt for several reasons. First, a potential attack may result in a large profit for those who can afford to take speculative positions. Second, the costs of belated flight to other financial market participants may be huge, whereas flight itself is cheap. Third, there are several types of speculative (uncovered, risky) positions in the economy to which regulatory authorities have no access, and the closing of these positions can launch catastrophic changes.

As far as fiscal policy is concerned, to avoid speculative attack without restricting capital flows, public debt must decline—not even in unfavourable circumstances should the upsurge of debt be allowed.

Sudden and large falls in asset prices may be dangerous if there are weak (risky) balance sheets in the economy. The most serious form of this is if the banking system takes excessive risk. The prudential regulation of the banking system in itself is not sufficient to prevent the formation of bubbles.

Figure 8.13 Hungary: correlation between the exchange rate and the spread on long bonds

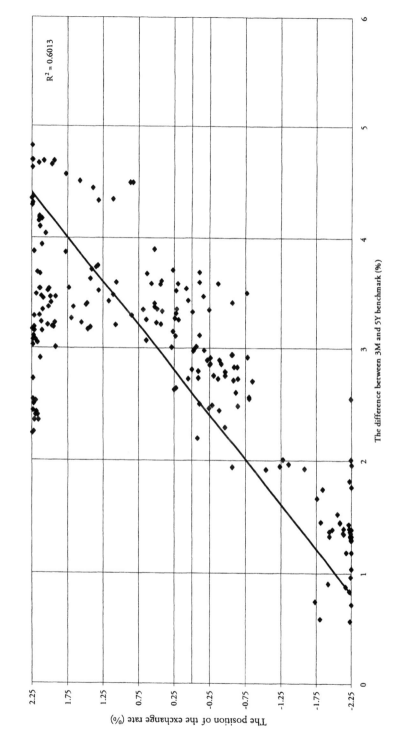

$R^2 = 0.6013$

The position of the exchange rate (%)

The difference between 3M and 5Y benchmark (%)

Source: Authors' own calculations based on data provided by the National Bank of Hungary.

The interest rate sensitivity of an economy is an important determinant of both the probability of an attack on the currency and the prospects for defense. Interest rate sensitivity may take several forms but the significant indebtedness of some agents always plays a part (for example, high interest payments on public debt or substantial indebtedness of households in the form of mortgage contracts).

Substantial appreciation of the real exchange rate and a large and persistent current account deficit are dangerous in a fixed exchange rate regime, not necessarily because they are unsustainable but because they increase the chance for an attack to be profitable in case of an unexpected shock (that is, the post-attack nominal exchange rate will be surely weaker than the previous fixed rate). In the 1990s, expansionary fiscal policy was not the only cause of currency crises (as an influential branch of theory suggests); however, if fiscal policy was loose, crisis was almost unavoidable.

Financial liberalisation contributes to the increased probability of speculative attack. Liberalisation and growth as well as deepening (for example, new forms of derivatives) of financial markets make speculation easier. Unsustainable public debt and exchange rate misalignments are penalised not only *ex post* (as in the past) but also *ex ante*. It must be emphasised that the faster and more dramatic reaction of financial markets is not due to their perfection or efficiency. On the contrary, changes in perfect and fully efficient markets would be much less drastic—catastrophic changes would occur less frequently. The real problem is that liberalisation itself does not eliminate every problem, but at the same time, the consequences of problems stemming from market imperfections are less and less borne by sophisticated market agents. If we believe that financial liberalisation is a good thing and contributes to the higher long-run growth of the world economy, then we have to live with the unpleasant side effects also, either accepting or minimising them.

The fact that open capital markets reduce the independence of domestic economic policies is not necessarily troublesome. On the one hand, open capital markets make it possible for less sophisticated investors to protect themselves from unexpected devaluation and inflation tax. On the other hand, less liberalised countries are able to maintain not only risky, but also explicitly unsustainable policies for quite a long time.

As far as monetary and exchange rate policies are concerned, rigid exchange rate regimes increase vulnerability. Since exchange rate stability plays an important role in small, indebted countries, a managed float may be a temporary solution.

9 Currency crisis in Russia in a wider context

*Vladimir Popov**

Were the recent crises in transition economies only the result of financial contagion spreading in the global economy or could this series of crises be attributed to domestic causes? Does the coincidence of crises justify the view that the causes of the crises in East Asia and in Russia and other transition economies were similar in nature? This chapter embraces a third explanation—currency crises in transition economies resulted mostly from domestic policy mistakes, but of a different nature than those in East Asia.

The Russian crisis was a trivial balance of payments crash resulting from inconsistency in macroeconomic policy objectives, as has been experienced many times in many countries. It would have occurred even without East Asian viruses, Russian fiscal imbalances and oligarchs' prodigality. The root of the crisis was the overappreciation of the ruble—from early 1992 to late 1995 the real exchange rate of the ruble grew more than seven-fold. This was more than in other transition economies and more than enough to kill the growth of exports, cause an unaffordable rise in imports and undermine the trade and current account surpluses, leading to the depletion of reserves.

Currency crises in post-communist countries are best explained by first generation currency crisis models—straightforward macroeconomic mismanagement manifested in an overvaluation of the exchange rate resulting from a combination of a nominal exchange rate peg and ongoing inflation. This leads to deterioration of the current account, outflow of capital in the anticipation of devaluation, depletion of the foreign exchange reserves and, eventually, currency collapse. In Russia the crisis was aggravated by the decision to default on short-term, and later, long-term debt. This was by no means necessary—the debt crisis was artificially manufactured by the government.

The East Asian story is more complex. It caught many economists by surprise: the East Asian currencies were not overvalued, macroeconomic policy was prudent and fundamentals were sound.[1] The collapse of these currencies arose from the private sector debt crisis—overextension of credit by banks and companies financed through foreign borrowing.

The lessons to be learned from the currency crises in transition economies regard the consistency of macroeconomic policy goals and the efficiency of different macroeconomic stabilisation programs. Perhaps the most important lesson is that the exchange rate, the single most important price in an open market economy, is far too important to be used only for fighting inflation (as done in some post-communist countries).

The lessons to be learned from the recent experience in East Asia concern the failure of the private sector to optimise the level of lending and borrowing and the need for appropriate government regulations to set not only the rules of the game, but also strongly encourage prudent behaviour. Perhaps the most obvious lesson is that twin liberalisations (of the capital account and the domestic financial system) can wreak havoc if carried out haphazardly and simultaneously.

CURRENCY CRISES: THEORY AND EVIDENCE

It may be useful to distinguish between simple currency (foreign exchange) crises and more complicated cases of debt (financial) and credit (banking) crises. The latter two, even in countries with strong currencies, usually lead to currency crisis as well.

Currency crises

A crisis of this type can occur even without capital flows, creditors, lenders and banks. The only necessary precondition for currency collapse is that the central bank is attempting to maintain the exchange rate at an unsustainable level. If domestic monetary policy is different from that of neighbours, the demand for and the supply of foreign exchange will not be in equilibrium at the original exchange rate, exerting downward or upward pressure on the currency.

The ability of the central bank to defend against downward pressure on the currency is limited by foreign exchange reserves, which are usually enough for at most several months of import financing or several days of financing capital outflows. In the case of upward pressure on the currency, the central bank's ability to contain the currency is constrained by the inflationary consequences of a growing money supply or by the readiness to proceed with sterilisation operations, which lead to higher interest rates (and thus, new capital inflows).

Once either a brisk devaluation or revaluation occurs, there is a shift in relative prices and terms of trade, which may provoke a supply-side recession. Changes in relative prices of assets denominated in foreign and domestic currencies may cause disruptions in the repayment of credits (debt and banking crises).

This type of currency crisis was described initially by Krugman as a balance of payments crisis; he later termed it a canonical currency crisis, in which crisis results from 'a fundamental inconsistency between domestic policies—typically the persistence of money-financed budget deficits—and the attempt to maintain a fixed exchange rate' (Krugman 1979:3).

This is exactly the type of currency crisis that occurred in Russia in August 1998—a straightforward 'plain vanilla' currency crisis caused by a ruble which had been overvalued since the introduction of the exchange rate corridor in mid 1995. Export growth slowed and eventually stopped completely, whereas imports continued to rise, so that the current account shrank and even turned negative in the first half of 1998, whereas capital outflow accelerated in view of the possible devaluation. This led to the depletion of the foreign exchange reserves, which were not large even before the crisis (US$15 billion at the beginning of 1998). The IMF emergency credits (the first tranche of US$4 billion was handed out in July 1998) were used in about four weeks and devaluation followed on 17 August.

The consequences of what should have been a pure currency crisis were aggravated, however, by the clumsy actions of the government, which overreacted by defaulting on its own short-term domestic debt and by imposing a ninety-day moratorium on the servicing of external debt by private banks and companies. These latter measures were by no means necessary since neither a debt nor a banking crisis was imminent. But after the government defaulted, both debt and banking crises broke out.

Government debt crises

A second type of the currency crisis is that caused by the inability of the government to honour its debt obligations. If the debts are denominated in foreign currency, like Mexican *Tesobonos* in 1994, the connection is obvious—the outflow of capital in the expectation of default and/or devaluation leads to a depletion of reserves and triggers devaluation. If the obligations are denominated in domestic currency, investors, fearing inflationary financing of public deficits (leading to inflation and devaluation), switch to foreign exchange. The Mexican peso in 1994 and many Latin American currencies in the early 1980s were undermined by exactly this kind of mechanism—the outflow of capital caused by mistrust in the ability of governments to pay back debt brought down even those currencies in Latin America that were strong and not overvalued.

Krugman (1997) argues that currency crises caused by mounting debt are explained by second generation models, which assume that governments weigh the costs and benefits of abandoning exchange rate pegs. Once investors realise that the advantages of the depreciation of the debt denominated in domestic currency are greater than the disadvantages associated with devaluation, they attack the currency and crisis breaks out.

Private sector debt crises

This third type of currency crisis occurs due to an overaccumulation of private debt. It was a crisis of this nature that occurred in 1997–8 in East Asia. Currency crises of this type have been rare since the abandonment of the gold standard in 1914.

In the words of Paul Krugman (1998), the currency crises in East Asia 'were only part of a broader financial crisis, which had very little to do with currencies or even monetary issues per se. Nor did the crisis have much to do with the traditional fiscal issues', but rather was related to issues 'normally neglected in the currency crisis analysis: the role of financial intermediaries (and the moral hazard associated with such intermediaries when they are poorly regulated), and the prices of real assets such as capital and land'. The East Asian crisis was not brought on by fiscal deficits, as in first generation models, nor by macroeconomic temptation, as in second generation models. It is really the story of a bubble in and subsequent collapse of asset values, with the currency crises more a symptom than a cause of the real underlying malady.

The Lawson doctrine (named after the UK Chancellor of the Exchequer Nigel Lawson) assumes that the government cares only about its own fundamentals (government debt and budget deficits)—current account deficits and private sector debt are dismissed to be taken care of by the market (Montes 1998). The assumption that the costs of risky private sector borrowing would be internalised proved to be wrong—non-government debt crises (which finally led to currency crises) broke out in East Asia. These economies had nearly perfect fundamentals—high saving ratios, strong growth, undervalued rather than overvalued currencies, low inflation, government budget surpluses and low government debt. It was the excessive borrowing of the private sector abroad (banks in Thailand, industrial companies in Indonesia and *chaebols* in South Korea) that caused the mistrust of investors and resulted in the outflow of capital.

Interaction between the three types of the currency crisis

The above classification is a rough scheme—every particular currency crisis is caused by a variety of factors and usually combines the features of all three. Sachs, Tornell and Velasco (1996) examine the predictive power of three indicators: real currency appreciation, the ratio of M2 to foreign exchange reserves (the indebtedness of the public sector) and strength of recent lending booms (the indebtedness of the private sector). Of the twenty emerging market economies they examined, those that were particularly hard hit by the 1994–5 crisis (Mexico, Argentina and Brazil) displayed in the preceding period not only low reserve ratios but strong real appreciations and lending booms. Similarly, rapid growth in the ratio of bank credit to GDP preceded earlier financial troubles in Argentina (1981), Chile (1981–2), Colombia (1982–3), Uruguay (1982), Norway (1987), Finland (1991–2), Japan (1992–3) and Sweden (1991).

The East Asian currency crises were unique in the sense that there were virtually no preceding disequilibria in the government sector. Macroeconomic strategy—fiscal and monetary policy and exchange rate and debt management—was prudent and by no means invited trouble.

EXCHANGE RATES IN TRANSITION AND DEVELOPING ECONOMIES

Real exchange rate appreciation: theory and evidence

Some hold the view that, unlike mature market economies, developing and transition economies may experience prolonged periods of real exchange rate appreciation. A possible explanation of appropriate long-term real appreciation is the Balassa-Samuelson effect—if productivity grows faster in the traded than in the non-traded goods sector, and if wage rates are equalised across sectors with the result that real wage increases lag behind productivity growth, then the real exchange rate can appreciate without undermining business profits. For transition economies, however, this explanation is hardly feasible, since the non-traded goods sector (services) was underdeveloped before transition and thus became the fastest growing sector after transition, showing stronger productivity gains than the traded goods sector.

For the transition economies, Halpern and Wyplosz (1997) explain the appreciation of the real exchange rate not only by traditional overshooting (undervaluation of currencies when establishing convertibility), but also by the nature of the transformation process itself. Grafe and Wyplosz (1997) suggest an alternative to the Balassa-Samuelson effect based on a model in which the real exchange rate alters the distribution of revenues between labour and firms—real appreciation sets in as the need for capital accumulation financed by savings declines. This model captures an important stylised fact about transition—the decline in the ratio of investment to GDP, which was abnormally high in the centrally planned economies due to the need to compensate for low capital productivity (Shmelev and Popov 1989). In virtually all transition economies investment-to-GDP ratios initially fell, and even after recovery did not return to the levels that existed before reform (Popov 1998a). However, since the decline in investment-to-GDP ratios has already come to an end in most transition economies, the impact of this factor on the real exchange rate is diminishing.

Halpern and Wyplosz (1997) argue that real appreciation in transition economies will continue until transition is over (which may be decades away). They conclude that any attempts to resist real appreciation are not only hopeless, but lead to potentially speculative capital inflows and interventions that, if not sterilised, lead to faster money growth and eventually inflation. (If sterilised, reserves will build up, fueling further inflows in a never ending spiral.) Even more destabilising would be a policy of nominal depreciation based on the purchasing power parity rule, which leads to a dangerous cycle of inflation and depreciation.

The view that the real exchange rate in transition economies is doomed to appreciate is a good starting point for the discussion of the currency crises in the region. One of the basic stylised facts in transition economies is the substantial appreciation of the real exchange rate after deregulation of prices and introduction of the convertibility. Out of the major eastern European and former Soviet Union economies, only in Slovenia has the real exchange rate been relatively stable—in other countries there have been prolonged periods of real appreciation.

However, in most countries real appreciation had slowed by the mid 1990s and in some had stopped completely. Moreover, in 1996–8 eight post-communist countries with previously rapidly appreciating real exchange rates (Bulgaria, Romania, Belarus, Ukraine, Russia, Kyrghyzstan, Georgia and Kazakhstan, in chronological order) witnessed the collapse of their currencies (Figure 9.1). In all these countries the currency crashes were no less significant than in East Asia in 1997–8 (with the exception of Indonesia, where the rupiah had at one point lost 80 per cent of its value) or Mexico in 1994–5. In Bulgaria and Russia, currencies depreciated by nearly two-thirds, and in Belarus, by even more than in Indonesia (Figures 9.1 and 9.2).

Why did these currency crises occur? This chapter argues that the overappreciation of exchange rates should be held responsible.

Equilibrium exchange rates in transition and development economies

Unlike in Latin America, post-communist governments were not considerably indebted, and unlike in East Asia, companies and banks in former centrally planned economies did not accumulate sizeable debts. Most communist governments were prudent in accumulating external debts; besides, for many countries external debts were written off on the eve of transition. (Russia assumed all debts of the former Soviet Union, so that other newly created former Soviet Union states started their existence with no debt at all.) On the other hand, companies and banks in transition economies (which under central planning were not allowed to borrow abroad) do not have much of a credit history and are just starting to accumulate foreign debt.

Only in four transition economies (Bulgaria, Hungary, Mongolia and Vietnam) were foreign debt-to-GDP ratios higher than 60 per cent (Table 9.1). Even in these

Figure 9.1 Exchange rates (per US$) in transition economies, 1997–8

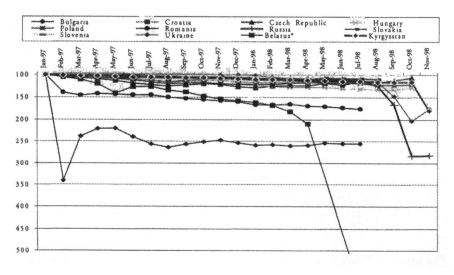

Note: 'CBR and street market rate.
Source: IMF, 1996. *International Financial Statistics*; Central Bank of Russia, *Economic and Financial Situation*, Central Bank of Russian Federation, Department of Research and Information, Moscow.

Figure 9.2 Exchange rates in Southeast Asia (national currencies per $US, January 1997=100) and Mexico (January 1994=100)

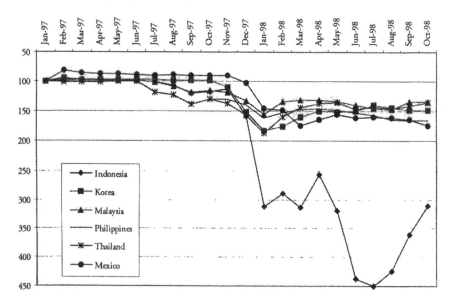

Source: IMF, 1996. *International Financial Statistics*; Central Bank of Russian Federation, Department of Research and Information, Moscow.

economies, however, debt service payments were quite low (because of debt restructuring), so that in no transition economy did debt service payments exceed 20 per cent of the export of goods and services in 1996 (except Bulgaria, with 20.5 per cent). By way of comparison, debt service payments amounted to 30–40 per cent of export revenues for major Latin American countries, and 20–30 per cent for the largest Asian developing economies. Short-term debt in transition states was relatively low compared to total foreign debt, and in most cases, foreign exchange reserves exceeded substantially outstanding short-term debt.

In three of the eight countries that experienced currency crises (Belarus, Bulgaria and Russia) reserves were barely enough to cover the short-term debt, which created an additional crisis potential. In Romania, Ukraine, Kyrghyzstan, Georgia and Kazakhstan all debt indicators were perfect, so their crises appear to be pure exchange rate crises. In Belarus, Bulgaria and especially in Russia, exchange rate overvaluation was most likely the major reason for the crisis as well.

Undervaluation of domestic currency is a common feature of most developing and transition countries since they usually need to earn a trade surplus to finance debt service payments and capital flight.[2] Unlike in mature market economies, the exchange rate is low compared to purchasing power parity (Table 9.2). For resource-rich countries, however, there is a danger of Dutch disease as resource exports are so profitable they allow a trade surplus even with an overpriced exchange rate. Thus, Middle East countries (mostly oil exporters) are the only major group of states in the developing world with exchange rates close to purchasing power parity.

Many developing countries (including those rich in resources) pursue a conscious policy of low exchange rates as part of their general export-orientation strategy. By creating a downward pressure on their currencies through building up foreign exchange reserves, they are able to limit consumption and imports and to stimulate exports, investment and growth. This was the strategy employed by Japan, Korea, Taiwan and Singapore to catch up with high income states, and is currently used in many new emerging market economies, especially China, which continues to keep the exchange rate at an extremely low level (five times lower than purchasing power parity) by the rapid accumulation of foreign exchange reserves. All very fast growing economies have high and rapidly growing international reserves—China (including Hong Kong), Taiwan, Singapore, Malaysia and Thailand account for at least 20 per cent of total world reserves. The reserves-to-GDP ratio for these countries is normally above 20 per cent, as compared to only 8 per cent for the world as a whole (World Bank 1997).

Sterilisation is often viewed as a self-defeating policy, since it is achieved only at a cost of higher domestic interest rates, which in turn lead to a greater inflow of capital, the need for further sterilisation and thus even higher interest rates. However, in practice sterilisation is usually carried out by countries exercising some kind of capital control, either administrative or in the form of the Tobin tax, which makes sterilisation policy efficient.

Relatively low exchange rates exist for two basic reasons—a low level of economic development and related capital flight and debt service payments (a non-policy factor), and a conscious policy to underprice the exchange rate in order to use it as an instrument of export-oriented growth (a policy factor). Thus the equilibrium level of the exchange rate is substantially below the purchasing power parity rate. A continuous appreciation of the real exchange rate will sooner or later result in currency crisis.

The view that transition economies were just the innocent victims of the East Asian contagion is not supported by evidence. First, Bulgaria and Romania experienced crises in 1996, before the first wave of the East Asian crisis broke out in July 1997 with the devaluation of the Thailand baht. Second, leeway for the real appreciation in transition economies was limited—crises would have occurred sooner or later anyway.

Exchange rate management in transition economies

The specifics of exchange rate policy in transition economies are determined by, among other factors, the challenge of macroeconomic stabilisation after the deregulation of prices. Economists and policymakers tend to disagree on the exchange rate policy best for economies in transition. Some stress the importance of maintaining a stable nominal exchange rate and using it as a nominal anchor to fight inflation—exchange rate-based stabilisation (Bofinger, Flassbeck and Hoffmann 1997). Others claim that it is the real exchange rate which should be kept stable (which implies constant devaluations, if inflation is higher than elsewhere). This would ensure that the actual rate is substantially below the purchasing power parity rate, stimulating exports and growth.

Each approach has advantages—while the first may be useful for fighting high inflation in the initial stages of macroeconomic stabilisation, the second may be better for overcoming transformational recession and promoting economic recovery by facilitating the transfer of resources from domestic demand to exports, a pressing need for all economies in transition.

The conventional shock-therapy approach to macroeconomic stabilisation recommends the use of a pegged exchange rate as a nominal anchor while pursuing an anti-inflationary policy (Sachs 1994 and 1995; Åslund 1994). There is some logic to this argument—high exchange rates increase import competition, helping to hold down inflation. In fact, this occurred in many eastern European and former Soviet Union countries, including Russia in 1995–8.

Some countries in the region introduced currency boards (Estonia, Lithuania, Bulgaria, Bosnia and Herzegovina) and were initially successful in fighting inflation and promoting growth. Other post-communist states exercised fixed exchange rate regimes (Czech Republic, Hungary, Poland and Slovakia), also with some degree of success.

However, virtually all transition economies experienced an appreciation of real exchange rate from the start of the transition, which undermined the competitiveness of exports, worsened the current account and forced the maintenance of high interest rates (to slow down capital flight and attract new foreign finance) at a time when exactly the opposite was needed. Even in countries which avoided the currency crisis, the real appreciation of the exchange rate has become a major policy concern. Overall, since the mid 1990s, the major problem in the region seems to be not the lack of stable exchange rates, but the overvaluation of national currencies, which hinders growth and creates the threat of currency crises. As a weapon to fight inflation, exchange rate management can play only a limited role, and at the end of the day inflation has

Table 9.1 *External debt and reserves ratios in selected transition, Asian and Latin American economies,*
1996 (per cent)

Country	Debt/ GDP	Debt service/ exports	Short-term/ total debt	Reserves/ GDP	Reserves/ short-term debt
Transition economies					
Albania	32	3.5	7.0	12.5	536
Armenia	27	10.7	0.3	11.6	14,265
Azerbaijan	10	1.3	3.6	5.8	1,606
Belarus	21	2.0	9.5	2.4	122
Bosnia and Herzegovina	53	-	-	-	-
Bulgaria	89	20.5	9.2	9.0	111
China	17	8.7	19.7	13.7	409
Croatia	24	5.5	10.0	12.8	533
Czech Republic	42	8.3	29.6	23.8	192
Estonia	9	1.3	26.4	14.7	619
Georgia	26	-	4.7	-	-
Hungary	62	41.0	12.5	21.9	283
Kazakhstan	14	9.9	7.6	9.4	888
Kyrghyzstan	37	9.2	1.1	298.1	73,248
Latvia	9	2.3	9.4	14.8	1,755
Lithuania	16	2.9	12.2	10.8	554
Moldova	39	6.2	3.2	17.4	1,394
Mongolia	65	9.7	1.3	16.6	1,960
Poland	31	6.4	0.2	13.4	21,612
Romania	23	12.6	9.8	8.9	393
Russia	25	9.6	9.5	3.7	155
Slovak Republic	41	11.9	38.3	20.5	131
Slovenia	21	8.7	1.4	12.4	4,210
Tajikistan	24	0.1	1.9	-	-
Turkmenistan	18	10.6	34.8	-	-
Ukraine	18	6.1	4.8	4.5	519
Uzbekistan	9	8.1	3.9	-	-
Vietnam	123	3.5	14.5	5.7	32
Latin America					
Argentina	31	44.2	13.0	6.7	166
Brazil	26	41.1	19.8	8.0	155
Chile	48	32.3	25.5	20.9	171
Mexico	44	35.4	19.1	5.8	69
Peru	43	35.4	22.1	18.0	190
Venezuela	51	16.8	8.2	23.8	569
Asia					
India	22	24.1	7.5	7.0	424
Indonesia	64	36.8	25.0	8.6	54
Malaysia	52	8.2	27.8	28.1	194
Pakistan	39	27.4	9.4	2.0	55
Philippines	51	13.7	19.3	14.0	142
Thailand	56	11.5	41.4	20.9	90

Source: World Bank, 1998. *World Development Indicators 1998*, World Bank, Washington DC.

Table 9.2 Ratio of the exchange rate to purchasing power parity rate (versus US$) for selected countries, 1993 and 1996 (per cent)

Country/region	Ratio		Country/region	Ratio	
OECD[a]	116		Transition economies[a]	81	
Germany	126	(133)	Central Europe[a]	54	
Japan	165	(158)	Bulgaria	30	(25)
United States	100	(100)	Croatia	65	(94)
Portugal	73	(77)	Czech Republic	36	(48)
Developing countries[a]	44		Hungary	62	(63)
Asia[a]	36		Poland	48	(59)
India	24	(23)	Romania	31	(34)
Indonesia	30	(33)	Slovak Republic	37	(47)
Korea	72	(81)	Slovenia	69	(78)
Malaysia		(44)	USSR[a]91		
Philippines	35	(34)	Armenia		(20)
Thailand	43	(45)	Azerbaijan		(32)
Turkey	54	(48)	Belarus	8	(30)
Latin America[a]	46		Estonia	29	(64)
Argentina		(90)	Georgia[b]		(29)
Brazil		(70)	Kazakhstan		(39)
Chile		(43)	Kyrghyzstan		(19)
Mexico	58	(45)	Latvia	27	(50)
Peru		(56)	Lithuania	19	(47)
Venezuela		(36)	Moldova	14	(28)
Middle East[a]	83		Russia	26	(70)
Kuwait		(67)	Tajikistan		(3)
Saudi Arabia		(68)	Turkmenistan		(45)
United Arab Emirates		(100)	Ukraine	19	(39)
Africa[a]	37		Uzbekistan		(22)
Ethiopia		(20)	China	22	(20)
Mozambique		(17)	Mongolia		(21)
Nigeria	36	(90)	Vietnam		(20)

Note: Figures in brackets are for 1996; [a] = 1990, [b] = 1995.
Source: UN International Comparison Project (Goskomstat, 1997. *Russian Statistical Yearbook 1997*, Moscow:698; *Finansoviye Izvestiya*, 10 November 1995); World Bank, 1998. *World Development Indicators*, World Bank, Washington, DC; EBRD (European Bank for Reconstruction and Development), 1997. *Transition Report 1997*, EBRD, London.

to be dealt with at its source—that is, high budget deficits, unregulated banking systems and fragile revenue collection (Desai 1998).

In countries which have exercised currency board arrangements longer than others (Estonia, since June 1992 and Lithuania, since October 1994), domestic prices continue to grow despite the stability of the nominal exchange rate. This real appreciation led to current account deficits in 1998 of over 10 per cent of GDP, and financing depends totally on the inflow of foreign capital. Both countries have until now managed to withstand the East Asian and Russian crises, but their growth rates in 1998–9 fell significantly and even turned negative.

The major problem in the region is the overvaluation of currencies hindering economic growth and creating the threat of currency crises. There is growing recognition that the exchange rate is far too important to be used only for fighting inflation, especially since most transition economies have achieved macroeconomic stability and are now preoccupied with economic growth.

The policy of keeping the real rather than the nominal exchange rate stable appears to appeal more to policy makers after the currency crises of 1996–8, particularly since countries pursuing this policy for some time are doing no worse than others. Zettermeyer and Citrin (1995) find that money-based stabilisation was successful in a number of countries (Albania, Slovenia, Croatia and FYR Macedonia) and there is no evidence that it is an inferior strategy to pegging the exchange rate for fighting inflation. With an appropriate monetary policy (at least partial sterilisation), inflationary pressure can be dealt with, as proven by the example of many emerging market economies.

While the technicalities of managing a low exchange rate are not discussed here, it is appropriate to mention that such a policy has some important practical advantages. Unlike other measures to promote growth, it can be implemented relatively easily since it favours the interests of powerful industrial groups (creating stimulus for the export-oriented sector, as well as providing protection from import competition in industries dependent primarily on the domestic market), whereas the costs of the policy (limits on consumption) are paid by unorganised and politically non-influential consumers. In addition, a low exchange rate policy is better than trade protectionism because it is not associated with corruption—it provides benefits to all exporters without leaving room for bureaucratic discretion in selecting priority industries and enterprises (devaluation cannot be stolen, as they say in Russia).

RUSSIA'S 1998 FINANCIAL COLLAPSE

Perhaps the most impressive of all currency crises that have affected transition economies was the one that broke out in Russia in August 1998. In a matter of days the exchange rate (stable during the preceding three years) lost over 60 per cent of its value (Figure 9.1). Prices increased by 50 per cent in two months, as compared to less than 1 per cent monthly inflation before the crisis (Figures 9.3 and 9.4). Real output, which before the crisis registered a small increase (0.6 per cent), fell by about 5 per cent in 1998 (Figure 9.5).

The macroeconomic stabilisation of 1995–8

The financial collapse in Russia marked the end of the macroeconomic stabilisation program that had been pursued for over three years, with a fair degree of success. After experiencing inflation of several hundred per cent a year during the period immediately following the deregulation of prices on 2 January 1992, Russia finally opted for the program of the exchange rate-based stabilisation. In mid 1995 the central bank, after accumulating foreign exchange reserves and managing to maintain a stable ruble for the first half of 1995, introduced a system of a crawling exchange rate peg—an exchange rate corridor with initially narrow boundaries (Figure 9.6).

The program was based on the government and central bank decision to lower the growth rate of money supply and thus to curb inflation. The key to the program was to contain the government budget deficit within reasonable limits and to find non-inflationary ways to finance it. On both fronts the government kept its promises for three years. It managed not to increase the budget deficit, even though this required drastic expenditure cuts since budget revenues, despite all efforts to improve tax collection, continued to fall (Figure 9.7). It also managed to finance the deficit mostly through borrowing—partly by selling short-term ruble-denominated treasury bills (which were also purchased by foreign investors) and partly by borrowing hard currency from international financial institutions, Western governments and banks and the Eurobond market. Under such conditions the central bank had the opportunity to ensure a reduction in the money supply growth rate and in the inflation rate (Figures 9.3 and 9.4).

The weak foundations of macrostabilisation

Macroeconomic stabilisation had become a reality. Inflation right before the crisis was running at only 6 per cent a year (July 1997 to July 1998), the fall in output had slowed down and Russia was looking forward to economic growth. However, macroeconomic stabilisation was based on an overvalued ruble and central bank policy to keep the real exchange rate intact through devaluing the nominal rate in line with ongoing inflation.

As a result, Dutch disease had developed since 1995, when the ruble approached some 70 per cent of purchasing power parity (Figure 9.6). Previously high export growth rates slowed substantially, from 20 per cent in 1995 to 8 per cent in 1996 for total exports and from 25 per cent to 9 per cent for exports to non-Commonwealth of Independent States economies. In 1997 total exports fell for the first time since 1992, with the already weak exports of manufactured goods most affected by the appreciation of real exchange rate. In 1996, among economies in transition, Russia (together with Slovenia, by far the richest country) had the smallest gap between domestic and international prices (Table 9.3; Popov 1996a, 1996b and 1998b).

Falling world oil prices in 1997–8 added insult to injury. The fall in exports accelerated in the first half of 1998, and combined with still rising imports, virtually wiped out the trade surplus, which in 1996 had amounted to US$20 billion (Figure 9.8). The current account turned negative in the first half of 1998 (Figure 9.9). Given the need to service the debt and the continuation of capital flight (which is partly captured in the errors and omissions in the balance of payments statistics (Smorodinskaya 1998)), the negative current account was a sure recipe for disaster.

The overvaluation of the ruble created the potential for currency crisis and caused the outflow of capital from Russia. A new source of ruble vulnerability developed in 1998 with respect to short-term capital flows. Since they were allowed by authorities in 1995, foreign investment into ruble-denominated government treasury bills increased rapidly, to nearly one-third of US$50 billion market for government treasury bills by 1997 (including investment in short-term government bonds through grey schemes (resident intermediaries)). From February 1998 the total amount of treasury bills held by the non-residents exceeded the value of the country's foreign exchange reserves (*The Economist*, 23 May 1998), just like in Mexico where, since 1994, the value of US dollar-denominated Tesobonos has exceeded total reserves (Griffith-Jones 1997).

Foreign investors also started to withdraw from the Russian stockmarket. They were estimated to control no less than 10 per cent of the shares in the booming Russian stockmarket, whose capitalisation surpassed US$100 billion in 1997. From

Figure 9.3 Russia: annual inflation rate, 1990–9

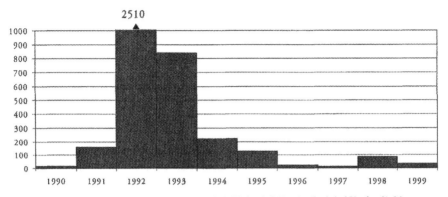

Source: Goskomstat, various years. *Rossiysky Statistichesky Yezhegodnik* (Russian Statistical Yearbook), Moscow.

Figure 9.4 Russia: monthly inflation rate, 1995–9

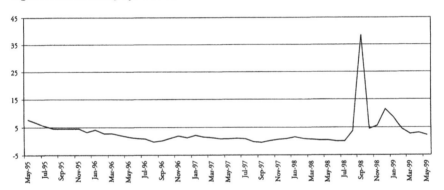

Source: Russian Economic Trends, RECEP, Moscow, monthly issues.

Figure 9.5 Russia: GDP growth rate, 1990–9

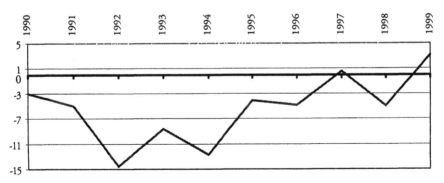

Source: Goskomstat, various years. *Narodnoye Khozyaistvo SSSR* (National Economy of the USSR), Moscow. Goskomstat, various years. *Rossiysky Statistichesky Yezhegodnik* (Russian Statistical Yearbook), Moscow.

then until mid 1998, about nine months, the stock prices in US dollar terms fell eight-fold to the lowest level since 1994 (Figure 9.10). The central bank decision to expand slightly the width of the exchange rate band from the beginning of 1998 was a cosmetic measure and has not yielded much room to manoeuvre. The central bank had to increase the refinancing rate to 150 per cent in May 1998 to prevent capital from fleeing at a rate of about US$0.5 billion a week at a time when foreign exchange reserves were at a level of only US$15 billion. Later the refinancing rate was lowered, but yields on government securities remained nearly 50 per cent in real terms and then again increased to over 100 per cent in August.

The central bank and the government, however, stood by the strong ruble policy, maintaining scandalously high interest rates that eliminated all prospects for economic recovery and negotiating a stand-by package with the IMF. This policy allowed Russia to maintain consumption and imports, avoid export-oriented restructuring and continue living beyond its means. The IMF finally provided the first instalment (US$4 billion) of the US$20 billion package. It went directly to the central bank to replenish vanishing foreign exchange reserves, but even this did not calm investors. Public officials' statements about the stability of the ruble, including that of Yeltsin made three days before devaluation, were not convincing.

In retrospect, it is obvious that the crisis was caused by the unrealistic and counterproductive attempts of the Russian government and central bank, as well as the IMF, to defend the unsustainably high ruble. This is not an argument against fixed exchange rates but rather against unrealistically high pegs. There is a difference between a stable and a strong currency—whereas the former is highly desirable for all countries, the latter may prove to be an unaffordable luxury for economies in transition trying to overcome transformational recession. It may well be that the central bank and the

Figure 9.6 Russia: consumer prices and the exchange rate (per US$), 1994–2000

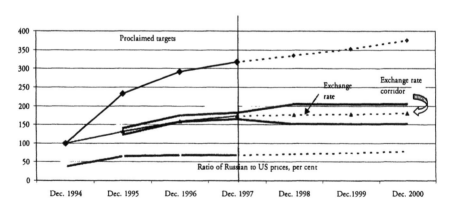

Source: Goskomstat, various years. *Narodnoye Khozyaistvo SSSR* (National Economy of the USSR), Moscow; Goskomstat, various years. *Rossiysky Statistichesky Yezhegodnik* (Russian Statistical Yearbook), Moscow; Central Bank of Russia.

government were right to establish a crawling peg for the ruble, but they were wrong to peg it at such a high level.

By pegging the ruble at a lower rate and continuing to build up foreign exchange reserves, the central bank could have killed more than two birds with one stone— Russian exports and the trade surplus would have increased, domestic interest rates would have fallen and there would have been an additional stimulus for the dedollarisation of the Russian economy and the inflow of foreign direct investment. A weaker ruble may have allowed higher saving rates without higher interest rates, and created an additional stimulus for production, investment and exports while limiting consumption and imports. Keeping the ruble at a lower level would thus not only have been a prudent policy to avoid currency crisis, but could also have been an instrument of export-oriented strategy, encouraging restructuring and growth.

Managing the August 1998 crisis

A number of economists strongly believed before the crisis broke out that the ruble was overvalued, arguing that if it was not devalued from above in advance, it was likely to get devalued from below, in the form of the currency crisis, with much greater costs (Illarionov 1998; Shmelev 1998; Popov 1996a, 1996b, 1997, 1998b and 1998e).[3] It was not difficult to predict the crisis—a number of scholars did so several months ahead of time. Even Jeffrey Sachs, earlier a strong advocate of the exchange rate-based stabilisation, in June 1998 spoke out publicly in favour of devaluation (*The New York Times*, 4 June 1998).[4]

What virtually nobody was able to predict was the way the Russian government handled the devaluation—declaring the default on domestic debt and part of the international debt held by banks and companies. This was by no means necessary, since basically there was no debt crisis, only a currency crisis, which could have been handled by devaluing the ruble.

The indebtedness of the Russian government had been growing, but not significantly compared to GDP (since GDP in US dollar terms was growing rapidly due to the real appreciation of the ruble) (Figure 9.11). In absolute terms total government debt by

Figure 9.7 Consolidated government revenues and expenditure, 1992–8 (percentage of GDP)

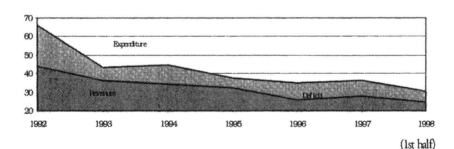

(1st half)

Sources: EBRD, 1996. *Transition Report 1996*, EBRD, London. EBRD, 1997. *Transition Report Update 1997*, EBRD, London. EBRD, 1998. *Transition Report 1998: Financial sector in transition*, EBRD, London.

Table 9.3 Ratio of the actual exchange rate to the purchasing power parity rate (versus US$), selected transition economies, 1990–9 (range of monthly averages)

	1990	1991	1992	1993	1994	1995	1996	1997	1998	1999
Slovenia	0.9–1.4	1.0–1.7	1.4–1.6	1.4–1.6	1.3–1.6	1.1–1.3	1.3–1.3	1.4–1.5	1.3–1.5	1.3–1.5
Hungary	1.9–2.4	1.9–2.0	1.7–1.8	1.6–1.8	1.6–1.8	1.5–1.6	1.7–1.8	1.6–1.8	1.7–1.8	1.7–1.8
Poland	2.1–3.9	1.6–1.9	1.8–2.0	1.8–2.0	2.1–2.3	1.8–2.0	1.8–1.8	1.8–2.1	1.8–2.0	1.9–2.1
Czech Republic	2.5–3.8	3.5–3.1	2.7–3.1	2.5–2.6	2.2–2.5	2.0–2.2	1.9–2.0	2.0–2.3	2.0–2.3	1.9–2.3
Slovak Republic	2.9–3.9	3.0–3.6	2.9–3.0	2.6–2.8	2.4–2.7	2.1–2.3	2.1–2.2	2.3–2.4	2.2–2.4	2.2–2.7
Lithuania	–	–	–	–	2.4–3.2	1.8–2.3	1.7–1.8	1.5–1.6	–	–
Romania	1.8–2.6	1.6–5.0	2.8–4.2	2.2–3.1	2.1–2.6	2.1–2.5	2.4–2.6	2.0–3.3	1.7–2.0	2.0–2.3
Bulgaria	3.3–5.1	2.9–10.9	3.0–4.7	2.3–2.8	2.3–3.1	1.8–2.2	1.9–2.8	1.7–3.2	16–1.8	1.6–1.9
Ukraine	–	–	–	–	–	1.8–2.5	1.3–1.7	1.3–1.4	1.3–2.1	2.0–2.7
Russia	–	33.0–131.0	10.2–45.7	2.5–8.0	2.4–2.8	1.4–2.4	1.4–1.5	1.4–1.5	15–2.8	2.7–2.9

Note: Data for the second half of 1998 are forecasts for Slovenia, Czech Republic, Romania, Bulgaria and Russia. For Slovakia all 1998 data are forecasts, for Poland data for March–December 1998 are forecasts, for Ukraine data for the fall of 1997 are forecast, for Lithuania all 1997 data are forecasts. For Hungary all 1997 data are forecasts. For Hungary data are for January–March 1998 only.

Source: PlanEcon, various years. Washington, DC.

Figure 9.8 Russia: foreign trade, 1993–8 (US$billion)

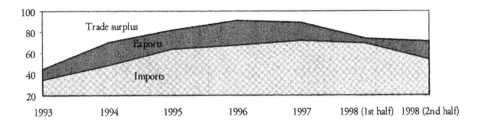

Source: Goskomstat, *Rossiysky Statistichesky Yezhegodnik* (Russian Statistical Yearbook), Moscow.

Figure 9.9 Russia: balance of payments and foreign exchange reserves, 1993–8 (US$billion)

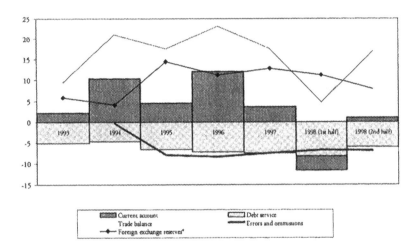

Note: End of period, excluding gold.
Source: Goskomstat, various years. *Rossiysky Statistichesky Yezhegodnik* (Russian Statistical Yearbook), Moscow.

mid 1998 had not even reached the threshold of 60 per cent of GDP. Even when the wage and payment arrears of the Russian government are taken into account, total indebtedness does not increase significantly: government wage arrears right before the crisis stood at 13 billion rubles, 0.5 per cent of GDP, whereas total government arrears, several times higher than wage arrears, were largely offset by tax arrears to the government.

Since early 1998, government short-term obligations (ruble-denominated but held by non-residents) exceeded total foreign exchange reserves, obvious mismanagement contributing to the crisis. However, the absolute value of the outstanding short-term debt held by foreigners was by no means substantial, US$15–20 billion. The problem rather was the negligible reserves (US$15 billion). Even so, it would have been possible

Figure 9.10 Stock price indexes for four transition economies (US$), 1992–9

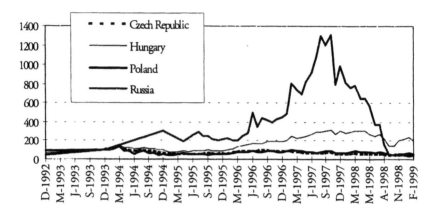

Source: *The Economist*, 1995–99; (author's estimates for Russia 1992–3).

to continue to service the debt after, say, a 50 per cent devaluation (which would cut debt service payments in two), not to mention the IMF credits.[5]

The mistrust of investors in the first half of 1998 was associated first and foremost with the low credibility of the government's ability to defend the ruble—the ability of the government to service its debt was not in question. The difference between the rates at which the Russian government borrowed abroad in hard currency (returns on Eurobonds were around 15 per cent) and the rates offered to the prime borrowers (7 per cent) was much lower than the gap between returns on ruble-denominated bonds (about 100 per cent in real terms) and Eurobonds (15 per cent). Because the first gap is the indicator of country risk (the risk associated with default by the government), whereas the second reflects the currency risk (the risk associated with devaluation), it is clear that the anticipation of the market at that time was devaluation, not default.

Unfortunately, the default was not the only mismanagement in handling the crisis. Shortly after the default the central bank provoked by its clumsy actions a run on the banks and a banking crisis. Banks were hurt by the devaluation (an inevitable cost), but also by the default (both because they held a considerable portion of their assets in short-term government securities and because they lost opportunities for external financing due to the ninety-day moratorium on servicing external debt). To make matters worse, the central bank in early September introduced a scheme to guarantee personal deposits in commercial banks, which implied losses for depositors, especially for the holders of US dollar accounts at private banks.[6] The run on the banks that naturally followed contributed to the developing paralysis of the banking system—in September 1998 banks were hardly processing any payments and businesses started to carry out their transactions purely in cash, barter and cash substitutes.

After the crisis

The response to the crisis, which was discussed for some time in early September 1998—after Chernomyrdyn succeeded Kiriyenko as an acting prime minister and before Primakov took charge—was the introduction of the currency board, an institution which has serious theoretical and practical shortcomings.[7]

The theoretical objection is the possible deflationary impact of the currency board as it requires the full (or nearly full) backing of the money supply by foreign exchange reserves. An outflow of capital inevitably results in a reduction of the money supply, and subsequently, a deflationary shock. Whether or not a currency board arrangement is efficient for a particular country depends on whether there is enough price flexibility to ensure that the deflationary shock does not affect real indicators. For small open economies, where domestic prices already depend heavily on world market prices, the answer may be positive, for medium and large countries (like Russia), there is still not enough evidence. There is evidence that the ability of the authorities to address banking problems through providing lender-of-last-resort support weakens considerably with the introduction of the currency board, making it risky for countries with vulnerable banking systems (Santiprabhob 1997).

The practical objection to the currency board plan for Russia is even more persuasive. It is generally recognised (Hanke, Jonung and Schuler 1993) that a necessary precondition for the successful introduction of a currency board is credibility in the government's ability to eliminate the budget deficit. It is also generally accepted that the current Russian government is among the least credible in the world.

The Primakov government that took office in September 1998 made it clear that the currency board option is no longer being considered. The central bank has continued to maintain a floating exchange rate and has succeeded in stabilising it at around 25 rubles per US dollar. The response of the real sector to the new exchange rate surprised many observers.

After the August 1998 financial crash, ailing Russian industry experienced a boom, registering growth rates that had not been seen for more than half a century. Industrial output was constant in 1995–7, declined by 15 per cent from the beginning of 1998 until August 1998, and has been growing at a rate of about 2 per cent per month, or over 25 per cent annually since September 1998 (Figure 9.12). In July 1999 industrial output was 11 per cent higher than in July 1998. Strong growth has started not because of, but despite government policy—prior to the crisis the overvalued ruble was undermining the competitiveness of domestically produced goods; since devaluation, domestic producers are taking advantage of new export opportunities and the shift in demand from foreign to Russian-made goods.

The 1998 recession was artificially manufactured by the poor policy of keeping the exchange rate at an unsustainably high level. The market moved to correct the IMF-backed government mistake—this is what the August 1998 crisis was all about. Different patterns of decline of output in Russia (before the currency crisis) and in East Asia (after the currency crisis) provide evidence of the different nature of the currency crashes: whereas in East Asia, devaluation, coupled with the collapse of overextended

Figure 9.11 Russia: government debt, 1994–8 (percentage of GDP)

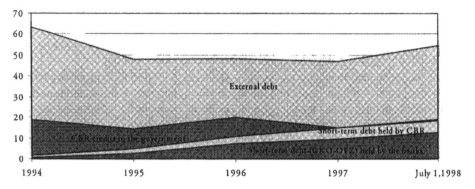

Source: Bank of Finland, Institute for Economies in Transition, 1998. *Russian Economy: The month in review,* 98/1, Helsinki; Goskomstat, *Rossiysky Statistichesky Yezhegodnik* (Russian Statistical Yearbook), Moscow.

credit, led to an adverse supply shock, in Russia devaluation of the previously overvalued currency restored competitiveness and led to the increase in capacity utilisation rates. The Russian economy experienced a boom rather than a recession after the currency crisis.

ALTERNATIVE EXPLANATIONS FOR THE RUSSIAN CRISIS

There are two prevailing (and not mutually exclusive) explanations for the August 1998 currency crisis in Russia. One stresses the unfortunate coincidence of events, including the East Asian virus, a drop in oil prices and political instability. Yevgeny Yasin (1999), the minister without a portfolio in the former Kirienko government and a respected academic economist, says 'the crisis is not just the result of the evil forces or incompetence, but is caused by the coincidence of circumstances, most of which were against us'. Sergey Kirienko himself, even now, believes that as late as June 1998, Russia might have avoided the crisis, had only the Duma accepted the tax increases suggested by the government (*Expert*, 18 January 1999). Åslund takes a similar stand, noting that by rejecting the government's sensible policies the Duma pushed the country 'over the brink into a financial abyss' (Åslund 1999b).

Another explanation (and the view taken by former high officials of the CBR) is that the crisis was caused by budgetary problems—specifically, persistent deficits resulting in mounting government debt, or the 'GKO pyramid' (see Russian Economy in 1998; GKOs are short-term government bonds). 'No doubt, the current financial crisis is mostly of budgetary and debt origin', states Sergei Alexashenko, the then deputy chairman of the central bank (Alexashenko 1999). Former government officials claim they knew about the problem, but were not able to force the Duma to accept the necessary tough measures to improve tax collection. Hence, the scapegoat is again the former parliament, which the government widely blamed for creating obstacles to the reforms. One variation on these views is the theory that the government debt pyramid was doomed to collapse. The returns on GKOs were many times greater than those available in the real sector (Nekipelov 1998). High financial returns that are not based on the healthy foundation of the real economy cannot continue for long; it was inevitable, under this view, that they finally came to an end in the form of a crisis. Western explanations of the Russian crisis—at least those that appear outside the regional studies field—are generally even more straightforward. The most popular explanations are associated one way or another with cronyism and the criminal nature of Russian capitalism. The government is accused of caving in to the interests of 'oligarchs'—heads of large financial-industrial groups in the Russian economy—that have effectively 'privatised' the state and care only about enriching themselves in the short term.

It seems the majority agrees that everything is so rotten in Russia that it would be strange if the crisis had not happened. It is often stated that funds obtained by the state through domestic and external borrowing were mishandled, if not embezzled or stolen, and that the inefficient and corrupt public administration could not ensure any kind of macroeconomic stabilisation, be it exchange rate-based or money-based. Oligarchs do not consider the long term and are unable to agree on measures to increase tax revenues, slow down capital flight and control indebtedness. As Paul Krugman puts it, 'there is no honor among the thieves' (Krugman 1998e), suggesting that the IMF–World Bank credits were wasted, if not stolen, by the short-sighted and *apres-nous-le-deluge*-minded oligarchs. Åslund (1999a) believes that the August 1998 crash was the outcome of intense competition over the evasive rent that decreased from 15–80 per cent of GDP in 1991–4 to 5–15 per cent in 1995–8.

Some go even further, seeing the root of all Russia's evils in the misunderstanding of the nature of money. References are being made to the Russian national character (described, for instance, in *The Gambler* by F. Dostoyevsky, who states that Russians are squanderers and like roulette so much because one can become rich effortlessly in two hours), as well as to seventy years of bolshevism, which virtually abolished money as a legal tender of predictable value, making the value of the ruble 'something stranger than zero' (*The Economist* 19 December 1998).

Figure 9.12 Russia: industrial output index, 1996–9

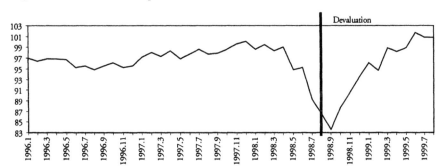

Institutional collapse

These explanations miss the point. First, although the role of money and credit in the Soviet centrally planned economy was limited compared to a market economy, the degree of monetisation (M2/GDP) and creditisation (bank credit outstanding as a percentage of GDP) was much higher in the 1980s than in the 1990s (about 50 per cent compared to less than 15 per cent). Soviet planners were quite prudent in their macroeconomic policies in the four decades from 1947 (Stalin's confiscatory monetary reform) to 1987 (the beginning of macroeconomic mismanagement under Gorbachev). The annual average inflation rate (open and hidden, that is, the increase in monetary overhang) was only 3 per cent, less than in most countries in this period. Government budget deficits were low or non-existent, government domestic debt was miniscule, external indebtedness was low and payments were made according to contracts. Neither the argument about the demonetised Russian soul nor that about the difficult Soviet heritage are convincing, since neither prevented Soviet planners from achieving a high degree of macro stability and monetisation.

Second, there is no doubt that Russian state institutions have been degenerating in recent years and that the weakening of the state institutions is the main long-term factor explaining the poor performance of the Russian and Commonwealth of Independent States economies as compared to China and Vietnam (with strong authoritarian institutions) and central European countries (with strong democratic institutions). A study comparing twenty-eight transition economies (including China and Vietnam) suggests that it is not the speed of liberalisation which should be held responsible for differing performances, but the institutional capacity of the state. This factor was overlooked by both schools of transition thought—the shock therapists and the gradualists (Popov 2000). This approach is gaining more and more support in the framework of the post-Washington consensus (Stiglitz 1998 and 1999, Kolodko 1999b).

In most former Soviet Union and Balkan countries the collapse of institutions is observable in the dramatic increase of the share of the shadow economy; the decline of government revenues as a proportion of GDP; the inability of the state to deliver basic public goods and an appropriate regulatory framework; the accumulation of tax, trade, wage and bank arrears; the demonetisation, dollarisation and barterisation of the economy, as measured by high and growing money velocity, and the decline of bank financing as a proportion of GDP; and the poor enforcement of property rights, bankruptcies, contracts and law and order in general. Most of the mentioned phenomena may be defined quantitatively with the remarkable result that China and Vietnam are closer in this respect to eastern European countries than to the Commonwealth of Independent States.

Under strong authoritarian regimes (like China), cuts in government expenditure have occurred at the expense of defence, subsidies and budgetary financed investment, while expenditure for ordinary government (Naughton 1997) as a percentage of GDP has remained largely unchanged (Figure 9.13). Under strong democratic regimes (like Poland), expenditure, including that on ordinary government, declined in the pre-transition period, but has increased during transition itself. Under weak democratic regimes (like Russia), the reduction of the general level of government expenditure has led not only to a decline in the financing of defence, investment and subsidies, but to the downsizing of ordinary government and the collapse of the institutional capacity of the state.

In China, while total budgetary expenditure and that for ordinary government are much lower than in Russia and Poland, they are sufficient to preserve functioning institutions since government financing of the social safety net has traditionally been low. Besides, due to GDP growth, real expenditure for ordinary government in China in the first seven years of the reform increased two-fold. In Russia, though expenditure for ordinary government is not that much lower than in Poland, the pace of reduction during transition exceeded that of GDP—while in Poland ordinary government financing grew by about one-third in real terms in 1989–96, in Russia, it fell almost three-fold! The Russian pattern of institutional decay has proved to be extremely detrimental for investment, and most importantly, for capital productivity and output.

The most striking feature has been the disintegration of state institutions. Although the government should be credited for cutting government expenditure in line with falling revenue and thus keeping the deficit under control (Figure 9.7), the sharp reduction of the share of government revenues in GDP is an obvious sign of institutional degradation. The reduction of government expenditure occurred in the worst possible way—chaotically and without a reassessment of government commitments. Instead of shutting down completely some government programs and concentrating limited resources on the others, the government kept all programs half-alive, half-financed and barely working. Poor administration of shrinking public funds has turned into a major problem. As a result, excessively wide social responsibilities have become financially unsustainable, and a huge gap between the obligations of the state and its ability to deliver has emerged.

Public education, health care, infrastructure, law and order institutions and fundamental research and development have slowly decayed. Virtually all services provided by the government, from collecting custom duties to regulating street traffic, are notorious for inefficiency. There have been numerous cases of government failure, further undermining the credibility of the state. Many government activities in providing public goods and social transfers are slowly dying, and have been replaced by private and semi-private business, which are not able to provide public goods with the same efficiency as the state.

In the former Soviet Union not only were government regulations pervasive, but the financial power of the state was comparable to that in European countries. This allowed the state to provide the bulk of public goods and extensive social transfers. In post-communist Russia (and other Commonwealth of Independent States countries) the state has found itself deprived of its former vast resources. On the one hand, government regulatory activities have only limited efficiency due to difficulties in enforcing regulations since the authoritarian regime was replaced by a weak democracy (in contrast to central Europe, where strong democratic regimes emerged). On the other hand, government revenues plummeted after the centrally planned economy was dismantled, falling below 30 per cent of GDP (including off-budget funds) in 1997. Though this is more than in East Asian countries and other economies with similar GDP per capita (Illarionov 1998; Mau 1998), it is less than needed to finance government commitments—large agricultural and housing subsidies, mostly free education and health care and universal pay-as-you-go social insurance.

Even though institutional weakness is the single most important long-term factor contributing to the extreme magnitude of the Russian recession, it is not linked directly with the collapse of the ruble and the failure of macroeconomic stabilisation program. The debt levels of the Russian government and Russian companies were very modest by international standards—embezzlement of borrowed funds could not lead to the debt and currency crises since debt was not excessive. There had been no major changes with respect to cronyism, corruption and institutional weaknesses (except, maybe, for some stabilisation), so references to the criminal nature of Russian capitalism cannot explain much either.

A goal of maintaining an appropriate exchange rate would have been perhaps the least politicised issue of government economic policy—keeping the ruble low through timely and gradual devaluations, the government and the central bank would not have faced opposition from either industrial lobbies or oligarchs. While there are reasons to believe that macroeconomic stabilisation in Russia did not materialise in 1992–4 because of the lack of consensus among powerful industrial lobbies on how to finance cuts in government expenditure (Popov 1996a, 1996b), there is no evidence whatsoever that a low ruble strategy in 1995–8 would have been politically unacceptable.

CONCLUSIONS AND POLICY IMPLICATIONS

The recent crises provide two important policy lessons for transition economies and other economies undertaking market reforms that almost instantly provide access to foreign capital. First, real exchange rate appreciation must be avoided. Second, in the face of increasing external debt, economies should draw lessons from more complex government debt crises (Latin American countries in early 1980s and in 1994–5) and private sector debt crises (East Asia in 1997–8) to avoid another episode of currency collapse.

Preventing the appreciation of real exchange rate

Unlike the currency crises in East Asia and Latin America, recent currency crises in transition economies were not caused by excessive private or government debt accumulation, but by excessive appreciation of the exchange rate. Theories offered to explain the trend towards real exchange rate appreciation in transition economies have proved to be of limited applicability. No currency can appreciate infinitely in real terms, and, if currencies grow too strong, crisis ensues.

The policy of keeping the exchange rate low through the accumulation of reserves seems not only prudent but also conducive to economic growth. For transition economies facing the challenge of export-oriented restructuring, it is highly desirable. The inflationary consequences of such a policy, as the example of East Asian countries shows, may be dealt with through sterilisation operations.

Exchange rate-based versus money-based stabilisation

Whereas exchange rate-based stabilisation may be successful in fighting inflation in the initial stages of transition, there is growing evidence that at later stages it becomes

Figure 9.13 Government expenditure in three transition economies, 1985–96 (percentage of GDP)

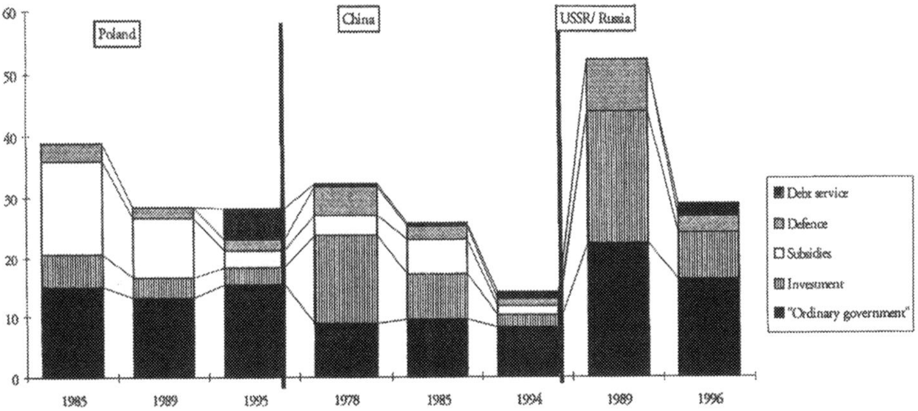

Notes: Data for China, Russia and Poland do not include off-budget funds, which are very substantial in all three countries and are used mostly for social insurance purposes. Defense expenditure are from official statistics, which are lower than Western estimates, which is likely to lead to overstatement of spending for investment and subsidies at the expense of defense outlays. For USSR/Russia investment and subsidies are shown together.

Sources: Data for China are from World Bank, 1996b; Russia from Goskomstat, *Narodnoye Khozyaistvo SSSR* (National Economy of the USSR), Moscow, and Goskomstat, *Rossiysky Statistichesky Yezhegodnik* (Russian Statistical Yearbook), Moscow; and Poland from Rocznik Statystyczny 1990, Warszawa and data from Institut Finansow provided by G. Kolodko.

an obstacle for economic growth and creates the potential for currency crisis by allowing the real exchange rate to appreciate.

Bringing inflation down to single digits in transition and other emerging market economies with many market imperfections and structural rigidities is itself a questionable policy. In countries with highly inflationary environments output growth is likely to be weak. However, it has been shown that 40 per cent a year inflation is sort of a threshold—there is no evidence that inflation below 40 per cent per annum is ruinous for growth, while there is even some evidence that inflation below 20 per cent a year is beneficial (Bruno and Easterly 1995; Bruno 1995; Stiglitz 1998). It may even be argued that the threshold for transition economies is higher than for other emerging markets because of the numerous structural rigidities. In most successful reformers inflation was by no means insignificant—it never fell below 20 per cent a year in the first five years of transition in Poland and Uzbekistan, while in China, though low most of the time, there were outbursts of inflation in 1988–9 and 1993–5 when it increased to about 20 per cent.

Russian authorities went from one extreme (the very high inflation of 1992–4) to the other, trying to be more catholic than the Pope. The exchange rate-based stabilisation program was pursued with great diligence: right before the crisis, in July 1998, year-on-year inflation was 6 per cent, less than in most transition economies. This low level of inflation did impose unnecessary strains on the economy, causing an avalanche of non-payments and leading to a demand-induced reduction of output. In fact, after the modest growth in 1997, output started to decline in the first half of 1998.

Fixed versus flexible rates

Given the relatively small size of most emerging market economies and their rapid integration into the world economy, floating exchange rates may provide more flexibility in adjusting to external shocks. Most developing and transition economies, with the exception of the smallest, like Hong Kong, Singapore and perhaps the Baltic states, are large enough to remain not completely exposed to competition on the world market and hence to retain some inflexibility in domestic prices with respect to the world market prices. Nevertheless, they are not large enough to create an appropriate cushion in the form of foreign exchange reserves, bringing down the vulnerability resulting from international capital flows to reasonable levels. In most emerging markets (with the possible exception of China) foreign exchange reserves are only enough to withstand several weeks, if not days, of currency attack. Moreover, because the major international banks, investment and hedge funds operate with pools of money comparable to or even exceeding the value of reserves in most countries, fluctuations of the exchange rate remain the only reliable and efficient safety valve providing protection from external shocks.

As fixed exchange rates and particularly currency boards effectively force countries to abandon independent monetary policy, they are doomed to adjust to the inflows and outflows of capital through real indicators—when the exchange rate is pegged and prices are not completely flexible, changes in the money supply (caused by the fluctuation of reserves) may affect output rather than prices. And as the recent experience of East Asian and transition economies showed, this kind of real sector adjustment is costly. Under a fixed exchange rate regime, neither changes in foreign exchange reserves nor domestic price changes in response to money supply fluctuations provide enough room to handle international capital flows.

Openness of capital accounts and strength of the banking system

For transition economies, where the currency crises were not triggered by the debt and lending boom, there is an important lesson to be derived from the East Asian experience about twin liberalisations of the capital account and the domestic financial system. As debt levels, both government and private, in these economies continue to grow, measures should be taken to ensure that the safety and reliability of banking institutions is not overrun by the openness of the capital account.

In Russia, for instance, the credit and banking crisis was by no means necessary and was in fact manufactured by poor policies (the government default on short-term debt and the central bank measures that undermined the credibility of commercial banks). Regardless of the source of the crisis, it revealed the long-known and discussed weaknesses of the domestic banking system. If the next shock comes from international capital flows, Russian banks will not be able to withstand it unless prudential regulations are tightened and a viable banking sector is created. Meanwhile, the continuation of the policy of nearly complete openness to capital flows may be an invitation for trouble.

NOTES

* This chapter draws heavily on my articles and papers listed in the References, and on Montes. and Popov (1999).

[1] The term fundamentals in this chapter is used to describe basic macroeconomic proportions; it does not pertain to variables such as the quality of corporate governance, the soundness of the financial system, explicit and implicit guarantees given to the creditors by the commitment of the government to maintain the fixed exchange rate and by the international financial institutions to bail out creditors in the case of the crisis.

[2] Hölscher (1997) makes a similar argument with respect to eastern European countries drawing on the West German experience with undervalued mark in the 1950s.

[3] This argument was also developed in newspaper articles. See 'Growth strategy', *Segodnya*, 14 March 1996 (in Russian); 'The currency crisis is possible in Russia', *Finansoviye Izvestiya*, 30 October 1997 (in Russian); 'An emerging economy's unaffordable luxury', *Financial Times*, 11 December 1997; 'What exchange rate of the ruble is needed for Russia?', *Nezavisimaya Gazeta*, 21 May 1998 (in Russian); and 'Arithmetic of devaluation: why do we need a rate of 12 rubles per dollar', *Nezavisimaya Gazeta*, June 1998 Supplement (in Russian).

[4] The other major proponent of exchange rate-based stabilisation and former adviser to the Russian government, Anders Åslund, like the IMF, continued to deny the need to devalue even in July ('Don't devalue the ruble', *The Moscow Times*, 7 July 1998).

[5] This was in sharp contrast to the Mexican situation in the second half of 1994. Like in Russia, the value of outstanding short-term government debt exceeded the amount of foreign exchange reserves. But unlike Russian short-term government bonds, Mexican Tesobonos were denominated in US dollars, so devaluation of the peso could not decrease the US dollar value of the debt.

[6] In the state-owned *Sberbank* (Savings Bank) that accounted for 75 per cent of all household deposits, savings were guaranteed by the state. The central bank, while extending the guarantees to the personal deposits at commercial banks, asked depositors to move them to *Sberbank*, promising to pay them back only in two months and only in part (US dollar deposits, for instance, were supposed to be converted into rubles at a 1 September rate of 9.33 rubles per US dollar, whereas the market rate was already two times higher).

[7] In recent years the plan was suggested by Hanke, Jonung and Schuler (1993). Among other things, the book tells an interesting story of the currency board in Northern Russia in 1918–20, during the period of the Civil War. It was set by the British occupational forces and designed by J. M. Keynes, then an official responsible for war finance.

Part 4
Latin American crises

10 The 1990s crisis in emerging markets

The case of Brazil

Eliana Cardoso and Ann Helwege

This chapter reviews the collapse of the Brazilian currency in February 1999. It discusses fiscal and monetary policies during an exchange rate based stabilization program and examines crisis management following a shift from an exchange rate anchor to a floating exchange rate regime.

In the mid 1990s, the combination of Brazil's tight monetary policy and declining primary fiscal balance led to a swelling stock of the net public debt. The net public debt increased from 20 per cent of GDP in December 1994 to 44 per cent of GDP in December 1998. Real interest rates remained extremely high during this period. Between 1994 and 1998, the average ex-post passive real interest rate was 23 percent per year. Monetary policy kept real interest rates high for two reasons: to safeguard the stability created by the exchange rate based Real Plan and to maintain a difference between the domestic and foreign interest rates that would attract foreign capital in order to finance a rising current account deficit. By 1998, concerns about Brazil's policy mix were growing and investors were not surprised by the collapse of the real in February 1999.

Brazil adopted the exchange rate anchor in 1994—the historical and political conditions that led to an inflation rate of more than 50 per cent per month at the beginning of the decade precluded further experimentation with alternative stabilisation options. Because the exchange rate can be used to synchronise expectations and stop mechanisms that perpetuate inflation, the exchange rate anchor rightly played a central role in the first stage of inflation stabilisation. However, because fiscal adjustment was politically difficult, the real plan continued to use the exchange rate as an anchor for far too long.

This strategy led to its own demise. Although overvaluation and current account deficits have been common threads throughout currency crises in the 1990s, the emergence of these problems in Brazil is strikingly different from those in Mexico and Thailand. In Mexico, trade imbalances were seminal elements of disequilibria; in Thailand, banking crises became manifest early. Although trade imbalances eventually emerged in Brazil, the root disequilibria lay in contingent liabilities and fiscal deficits that were, in large measure, bloated by the high interest rates needed to support the currency. These imbalances posed policy dilemmas in the management of interest rates, exchange rates and capital controls. Massive capital inflows financed current account deficits, while fiscal deficits were financed by increases in public debt, initially denominated mainly in local currency. The high interest rates that attracted capital also fueled debt service. As the primary surplus declined and debt service increased, the ratio of net public debt to GDP doubled between 1994 and 1999 despite economic growth of about 3 per cent per year. Capital flows in turn supported the overvalued currency and the large current account deficits.

Growing trade imbalances caused by overvaluation and rising debt service fueled speculative attacks against the real. In the year leading up to January 1999, financial investors positioned themselves to take advantage of an expected devaluation: this betting game cost the central bank more than US$6 billion in January 1999. Policy makers were finally forced to take action.

Having stumbled away from its currency anchor, Brazil faces the challenge of defining a credible economic strategy for the future. By delicately negotiating the relationship between interest rates, inflation and exchange rates, policymakers have temporarily contained speculative attacks on the real. A return to sustained growth is less certain. This is complicated by a lack of progress in resolving the distributional issues behind Brazil's fiscal deficits. The illusion that macroeconomic growth under the real plan can satisfy all competing demands is gone. At the same time, the international investment community is increasingly agile in the face of currency risk and potential default. Brazil's next steps must look less like a quick fix and more like steady progress toward resolution of its fundamental problems.

RECENT AND NOT-SO-RECENT ECONOMIC DEVELOPMENTS

Sustained long-run growth—enough to warrant the use of the term Brazilian miracle— is a receding memory. Brazil's rapid growth after World War II ended in a crisis and triple digit inflation in 1964, but a period of sustained stabilisation then followed. Despite the OPEC oil shock, the economy kept growing at fast rates—between 1968 and 1980, GDP per capita rose by over 6 per cent per year. In the same period, exports became more diversified and grew by an average of 22 per cent per year. High public savings and expanding public enterprises also characterise the early half of this period. However, reliance on commercial loans to finance both public investment and expensive oil imports led to the debt crisis of the early 1980s. Since then, growth has faltered. Between 1980 and 1998, the annual real GDP growth rate was 2 per cent, a very mediocre performance for an economy that, since 1949, had grown on average 7.3 per cent annually for thirty-two years.

The end of rapid growth compounded distributional challenges posed by greater democracy. As military regimes ceded power to voters and the literacy requirement for voting was lifted in the 1980s, Brazil's extreme income inequality subtly contributed to fiscal paralysis. With a Gini coefficient of 0.59, Brazil is among the most unequal countries in the world. Neither revolution nor guerrilla insurgency has threatened stability. Instead, the constitution of 1988 embedded privileges for a host of special interests and undermined the capacity of democratic regimes to mediate economic demands. Inflation served to resolve economic imbalances that politicians could not or would not close.

Between 1981 and 1994, the annual rate of inflation exceeded 100 per cent in all years except 1986. The containment of chronic inflation became the focus of economic policy. Yet despite a spectacular series of failed stabilisation plans—involving six monetary reforms in ten years—megainflation did not destroy the Brazilian economy. Indexation, the adaptive policy response, became pervasive throughout the economy. Taxation revenue did not fall significantly and remained high relative to other Latin American countries. Brazil's financial sectors and industrial businesses kept functioning well. Except during short periods, policy makers kept the exchange rate competitive and the country was able to generate substantial trade surpluses until mid 1994. This capacity to accommodate inflation may partially explain Brazil's failure to engage in serious structural change.

A ratchet pattern characterised the behaviour of inflation in the late 1980s, as a series of heterodox policy interventions resulted in lower inflation rates for a few months, after which inflation would climb up again. The cruzado plan, started in February 1986, lasted sixteen months. This plan froze prices, prohibited indexation in financial markets and, after a wage increase, froze both wages and the nominal exchange rate. Lacking fiscal and monetary discipline and unable to arrest growing trade deficits, the government was forced to dismantle price controls and change to an exchange rate regime using daily devaluations. Inflation returned and a new stabilisation attempt was imposed, the Bresser plan of June 1987, which also relied on price freezes and a new wage indexation scheme. In 1988, a stand-by agreement with the IMF was approved but failed because of inadequate fiscal performance. In January 1989, the summer plan introduced yet another price and wage freeze, which was relaxed in April with a return to formal indexation. By early 1990, inflation was close to 3,000 per cent per year.

In the face of inflation that could not be easily accommodated through indexation, the Collor plan of March 1990 drastically cut liquidity. An arbitrary freeze was imposed for seventeen months on nearly two-thirds of the money supply (M4), broadly defined to include demand deposits, mutual funds, federal bonds, state and municipal bonds, saving deposits and private bonds. Although Brazilians eventually managed to circumvent some of these controls, the financial freeze took over personal assets and was wildly unpopular. Fiscal policy was tightened, price controls were set in place and indexation rules modified. Public debt was also cut because the official inflation correction of indexed debt (the monetary correction) was set below the actual inflation rate in March and April. The plan contained important components of structural reform, including trade liberalisation and privatisation of public enterprises, that have been sustained throughout the decade. By 1992, however, President Fernando Collor was ousted from power in a corruption scandal, and inflation touched 1,000 per cent per year.

By the time Collor left power, the economy's resilience had been sapped—GDP declined by 4 per cent in 1990 and again by 0.5 per cent in 1992. A stand-by agreement with the IMF in January 1992 temporarily shifted the regime from heterodoxy to orthodoxy, with an emphasis on high real interest rates. This was short-lived, however, as nominal interest rates fell in 1993, GDP increased and inflation accelerated again. The IMF stand-by agreement expired in August 1993 and was not renewed. Inflation exceeded 2000 per cent, and the real plan was launched in December 1993.

Under the real plan, stabilisation went through three stages: a brief fiscal adjustment, monetary reform and the use of the exchange rate as a nominal anchor. In January 1994, Brazil's congress approved a fiscal adjustment plan that included cuts in current spending and creation of the emergency social fund. The fund—financed by redirecting federal revenues, limiting the ability of states and municipalities to access credit and recovering mandatory social security contributions—allowed the government to break some of its mandated links between revenue and expenditure. Twenty per cent of previously earmarked revenues were freed. This increased flexibility led to an operational surplus in 1994.

The second component of the real plan, a temporary monetary reform measure, linked contracts, prices, wages and the exchange rate to a single daily escalator and unit of account, the *unidade real de valor*. The adjustment, which started on 1 March 1994, lasted four months. The central bank determined a daily parity between the cruzeiro real and the *unidade real de valor* based on the current rate of inflation, as reflected in the three most closely-watched price indexes.

Finally, since the cruzeiro real and the *unidade real de valor* depreciated relative to the US dollar at roughly the same rate, most prices and contracts were implicitly in US dollars. On 1 July 1994, a new currency, the real, was introduced by converting contracts denominated in *unidade real de valor*s into reais at a rate of one-to-one. The cruzeiro real ceased to exist, and was converted at 2,750 cruzeiro reais per real.

THE REAL PLAN

The real plan brought inflation under control with remarkable speed—it fell from four digits in 1994 to two digits in 1995 and to less than 2 per cent in 1998. Indeed, Cardoso's success in securing the right to run for re-election in 1998 drew on popularity derived from sustained price stability. Economic growth was also strong—GDP growth averaged 4 per cent per year between 1994 and 1997, compared to flat or declining output in the prior five years. The economic boom that began in 1994 did not originate from a decline in real interest rates, as happened in the first phases of other exchange rate-based disinflation programs. In fact, real interest rates remained high throughout the period— between June 1995 and December 1998, the passive real interest rate averaged 22 per cent per year. Instead, the Brazilian boom appears to have originated with an increase in real wages. Between 1993 and 1995 several wage adjustments (including increases in minimum wages and in government wages and salaries) took place. These gains in income were reflected in booming imports and durable goods consumption (De Gregorio, Guidotti and Vegh 1994). High real interest rates drew in capital to finance growing imbalances. Policy makers faced complex, often contradictory policy choices as they attempted to deal with fiscal and trade deficits and volatile capital flows.

FISCAL DEFICITS: PRIMARY, OPERATIONAL, QUASI AND INVISIBLE

The new plan started with an apparent commitment to control fiscal deficits, but any fiscal adjustment achieved in 1994 was lost in subsequent years (Table 10.1). The operational deficit, which includes real interest payments, moved from a surplus in 1994 to a deficit equal to 5 per cent of GDP in 1995; it remained around 4 per cent of GDP in 1996 and 1997, and deteriorated further in 1998. The primary surplus, which

Table 10.1 Brazil: public sector deficits, 1994–8 (percentage of GDP)

	1994	1995	1996	1997	1998
Primary balance (A)	-5.2	-0.3	0.1	1.0	0.0
Real interest (B)	4.1	5.3	3.7	3.4	7.5
Operational balance (A+B)	1.1	5.0	3.8	4.4	7.5
Interest (D)	32.2	7.5	5.8	5.1	8.0
Public sector borrowing requirement (A+D)	27.0	7.2	5.9	6.1	8.0

Notes: The public sector borrowing requirement is equal to total revenues less total expenditures of the public sector, which includes all government levels, the central bank and public enterprises, but excludes state and federal banks.
Source: Conjuntura Econômica, "Encarte: Conjuntura Estatística," page XXII, Rio de Janeiro: Fundação Getúlio Vargas, October 1999.

excludes interest payments, declined in 1995, reflecting the significant increase in payroll outlays, and turned into a deficit in 1996. Factors that contributed to the primary imbalance include a 43 per cent increase in pensions following the increase in the minimum wage in May 1995 and the significant growth of other expenditures, particularly as the 1998 elections were approaching. In 1998, the budget deficit reached 8 per cent of GDP.

Fiscal problems were compounded by the emergence of substantial quasi-fiscal deficits in federal and state banks. For example, the federally owned Banco do Brasil (a traditional source of subsidised credit to agriculture) and the National Bank of Development introduced programs of subsidised credit to exporters in 1996. Partly to finance these programs, the treasury recapitalised Banco do Brasil by R$7.9 billion (over 1 per cent of GDP). Such intergovernment transfers contributed to an increase of total net public debt from 30 per cent of GDP in 1995 to 35 per cent in 1996.

Furthermore, with the end of inflation, bad loans from state banks to state governments became a serious problem. In the case of BANESPA (one of the banks of the state of Sao Paulo), the federal government agreed to swap bonds of its own for the obligations of Sao Paulo to BANESPA (about R$33 billion). Although this did not directly increase the net federal debt (for its bonds were offset by state obligations), such measures to stabilise weak state banks further increased the federal government's vulnerability to capital shocks.

Although the economy was growing on average above 3 per cent per year between 1994 and 1998, the ratio of net public debt to GDP increased from 28 per cent in 1995 to 44 per cent in 1998, and jumped to more than 50 per cent after the devaluation in January 1999.

ADJUSTING TO THE LOSS OF INFLATION AS A TOOL TO BALANCE BUDGETS

The end of inflation made fiscal problems more transparent. Economists think of extreme inflation as an unstable process, the instability reinforced by the Tanzi effect— a decline in real tax revenues as inflation rises. But empirical evidence suggests that a powerful effect runs in the other direction through declining real spending levels— the Patinkin effect (Cardoso 1998).

Observed aggregate budget data on nominal, operational and primary deficits contain very little information about the true fiscal position of the public sector when inflation exceeds 500 per cent a year. The Tanzi effect predicts that real tax revenues decline as inflation rises because collection lags inflation, and thus the budget deficit is higher at higher inflation rates. But there is also a reverse Tanzi effect—the Patinkin effect. If the Patinkin effect dominates at high inflation rates, real expenditures are lower than they would be if there were no inflation, and real expenditures tend to increase when inflation disappears. Thus, the fiscal adjustment needed once inflation disappears is usually underestimated. Several factors explain this phenomenon.

- Real interest rates decline with increasing inflation rates and usually rise following stabilisation. This rise in real interest rates contributes to the increase in real government expenditures once inflation disappears.

- During periods of high inflation, local governments' payments of salaries and wages lag inflation. When inflation exceeds 1,000 per cent a year, this delay produces a substantial decline in real expenditures.

- Although governments have learned to lessen gaps in tax collection and index delayed tax payments to inflation, they still program expenditures with a forecast for inflation that is usually lower than observed inflation. As a consequence, realised real expenditures are much lower than programmed expenditures. When inflation disappears, actual expenditures will be closer to their programmed levels.

- The inflationary revenue of state banks can finance credit subsidies that are not recorded. This revenue disappears when inflation disappears. Furthermore, if inflation has been concealing banks' weaknesses, and these weaknesses are accentuated by the rise in real interest rates that follows stabilisation, the government will have to use fiscal revenues to rescue banks, and recorded real expenditures will increase with stabilisation.

- Because inflation reduces real expenditures but not real taxes when governments fully index taxes, inflation can be used to accommodate conflicting spending demands from different government levels. Thus inflation produces operational budget deficits consistent with the amount of real seigniorage that the government needs to finance the deficit.

The Patinkin effect is only a partial explanation for the resurgence of large fiscal deficits after inflation disappeared with the real plan. Of course, high real interest rates—a factor in the Patinkin effect—did undermine fiscal efforts. But problems inherent in the constitution of 1988, the failure to rein in excessive pension payments and increased expenditures during the 1998 election year lay at the core of the fiscal fragility in the second half of the 1990s. Prior to the real plan, unresolved distributional issues had been masked in policy deliberations by passing unfeasible budgets, while inflation served as an equilibrating mechanism. With the end of inflation, policy makers were forced to undertake structural reforms to contain fiscal deficits.

USING MONETARY POLICY AS A SUBSTITUTE FOR FISCAL REFORM

Stabilisation under the real plan was supported by tight monetary policy, including an increase in reserve requirements. The required reserves-to-deposit ratio rose from an average of 26 per cent during January–June 1994 to 64 per cent during November 1994–April 1995. This increase in required reserves and the decline of inflation led to a substantial decline in the inflationary revenues of deposit banks.

With the rise in lending restrictions under the real plan, the share in total seigniorage seized by the central bank increased from an average of 60 per cent in the first half of 1994 to 84 per cent a year later. As a consequence, the share in GDP of seigniorage seized by deposit banks fell from 2 per cent to close to zero (Cardoso 1998).

The increase in required reserves and the decline in seigniorage of the banking sector in part explains rising interest rate spreads, the high active real interest rates and the increase in non-performing loans after stabilisation. The spread between active and passive rates (that is, between rates on government bonds and lending rates) increased from 4 per cent per year in early 1994 to 86 per cent in early 1995 (Campelo 1997). Required reserves were gradually reduced, but other factors contributed to keeping the spreads high, such as taxes on financial transactions and the increase in non-performing loans caused by higher real interest rates.

Stabilisation was not achieved through a tightening of fiscal policy, which would have reduced financing of the deficit through seigniorage collected by the central bank. Instead, seigniorage collected by the central bank rose from 1.8 per cent of GDP in 1993, the peak inflation year, to 3 per cent in 1994, the year of the real plan, and was 2 per cent in 1995, the average level of seigniorage during the high inflation years.

This appropriation of seigniorage from the banking sector to the central bank helped to finance government spending as inflation ebbed, but it also put the banking sector at risk. A more balanced policy would not have transferred the revenues from money creation so drastically from deposits banks to the central bank, and thus would have avoided the increase in interest rate spreads and non-performing loans. The elements exposed banks' weaknesses, particularly those of public banks, further straining fiscal resources needed for restructuring. Since July 1994, the central bank has intervened in fifty-one banks and 140 other financial institutions. The failure of two big banks (Banco Economico and Banco Nacional) prompted the creation of a program of assistance to private banks (known as PROER).

MANAGING THE EXCHANGE RATE

Brazil's success in bringing down inflation was associated with real exchange rate appreciation (Figure 10.1). Between 1994 and 1998, the average real exchange rate was 31 per cent above the average of the prior fourteen years—the only comparable peaks occurred prior to the debt crisis and in the wake of failed heterodox plans.

Rapid appreciation under the real plan occurred at the end of 1994. Despite minor devaluations between 1995 and 1998, the real exchange rate at the end of 1998 was still as high as it was at the beginning of 1996. This overvaluation is even more dramatic

Figure 10.1 Brazil: real exchange rate, 1980–99 (1990=100)

Source: J.P. Morgan website: www.jpmorgan.com.

if we compare industrial wages. During the second quarter of 1996, the ratio of Brazil's industrial wages to industrial wages in reais of its major trade partners was at least 40 per cent above the average ratio for the entire period 1988–96 (Faria 1997).

There were no structural changes or anticipated growth to justify such a large real appreciation. On the contrary, sustained long-run growth would have been inconsistent with the large current account deficits that were bound to prevail at that real exchange rate. The behaviour of the trade balance reinforces this observation. During 1995 Brazil's trade deficit increased during the first semester and started to decline during the second semester as the economy contracted. A small recovery after June 1996 was enough to produce further deterioration of the trade deficit, producing a deficit of US$8.4 billion in 1997 and US$6.5 billion in 1998. Evidence of overvaluation was also apparent in the slow growth of exports. Between 1995 and 1998, the growth rate of exports in US dollar terms was 4.2 per cent per year compared to an average of 11.3 per cent per year between 1991 and 1994.

The strong currency harmed the industrial sector and increased unemployment. The government reacted by creating subsidised credit to exporters through the National Development Bank and by approving legislation to exempt primary and semi-manufactured exports from indirect taxes (manufactured goods were already exempt from indirect taxes). Neither was sufficient to offset the effects of overvaluation.

This phenomenon of accumulated real appreciation has been evident in other Latin American stabilisation programs using the exchange rate as a nominal anchor— Chile during the period 1975–81, Mexico during 1987–93 and Argentina during 1990–5. Among the early experimenters with neoconservatism, Chile used the exchange rate to reduce inflation. It experienced real appreciation, sizable capital inflows, large external deficits, and in 1982, a sharp devaluation and recession. Mexico and Argentina recently followed a similar stabilisation path, building up fiscal surpluses, pursuing trade liberalisation and supporting privatisation. Both countries enhanced productivity by reforming goods and labour markets, but productivity growth is rarely enough to counterbalance an overvalued exchange rate.

The problem with exchange rate overvaluation is that it is often associated with a boom in consumption involving a large increase in imports and a decline in private savings. An overvalued exchange rate encourages agents to bring forward imports which they fear may become more expensive later. When this takes place at the same time as trade liberalisation, the effects are multiplied, leading to a jump in imports as controls are dismantled. If reforms face a credibility problem, firms and households doubt that trade liberalisation will be maintained and go on a precautionary import binge. For these reasons, a boom in imports is often characteristic of periods of economic reform. Even where exports have grown fast, as in Mexico during the early 1990s, exchange rate anchors foster trade deficits.

A second, less obvious problem with overvaluation is that it encourages a decline in private savings as residents substitute present for future consumption. Mexico's exports were growing strongly in 1994, but national savings had declined to very low levels (13.7 per cent of GDP) (Naim 1995). Between 1978 and 1981, overvaluation in Chile was also characterised by a low level of savings, averaging just 10 per cent of GDP (Milesi-Ferretti and Razin 1996). By undermining savings, overvaluation hinders economic activity because high interest rates are needed to maintain the capital inflows to support the exchange rate. As growth dwindles, savings decline further, leading to a vicious circle of low savings and low growth.

Both of these problems—growing trade deficits and declining savings—emerged in Brazil. Imports nearly doubled between 1994 and 1997, climbing from US$33 billion to US$61 billion. Combined with the slower growth of exports, the trade balance turned from a healthy surplus of US$10 billion to a deficit of US$8.4 billion. At the same time, gross national savings declined from 19.7 per cent of GNP in 1994 to 16.8 per cent in 1997.

These problems point to the need for an exit strategy in exchange rate-based stabilisation plans. Sustained stabilisation depends on fiscal equilibrium and modest current account deficits. But fiscal austerity is difficult to achieve and requires time-consuming reforms. Thus it is essential to develop a short-term strategy to make the transition from high inflation (with periods marked by large fiscal and quasi-fiscal deficits, capital flight and mechanisms that perpetuate inflation) to low inflation (consistent with small and sustainable deficits). It is appropriate to use the exchange rate during the first stage of easing four-digit inflation because it synchronises expectations and stops mechanisms (such as formal indexation) that tend to perpetuate inflation. After inflation has been brought down to double digits, however, continued use of the exchange rate produces serious distortions.

To sustain external equilibrium and reduce trade deficits as the real exchange rate appreciates, policy makers often use monetary policy to reduce aggregate demand. Unfortunately, high real interest rates make fiscal adjustment even more difficult because they increase public debt servicing. They also contribute to the deterioration of bank portfolios and increase the need for subsidies to recapitalise banks. The difference between domestic and foreign interest rates increases external borrowing and sustains real appreciation, providing apparent stability. But Sargent and Wallace's (1986) unpleasant arithmetic has shown that tight monetary policy cannot kill inflation where persistent budget deficits are present. Nor are current account deficits tolerated indefinitely by international capital markets. The problems created by overvaluation will not disappear without devaluation. The longer the correction is postponed, the worse the delayed adjustment will be.

The Mexican experience, reconfirmed by Brazil in 1999, showed that the costs of real appreciation compound slowly and explode suddenly (Goldfajn and Valdes 1996). The run on the Mexican peso highlighted the risks that arise when foreign capital sustains exchange rate overvaluation and current account deficits. In Brazil, as in Mexico, the crisis took years to develop because interest rate policies allowed overvaluation to persist. As long as reserves and capital flows are available, the temptation to continue to use the exchange rate to keep inflation under control seems irresistible.

CAPITAL FLOWS: MAINTAINING CREDIBILITY AS THE FUNDAMENTALS DETERIORATE

The real plan's strategy to contain inflation by using monetary and exchange rate policies reduced domestic savings and created unsustainable current account deficits. These policies, in turn, led to a boom in capital flows that initially helped stabilisation. Capital flows that averaged US$39 million per month between 1988 and 1991 mushroomed into a monthly net flow of US$970 million between 1992 and 1995. In 1996 and 1997, total net annual capital flows reached US$33 billion and US$26 billion. In the end, by supporting the exchange rate overvaluation, these flows brought about the collapse of the economy. Accumulating reserves, fed by capital flows, masked the severity of the current account deficits and the decline in private savings. As capital continued to enter Brazil, it sustained currency overvaluation and clouded policy makers' perception of the maturing crisis.

The pace of accumulating net foreign liabilities is a reflection of deficits and surpluses in the current account (Figure 10.2). Four periods can be clearly distinguished

- between 1953 and 1970, a period of severe foreign capital constraints, Brazil generated a current account surplus of almost 1 per cent of GDP
- with the recycling of petrodollars between 1971 and 1984, foreign capital flows flooded into Brazil and financed current account deficits of 3.2 per cent of GDP
- in the aftermath of the debt crisis (1985–92) current account balances moved between surpluses and deficits, resulting in a balanced current account for the period as a whole
- between 1993 and 1997 current account deficits returned to Brazil with renewed strength, financed by unprecedented capital inflows.

The obvious two periods of capital inundation, between 1975 and 1982 and between 1993 and 1998, both ended in a balance of payments crisis and an IMF program (Cardoso and Leiderman 1999).

In the two years prior to the inception of the real plan, Brazil's interest differentials *vis-à-vis* the United States far exceeded expected currency depreciation in the short run and attracted foreign capital. A desire to counteract the pressure for exchange rate appreciation in the face of large, potentially volatile capital inflows led to central bank intervention. Capital controls were used to discriminate between investment

Figure 10.2 Brazil: stock of net foreign liabilities, 1953–97 (current US$)

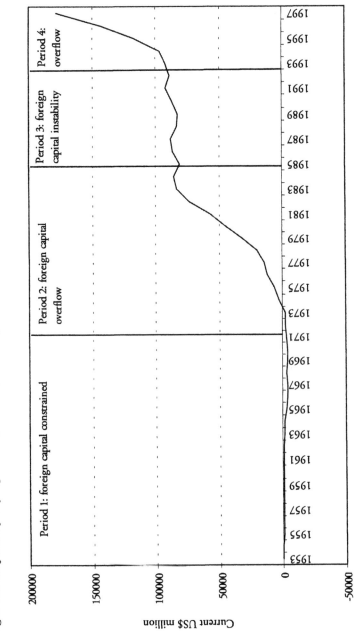

Note: Assuming net foreign liabilities were 0 in 1952.
Source: Cardoso, E. and Lederman, D, 1999. 'Brazil: Short Stories of a Ménage à Trois', The World Bank, Washington, DC, mimeo.

believed to make the economy more productive and competitive (such as foreign direct investment) and potentially volatile investment motivated by short-term gains. Authorities turned restrictions on and off during the 1990s, applying selective taxes to limit such capital inflows (Cardoso and Goldfajn 1998). For example, once capital inflows returned after the Mexican peso crisis, the tax on foreign investment in fixed-income instruments was raised from 5 per cent to 7 per cent, and on bond placements from zero to 5 per cent. New foreign investment in stock options and futures markets was prohibited. Despite such efforts, capital inflows consisted primarily of short-term resources tied to portfolio investments and other short-term investments. In 1995, net capital flows amounted to more than US$29 billion, of which US$20 billion were short-run capital—US$2.3 billion were equity and special investment funds and approximately US$18 billion were short-run capital not classified under a specific category. As some of the restrictive measures were eased, foreign direct investment increased significantly, amounting to US$9 billion in 1996 and US$16 billion in 1997. The increase in foreign direct investment was partly due to privatisation of public enterprises and to increased mergers and acquisitions in the private sector.

The Brazilian evidence is consistent with evidence from other countries, showing that controls can generate interest rate differentials for extended periods of time (Obstfeld 1995). Controls have also changed the composition of flows, at least temporarily. They have been less effective in affecting the quantity of flows or in avoiding the final collapse of the real.

To avoid a monetary expansion induced by capital flows, inflows were partly sterilised. Sterilisation created significant fiscal costs in financing high levels of reserve holdings, both because of the scale of the operations and the size of the interest differential *vis-à-vis* US dollar rates (and rates in other reserve centres). The rise in monetary authorities' gross foreign assets in relation to the increase in the monetary base suggests that sterilisation operations were large and costly in Brazil in the 1990s.

The sustainability of such a situation should not have been in doubt. Yet few governments will resist the temptation to let the real exchange rate appreciate as long as money is flowing in to finance current account deficits. The common argument is that productivity growth in the tradable goods sector is sufficient to justify real appreciation, and that the current account deficit reflects capital good imports that will generate future exports to pay for the accumulated liabilities. The hard truth is that productivity growth in the tradable goods sector would have to be well above what is credible to justify the real appreciation that occurs at the beginning of exchange rate-based stabilisation programs. Under a freely floating exchange rate regime, the risk of such optimism is borne by private portfolios. Under an exchange rate-based stabilisation scheme, this self-deception by the government entails an increasingly expensive commitment to guarantee an untenable outcome.

When the Mexican peso crisis erupted in late 1994, the initial reaction of investors suggested that the Mexican financial crisis would compromise all emerging markets—stock prices plunged, particularly in Argentina and Brazil. During the fourth quarter of 1994 and the first quarter of 1995, the net flow of capital into Brazil was insufficient to finance the current account deficit, and the central bank lost reserves of about US$9.8 billion. The rescue operation led by the United States and the IMF to support Mexican reform successfully insulated financial markets from the crisis and capital returned to Brazil. By the end of 1995 net capital flows reached US$29 billion, and by 1996, US$33 billion.

Although stability under the real plan survived the Mexican shock, by mid 1995 policy makers faced the same fundamental challenges as before the shock. In broad terms, insufficient fiscal adjustment continued to impose a burden on monetary, credit and exchange rate policies. In particular, covered interest differentials increased sharply and remained high. These unusually high real interest rates partly reflect the difficulty of establishing credibility in a country with a history of hyperinflation lacking fiscal balance.

High interest rates accompanied a sharp increase in public sector debt. In 1995, the stock of central bank securities and treasury securities outside the central bank grew 53 per cent in real terms. Between 1994 and 1996, the ratio of the net debt of the public sector to GDP increased from 28.5 per cent to 35 per cent, as high real interest rates allowed a weakening of the fiscal stance for two years in a row. Net debt continue to grow in the following years, reaching 44 per cent of GDP in 1998.

Lack of confidence in the ability of the regime to sustain the exchange rate anchor and to meet its obligations was reflected in the increasing use of US dollar-denominated and floating rate debt. Prior to the problems of 1998, most domestically denominated debt was at fixed rates and about 15 per cent was US dollar-indexed. By early 1999, 21 per cent was US dollar-denominated and 70 per cent was indexed to the overnight interest rate. Moreover, maturities fell—the interest due on domestic debt in January 1999 alone exceeded 6 per cent of GDP.

MANAGING THE COLLAPSE OF 1999

The Mexican crisis led to a significant loss of investor confidence, which gradually returned over the course of 1995. The 1997 East Asian crisis caused a brief panic, but the real jolt came with the Russian crisis in August 1998. Brazil's foreign currency reserves fell by US$30 billion as the government struggled to defend the real.

The IMF moved quickly to set up a loan package, but domestic politics (including the timing of presidential and gubernatorial elections and the relationships between the central and state governments) delayed negotiations. Finally, in December 1998 Brazil signed a US$41.5 billion financial assistance package. Contributions were to come from the IMF (US$18 billion), the World Bank and the Inter-American Development Bank (US$4.5 billion each), and bilateral creditors (US$5 billion of which would be provided by the United States and US$9.5 billion by European governments).

About US$9.2 billion was disbursed in mid December. Further disbursements from the assistance package (to be made through the Bank for International Settlements) were conditional on compliance with a three-year IMF stand-by program, which focused on fiscal adjustment. The initial program aimed at reducing the public sector borrowing requirement from 8 per cent of GDP in 1998 to 4.7 per cent in 1999.

This IMF program gave the financial sector time to reduce its exposure in Brazil. It was soon overtaken by events, however, as monetary policy failed to prevent a collapse of the exchange rate. Capital outflows, lack of fiscal progress, strong resistance by the domestic business community to the record high interest rates and growing demands for correction of the overvalued exchange rate forced the government to adopt a new exchange rate regime. The real was floated on 15 January 1999, and by the end of February it had depreciated by more than 35 per cent. In the three-week period between 13 January and 2 February, twenty-four banks made a profit of US$10 billion with sale and buy operations in the futures exchange (BM&F) due to a combination of the weaker real and high interest rates. Citibank and Morgan Guaranty Trust had the largest stakes in operations in the futures exchange. The big loser was Banco do Brasil, operating on behalf of the central bank.

PREVENTING A FREE-FALL OF THE REAL

Although most economists would agree that the real was overvalued throughout the plan, there was no consensus on the size of the overvaluation. (Part of the reason for this is a controversy over the choice of price indexes and the relevant period for comparison.) After its collapse, the average real exchange rate in the first quarter of 1999 was close to that which prevailed prior to the real plan (Figure 10.1). But it was not stable—between mid January and the end of March, its value against the US dollar fluctuated to as high as R2.2/US$ before settling at a rate of R1.68/US$ in early May.

The new exchange rate regime allowed the government to adopt a more balanced policy mix, but it imposed the need for a new monetary framework and a new nominal anchor. The most difficult problem was in setting monetary policy during the first few weeks following the collapse of the exchange rate, when financial market conditions and expectations were unsettled. Inflation can increase sharply after a speculative attack on the currency, as substantial depreciation causes a one-time adjustment in many prices. This temporary increase in inflation would then reduce real interest rates on debt denominated in domestic currency, and thus fuel capital flight. To offset, at least partially, this near-term effect, it is appropriate for policy makers to raise nominal interest rates to avoid further depreciation and the danger of igniting a spiral of depreciation and inflation.

On the other hand, policy makers also have to pay attention to the debt denominated in foreign currency. The larger this debt is, the greater the impact of the devaluation on the debt-to-GDP ratio. In the case of Brazil, that ratio had reached 53 per cent by January 1999.

The relationship between interest rates, devaluation and inflation is a matter of considerable debate. Proponents of tight monetary policies argue that domestic interest rates must be maintained above the expected rate of devaluation in order to relieve pressure on the exchange rate. If the gap between domestic interest rates and the expected rate of devaluation is not sufficiently high, people will borrow in domestic currency in order to buy foreign currency, thereby creating pressure for devaluation.

Even opponents of tight monetary policies concede that higher interest rates serve as an obstacle to currency speculation. Their objection to high interest rates is that, sustained over a long period of time, they can become counterproductive. According to this view, high interest rates increase the chance of default, raise debt service requirements and may signal more inflation for the future. In countries in which short-term domestic debt or domestic debt based on floating interest rates is sizable, high interest rates severely increase debt service requirements. Such an effect is relevant in countries (such as Mexico in 1994–5 and Brazil and Ecuador more recently) where a large stock of very short-term debt has been at the centre of policy discussions. Indeed, many analyses of the sustainability of the Brazilian program focus on whether interest rates can fall quickly enough to ensure a swift convergence of the debt-to-GDP ratio while avoiding an inflation–devaluation death spiral.

DEVALUATION, INFLATION, INTEREST RATES AND THE BUDGET

The IMF agreement announced on 8 March 1999 set two clear objectives—to limit the inflationary impact of the devaluation by raising interest rates and to prevent the ratio of debt to gross domestic product from exploding by producing substantial primary surpluses in the fiscal accounts.

The agreement recognised that the likely cost of these policies would be a recession and estimated a decline in GDP of 3.5–4 per cent. Discussion, however, centred around a strategy that critics call contradictory—the use of high interest rates can subdue inflation but aggravates the fiscal deficit by increasing the debt burden and reducing tax revenues. Following the float of the real on 15 January, short-term rates were raised steadily, from 29 per cent in mid January to around 39 per cent by the beginning of February and to 45 per cent on 4 March, declining to 29 per cent by early May. Does the apparent success of this strategy in Brazil validate the use of high interest rates in such crises?

Using a model of deficit finance, it is possible to examine situations in which higher interest rates lead to more monetisation of government debt, higher inflation and still higher interest rates. The challenge is to avoid this self-reinforcing explosion of inflation and interest rates after an inflationary shock, and to move the economy toward a stable low inflation, low interest rate equilibrium.

Suppose that bondholders develop doubts about the government's capacity to service and rollover debt. As investors begin to refuse to hold government bonds, the government can do two things. It can increase interest rates further, creating an incentive for investors to increase holdings of government debt, or it can monetise part of the budget deficit. Increasing interest rates has costs, including recession and political costs. Higher interest rates also raise the cost of servicing the debt and exacerbate the need to raise taxes. Thus, the higher interest rates are, the greater the temptation to monetise the debt. We can assume that the part of the budget deficit that is monetised, G, is an increasing function of the interest rate, i

$$G(i) = \Delta M \qquad (10.1)$$

where DM is seigniorage or the increase in the monetary base. The remainder of the budget deficit is covered by increases in public debt.

Dividing both sides by the monetary base, M, we can rewrite Equation 10.1 as

$$g(i)\, v(i) = \Delta M/M \qquad (10.2)$$

where $g(i) = G(i)/Y$, the budget deficit financed by money creation as a share of national income, and $v = Y/M(i)$, velocity. Velocity is a positive function of the nominal interest rate. In the model, the opportunity cost of holding money is the interest forgone by not holding public bonds. Empirical evidence shows that money demand

M(i) is inversely related to the nominal interest rate. We could also enter the inflation rate independently as an argument in the money demand function without affecting the results discussed here.

In a steady state, the inflation rate, p, is equal to monetary growth rate, $\Delta M/M$, and thus

$$\pi = gv \tag{10.3}$$

Thus, there is an upward sloping relationship between monetisation of the budget deficit, interest rates and inflation (Figure 10.3). The slope reflects the assumption that as interest rates rise and debt service increases, the political costs of conventional finance (for example, debt) become increasingly less tenable. It is easier to print money than to convince investors that extremely high interest rates do not carry a default risk. At the same time, as interest rates increase reflecting higher inflation, holding money becomes more costly and people economise on their real cash balances, further increasing inflation and money growth.

Points below the schedule $\pi = gv$ correspond to combinations of inflation and money growth that are inconsistent with the equilibrium condition of constant real cash balances—money growth exceeds inflation. Thus the interest rate is declining at any point below the schedule $\pi = gv$. Declining interest rates provide the incentive for people to hold higher real cash balances, reducing velocity and moving the economy to a new combination of lower interest and inflation rates on the schedule $\pi = gv$.

Figure 10.3 Phase diagram for inflation and interest rates

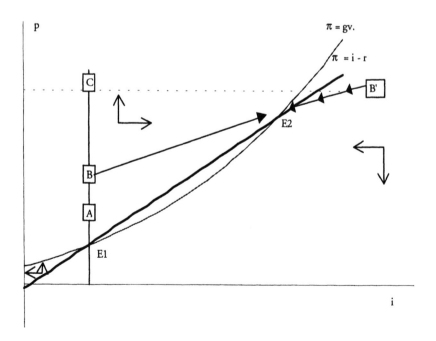

Points above the schedule $\pi = gv$ correspond to combinations of inflation and money growth rates such that the inflation rate exceeds money growth and the interest rate is increasing. Real cash balances and nominal interest rates are low relative to real cash balances and interest rates on the schedule $\pi = gv$ for the same inflation rate. Increasing interest rates reduce desired real cash balances and increase both velocity and the budget deficit, moving the economy to a new combination of both higher interest and inflation rates on the schedule $\pi = gv$.

The next question concerns the dynamics of inflation. We assume that inflation depends on the level of economic activity and inflation increases whenever the actual real interest rate, $i - \pi$, is below the long-run equilibrium real interest rate, r

$$\Delta\pi/\pi = F(r - (i - \pi)) \tag{10.4}$$

Note that Equation 10.4 implies both inflation inertia and scope for monetary policy to affect inflation.

In steady state, the inflation rate is constant, $\Delta\pi = 0$. Thus, in steady state

$$\pi = i - r \tag{10.5}$$

The schedule $\pi = i - r$ shows all the combinations of the inflation rate and the nominal interest rate for which the actual real interest rate is equal to the steady state real interest rate (Figure 10.3). Points to the right of the schedule $\pi = i - r$ correspond to points where the observed real interest rate exceeds the steady state interest rate, that is, points of unemployment and falling inflation rates. Points to the left of the schedule $\pi = i - r$ correspond to real interest rates that are lower than in steady state, fueling economic booms and rising inflation.

There are two steady state equilibria, labeled E_1 and E_2. The phase diagram shows that for stability the schedule $\pi = gv$ must cut the schedule $\pi = i - r$ from above (Figure 10.3). E_1 can be a stable, low inflation equilibrium. The nature of the time path around the low inflation equilibrium is one of oscillation as in a cobweb model. The cobweb would be converging depending on the relative slopes of the two schedules.

On the other hand, E_2 is a saddle point. This high inflation equilibrium can be easily disrupted. Even a small increase in the nominal interest rate at this level can sharply increase the share of the deficit that is monetised. This in turn fuels inflation and drives the economy away from E_2. The position of the saddle path, represented by the line B to B', is driven by the relative slopes of the two schedules, or by the inflection point in the schedule $\pi = gv$.

Assume an inflationary shock, such as a sudden devaluation. This shock would immediately push the inflation rate up to a point such as A or C. The inflation path following the initial jump will depend on the size of the initial shock and on the policy response. If the shock is small, and the inflation initially jumps to point A, the economy will go through a period of rising inflation and rising interest rates and then oscillate around the initial equilibrium to which it will eventually return.

Suppose the shock is very big and moves the inflation rate to a point such as C, above the saddle path defined by the points B and B'. To bring such a situation under control, monetary policy will have to increase the interest rate by enough to move the economy toward a point such as B' on the saddle path. The real interest rate shock, coming on the heels of devaluation and accelerating inflation, will cause a significant increase in unemployment. If inflationary expectations can be lowered, both inflation and interest rates will start to come down. In the new equilibrium, E_2, the inflation rate is higher than at the initial equilibrium. To further reduce inflation and move to E_1, action on the fiscal front would require the creation of primary surpluses to finance part of the interest payments that were initially monetised.

Things could easily go the other way if inflationary expectations were not lowered. Higher real interest rates can lead investors to fear that the government will not be able to service its debt, and will thus resort to the printing press, or that the government will not be willing to risk the political fallout of a severe recession. Inflationary expectations can then drive nominal interest rates up even further. To succeed in its strategy, the regime must survive what amounts to a test of willpower, enduring high real interest rates until investor confidence is secured.

Once an exchange rate anchor is abandoned, inflationary expectations affect the exchange rate. Thus the dynamics of the model presented above have implications for the exchange rate. After a collapse of the currency, the central bank must tighten monetary policy to avoid a deadly devaluation–inflation spiral. If monetary policy is too loose, people will use cash to buy US dollars, bringing about further devaluation and inflation. Interest rates have to increase; by how much is the crucial question. If the central bank increases the interest rate too little too late, inflation picks up and the economy returns to its history of persistent inflation. Inflation might once again hide some structural imbalances, but it would certainly destroy external confidence. If the central bank increases the interest rate too much, the resulting recession might be too severe, and inflation could decline ahead of interest rates, leading to higher real interest rates. The combination of recession and high real interest rates would increase the budget deficit and reduce confidence in government capacity to service debt without resorting to monetisation. Moreover, the prospect of a severe recession can undermine confidence in the government's resolve to sustain tight monetary policy, and thus set off a new round of inflationary expectations.

The recovery of credibility is everything. As the government raises interest rates, inflationary expectations must be declining for markets to bring nominal interest rates back down. But if there is a large public debt that is both short-term and carries floating interest rates, as in Brazil, investors may worry that higher interest rates will force the regime into debt monetisation.

The short-run task, then, is to negotiate a path of declining inflation and interest rates to avert a collapse of the exchange rate. Failure to stay within this path has implications for the budget and vice versa—the smaller the primary deficit the greater latitude policy makers have in setting monetary policy. However, it is difficult to achieve dramatic changes in the primary budget, especially where constitutional changes are required, and operational deficits, which reflect interest payments on outstanding debt, may be outside the regime's control. For this reason, support from multilateral institutions can be essential to restoring credibility and stability.

WAS THE DEVALUATION SUCCESSFUL?

Brazil has negotiated its way through the real crisis with extraordinary ease and speed. By May 1999, the real had risen to R1.67/US$, compared to a low of R2.21/US$ in March. Short-term interest rates had fallen from 45 per cent in March to just 23 per cent by 25 May, and inflation, measured by the national consumer index, had declined from an annualised rate of 16 per cent in March to 6 per cent in April (Table 10.2). Far from slipping into a deep recession, the Brazilian economy actually grew by 1 per cent in the first quarter of 1999 and forecasts of a serious decline in output were revised.

What explains the rapid turnaround? Certainly a dose of good luck has to be acknowledged. Interest rates in the United States had remained low. Agricultural output grew by 18 per cent in the first quarter of 1999, thanks to a record harvest following good weather conditions. But central to the restoration of investor confidence was fiscal action and shrewd monetary policy. Awareness of the risk of a grave collapse among even intransigent legislators and governors helped—in February, the collapse of the real galvanised congress into passing pension reform legislation that it had rejected in 1998. Congress also approved an increase in a temporary tax on financial transactions. Measures were introduced to rein in expenditures by state and local authorities. By the end of the first quarter of 1999, a central government primary fiscal surplus of US$5.6 billion was achieved.

Monetary policy, as suggested in the model described above, played the critical role. Following the inflationary shock of the mid January devaluation, inflation immediately increased, pushing real interest rates down (Table 10.2). The central bank reacted by increasing interest rates, resulting in extraordinarily high real interest rates for March. As inflationary expectations fell, nominal interest rates were allowed to decline. Yet real interest rates in April and May still remained among the highest in the world. This strategy successfully shifted the economy from a potentially explosive situation to a path of steadily declining inflation, allowing real interest rates to decline gradually.

Table 10.2 Brazil: inflation, nominal and real interest rates, 1998–9 (per cent per month)

	12/98	*1/99*	*2/99*	*3/99*	*4/99*	*5/99*ª
Nominal interest rate (Overnight-selic) (A)	2.40	2.10	2.38	3.31	2.44	1.85
Inflation rate (IGP-DI) (B)	0.98	1.15	4.44	1.98	0.03	0.00
Inflation rate (INPC) (C)	0.42	0.65	1.29	1.28	0.47	0.00
Real interest rate ((1+A)/(1+B))-1	1.41	0.94	-1.97	1.30	2.41	1.85
Real interest rate ((1+A)/(1+C)) -1	1.97	1.44	1.08	2.00	1.96	1.85

Note: ª projected.
Source: Fundação Getúlio Vargas, Conjuntura Economica, 'Encarte: Conjuntura Estatística: Taxa Selic', Fundação Getúlio Vargas, Rio de Janeiro, October 1999:XXV.

Table 10.3 Brazil: external balance, 1996–9 (US$billion)

	1996	1997	1998	1999
Exports (A)	48	53	51	48
Imports (B)	53	61	58	49
Trade balance (A-B)	-5	-8	-7	-1
Current account balance (C)	-24	-33	-35	-24
Net capital flows (D)	33	25	18	17
Balance of payments surplus (C + D)				
(gain in reserves)	9	-8	-17	-7
Memo items				
Net interest payments	-9	-10	-12	-15
Foreign direct investment	9	16	24	30
Amortisation	-14	-29	-34	-52

Source: Fundação Getúlio Vargas, *Conjuntura Econômica*, 'Encarte: Conjuntura Estatística: Setor Externo Dados Acumulados', Rio de Janeiro: Fundação Getúlio Vargas, December 1999, and Brazil Central Bank's website: www.bcb.gov.br/htms/notecon1.htm.

The central bank demonstrated its commitment to restraining inflation through tight monetary policy, even as official forecasts pointed to a 4 per cent contraction in GDP and rising unemployment. This resolve restored confidence partially and by April short-term capital was flooding back attracted by the high yields in Brazil's financial markets.

External endorsement of these measures by multilateral institutions lent credibility. In March, the government of Brazil and the IMF announced that they had agreed on a revised economic program. The IMF strongly endorsed the government's commitment to keeping inflationary expectations low, protecting expenditure on social programs and maintaining structural fiscal reform (at the national and subnational levels) on which credibility and the recovery of growth would be based. Once the fiscal measures that had been rejected were ratified, the central bank could confidently count on access to the remainder of its US$41.5 billion in IMF credit. The World Bank also provided a package of US$4.5 billion in loans to support social spending and state-level reforms.

Brazil's banking sector was also a factor in this recovery—many banks had anticipated the devaluation and had both positioned themselves to profit from it through currency futures contracts and hedged by holding US dollar-linked government bonds. As a result, the risk of a banking sector collapse did not threaten fiscal balance, as it had in East Asia and Mexico. The agility of the financial sector in assessing and acting on changes in inflation also facilitated the steady reduction in interest rates—renewed capital inflows allowed the central bank to reduce nominal interest rates six times in seven weeks without creating the impression that it was abandoning tight monetary policies.

By the end of May, markets were once again shaken by contagion, despite efforts by Argentina's government to slay rumours that it would be forced to abandon its eight-year pegging of the peso one-for-one against the US dollar. If volatility subsides, Brazil's success in stopping a spiral of rising inflation and depreciation of the exchange rate will mean more than the recovery of a profitable stockmarket. Provided there is no return of financial market turbulence and excessive delays on the fiscal front, the economy should continue to expand modestly. Averting recession will have profound implications for Brazilian workers, and would make Brazil's 70 million people who live on less than US$2 a day at least no worse as a result of the central bank's gamble that pitted their livelihood against the fickle opinion of world financial markets.

Nonetheless, the program's success does not fully address the substantial reforms that have eluded Brazil for more than a decade. The operational deficit is still large due to accumulated interest obligations and external finance remains vital to service external liabilities accumulated during the past five years (Table 10.3). Should exports fail to pick up, confidence could evaporate. Thus the regime remains vulnerable to external shocks. Until now, Brazil has been inclined to take risks and build asset and liabilities positions that are sensitive to exchange rate changes. Economic recovery can provide an opportunity to reverse this by converting debt denominated in foreign currency to locally denominated debt. The regime must also avoid the temptation to target the exchange rate as a way of securing stability—one of the advantages of floating rates is that they minimise the accumulation of foreign exchange assets and limit the government's lender-of-last-resort commitment to maintain the domestic value of bank assets (Dooley 1999).

CONCLUSIONS

Contrary to the pessimistic scenario envisaged in early 1999 by many analysts, the adjustment to the depreciation of the real has been faster and smoother than expected. Monetary policy played a critical role. The central bank reacted to the currency collapse by increasing interest rates and keeping inflation under control. The decline in the level of economic activity was small compared to the fall in other countries suffering from similar currency crisis. Two factors account for this favorable development: the depreciation of the real increased profitability in import-substituting activities and the agriculture sector showed an exceptional growth in the first quarter of 1999. Equally important, the domestic banking sector was less vulnerable to large exchange rate shocks than in other emerging markets. Now that the turbulence associated with the collapse of the currency is over, Brazil faces the challenge of defining its strategy for sustained growth.

At a deeper level, corruption scandals threaten the credibility of government at all levels. They also undermine confidence in the ability of congress to move beyond solutions to the budget deficit that include distortionary measures such as the financial transaction tax. The overall tax burden is not small by Latin American standards, but revenues are not progressively collected and spent. The result is that productivity growth is restrained by an average level of education that is close to that in much poorer countries.

Realisation of the Brazilian miracle—a resumption of sustained rapid growth— requires an investment in human capital, institution building and the restraint of special interests that undermine economic progress. When will Brazil return to the challenge of these more enduring reforms? Without the successful containment of the real crisis, one could not even pose this question, but nor does it seem likely that new crises will be averted unless fundamental reforms are brought forward.

11 Foreign capital flows, economic crisis and policy regime in Mexico in the 1990s

Lessons and challenges

Rogelio Ramirez de la O

Mexico was the first of the emerging economies to suffer financial crisis in the 1990s. The main cause of this crisis was domestic policy, although the increase in United States interest rates early in 1994 and political assassinations undermined confidence. These were, however, triggers rather than fundamental problems. Mexico was lucky that at the time there was no international contagion (as there was in 1997 from East Asia) and that the United States economy was growing robustly. That domestic policies were fundamental to both the crisis and recovery was amply demonstrated in the following years when Mexico showed stronger economic performance and managed relatively well during strong international contagion from East Asia in 1997, Russia in 1998 and Brazil in 1999. Such good performance is explained by a set of domestic policies that minimises macroeconomic imbalances and vulnerability.

This chapter examines the policy setting before, during and after the crisis of 1994–5, in particular, the response of capital flows to government policy. It also examines Mexico's needs for foreign finance over the medium term and points to potential problems.

Because it was the first crisis in emerging markets exhibiting high current account deficits and vulnerability to short-term capital flows, Mexican policies deserve special consideration. The thinking behind policy and the way in which it was rationalised is discussed comprehensively, for much of this thinking influenced policy in other countries that later suffered from similar crises.

POLICIES BEFORE THE 1994 CRISIS

Financial policies prior to the 1994 crisis were a by-product of stabilisation policies implemented shortly before the new presidency of Carlos Salinas. Salinas and his team of policy makers, in particular Pedro Aspe, were the architects of the stabilisation and exchange rate policy implemented since December 1997. Such strategy was set in the framework of a political and social pact between government, unions and business revolving significantly on a fixed exchange rate. When the peso collapsed the pact and policy went into a vacuum.

Aspe (1995) illustrates government thinking, describing the 'new mechanism of transmission' and argues that policy makers in the 1990s should not be preoccupied with current account deficits. In contrast to the 1980s, in which this deficit arose because of 'an overheated economy and higher government spending…in the new mechanism of transmission, the sequence is from improved investment opportunities…to greater private investment financed with capital repatriation, foreign direct investment, supplemented by increased domestic savings' (Aspe 1995:192).

Readers will recognise in this argument the view of Nigel Lawson, UK Chancellor of the Exchequer, who used the same reasoning to justify the similarly large current deficit in the United Kingdom in the late 1980s and early 1990s. When the sterling pound was ejected from the exchange rate mechanism, this view was finally exposed as flawed. Aspe and the authorities, however, insisted that the current deficit was privatised, as the government was not running a fiscal deficit. It was, therefore, self-financed and would adjust automatically when capital inflows fell. Thus, 'the trade balance confirms the idea that its deterioration is related to a healthy economic recovery' (Aspe 1995:47).

To back his argument, Aspe used a four-equation model of private investment financing. In this model, private investment, financial savings, foreign direct investment and capital repatriation (part of portfolio short-term capital) are endogenous. He tested for an increase in the government deficit using monthly data for 1980–91 and for 'good news'. Using this model, he concluded that 'private capital inflows are linked to real investment and are not only financial speculation' and 'any increase in private investment is financed in its totality by capital repatriation or foreign indebtedness' (Aspe 1995:204). Thus, the model ignored the high current account deficit.

Ironically, in the model the real exchange rate had a positive sign in affecting foreign capital inflows as well as capital repatriation. Moreover, from the beginning of the pact to 1991 (the data used by Aspe) the real exchange rate appreciated by 46 per cent. Aspe, however, considered the real exchange rate as an exogenous variable, losing a very powerful link with other variables. Another grave error was to confuse permanent capital repatriation with short-term foreign capital and to lump together all foreign investment. As for the effects of good news, such as the positive impact on capital inflows from NAFTA, he did not explore the duration of the effect and whether such inflows would increase the vulnerability to outflows later on.

It was another member of the same Salinas team (although not as prominent as Aspe), Ernesto Zedillo, who in December 1994 called the error, stating 'ignoring the current account deficit was a grave error'. The stabilisation program started in 1987 resulted very soon in a very strong peso and rising current account deficits. The Salinas administration reinforced market confidence by starting with a program of structural reforms, which mobilised investments and improved business expectations. One was the acceleration in trade liberalisation. A second was the renegotiating of the foreign debt owed to foreign commercial banks, leading to the substitution of old securities by new Brady bonds. A third was the push given to deregulation and privatisation. A fourth was the change in the foreign investment legislation aimed at opening opportunities for equity investment in most industries. The umbrella of all these reforms was a macroeconomic policy that eliminated the fiscal deficit and a monetary policy maintaining the nominal exchange rate. Eventually, the effect of these positive changes was an increase in investment and domestic consumption.

By ignoring the current account deficit and treating the real exchange rate as exogenous, the authorities lost important warning signals on changes in economic fundamentals and of excessive reliance on short-term capital.

Another flaw was to ignore the role of a credit boom in contributing to the deterioration in the current account balance. This was very much a function of the real exchange rate signalling investors that returns would be higher if they produced for the domestic sector rather than for export. Another problem associated with the credit boom is that banks acquired large foreign debts that increased vulnerability and deepened the crisis in 1995.

The central bank repeated the same arguments as Aspe—'the large inflows of foreign capital have induced an expansion of the current account on the balance of payments' (Bank of Mexico 1994:28–9). That is, causality runs from confidence increasing capital inflows, which became investment and showed up as a current account deficit that would, however, not be a problem in the medium term.

PESO EXCHANGE RATE POLICY

The legacy of the devaluation-ridden late 1980s was that a systematic appreciation of the peso ought to be avoided. During the first year of the economic pact (1988), the peso was pegged to the US dollar. As inflation did not fall quickly to United States levels, the real exchange rate appreciated 41 per cent against the US dollar (Table 11.1). Starting from an undervalued rate in terms of purchasing power parity, the peso quickly appreciated, reaching a peak in 1993. Considering that one of the structural reforms was a dramatic reduction in trade protection, the pressure on the real exchange rate was exacerbated.

A stable peso proved the key to reconquering business confidence, which had been badly shattered during the 1980s. The authorities initially were concerned about the high inflation and determined a daily slippage in the exchange rate. In 1989, this was of 1 peso per day, representing 15.9 per cent annual depreciation (against inflation that year of 19.7 per cent). In 1990, the slide was reduced to 0.80 peso per day, or only 10.9 per cent annual depreciation (against inflation of 29.9 per cent).

Table 11.1 Mexico: inflation and exchange rates, 1987–94 (December)

	Nominal rate (Ps/US$)	Inflation (%)	Real exchange rate (US$/Ps)
1987	2.241	159.2	0.660
1988	2.298	51.7	0.933
1989	2.667	19.7	0.913
1990	2.938	29.9	1.026
1991	3.073	18.8	1.119
1992	3.121	11.9	1.200
1993	3.107	8.0	1.262
1994	5.150	7.0	0.794

Source: Bank of Mexico and Ecanal.

As economic growth picked up, the current account shifted from a surplus of US$3.8 billion in 1987 to a deficit of US$6.1 billion in 1989.

As the reforms and privatisations of the Salinas administration started to attract foreign investors, authorities became more complacent. In November 1991 they inaugurated a band system inspired by the European Exchange Rate Mechanism bands, with the lower limit fixed at Ps3.05/US$. During the first year of the band, the upper limit increased by 0.0002 peso per day or 2.4 per cent per year (against inflation of 11.9 per cent). During the second year of the band, the slippage was increased to 0.0004 peso daily (4.6 per cent per year), signalling the authorities wanted to allow for adjustment and prevent excessive real appreciation (inflation was 8.0 per cent). During the last year of the band, 1994, the same slippage was maintained.

THE MICRO BAND FOR THE EXCHANGE RATE

Despite the daily upward movement in the band, the Bank of Mexico and the Ministry of Finance wanted a strong peso as a means to control inflation. Thus, in 1993, the central bank introduced a micro band within the band to limit the daily movement in the exchange rate—the central bank would intervene when the peso moved more than 1.5 per cent in any single day. As the peso remained at Ps3.1/US$ during most of the pre-crisis period (the same rate as at the beginning of the band), in practice this instrument signalled to investors that the authorities wanted to limit nominal depreciation.

That this refinement in policy took place in 1993, when portfolio foreign investors were most active in peso investments, was critical to the momentum of capital flows before the crisis. Investors read this as an implicit guarantee that they would have a strong peso through their investment term. This translated into low interest rates as the perceived exchange rate risk diminished. By inducing such a reduction, the system contributed to the boom in bank credit and to the high indebtedness in international markets incurred by banks.

The features of band systems have been extensively criticised (see Walters (1990) for an early warning against the band system of the European Exchange Rate Mechanism). The band system gave short-term portfolio investors the best of two worlds—high interest rates (justified by the high inflation) and a predictable nominal exchange rate. The bonus was that the peso could become even stronger than the upper limit of the band.

Investors could at any time, liquidate peso assets if they thought that the peso would approach the upper limit of the band. And vice versa, if capital was flowing in and the nominal rate remained substantially below the upper limit. Portfolio foreign investors could not have responded in any other way to the policy setting. They validated the band system and the exchange rate fundamentals and further contributed to the peso appreciation.

Not surprisingly, the peso remained at Ps3.1/US$ for most of the period until the crisis hit. The exception was 1994, when the authorities tolerated depreciation from Ps3.1 to Ps3.5/US$ (closer to the top of the band) after there had been an uprising in Chiapas and the Partido Revolucionario Institucional (PRI) candidate to the presidency, Mr Luis Donaldo Colosio, had been assassinated. This relaxation came too late to improve the economic fundamentals of the economy.

ACCESS TO FOREIGN CAPITAL IN THE EARLY STAGE

During the early stage of the Salinas administration Mexico's access to foreign capital was very limited (Table 11.2). This was partly because the success of the stabilisation program remained to be seen and partly because of the need to renegotiate the public foreign debt to reinstill confidence in Mexico's future capacity to service such debt. Foreign direct investment reacted relatively early, with an inflow of US$3.2 billion in 1989, while portfolio investment was only US$493 million.

INTERNATIONAL RESERVE POLICY

Mexico has never had an explicit policy, let alone a target, for international reserves. During the period 1990–4, the implicit policy was to increase reserves, as this would enhance the credibility of the exchange rate regime. In addition, in 1993 the central bank tried to limit the impact of capital inflows on domestic credit expansion, which reinforced this policy.

In March 1994 there was a large outflow of capital owing to the assassination of Mr Colosio, such that in the second quarter of that year international reserves had fallen by US$8.7 billion from US$24.7 billion at the beginning of the year. The government negotiated with the United States and Canadian treasuries to arrange special credit lines for US$6.8 billion, to be used in an emergency. This agreement, the North American Financial Agreement, remains in place today.

During 1995 the policy was to rebuild international reserves from the low level of US$6.2 billion, largely motivated by the political need to repay the 1995 United States treasury loan. Mexico also repaid the IMF ahead of schedule.

CAPITAL INFLOWS IN THE LATE STAGES

Foreign direct investment responded positively to the structural changes of the Salinas administration and for some time ignored the strong peso. Despite the potential risk posed by the peso, investors were attracted by the rapid increase in domestic demand and the prospects of NAFTA, whose negotiation started in 1991. Foreign direct

Table 11.2 Mexico: foreign finance, 1989–98 (US$billion)

	1989	1993	1995	1998
Current account	-6.1	-23.5	-1.6	-15.8
Capital account	-1.2	32.5	15.4	16.2
Foreign direct investment	3.2	4.4	9.5	10.2
Portfolio investment	0.493	28.9	-9.7	1.3
Equity	0.493	10.7	0.5	-0.7
Securities		18.2	-10.2	2.0
Bank of Mexico	1.7	-1.2	13.3	-0.2
Non-banking public	0.4	-2.4	10.5	-1.1
Private sector	-1.1	2.8	3.1	1.3

Source: Bank of Mexico.

investment contributed with inflows between US$2.6–4.3 billion during 1989–94. Such inflows, however, were very small compared to the expanding current account deficit, which rose from US$6.1 billion in 1989 to US$29.6 billion in 1994.

The bulk of the current account deficit during this period was financed by portfolio investment. In addition, there was heavy foreign indebtedness by Mexican banks (recently privatised) and the non-banking private sector. Much of this financing would represent in the end open positions to exchange rate risk, as most of the investments generated peso revenues.

The critical period of these developments was between 1992 and 1994. In 1992 the current account deficit jumped to US$24.5 billion from US$14.9 billion the year before. The boom in credit for consumption, which usually accompanies an overvalued currency, gathered speed in 1992. Between 1987 and 1994 bank credit for housing jumped 966 per cent in real terms, consumer credit grew by 458 per cent and credit for retailers by 513 per cent.

Thus, the large capital inflows in portfolio investment and indebtedness by the private sector and Mexican banks were intimately related to the security afforded by an exchange rate system biased in favour of a strong peso (Table 11.3). Portfolio investment contributed US$18.1 billion in 1992 and US$28.9 billion in 1993 of the capital account in those years of US$26.5 billion and US$32.5 billion respectively.

During the critical period, 1993–4, some of the flaws of the Salinas strategy became evident. One was that the opening up to foreign direct investment had not been sufficient and that was one reason why it had not surpassed US$5 billion. This was partly because some of the most promising sectors remained closed to foreign investors—not only the traditional petroleum and electricity sectors, but the new privatisations, telephones, telecommunications and banks were mainly for the benefit of Mexican investors.

Another problem was that the strong peso combined with high interest rates. This was interpreted by Mexican banks as a license to maintain very high differentials between deposit and lending rates. In response, the manufacturing sector began to decelerate. Combined with trade liberalisation, this resulted in a somewhat paradoxical situation—by 1993 GDP growth had slowed down while foreign capital inflows were at a record high.

Through the first quarter of 1994 there were heavy inflows of portfolio investment, a sharp increase in private foreign indebtedness from security placements (particularly strong in 1993) and heavy indebtedness by banks and the private sector (Table 11.4). Private sector indebtedness was very risky as it was used for bank lending to sectors and borrowers that would prove extremely sensitive to exchange rate devaluation and recession. Much of the investments were in highly cyclical sectors (such as construction) or dependent on domestic activity and peso revenues. The classic example is toll road construction following privatisation of toll roads, ending with the virtual bankruptcy of most construction companies in Mexico.

TESOBONOS

Although short-term portfolio investment in 1993 responded positively to the policy setting, despite the slowdown in economic growth, portfolio investors started to perceive risks. Such risks became more evident by the assassination of the PRI presidential candidate Mr Luis Donaldo Colosio in March 1994. Investors responded by switching their investments from peso instruments to Tesobonos, a US dollar-indexed instrument. Holdings of Tesobonos jumped from US$1.8 billion in January 1994 to US$18.0 billion in November 1994 (before devaluation) and US$20.8 billion in December 1994. Contrary to arguments by the government that the perception of risk increased only because of the exogenous event of the Colosio assassination, a large jump in Tesobonos, from US$9.1 billion to US$18.4 billion, took place after the presidential election in July 1994, despite the fact that the PRI had been a clear winner and that Ernesto Zedillo was regarded as the guarantor of continuity in economic policy. That the president elect, Zedillo, co-signed and validated the economic pact for 1995 in October 1994 with no change in exchange rate policy was not reassuring to investors.

By the end of 1994 Mexican portfolio investors had concluded that it would be extremely difficult for the new Zedillo government to maintain exchange rate policy. The election of a new government with a new cabinet marked the point at which they perceived a change in policy to be imminent, regardless of what the elected president said in public.

Foreign portfolio investors were much slower in seeing the constraints on the new government, largely because of disinformation by Wall Street analysts. Nevertheless, much of their holdings were already in Tesobonos, suggesting that they had gradually become more cautious.

THE CRISIS AND HOW POLICIES WERE TRANSFORMED

The crisis started with the devaluation of the peso. The large holdings of Tesobonos and their immediate redemption together with other foreign debt maturities forced the government to seek direct assistance from the United States government. The United States treasury stabilisation fund offered US$20 billion, while the IMF granted an extraordinarily large US$17.8 billion. Other funds were said to be available from the Bank for International Settlements (US$10 billion) and commercial banks (US$3 billion), though these did not materialise in actual financing flows. The official announcement, however, of a major package of US$50.8 billion contributed much to stabilise expectations in the short run.

At that point, Mexico faced redemptions from Tesobonos and other debts of US$41 billion. The foreign finance package seemed sufficient, provided Mexico converted its current account deficit into a surplus. Mexico applied a sharp fiscal adjustment to raise the primary fiscal surplus from 2.3 per cent of GDP in 1994 to 4.4 per cent in 1995. This included a large increase in value-added tax rates from 10 to 15 per cent.

The greatest change in policy took place in the formulation of exchange rate and monetary policy. The authorities adopted a floating rate with minimum intervention. Monetary policy, focused on the nominal monetary base but enhanced by other measures, became very tight. Before 1995, under the governorship of Miguel Mancera, the monetary base had been the target for monetary policy. During 1994 the central bank interpreted this target too literally—in the presence of large capital outflows, it injected net domestic credit and thus maintained the nominal base.

Table 11.3 Mexico: annual flows in the current and capital accounts of the balance of payments, 1990–8

	1991	1992	1993	1994	1995	1996	1997	1998
International reserves (beginning of period)	9.1	17.2	18.4	24.5	6.2	15.7	17.5	28.1
Foreign direct investment	4.8	4.4	4.4	11.0	9.5	9.2	12.8	10.2
Foreign portfolio investment (detail below)	12.7	18.0	28.9	8.2	-9.7	13.4	5.0	1.3
Loans and deposits	8.4	-1.4	2.9	1.1	23.0	-12.2	-8.8	3.9
Change in foreign assets held by Mexican residents	-1.0	5.6	-3.6	-5.7	-7.4	-6.3	6.7	0.8
Capital account change	24.9	26.6	32.6	14.6	15.4	4.1	15.8	16.2
Errors and omissions	-1.9	-1.0	-3.1	-3.3	-4.2	0.0	2.2	1.7
Current account deficit	-14.9	-24.4	-23.4	-29.6	-1.6	-2.3	-7.4	-15.8
Change in international reserves	8.1	1.3	6.1	-18.3	9.5	1.8	10.6	2.2
International reserves (end of period)	17.2	18.4	24.5	6.2	15.7	17.5	28.1	30.3
Private sector and banks (part of loans and deposits)	8.6	2.6	6.3	2.7	-1.8	0.2	0.7	3.5
Detail of foreign portfolio investment								
Foreign residents' investments in stockmarket (hot)	6.3	4.8	10.7	4.1	0.5	2.8	3.2	-0.7
Foreign residents' investments in peso-denominated govt securities (hot)	3.4	8.1	7.4	-2.2	-13.9	0.9	0.6	0.2
Govt securities denominated in foreign currencies	1.7	1.6	4.9	4.0	3.0	8.9	-1.7	0.2
Private security placements (commercial banks + non-financial private sector)(hot)	1.3	3.6	5.9	2.3	0.6	0.8	2.9	1.5
Foreign portfolio investment	12.7	18.0	28.9	8.2	-9.7	13.4	5.0	1.3
'Hot' money (excludes govt securities denominated in foreign currencies)	11.1	16.5	24.0	4.2	-12.7	4.5	6.7	1.1
Trade balance	-7.3	-15.9	-13.5	-18.5	7.1	6.5	0.6	-7.7
Various services (tourism, royalties, etc.)	-1.2	-2.2	-2.6	-3.1	0.9	0.0	-0.8	-1.6
Net transfer surplus (Mexicans working abroad, money repatriated to Mexico)	2.7	3.4	3.6	3.8	4.0	4.5	5.2	6.0
Foreign interest, dividends	-9.2	-9.6	-10.9	-11.8	-13.6	-13.4	-12.4	-12.4
Current account deficit	-14.9	-24.4	-23.4	-29.6	-1.6	-2.3	-7.4	-15.8

Note: Owing to the rounding of figures, the total may not coincide with the sum of quarterly figures.
Source: Bank of Mexico.

Table 11.4 Mexico: quarterly capital inflows, pre-crisis and crisis

	1993				1994				1995			
	Q1	Q2	Q3	Q4	Q1	Q2	Q3	Q4	Q1	Q2	Q3	Q4
International reserves (beginning of period)	18.4	20.7	22.3	22.4	24.4	24.4	15.8	16.0	6.0	6.6	9.9	14.5
Foreign direct investment	1.1	1.0	0.6	1.7	3.2	3.3	2.8	1.7	2.0	2.9	2.3	2.4
Foreign portfolio investment (detail below)	6.5	6.2	7.0	9.3	8.6	1.4	3.6	-5.5	-7.4	-3.8	-0.2	1.7
Loans and deposits	2.5	1.0	-0.9	0.3	1.8	-0.3	-1.7	1.4	9.3	3.7	6.5	3.5
Change in foreign assets held by Mexican residents	-0.8	-1.0	0.4	-2.2	-2.1	-1.7	-0.6	-1.3	0.0	-0.6	-4.0	-2.8
Capital account change	9.3	7.1	7.0	9.2	11.4	2.7	4.1	-3.7	3.9	2.2	4.6	4.7
Errors and omissions	-1.4	0.3	-0.3	-1.7	-4.5	-3.9	3.9	1.2	-1.9	0.7	0.5	-3.6
Current account deficit	-5.7	-5.7	-6.6	-5.4	-6.8	-7.5	-7.9	-7.5	-1.4	0.4	-0.4	-0.1
Change in international reserves	2.3	1.7	0.1	2.0	0.1	-8.6	0.1	-10.0	0.6	3.3	4.6	1.1
International reserves (end of period)	20.7	22.3	22.4	24.4	24.6	15.8	16.0	6.0	6.6	9.9	14.5	15.5
Private sector and banks (part of loans and deposits)	1.9	2.3	0.5	1.4	2.7	0.4	-0.9	0.5	-1.9	-0.9	0.4	0.5
Detail of foreign portfolio investment:												
Foreign residents' investments in stockmarket (hot)	1.3	1.3	1.9	6.3	3.5	0.2	0.7	-0.4	0.1	0.1	-0.1	0.4
Foreign residents' investments in peso-denominated govt securities (hot)	3.7	1.2	2.0	0.5	1.5	0.0	1.0	-4.6	-4.7	-3.4	-3.8	-1.9
Govt securities denominated in foreign currencies (hot)	0.5	1.8	1.4	1.2	2.2	1.1	1.3	-0.6	-1.9	-0.2	2.4	2.7
Private security placements (commercial banks + non-financial private sector) (hot)	1.0	1.9	1.7	1.4	1.5	0.1	0.6	0.1	-0.9	-0.4	1.3	0.6
Foreign portfolio investment	6.5	6.2	7.0	9.3	8.6	1.4	3.6	-5.5	-7.4	-3.8	-0.2	1.7
'Hot' money (excludes govt securities denominated in foreign currencies)	6.0	4.4	5.5	8.1	6.4	0.4	2.4	-4.9	-5.4	-3.6	-2.6	-1.0
Trade balance	-3.6	-3.4	-3.4	-3.1	-4.3	-4.6	-4.8	-4.8	0.6	2.6	2.2	1.4
Various services (tourism, royalties, etc.)	-0.2	-0.8	-1.0	-0.6	-0.3	-1.1	-1.0	-0.8	0.2	0.1	0.1	1.1
Net transfer surplus (Mexicans working abroad, money repatriated to Mexico)	0.8	1.0	1.0	0.9	0.8	1.0	1.0	0.9	0.9	1.1	1.1	0.9
Foreign interest, dividends	-2.6	-2.5	-3.1	-2.6	-3.0	-2.8	-3.2	-2.8	-3.1	-3.4	-3.8	-3.5
Current account deficit	-5.7	-5.7	-6.6	-5.4	-6.8	-7.5	-7.9	-7.5	-1.4	0.4	-0.4	-0.1

Note: Owing to the rounding of figures, the total may not coincide with the sum of quarterly figures.
Source: Bank of Mexico.

From 1995 onwards, under IMF and United States treasury supervision, the central bank reformulated its monetary base target to exclude the effect of the large international loans. This automatically set limits to domestic credit creation, despite the fact that commercial banks needed large amounts of liquidity to maintain operations as most borrowers found it impossible to service their bank debts at the high interest rates. Thus a new crisis began, the virtual bankruptcy of the Mexican banking system.

NEW AND ENHANCED MONETARY POLICY

Monetary policy based on a floating exchange rate has been successful since 1995 largely because the current account deficit has been moderate. This has made it unnecessary for Mexico to try to attract large portfolio investment and therefore allowed monetary policy more autonomy to pursue domestic economic priorities.

At the same time, interest rates, as high as 48 per cent in 1995, have made it necessary for the central bank to adopt a nominal target in order to induce lower inflation expectations. This target was the monetary base, but has been supplemented with other indicators—surveys on inflation expectations, wage increases, the peso exchange rate, producer prices and the balances on the current and capital accounts.

To implement its policy, the central bank has pursued an average level of settlement balances on the commercial banks' accounts with the central bank. To signal that it does not want positive or negative balances in banks' current accounts, the central bank follows a reserve requirement of zero averages, considered to be neutral, as punitive interest rates apply to excess overdrafts while no interest is paid on balances above zero.

In applying this policy the central bank uses the accumulated balance of commercial banks' accounts for twenty-eight-day periods. At the end of the period, the banks must show a zero balance. To avoid banks running large overdrafts during the month, the central bank has limits on the daily positive balance that banks can carry. These limits mean that the accumulated negative balances that banks can offset in the days before the end of the month are also limited. Positive and negative limits are set for each bank considering its capital and liabilities.

According to the need to tighten or relax monetary policy, the central bank signals that it wants to leave the banking system 'short' or 'long' of the estimated demand for base money. By sending a signal on changes in the accumulated balance of the whole system, the central bank induces banks to cut or expand credit and indirectly affects overnight interest rates. Market expectations adjust accordingly.

The central bank estimates the demand for base money daily, following seasonal patterns. The central bank offers facilities enabling banks to overdraw their current accounts and intervenes in the money market through sales and purchases of government securities through auctions and credit and deposit offers or repurchase agreements. It provides daily information on previous daily balances, the accumulated balances of banks, the projected pre-intervention cash position of banks in their current accounts and, consequently, the intended intervention by the central bank in the money market.

THE NEW AND ENHANCED FLOATING EXCHANGE RATE POLICY

A floating exchange rate has proven to be an excellent policy, especially after the central bank lost credibility in 1994 and recovery of international confidence had been slow. More important, Mexico has had a rate of inflation higher than in the United States.

The floating rate has been relatively volatile during periods of international turmoil. Volatility has generally been of short duration but has still had disturbing effects. Similarly, the peso appreciated in real terms during part of 1997 and more markedly in 1999. At present the peso is at a level of strength that is not sustainable in real terms without causing concern.

To partly minimise the volatility and signal the market on where it believes the peso should be, the central bank instituted in August 1996 an auction system to sell warrants for sales of US dollars by credit institutions to the Bank of Mexico. This was with the purpose of accumulating international reserves. Over time, however, the central bank has found that such purchases may serve other purposes as well, such as signalling that it wants to halt an appreciation of the peso.

The auctions started at US$130 million and have increased to US$500 million per month. At particular times, however, the central bank has auctioned more, when 80 per cent or more of the amount of warrants are executed before the sixteenth day of the month.

This mechanism was supplemented in February 1997 by auctions of US dollars sold by the central bank to credit institutions of up to US$200 million daily. Institutions bid for the US dollars and the sale materialises if they pay at least 2 per cent more than the exchange rate of the previous day.

FEATURES OF THE PRESENT POLICY REGIME

The present regime is a logical evolution of a floating exchange rate with minimum intervention. The monetary policy regime, similarly, has evolved from targeting the monetary base to a system of signals to affect liquidity and thus interest rates. When the central bank decides to leave the banking system short of liquidity, it has to intervene early, soaking up liquidity through auctions and pushing interest rates up.

Since early 1997, the central bank has been in a debtor position against the banking system. This means that at the beginning of the day the market has excess liquidity, which leads the central bank to engage in open market operations in order to reduce it. Because these operations are through auctions, the central bank places its paper with those institutions that offer the lowest interest rates. The mechanism introduces a downward bias in rates. Given the fact that the central bank is now in a debtor position with respect to the market, it is more difficult to induce increases in interest rates by using the mechanism known as short. This may be one reason why the response of interest rates to the short of the central bank during 1998 was smaller and of shorter duration than in the past—before 1997, the central bank had a creditor position in the market.

The new policy regime has responded relatively well to the needs of overcoming the crisis and putting the current account balance on a sustainable path through a realistic exchange rate. It also has certain limitations. One of them is that limiting the appreciation of the peso can be very difficult at times. Similarly, the regime has not managed to bring interest rates down for a period of time sufficiently long to permit recovery of the banking system.

The regime is flexible enough to include changes in some of the operational tools of monetary and exchange rate policy. For example, purchases and sales of US dollars could be carried out in a different way or in different amounts without hurting the basic characteristics of the floating rate. Similarly, the nominal target of the monetary base is a good guideline, but it is far from being the mechanical tool that it was before the crisis.

In 1998 the central bank did not deliver on the inflation target. One of its explanations was the depreciation of the peso of more than 20 per cent. Nevertheless, it has now started to recognise that the transmission between the exchange rate and prices is less clear-cut than it was in the past. It has also started to focus more on wages and monopolistic pricing, with the result that limitations of monetary policy to control inflation are being recognised. This is an implicit indication that it will not try to use the exchange rate to force inflation down.

The central bank is also limited in its ability to follow a stringent monetary policy resulting in very high interest rates for a prolonged period—the banking system has not recovered and the cost of rescuing it will eventually hurt the fiscal balance. Thus, a policy of high interest rates today might be detrimental tomorrow if the fiscal outlook deteriorates.

The present regime is likely to evolve in the future. Some entrepreneurs have challenged the floating exchange rate despite its excellent results. A proposal to adopt the US dollar as the currency has been presented as a definite solution to exchange rate risk. The present regime has started to receive public support but will need more time to consolidate. While this continues, the regime will probably be enhanced further.

Table 11.5 Holdings of (Peso) Cetes and Tesobonos (dollar-indexed) by the private sector, 1994 (US$billion)

	Cetes	Tesobonos
January	22.6	1.8
February	25.8	2.1
March	21.3	3.5
April	12.7	9.1
May	12.9	10.9
June	11.9	12.0
July	9.8	15.1
August	8.9	18.4
September	8.6	17.6
October	8.7	16.8
November	7.1	18.0
December	3.6	20.8

Source: Bank of Mexico.

MEXICO'S FOREIGN CAPITAL NEEDS, AND FOREIGN INVESTMENT

Mexico needs foreign finance to cover a steady current account deficit in the range of US$15–20 billion per year for the next three years (Table 11.6). This estimate is based on the assumption that there is no explosion in domestic credit, that the government maintains public finances under control and that oil prices remain within the band of US$10–15 per barrel for the Mexican mix. In addition to these flows, Mexico needs an average of US$12–15 billion to refinance foreign debt maturities. In total, its financing needs are in the range of US$27–35 billion per year, with some repayments lumping in some years.

Realistically, Mexico could receive US$10 billion in foreign direct investment—a higher amount would require a significant improvement in the business climate and further deregulation by the government. Estimating modest amounts for public and private indebtedness are consistent with the recent trend results in a requirement for portfolio short-term finance in the order of US$12–13 billion per year.

A level of US$5 billion in portfolio investment is sustainable and feasible if Mexico maintains sound economic management, but higher levels would present problems. For one thing, high levels of short-term flows could again become destabilising if they lead to a setting of policy that is not consistent with domestic stability in the medium term (as in 1992–4). For another, in contrast to the low levels of portfolio investment during 1995–8, they create the potential for large capital outflows.

Mexico must reinforce its structural reform and encourage foreign direct investment. If it does this and attracts large inflows of capital, the floating exchange rate would be the best option to moderate short-term capital inflows, signalling no commitment to any nominal target. In the absence of larger inflows of foreign direct investment, it would be forced to slow down economic growth or reformulate its policies to attract short-term inflows, with a consequent increase in risk.

Table 11.6 Possible range of Mexico's external financing requirements over the medium term, 1999–2002 (US$billion)

Current account	-15	-20
Foreign debt maturities	12	15
Public sector	8	9
Private sector	4	6
Sum of requirements	27	35
Foreign direct investment	8	12
Public debt	2	3
Private debt	1	2
Commercial banks	1	2
Public debt dollar securities	1	2
Private debt dollar securities	1	2
To be financed by portfolio investment	13	12

Source: Ecanal estimates.

REASSESSING MEXICO

Foreign direct investors have reassessed Mexico as a good location for manufacturing and export investment. Mexico has given large multinational firms the appropriate signals that it has the right ingredients for a successful manufacturing industry linked to global markets. This largely explains the large inflows of foreign direct investment since 1995. In some sectors, however, the Mexican government is seen to be too protective of domestic business interests, with the consequence that foreign direct investment is not realising its true potential.

Portfolio investors failed in 1994 to understand the need for an exchange rate correction and the benefits of the new floating system. This explains that they have been absent from peso money markets for most of the period since 1995, despite the fact that yields have been extremely high. Investors in equities have been absent during most of the post-crisis period, although they have tended to maintain positions in well known shares. In many instances, equity investors were justified in staying out of the Mexican Bolsa, as many of the firms listed suffered from misguided investments made during the Salinas period. For example, toll road construction, banks and stockbrokers and consumer goods producers had to absorb much of the increase in import costs with domestic profits. Given the large presence of these industries in the Bolsa, the equity market has systematically failed to attract inflows of portfolio investment. The potential is there, but investors must be convinced that Mexico is on the right path and that the issuers are healthy companies.

Portfolio investors have reassessed the soundness of Mexican macro policy due to its superior performance during the East Asian and Russian crises relative to other economies in Latin America. Ironically, part of the explanation lies in the fact that it has had no large inflows of short-term capital. Gradually investors have abandoned their conception of fixed exchange rates as synonymous with stability and concluded that a floating exchange rate may perform better in the long term. They have not, however, gone as far as to differentiate emerging markets and have not yet concluded that Mexico deserves greater concentration of assets.

One problem is poor corporate governance of the largest Mexican issuers. The problems with refinancing debt and disposing of assets after the 1994 crisis exposed a corporate sector with many vices inherited from a closely knit system of controlling shareholders unwilling to share information with minority shareholders. This problem will only be overcome as the Mexican government enacts new laws to provide more guarantees of fair treatment to foreign minority investors, and more importantly, when the government signals that it is no longer interested in protecting domestic business interests against the interests of the economy.

An additional problem is Mexico's politics. Dominated by a one-party system that only in 1997 had a Lower House in congress with a majority of opposition parties, politics carry an additional risk. This was particularly true with presidential elections in July 2000. Investors have not forgotten the 1994 election and the accompanying violence and tension. Investors want to see a peaceful political transition and expect the dominant party (the PRI) to be significantly weakened in order to contribute to a more transparent system, in tune with a modern market economy.

The third problem is the banking system, whose portfolios had deteriorated badly even before the 1994 peso crisis because many loans lacked the appropriate collateral and risk analysis. The government has so far injected US$70 billion into the banking system and opened up the doors to foreign banks. But banks have not been recapitalised, partly because shareholders fear that rescue will produce a political backlash. In effect, the government used promissory notes to buy bad loans and such notes face redemption between 2001 and 2003, with the risk that the government may want to restructure them. The budget does not register the accrued interest on this debt, partly because the government argues it is a contingent debt, but the official fiscal deficit has lost credibility. This crisis is still unfolding and will hit the next government while it greatly reduces the room for manoeuvring.

Part 5

The East Asian crisis economies

12 Lessons from Indonesia's crisis

Ross H. McLeod

The objective of this chapter is to review Indonesia's experience during the current crisis, with a view to suggesting policy changes that might prevent a repetition. High international mobility of capital is taken as given. The defeatist Mahathir–Krugman approach of imposing capital controls is not considered here, as it is obviously not a first-best policy. Many countries with open capital accounts have not experienced financial crises. Why were they not susceptible to the contagion? What is it about their economic policies that is better than those of countries like Indonesia? Unfortunately, the list is long, and one problem of analysing the crisis is that one can focus on virtually anything that Indonesia did not do well and blame it for the crisis. For example, some find *the* explanation in Indonesia's high degree of corruption. Alternatively, one can attribute blame to *everything* Indonesia does not do well. Neither approach is very helpful. It is easy to point out poorly designed economic policies; it is another to demonstrate convincingly that one in particular can be blamed for the crisis.

Nor is there good reason to backtrack on financial liberalisation. Crisis often follows liberalisation, but it is not an inevitability. Australia experienced a mini-crisis within a few years of financial deregulation in the 1980s, but survived without the drastic decline experienced by Indonesia (Gruen *et al.* 1998:207–23). It is necessary to understand the factors behind this in order to ensure that when countries like China and Vietnam eventually liberalise their financial systems, there will be a relatively smooth transition.

The concern of this chapter is to identify policies that reconcile the reality of highly mobile capital, the desirability of financial liberalisation, and the objective of domestic stability.

EVOLUTION OF THE CRISIS

Indonesia's crisis can be divided into three main phases.[1] The first phase extended from July 1997 through October 1997—the time at which the IMF became involved. The second phase extended from November 1997 through July 1998, and the third extends from about August 1998 until the present.

The exchange rate depreciation in the first phase seemed astonishing at the time, given the previous high degree of stability and excellent performance of Indonesia's economy over many years. In retrospect it pales almost to insignificance by comparison with the violent upheavals of the second phase (Figure 12.1) which, in addition to

Figure 12.1 Indonesia: exchange rate (Rp/$US)

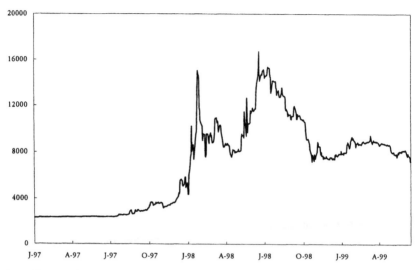

Source: Kompas, Indonesia.

economic misery, saw the unexpected demise of Indonesia's dominant leader of more than three decades. Figure 12.2 suggests the extent of the damage, by comparing actual real GDP with extrapolated values based on the pre-crisis trend of 7.5 per cent per annum. On this basis, output was about 38 per cent lower by mid-1999 than might have been expected on the basis of past performance. The third phase has seen the return of stability and indications of the beginnings of a recovery.

A FRAMEWORK FOR UNDERSTANDING THE CRISIS

A useful framework for interpreting the Indonesian crisis is provided by a model that relies on the fear of inappropriate government macroeconomic policy in response to some adverse change in the country's circumstances ('policy risk') (McLeod 1998b:335). Specifically, it is expected that the government will step in when faced by a disturbance and take actions that dramatically increase the money supply. This will generate a fear of devaluation, and thus provide the basis for currency speculation that will appear self-fulfilling. There is nothing irrational about this behaviour; it is entirely rational, given the premise that the government is likely to handle an adverse shock badly. Nor is it in any real sense self-fulfilling, since the end result will be an exchange rate that reflects the government's monetary policy rather than the actions of speculators: speculators merely hasten the process to its inevitable conclusion.

In this framework, the focus is much less on the initial disturbance than on what turns this disturbance into a crisis—the negative perception of the government's ability to handle an adverse shock. The model is therefore fundamentally different from approaches that focus on sources of vulnerability (for example, Athukorala and Warr 1999; Kenward 1999a). Here, the basic source of vulnerability has little to do with

Figure 12.2 Indonesia: crisis impact on quarterly GDP (March 1995=100)

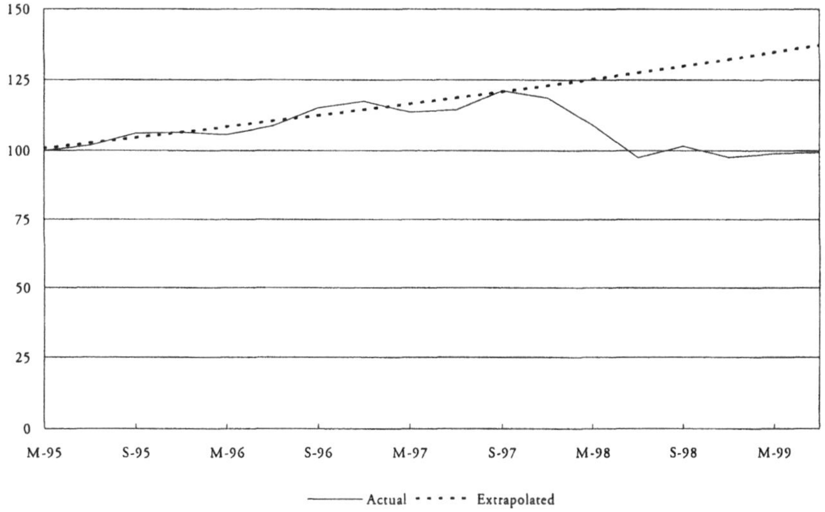

Source: CEIC Data Ltd, Hong Kong.

variables that can be observed and measured prior to any crisis; rather, it lies in the unobservable perception of how governments will react in response to an event yet to occur. The policy implications from this model will presumably differ also. The focus on certain variables or ratios that seem successful in predicting crises (if not their timing) invites government intervention that is likely to be counterproductive—for example, controls on foreign capital flows and the growth of banks. This intervention does little to dispel fears as to what the government might do in response to some adverse shock.[2]

Perhaps even more important, the key to whether crisis takes off is the government's actual ability, as distinct from the prior perception, to handle the disturbance properly. It is argued here that this is why some countries were severely affected and others hardly affected at all by the East Asian crisis, even though virtually all countries faced temporary shocks (as when the East Asian crisis seemed to bounce around the world after the Hong Kong dollar came under speculative pressure in October 1997). The model described above seems more helpful than the vulnerability approach because the latter focuses on trying to predict crises, but has little if anything to say about how they evolve.

THE MODEL AND THE REALITY

The data fit this model very well. The Indonesian government was in a state of utter confusion as to how it should react to the initial shock. Eventually it did exactly that which drives the crisis outcome in the model—it allowed money growth to get out of hand. Figure 12.3 shows the target growth trajectories for base money that were set in each of the first several Letters of Intent from the government to the IMF in 1997–8.

Figure 12.3 Indonesia: base money targets and outcomes (Rp trillion)

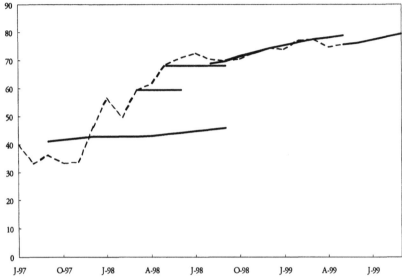

Notes: Solid lines show successive growth trajectory targets in Letters of Intent to the IMF. Broken line is actual outcome.
Source: CEIC Data Ltd, Hong Kong; Letters of Intent from Indonesian government to the International Monetary Fund (various).

These were missed by very wide margins until control was regained in mid-1998. Policy incoherence was in part a reflection of increasing political instability as the end of the Soeharto era drew closer. Amongst other things, this saw the removal of the entire board of directors of the central bank over the few months prior to Soeharto's re-election in March 1998 (Kenward 1999b:122). Nevertheless, in order to focus on the economic issues, the following discussion abstracts from the political processes that generated the economic policies followed during this period.

Perceptions of government's skills as macroeconomic manager

The negative perception of the government's ability to cope with the adverse shock generated by the sudden float of the Thai baht in July 1997 may seem somewhat surprising. Indonesia had a good record of macroeconomic management, with sustained high growth and moderate inflation, a steadily but slowly depreciating currency, and conservative fiscal policies that were allowing the government to prepay some of its foreign debt. Moreover, it had handled some severe shocks effectively in the past—notably the crisis of the mid 1970s caused by the uncontrolled borrowing of the giant state oil company, Pertamina (McCawley 1976), and the drastic decline in world oil prices in the mid 1980s. Thus Feridhanusetyawan (1997:8) argued strongly, in the short interval between the baht and rupiah floats, that 'Indonesia [was] not Thailand', while this writer saw little reason to panic, even six weeks after the rupiah float (McLeod 1997a:100).

Market participants were less than fully confident in the government's ability as macroeconomic manager. First, even though the rate of depreciation of the rupiah was held reasonably steady from September 1986 until July 1997, there were frequent, rumour-driven bouts of speculation against the currency during this time. There had been several large devaluations during the New Order regime of President Soeharto, and not everyone believed the government's reassurances that it would never do so again.

Second, a good deal of business was done in Indonesia in US dollars, reflecting market participants' greater confidence in its stability. It was common for contracts in the upper end of the rental market (for housing, office and retail space), and for international-standard hotel room rates, to be US dollar-denominated. Also, the state electricity utility, PLN, had contracted with several private sector power generation companies to purchase electricity at prices denominated in US dollars in the years prior to the crisis. In particular, a large proportion of deposits with, and loans from, the banking system were US dollar-denominated. There were large differentials between rupiah and US dollar interest rates—far in excess of the promised 4–5 per cent per annum rate of depreciation. The apparent penalties for those who preferred to borrow in rupiah and to hold deposits in US dollars can only be explained in terms of significant concerns that the government would not in fact keep the rate of depreciation down to this level.

Conflicting policy objectives

One good reason for the lack of faith in the Indonesian government's exchange rate promises was that it had always tried to achieve the impossible—to control more than a single macroeconomic variable from a large group that included the nominal exchange rate, the inflation rate, several monetary aggregates, interest rates and the current account deficit (McLeod 1997b). The policy stance just prior to the crisis was to aim for 4–5 per cent per annum depreciation, an inflation rate no greater than 5 per cent per annum and a current account deficit no greater than 2 per cent of GDP. Target growth rates for narrow and broad money and bank lending were also specified (of the order 19–20 per cent per annum in the mid 1990s). And although direct controls on bank interest rates had been abandoned during the 1980s, the central bank had never allowed the rates on its open market operations instruments to be entirely market determined.

As theory indicates and practice demonstrates, there are inevitable conflicts between these policy objectives and, while it may be possible to achieve all of them for some time, in the long run some will need to be sacrificed in order to achieve others. During most of the 1970s, keeping the nominal exchange rate constant was the top priority, but high oil prices generated balance of payments surpluses, rapid money growth and inflation. Exchange rate stability was sacrificed in November 1978 in an attempt to restore the competitiveness of non-oil exports.[3] During the 1980s, slow and steady depreciation of the nominal exchange rate was still accorded highest priority amongst the various policy objectives, but this was again sacrificed in March 1983 and September 1986 when declining oil prices generated payments deficits, threatening monetary contraction and deflation in the absence of devaluation. The reductions in the value of the rupiah on these three occasions were 33 per cent, 28 per cent and 31 per cent respectively (McLeod 1997a).

From 1987 on, steady depreciation of the exchange rate continued to dominate as the top policy objective. This policy generated persistent payments surpluses and high money growth. Inflation in the range of 5–10 per cent per annum was regarded as tolerable, even though not within the specified ceiling; and in the absence of any means of controlling the current account deficit, nothing more than lip service was paid to the 2 per cent target ceiling. The attempt to meet money growth targets and hold inflation within the tolerable range involved sterilisation of the payments surpluses by issues of central bank certificates and the accumulation of government deposits at the central bank. The large difference between rupiah rates of interest on central bank certificates and US dollar rates of return on international reserves implied a negative spread for the central bank, causing large losses. Probably for this reason, the central bank ceased publishing its profit and loss statement for a number of years in the early 1990s.

The floating exchange rate myth

When the baht was floated, many thought the Indonesian government would devalue the rupiah in response to the resulting surge of capital outflow, rather than sacrifice monetary stability by allowing sales of foreign exchange by the central bank to contract the money supply and push up interest rates. Much to the surprise of most, the government went one step further, abandoning any target for the rupiah by floating— or so it proclaimed. The new policy promised an end to the disruption of monetary policy by payments imbalances—a welcome, if belated, recognition of the inherent conflict between exchange rate and inflation targets. But the policy switch was more apparent than real, doomed from the start by the government's conviction that controlling a single macroeconomic variable, such as a monetary aggregate or the price level, is insufficient to ensure overall stability. The idea of leaving the other variables to be determined by market processes has been, and remains, anathema.

The most recent evidence for the existence of this mindset is contained in the new Law on Bank Indonesia (No. 3, 1999; McLeod 1999b). This states that the central bank's sole objective is to 'maintain the stability of the rupiah', *both* in terms of its purchasing power and its rate of exchange for other currencies (Article 7, including its elucidation). The implicit assumption is that it is possible to set both prices and the exchange rate, which is refuted by both theory and experience. Moreover, this statement appears to rule out even the possibility of a genuinely floating exchange rate policy, since the exchange rate cannot be both floating and stable.

The elucidation of Article 12 of the law discusses exchange rate policy in more detail, although the term 'elucidation' proves to be a misnomer. It confuses rather than clarifies the issues involved by unnecessarily making a distinction between the 'exchange rate system' and 'exchange rate policy' ('Bank Indonesia implements exchange rate policy based on the exchange rate policy that has been determined in accordance with the exchange rate system which is followed, including, amongst others…'). It then mentions three possible exchange rate systems—all of which involve intervention in the market by the central bank. One is a fixed exchange rate system, in which exchange rate policy is limited to devaluing and revaluing the currency. Another is a managed floating exchange rate system, in which exchange rate policy is to determine a rate each day, together with an intervention band. The third is a floating exchange rate system, in which exchange rate policy is market intervention, but without any exchange rate target—or at least, none that is known outside the central bank! To have a floating rate system and not intervene seems to be regarded as not having a policy: allowing the exchange rate to be determined by market forces without any intervention is simply not recognised as a policy option (although it must be noted that this list of three possible systems *cum* policies is not intended to be exhaustive).

'Floating rate' as used to describe the policy introduced in August 1997 is a misnomer. The policy is more appropriately described as a temporary, augmented currency board policy. Under standard currency board arrangements, purchases of foreign exchange by speculators reduce the money supply commensurately, driving interest rates higher, thus making it more costly to speculate; the increase in interest rates provides an equilibrating mechanism. Under Indonesia's temporary, augmented currency board policy, this automatic market mechanism was amplified by the deliberate withdrawal of base money from the system by the forced issue of central bank certificates to a number of state enterprises. The liquidity squeeze was so severe as to reduce banks' deposits at the central bank by no less than two-thirds. This made it impossible for them to meet the required reserve ratio, because they could not cut their deposits and loans overnight by such a large proportion.

Policy confusion

Rather than restoring liquidity to the system, the government chose to allow the banks to ignore the reserve requirement, and even to overdraw their accounts with the central bank, thus taking the pressure off interest rates. This policy blunder (which seems partly the result of a lack of communication between the Ministry of Finance and the central bank) (Kenward 1999b:122–3) could only have heightened perceptions of inability on the part of the government to respond calmly and appropriately to currency speculation.

The floating rate policy was therefore stillborn, although there has been no acknowledgement of the fact. In October 1997, after the short period during which the true policy was to sacrifice monetary stability to try to avoid further depreciation, there was a further unannounced change—a return to direct intervention in the foreign exchange market. At the same time, monetary policy underwent another major shift, from drastic liquidity squeeze to a reinstatement of sterilisation of the monetary impact of balance of payments disequilibria, involving the restoration of base money to its previous level. Foreign exchange reserves began to decline rapidly; those who had taken speculative positions on the basis of doubts as to the government's macroeconomic management capacity could almost be heard licking their lips.

The IMF and the run on private banks

By late October 1997 the IMF had become an important player in the unfolding tragedy. One of its conditions for the provision of financial support was that the government should close down a number of private banks that had such large volumes of non-performing loans that their capital was exhausted and/or that had vastly exceeded the limits on lending to affiliates. The government had been saying for some years that it did not guarantee the safety of bank deposits, although it seems doubtful that this was taken at face value. When the first sixteen banks were closed at the end of October 1997, the government overturned this policy also, promising that it would back all deposits up to an amount of Rp20 million per depositor. But at that time this figure was only equivalent to about US$5,000, so the promise meant little to large depositors—in particular, those at other private banks, since it was an open secret that the IMF had been pushing for about two dozen more private banks to be closed.

Having just had to restore the liquidity the government had unthinkingly withdrawn from the system in August, the central bank now found itself having to restore liquidity to a number of private banks experiencing a rush by depositors to withdraw funds.[4] At this point, the government sailed into uncharted waters. On various occasions during the 1980s and 1990s it had faced and dealt with runs on the currency by pushing interest rates to high levels for periods of a few days (Cole and Slade 1996:131–3). Now, the disturbance had acquired the additional characteristic of a simultaneous run on the banks. What should be done? Banks were in trouble because many of their borrowers had defaulted on US dollar-denominated loans: further depreciation would worsen this problem. They were also in trouble because the high interest rate regime created by the authorities had made it extremely difficult for rupiah borrowers to service their loans as well; again, any further tightening of liquidity seemed likely to worsen the problem.

Perceptions vindicated

Earlier perceptions of the authorities' inability to manage a crisis began to be convincingly vindicated. Fear of widespread failures amongst the private banks led the central bank to accommodate requests for additional funds, apparently with little hesitation (and, it would appear, with inadequate security). This was too great a temptation to ignore. Most of the private domestic banks by this time were technically insolvent. From shareholders' point of view, there was nothing to lose by taking on any investment that promised a positive return, no matter how risky. The corporate sector was by now in such deep trouble that there were few borrowing proposals in support of normal business activity, but one kind of investment was particularly inviting—investment in foreign currency (or prepayment of foreign currency liabilities).

Several of the tightly owned private banks began to lend heavily to affiliated entities. The deposits thus created were drawn down immediately and used to purchase foreign exchange from the central bank (directly or indirectly), following which the banks turned to the central bank for new lender-of-last-resort loans, allegedly needed to offset a run on deposits caused by loss of confidence in the banking system. By the time policy makers realised what was going on and were able to put a stop to it, the central bank had made liquidity support loans amounting to some Rp165 trillion (Pardede 1999:26). To put this in perspective, this was about five times the level of base money in October 1997—something of the order of US$40 billion at the exchange rate of late November 1997, approaching twice the nation's international reserves.

In effect, the central bank provided funds to the private sector to speculate against the rupiah. Despite still officially adhering to a floating exchange rate policy, the government was doing nothing of the kind, and its futile attempt to shore up the currency by selling foreign exchange resulted in a US$12 billion reduction in international reserves. Not all the money it injected into the system was used for this purpose, however. Base money doubled, and as a result, prices doubled in much the same period (Figure 12.4). The price of US dollars rocketed to more than Rp10,000 in January 1998, by comparison with just Rp2,450 in June 1997.

Explaining the sudden decline in the quality of macroeconomic management

Seen in historical context, this sudden evaporation of the conservative macroeconomic management for which Indonesia had become known seems extraordinary. The nation had a bitter experience with hyperinflation in the 1960s—another financial crisis that resulted in the demise of a president—and this had shaped macroeconomic policy throughout more than three decades of Soeharto's New Order. Unfortunately, however, the main lesson of the 1960s had been misinterpreted. The conventional wisdom was that hyperinflation had resulted from a lack of fiscal discipline—from large, persistent budget deficits. As a result, the government adopted the 'balanced budget policy', under which all cash outflows (including debt repayments) had to be fully covered by current revenues plus foreign borrowing.

Inflation is not caused by budget deficits, however, but by excessive money supply growth. Budget deficits only cause money growth if they are financed by borrowing from the central bank. Thus the balanced budget policy stood Indonesia in good stead over three decades not because it precluded deficits, but because it precluded the *monetisation* of deficits. The lack of appreciation of the role of money in the inflation process meant, however, that too little emphasis was placed on other central bank actions that cause money to grow. Thus Indonesian macroeconomic management

Figure 12.4 Indonesia: inflation and base money (per cent per annum, Rp trillion)

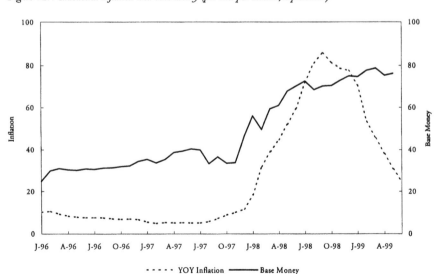

Source: CEIC Data Ltd, Hong Kong.

in late 1997 presents an absurd spectacle—a government striving to keep its budget balanced by drastically cutting back expenditure (in anticipation of a decline in revenues and despite weakening aggregate demand), while the central bank was pumping liquidity into the banking system at a rate that almost beggars belief.

THE APPROPRIATE RESPONSE TO A SUDDEN REVERSAL OF CAPITAL INFLOW

How should the initial disturbance have been handled, following the float of the baht? Adoption of a genuinely floating exchange rate would have been sensible—a long overdue recognition of the impossibility of controlling both the nominal exchange rate and the money supply (and/or prices) in an open economy and in a world of increasingly mobile capital. Such a decision would need to have been complemented by a commitment to either a target rate of money growth or a target rate of inflation as the new nominal anchor for the macroeconomy.

Given that this would have put a spotlight on the risk to which unhedged borrowers and investors were exposed, it could have been expected that this would result in a significant depreciation of the currency as these entities rushed to cover their exposures and speculators rushed to capitalise on their misfortune. There would have been no need for the government to respond to the ensuing depreciation of the rupiah. As soon as it had progressed to a sufficient extent it would have stopped of its own accord: the greater the actual depreciation, the less likely further depreciation would have become. In the short term, trade flows would not have been able to respond to the change in the exchange rate, but in the longer run exports would have expanded and imports contracted, which would have tended to cause some appreciation. If the government had been able to demonstrate its intention to stick to its money growth target, expectations of further weakening of the currency would have dissipated, making appreciation even more likely.

The folly of increasing interest rates

The actual policy of raising interest rates to defend the currency—confusing, to say the least, given the decision to float the exchange rate—reflects not only the Indonesian government's, but also the IMF's, inability to come to terms with a world that for years has been moving inexorably in the direction of floating exchange rates. It is surprising that there has been so little discussion as to the relative merits of having a genuinely floating exchange rate in combination with a fixed money growth or inflation target, and having a quasi-fixed exchange rate policy and an unstated commitment to manipulate interest rates in order to meet an unannounced target exchange rate. No doubt the fate of unhedged borrowers was of great concern, but on what basis was it decided that pushing up interest rates could save the rupiah, and that the implied interest burden to the business sector would be tolerable?

The policy has been a spectacular failure. The rupiah can hardly be said to have been saved, having depreciated from Rp2,450 in June 1997 to Rp15,000 a year later, despite keeping the one-month central bank certificate rate above 30 per cent per annum for fourteen months—and above 50 per cent per annum for eight months (Figure 12.5). Moreover, the business community and the banks have suffered enormously from the cash flow problems associated with the high nominal interest rate environment.

The presumption that the exchange rate could be stabilised by pushing interest rates to high levels is best described as wishful thinking. If there is a strong expectation of a large depreciation within a short period, interest rates have to be at astronomical levels if they are to dissuade speculators from borrowing in order to purchase foreign currencies. For example, the *ex post* rupiah rate of return on US dollars purchased at the start of November 1997 and held for three months was well over 6,000 per cent per annum. It was not high interest rates but an eventual change in expectations about depreciation that was primarily responsible for bringing the decline of the rupiah to a halt: once the currency had fallen so far that few could see any reason to believe it would fall further, speculation ceased.

Dealing with banking system problems

How should the problems of the banking industry have been handled? The run on the private banks probably would never have eventuated if the government had taken control of, rather than closing, the sixteen banks in October 1997. Indeed, the main thrust of bank restructuring throughout the crisis has been to close and liquidate troubled banks, rather than to try to rebuild their capital to enable them to stay in business—if necessary, with new owners and under new management. This flies in the face of a well established trend in bankruptcy law (as reflected in the Chapter 11 provisions of US bankruptcy law, for example) which recognises the fact that the going concern value of firms often exceeds their value in liquidation.

Rather, the IMF approach (which the government reluctantly followed), reflects the simplistic view that there were too many banks in Indonesia prior to the crisis, so that recovery would be best served by taking the opportunity to close many of them

Figure 12.5 Indonesia: one-month SBI rates (per cent per annum)

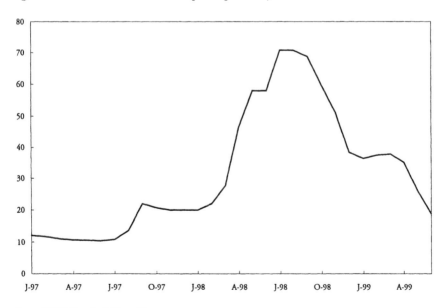

Source: CEIC Data Ltd, Hong Kong.

down. The desirability of having less banks was simply taken as given, although empirical evidence to support this view is lacking. The number of firms appropriate to any industry, banking included, depends on economies of scale. The market mechanism determines this number automatically, since firms operating at an inefficient scale will not be able to compete successfully with those whose scale permits minimum cost of production. There was therefore no need for the government to be concerned with this issue.

There is no evidence to show that small banks could not compete; in fact, there is strong evidence to the contrary. This comes in the form of several thousand 'peoples' credit banks'. These banks' operations are very simple: they usually have only a single office and are not part of the national clearing system. Banks of this type have existed for decades and show no signs of dying out, despite the rapid expansion of the larger commercial banks. It is important also to note that *all* of the largest private banks have been brought down by the crisis, while many of the smaller ones have fared much better. It is the large state banks—which have incurred huge losses on several occasions in the past—that account for the lion's share of losses of the banking industry during the present crisis (Pardede 1999:26–7). Devoting high level skills to the task of wiping out small private sector banks was a gross waste of resources that would have been better used in privatising the state banks.

Handling the bank run

Setting aside the question of whether large numbers of banks should have been closed, how should the government have handled the run on the remaining private banks? For brevity, it is assumed here that abandoning them and their creditors to their fate was not a politically feasible option. Given that depositors have lost confidence in the safety of their deposits, the government response most likely to maintain economic stability is to provide them with close substitute financial instruments. In the case of demand deposits, this means the other medium of exchange, cash. Indeed the authorities did succeed in ensuring that those who wanted to shift into cash were accommodated: the data show a significant increase in the ratio of cash to demand deposits in narrow money. There has been no suggestion that bank customers had any difficulty in converting their deposits to cash (Pardede 1997:21).

In the case of the quantitatively more important rupiah-denominated 'quasi-money' (time and savings) deposits, however, cash was not a close substitute—especially when runaway inflation was threatening and nominal interest rates had already increased dramatically. Supplying base money to the banks, therefore, was not the answer. This merely created an excess supply of base money, resulting in inflation and accommodating speculation against the currency. The authorities could and should have supplied interest-yielding instruments such as central bank certificates to depositors who had lost confidence in the private banks (or to the state-owned and foreign banks, to the extent deposits were shifted to them). Funds raised in this manner could then have been loaned to the banks from which they were withdrawn, at a rate sufficient both to cover the interest cost to the government and to impose at least some penalty on the banks. Disruption would have been minimal: the public would have ended up holding government instruments instead of bank deposits and the banks would still have been able to fund their existing portfolios of assets. In effect, the government would have been acting as intermediary between the public and the banks.[5]

Thus, although we may accept the view that the government had no choice but to provide liquidity support to the banks when there was a rush to withdraw deposits, there was no reason for doing this in such a manner as to increase the money supply (except to the small extent the public's demand for cash had increased). The fear that sterilising the monetary impact of last resort loans by issuing central bank (or government) debt would increase interest rates was unfounded: these would simply have served as a substitute for interest-bearing deposits in the public's asset portfolio.

CONCLUSIONS

The simple model described here fits the Indonesian experience very well. It suggests that the particular severity of Indonesia's crisis can be best explained by the course of government policy *after* the initial disturbance, which was incoherent from the beginning, and which took a decided turn for the worse after the IMF became a major player. The important lesson to be drawn is that governments need to establish and maintain sound macroeconomic policies, since the driving force for instability is perceived weakness of the government as macroeconomic manager. Key to such soundness is abandoning the belief that stability requires governments to control many macroeconomic variables rather than a single one, and, indeed, that they have the ability to do so.

It seems inevitable on occasions when economic policy has been seen to fail that there will be two contradictory policy responses. Those who are favourably disposed to government intervention will conclude that more and better intervention is needed. In the present context, the solution to policy failure at the national level is to redesign the international financial architecture and to expand the scope of operations of the IMF so as to compensate for national policymaking inadequacies with supranational policy responses. On the other hand, those who are more inclined to see government intervention as the source of problems rather than the solution will conclude that better outcomes will be achieved by cutting back on the offending interventions. The analysis presented here belongs clearly to the latter school.

Appendix: A chronology of Indonesia's crisis

Condition prior to July 1997 was good, as indicated by

- high output growth over many years
- moderate inflation for many years, and declining
- slowly depreciating exchange rate over more than a decade
- high and rapidly rising international reserves
- conservative fiscal policy for three decades
- stable or declining government debt
- high and rising share prices
- US$1 costs about Rp2,450 at the end of June 1997

July 1997

- Thai baht float immediately results in speculation against the rupiah
- government widens intervention band
- US$1 costs Rp2,600 at the end of the month

14 August 1997

- Rupiah 'floated'

Late August 1997

- Rupiah depreciates quickly
- government sacrifices monetary stability to halt depreciation
    huge increase in short-term interest rates as government squeezes liquidity[6]
    SBIs on issue up Rp2 trillion; SBPUs[7] down Rp300 billion
    base money falls Rp6.5 trillion from Rp40 trillion (16 per cent) during the month
- US$1 costs Rp3,035 at the end of the month

September 1997

- government cuts spending to maintain balanced budget and strengthen the rupiah
- US$1 costs Rp3,275 at the end of the month

October 1997

- government abandons 'floating rate policy' (without announcement), and intervenes in foreign exchange market to prop up the rupiah
- reserves fall by $3 billion (11 per cent) during the month
- US$1 costs Rp3,670 at the end of the month

November 1997–January 1998

- central bank loses control over base money, which rises by Rp22 trillion (66 per cent) in two months
- Bank Indonesia lends huge sums to banks: Rp41 trillion in the three months to January 1998, according to its published balance sheet

- reserves fall by a further $5 billion (20 per cent) in the two months to January 1998
- US$1 costs Rp4,650 at the end of the year, and Rp10,375 at the end of January

First half 1998

- interest rates surge

    rates on 1-month central bank certificates (SBIs) rise from 20 per cent per annum in January to 58 per cent per annum by mid year

    overnight interbank rate rises from 40 per cent per annum in February to 60 per cent per annum by mid year

- GDP falls by 8 per cent in Q1, then a further 10.6 per cent in Q2, compared with a decrease of 2.1 per cent in Q4 1997
- inflation surges to 12.7 per cent per month in February compared with an average monthly price increase of 0.8 per cent throughout 1997
- base money increases by a further Rp19 trillion (35 per cent) in the six months through July
- consumer prices increase by 57 per cent in the year to June 1998, compared with 5 per cent in the year to June 1997
- reserves held roughly constant thanks to disbursement of IMF and other loans
- US$1 costs Rp14,900 by mid year

Second half 1998

- interest rates peak in July–August

    1-month SBI rate peaks at 71 per cent per annum, falling to 38 per cent per annum at end of year

    overnight interbank rate falls from 60 per cent per annum to 30 per cent per annum at end of year

- decline in output slows to about 4 per cent in each of Q3 and Q4
- base money growth is brought under control
- inflation quickly subsides
- reserves increase by about US$4 billion thanks to disbursement of IMF and other loans
- Rupiah recovers strongly
- US$1 costs Rp8,025 by end of the year

First half 1999

- growth turns slightly positive in Q1 and Q2
- inflation slightly negative March through June
- stock price index recovers to pre-crisis levels
- Rupiah continues to recover, especially mid year
- US$1 costs Rp6,854 by mid year

NOTES

[1] More detailed treatments may be found in McLeod (1998a and 1999a).

[2] One of the unhappy experiences of Indonesia's crisis is that policy makers assumed that by committing themselves to 'responsible' policies, perceptions would change for the better. Often this has not been the case—witness subsequent adverse exchange rate movements after the release of the first few Letters of Intent from the government to the IMF.

[3] And import substitutes, although for some reason these were never mentioned.

[4] Depositors' concerns did not extend to the state-owned and foreign banks, to which many deposits were transferred.

[5] To the extent the public wished to withdraw foreign currency deposits from the private banks, it would also have been appropriate for the central bank or the government to issue foreign currency debt to the public and make foreign currency loans to the banks.

[6] The available data on this are inconsistent. BI's balance sheet shows its holding of banks' deposits down by Rp8 trillion (from Rp12 trillion) in August; but the consolidated balance sheet for the commercial banks shows banks' deposits at BI down Rp4 trillion (from Rp13 trillion).

[7] Money market securities purchased from the private sector by BI in order to inject liquidity to the system.

13 Capital mobility and the Thai crisis

Peter G. Warr

Thailand's crisis was the collapse of a boom. Over the decade ending in 1996 the Thai economy was the fastest growing in the world, with annual growth of real GDP averaging almost 10 per cent. Although growth at these stellar rates was new for Thailand, sustained economic growth had been the norm throughout the second half of the twentieth century. Growth of Thailand's real per capita GDP was positive in every single year from 1958 to 1996 (Figure 13.1), a unique achievement among developing countries. By the mid 1990s, Thailand's performance was being described as an example others might emulate and its principal economic institutions, particularly its central bank, the Bank of Thailand, were cited as examples of competent and stable management.

The currency crisis of 1997 changed this rosy picture and capital movements played a central role in the process. The principal task of this chapter is to describe the manner in which capital movements generated the collapse of the Thai economic boom. The rapid capital outflows of early, 1997 placed pressure on the reserves of the Bank of Thailand, inducing a float of the currency and producing the subsequent macroeconomic instability. But more importantly, it is the manner in which short-term capital inflows were managed over the preceding four years of economic boom that culminated in these problems. They did this by rendering Thailand vulnerable to a currency crisis. The lesson from this experience is certainly not that capital flows are bad, whether short-term or long-term, but that they need to be well managed.

A secondary task of the chapter is to consider the role played by a less well known feature of the Thai crisis—it was preceded, in the early 1990s, by a relaxation of controls on capital movements into and out of Thailand. How important was the relaxation of these controls in causing the Thai crisis? Would their retention have averted the crisis?

The analytical core of the discussion is the distinction between vulnerability to a crisis and the trigger which actually provokes it. For now, assume a fixed exchange rate regime. A trigger is a disturbance which increases the perceived likelihood of a devaluation. This trigger may arise from many possible sources, both external and internal, including changes in the external or internal economic environment, political events and natural disasters. Vulnerability is a set of economic conditions under which a small disturbance will induce the expectation of a large devaluation. The result is that mobile capital will flee the country to avoid the large capital losses that will accrue to assets denominated in the devalued currency, or whose value would be reduced by policy responses to capital flight. For a crisis to occur there must be both a state of vulnerability and a trigger. As Dornbusch (1997) puts it, vulnerability does not mean that things will go wrong; it means that 'if they go wrong, then suddenly a lot goes wrong'.

The empirical core of the analysis is a review of the long-term factors that made Thailand vulnerable to a financial crisis and the role played by international capital mobility in that process. The newly emerging literature on macroeconomic vulnerability has stressed three predisposing conditions for vulnerability to a crisis. These are inadequate international reserves, real appreciation in excess of the natural rate and high levels of bank exposure. If these conditions exist, then a relatively small trigger could cause a major crisis because it could lead market participants to make a large upwards revision to their perceived probability of a devaluation.

By 1995, Thailand was already highly vulnerable to a financial crisis according to each of these three indicators. The short-term trigger—a slowdown of export growth in 1996—led to the expectation of a devaluation and in turn produced the crisis. The policy relevance of the discussion is that the set of disturbances that could potentially serve as triggers is endless and many cannot be avoided. What can be avoided is the circumstance under which a small or moderate disturbance will lead to a crisis— vulnerability is what must be managed. First, we must understand it.

Figure 13.1 Thailand: per capita GDP, 1951–99 (constant 1987 prices)

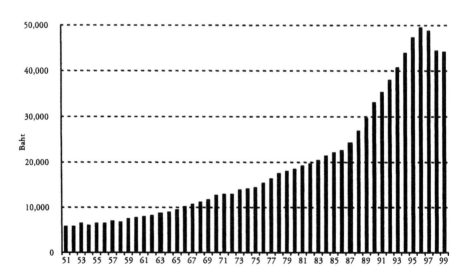

Note: Data for 1999 are based on Bank of Thailand projections.

HOW CAPITAL INFLOWS PRODUCED VULNERABILITY

The origins of the Thai crisis of 1997 must be understood in the context of the protracted boom which preceded the crisis. What fueled the growth of 10 per cent per annum which occurred from 1988 to 1996? Growth at this sustained, high rate could not result from an enormous, exogenous increase in productivity. To explain the boom we must examine the growth of the factors of production employed in Thailand.

EXPLAINING THE BOOM

Improvements in the quality of the labour force were not the source of Thailand's boom—the performance of Thailand's educational sector has been among the weakest in East Asia. Secondary school participation rates are low and have not improved greatly in the past two decades (Khoman 1993). Similarly, since the 1960s the expansion of the cultivated land area has been small, so growth of the stock of land was not the source either. The answer must lie with the capital stock. Thailand's capital stock has grown dramatically in the years since 1987, both in terms of foreign direct investment and domestic investment. Growth of foreign direct investment began first and was proportionately much larger (Warr 1993).

Studies of total factor productivity growth in Thailand reveal a crucial point. Over the twenty-year period ending around 1987, and therefore preceding the boom beginning in 1988, growth was explained reasonably well by growth accounting methods. The unexplained residual, total factor productivity growth, was less than 1 per cent per annum. But over the period of the boom of the late 1980s and the first half of the 1990s, the unexplained residual increased to around 5 per cent (Warr 1993). Growth of factor supplies, as conventionally measured, did not account for the growth that was occurring.

A clue to the difference between these two periods is provided by the behaviour of incoming foreign direct investment. Beginning in 1987, foreign direct investment increased dramatically. From annual rates of inflow varying between US$100 and US$400 million over the fifteen years prior to 1987, the annual rate of inflow rose more than five-fold, to over US$2 billion per year, and remained at roughly these levels over the next eight years. Rates of domestic saving and investment were also high, but the stock of capital represented by foreign direct investment was increasing much more rapidly than the stock represented by domestic investment.

The capital stock is measured in total factor productivity studies by adding the value of capital from all sources, foreign and domestic. The Thai experience exposes a flaw in that procedure. If foreign capital embodies forms of technological know-how which domestic capital does not, then the two forms of capital are imperfect substitutes. According to the author's econometric estimates using Thai data, the elasticity of substitution between the two is about 0.45, certainly not infinity, as implied by the usual aggregation. This implies that the two forms of capital are strongly complementary—an increase in the stock of foreign capital will increase the productivity of domestic capital. Simple aggregation of these two capital stocks is inappropriate because it excludes this effect.

This argument implies that when the foreign component of the total capital stock is increasing rapidly, the productivity of the domestic capital stock will in fact be increasing in a way that the conventional approach to measuring capital stocks does not recognise. Increased foreign investment thus increases the level of domestic investment because it raises the productivity of the domestic capital stock. When these two components of the capital stock are separated, the unexplained residual in total factor productivity growth studies becomes much smaller. To explain the Thai boom we must take note of the massive inflow of foreign capital and abandon the notion that foreign and domestic capital are perfect substitutes. But this inflow of foreign capital did not merely fuel the boom—its magnitude and its changing composition, combined with the policy environment of the time, also created the foundations for the collapse of 1997.

BANK OF THAILAND RESPONSE: STERILISATION AND LIBERALISATION

Thailand has a long and proud history of stable monetary policy and low inflation. The Bank of Thailand sees its major role as controlling inflation and for decades it had viewed the maintenance of a fixed exchange rate as central to achievement of that outcome. Prior to 1990, financial capital movements into and out of Thailand had been subject to extensive controls, a policy which had allowed Thailand a significant degree of monetary independence in spite of its fixed exchange rate (Warr and Nidhiprabha 1996). These controls were largely dismantled during the early 1990s. In part, it was hoped that Bangkok might replace Hong Kong as a regional financial centre following the restoration of Chinese sovereignty in Hong Kong in 1997, but the liberalisation of capital controls was also apparently supported by the IMF. Following this liberalisation, both the entry and exit of foreign funds became much easier. As foreign investment poured into the booming Thai economy, the Bank of Thailand attempted to sterilise its effects on the domestic money supply. Domestic interest rates were bid up, despite the fixed exchange rate and the increased openness of the capital market, confirming that foreign and domestic assets were imperfect substitutes. The result was an increased level of short-term foreign investment, which entered the country in response to the increased rate of return.

Suppose the foreign investment were long-term. If sterilisation was not occurring, the nominal prices of traded goods would not be affected, since they are determined (with lags) by international prices and the fixed exchange rate, but non-traded goods nominal prices would be bid up by the increased domestic demand. That is, the capital inflow would produce a real appreciation—an increase in domestic non-traded goods prices relative to domestic traded goods prices, the phenomenon now known as the Dutch disease (Corden 1984). The current account deficit would increase, reducing the amount by which foreign exchange reserves would be increased by the initial capital inflow.

The outcome would be much the same if the monetary authorities were attempting to sterilise but the exchange rate was fixed, capital movements were unimpeded and foreign and domestic assets were perfect substitutes. Any attempt to sterilise by raising domestic interest rates through sale of bonds would be defeated because it would produce an inflow of portfolio investment sufficient to drive the domestic interest rate down to its previous level. Demand would be increased by the monetary consequences of this inflow, producing the real appreciation described above. This is the familiar Mundell-Fleming model.

In the hypothetical case where sterilisation was completely effective, the monetary effects of the capital inflow would be exactly offset by the sale of bonds. Bond prices would be forced down and domestic interest rates would rise relative to international rates. The money supply would not increase and relative domestic prices would not be affected. Reserves would increase by the amount of the capital inflow. This outcome assumes, however, that additional short-term capital inflow is not induced by the rise in domestic interest rates. For this reason, complete sterilisation would be highly improbable in the early 1990s Thai context, because by then capital movements had been liberalised significantly. There was very little to prevent capital inflow in response to higher domestic interest rates.

Incomplete sterilisation implies an intermediate outcome, leading to capital inflows which only partially offset the attempts to sterilise. This might be observed if domestic and foreign assets were imperfect substitutes and/or where some residual controls on capital movements were limiting mobility. We would then expect the coexistence of the following phenomena, relative to what would otherwise have occurred

* increased levels of foreign exchange reserves
* increased current account deficits
* increased domestic interest rates
* increased inflows of foreign short-term capital
* increases in prices of non-tradables relative to tradables—a real appreciation.

This combination is what occurred in Thailand. The first three are obvious from inspection of Thailand's macroeconomic data. We therefore concentrate on the latter two.

ADEQUACY OF RESERVES

The Bank of Thailand was attempting to maintain a (nearly) fixed exchange rate relative to the US dollar. Were its reserves of foreign exchange adequate for this task? The conventional measure of reserve adequacy, the number of months of imports that reserves could finance, relates a financial stock, international reserves, to a trade flow, the monthly value of imports. Based on this measure, reserve adequacy increased steadily throughout the pre-crisis period from three months of imports in 1988 to over six months in early 1997. This measure signalled no problem regarding reserve adequacy at the time of the crisis. On the contrary, it suggested a steady improvement in the adequacy of Thailand's reserves as the boom progressed. But this indicator is conceptually of little relevance as an indicator of vulnerability to a financial crisis.

At a time of financial panic it does not matter how many months of imports could be financed from reserves. What matters is whether reserves can withstand capital outflow. Under a fixed exchange rate regime, the relevant magnitudes are the stock of foreign currency available to the central bank to finance transactions which convert domestic currency to foreign currency, namely its international reserves, compared with the stock of financial capital which could be presented to the central bank at short notice for such conversion. The accumulated stock of foreign-owned short-term capital is a major component of the latter. It is not the only component, in that it does not include volatile capital held by domestic residents, but it is one of the most volatile and focusing on it has the advantage that it can be isolated using balance of payments data.

Figure 13.2 compares the stock of the Bank of Thailand's reserves with the estimated cumulative stock of short-term foreign-owned capital. The latter includes foreign-owned portfolio capital, short-term bank loans and non-resident accounts held in Thai banks. This short-term capital is to be distinguished from long-term foreign-owned capital, which includes foreign direct investment and long-term loans from abroad. Monthly balance of payments data from the Bank of Thailand on net flows of financial capital are used to construct these stocks. The data are accumulated from January 1970, prior to which flows of foreign-owned capital were very small.

The longer the boom continued, the greater became the accumulated stock of mobile funds relative to long-term capital and, much more significantly, relative to reserves. There was a significant increase in vulnerability to a crisis in the years preceding 1997, especially from 1993 onwards. From 1994, the stock of short-term foreign capital exceeded the value of reserves and the discrepancy increased steadily. By early 1997 the stock of short-term foreign-owned capital exceeded reserves by 80 per cent. Both portfolio capital and non-resident accounts increased significantly in the years prior to the crisis, but the most significant component of the increase was in bank loans from abroad (Figure 13.3).

Figure 13.2 Thailand: international reserves and foreign-owned capital stock, 1980–98 (US$million)

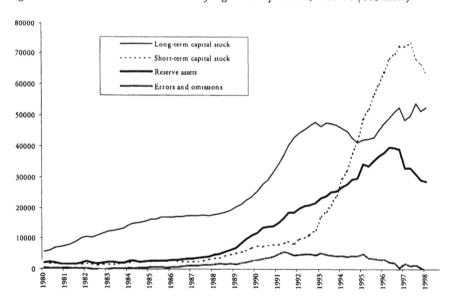

Source: Author's calculations using monthly data from the Bank of Thailand's balance of payments databank.

Clearly, the adequacy of Thailand's reserves had declined dramatically when these reserves are measured in relation to the stock of volatile funds that could be presented against them in the event of a loss of investor confidence. Moreover, this vulnerability did not develop suddenly, immediately prior to the crisis, but steadily, over a period of several years. That the subsequent outflow of this stock of short-term foreign-owned capital was the cause of the decline in reserves which accompanied the crisis is confirmed by comparing the decline in reserves during 1997 and 1998 with the decline in the stock of short-term foreign-owned capital during the same period (Figures 13.2 and 13.3).

The growth of volatile foreign capital relative to reserves rendered Thailand increasingly vulnerable to a speculative attack, but few observers, if any, were looking at the appropriate indicators. Prior to the crisis, both the absolute value of reserves and the number of months of imports they could finance had been increasing, but the growth of reserves was far exceeded by the growth of volatile foreign capital, thereby increasing Thailand's vulnerability to a financial crisis.

THE BUBBLE ECONOMY

What caused the massive inflow of volatile foreign capital in the years preceding the crisis? Large returns were being made from investing in Thailand and this situation had been sustained over several years. Euphoria induced by almost a decade of high growth produced overconfidence. In addition, the government was assuring the public that reserves were adequate to maintain the fixed exchange rate and the IMF also seemed satisfied, judging from its public statements. Investing in Thailand seemed both safe and profitable—not to participate was to miss out.

Figure 13.3 Thailand: international reserves and short-term foreign capital stock, 1980–98 (US$million)

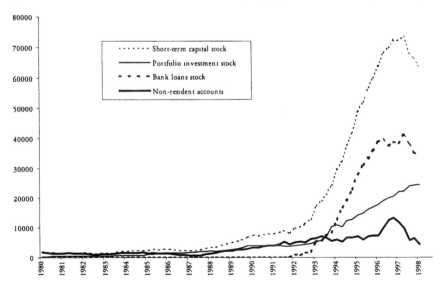

Source: Author's calculations using monthly data from the Bank of Thailand's balance of payments databank.

Through the first half of the 1990s, investment in real estate and commercial office space soared. The rate of inflow was so rapid that the quality of investment inevitably declined. Much proved to be financially non-performing, destroying the companies which had financed it. Why had investors acted so imprudently? Overconfidence was an important part of the story, as was the underlying real appreciation. The classic bubble economy is one in which real estate prices continue to rise well beyond levels justified by the productivity of the assets. As long as the prices continue to rise existing investors are rewarded and collateral is created for new loans to finance further investment—this cycle repeats until the inevitable crash.

Unrealistic expectations of continued boom underlie this process. These expectations are generally possible only after several years of sustained boom. The boom therefore generates the mechanism for a crash. This is why economic booms almost never peter out gradually. They collapse. In these respects, Thailand's financial panic was similar to many previous examples around the world, including the Mexican crash of 1994 (Edwards 1998).

In the Thai case, there were three other less well understood causes of overinvestment, each of which was policy-induced. First, the Bank of Thailand was attempting to sterilise the monetary consequences of capital inflows, despite the relaxation of capital controls. The increasing domestic interest rates encouraged further short-term capital inflows.

Second, beginning in 1993 the Thai government encouraged banks to borrow short-term through the establishment of the Bangkok International Banking Facility, again with the apparent approval of the IMF. This development made short-term borrowing from abroad easier and more attractive for domestic banks and from the point of view of the foreign lender, these loans were protected by implicit guarantees from the Bank of Thailand. The dramatic increase in short-term bank loans began at this time (Figure 13.3). In addition to new short-term loans, significant substitution of short-term loans for longer-term loans also occurred (Figure 13.2). Beginning in 1993, the stock of long-term loans actually declined for around two years while short-term loans accelerated.

Third, the Bank of Thailand also indirectly encouraged short-term borrowing by non-bank financial institutions. For many years prior to the crisis, banking licenses in Thailand had been highly profitable. The issuance of new licenses was tightly controlled by the Bank of Thailand but it had become known that the number of licenses was to be increased significantly. Thai finance companies immediately began competing with one another to be among the lucky recipients. To project themselves as significant players in the domestic financial market, many companies were willing to borrow large sums abroad and lend domestically at low margins, thereby taking risks they would not ordinarily contemplate. With lenders eager to lend vast sums, real estate was a favoured investment because purchase of real estate requires almost no specialist expertise, only the willingness to accept risk.

REAL APPRECIATION

A dramatic real appreciation was occurring throughout the 1990s (Figures 13.4, 13.5 and 13.6). Data on traded prices, non-traded prices and relative prices over a thirty-year period from 1968 to 1998 update the series explained in Warr and Nidhiprabha

Figure 13.4 Thailand: index of traded goods prices, 1968–98

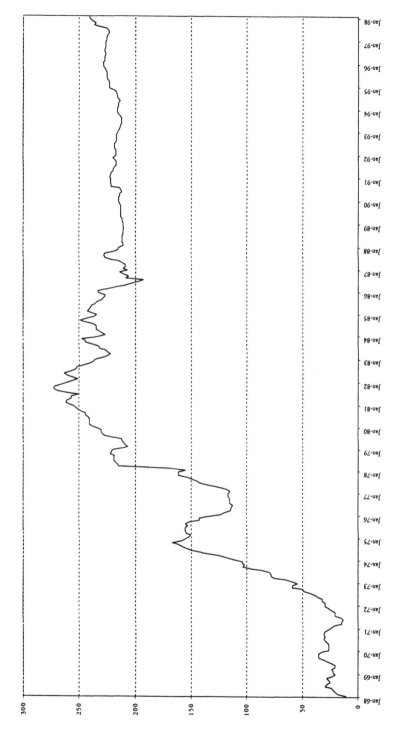

Source: Author's calculations using data from Department of Business Economics, Ministry of Commerce, Bangkok.

Figure 13.5 Thailand: index of non-traded goods and services prices, 1968–98

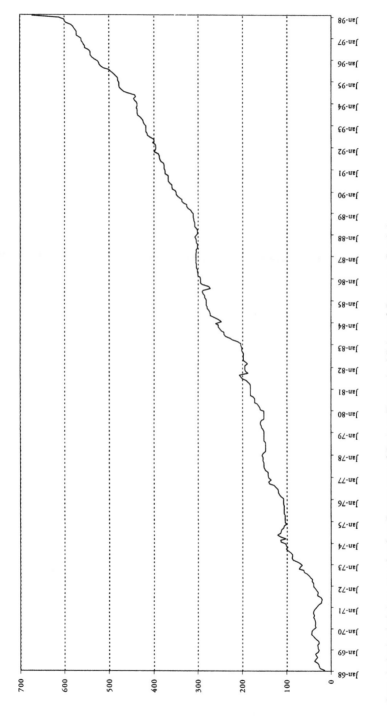

Source: Author's calculations using data from Department of Business Economics, Ministry of Commerce, Bangkok.

Figure 13.6 Thailand: index of traded/non-traded goods prices, 1968–98

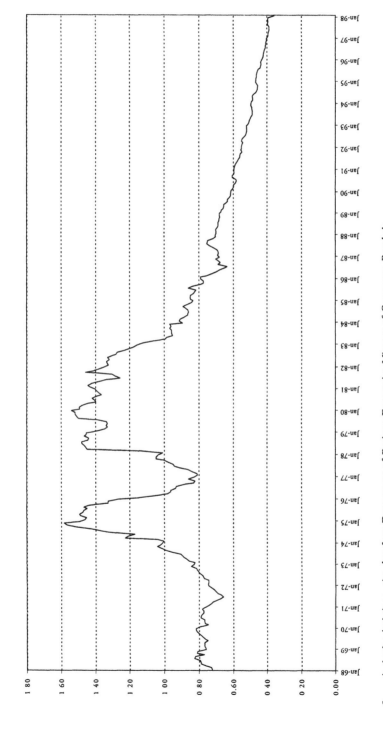

Source: Author's calculations using data from Department of Business Economics, Ministry of Commerce, Bangkok.

(1996), which used monthly domestic price data for Thailand to obtain an index of traded goods prices (using thirty-three individual wholesale prices) relative to non-traded goods (using forty-two individual consumer prices). In the earlier study, the data were presented for the twenty years from 1968 to 1988. The traded/non-traded goods price ratio rose sharply with the international inflation induced by the two OPEC oil price shocks of the 1970s, but a steady and rapid decline in the relative price series occurred from 1987 onwards (Figure 13.6).

Focusing on the decade 1988 to 1998, first consider the relative prices of traded to non-traded goods (the same index shown in Figure 13.6) (Figure 13.7). Over the preceding two decades the index took values between a maximum of 1.7 and a minimum of 0.68 (indexed to August 1973 = 1). In January 1988 the value of this index was 0.7.

For convenience of comparison with the earlier series, the relative price series shown in Figure 13.7 is indexed to begin at 0.7 in January 1988 and its composition and construction are identical to the earlier study. Leaving aside short-term fluctuations, the index declined steadily from 1990 onwards. By April 1997 its value was 0.38. A very large real appreciation had occurred—the real exchange rate had fallen to only 55 per cent of its lowest value over the two decades prior to the boom. Do external exchange rate changes explain this outcome? The question arises because it is now well understood that the depreciation since 1995 of the Japanese yen and other currencies relative to the US dollar meant that any currency pegged to the dollar would suffer a real appreciation.

Figure 13.7 Thailand: real exchange rates, 1988–97

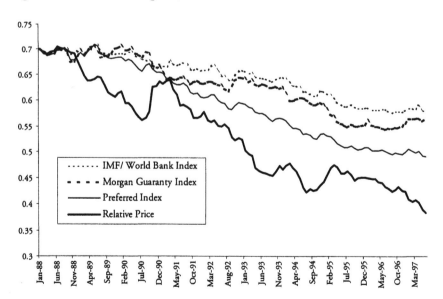

Source: Author's calculations using data from Thai government sources and International Monetary Fund, *International Financial Statistics*, Washington, DC, various issues.

It should be noted that the real appreciation within Thailand was not confined to the period after 1995, when the US dollar was appreciating. A large real appreciation within Thailand can also be seen in the first five years of the 1990s when the US dollar was depreciating relative to the yen and other currencies. Most of the real appreciation from 1990 to mid 1997 was already evident by mid 1994, well before the appreciation of the US dollar began. External exchange rate changes were clearly relevant, but they were not the main causal factor.

The principal source of Thailand's real appreciation resided in forces operating within the Thai economy—the demand effects of very large foreign capital inflows, only partially sterilised. The real appreciation undermined the competitiveness of Thailand's traded goods industries, meaning that their capacity to attract resources within the domestic economy in competition with non-traded goods sectors fell.

Three other measures of the real exchange rate, also commonly called measures of competitiveness, are also presented (Figure 13.7). All three are based not on domestic relative prices but on nominal exchange rates adjusted by foreign and domestic price levels. The two most commonly used in the literature are labeled the 'IMF/World Bank index' (the export share-weighted sum of trading partner consumer price indexes, each multiplied by the bilateral exchange rate, divided by the domestic consumer price index) and the 'Morgan-Guaranty index' (in which the two consumer price indexes described above are replaced by foreign and domestic wholesale price indexes, respectively).

Finally, the series labelled 'Preferred index' replaces foreign consumer prices in the numerator of the IMF/World Bank index with foreign wholesale prices, but retains the domestic wholesale price index in the numerator. This index is preferable to either of the other two as a proxy for traded goods prices relative to non-traded goods prices because the share of traded goods in wholesale price indexes is higher than its share in consumer price indexes. Thus the numerator of this index, the export share-weighted sum of foreign wholesale price indexes, each multiplied by the bilateral exchange rate, may be taken as a (very rough) proxy for domestic traded goods prices, and the denominator, the domestic consumer price index, may be taken as a (very rough) index of domestic non-traded goods prices.

For the reasons demonstrated in Warr (1986), all three of these measures, but especially the first two, may be expected to understate the magnitude of a real appreciation, compared with changes in the domestic relative prices of traded goods to non-traded goods. All four measures confirm that a real appreciation did occur but that the magnitude is understated in particular by the IMF/World Bank and the Morgan-Guaranty measures (Figure 13.7).

BANK EXPOSURE

The implication of the above phenomena was a large increase in the exposure of the Thai banking sector to both exchange rate risk and domestic default (Figure 13.8). First, the increased level of banks' foreign indebtedness relative to the lending base of the banks increased their exposure to exchange rate risk. Second, the increased level of bank credit relative to GDP increased their exposure to a domestic contraction. Poor supervision of Thai banks has been widely blamed for their difficulties. There seems little doubt that standards of prudential control were indeed lax, a product of the overconfidence on the part of monetary authorities that also characterised the private sector.

HOW THE 1996 EXPORT SLOWDOWN PRODUCED THE TRIGGER

The underlying causes of the Thai crisis were long-term. The trigger that actually undermined confidence sufficiently to induce a speculative attack on the baht was the collapse of export growth in 1996. Export growth declined from over 20 per cent per year in previous years, a performance which made the high current account deficits of the time seem (almost) sustainable, to around zero in 1996 (Table 13.1). This provoked capital outflow and speculation against the baht because it produced the expectation of a devaluation. Once this expectation developed and portfolio capital exited, the process was unstoppable. The slowdown was widespread among Thailand's export destinations but was greatest in exports to Japan, NAFTA and the Chinese economies. By looking at the composition of exports by commodity it can be seen that the slowdown was concentrated in manufactured exports from labour-intensive industries.

Table 13.1 Thailand: major exports by commodity, 1994–6

	1994	*1995*	*1996*
Total exports (million baht)	1,137,602	1,406,310	1,401,392
Growth rate (%)	20.9	23.6	-0.35
Growth rate by commodity			
Computer and parts	44.9	38.7	31.3
Garments	12.4	1.3	-21.9
Rubber	43.3	46.5	1.4
Integrated circuits	27.5	28.4	3.4
Gems & jewellery	8.3	11.5	8.4
Rice	18.9	24.1	8.4
Sugar	41.2	67.2	11.7
Frozen shrimp	29.9	2.3	-17.8
Television & parts	26.2	12.7	14.1
Shoes & parts	40.5	37.0	-40.9
Canned seafood	24.7	4.1	-0.3
Air conditioner & parts	62.1	49.6	33.6
Plastic products	-29.1	102.2	51.4
Tapioca products	-13.6	-2.8	16.7
Textiles	4.5	22.1	-4.4
15 commodities subtotal (million baht)	611,536	765,734	740,683
Growth rate (%)	20.7	25.2	-3.27
Share in total exports (%)	53.8	54.4	52.9

Source: Bangkok Post, *Year-end Economic Review,* December 1996.

Figure 13.8 Thailand: bank exposure, 1988–98

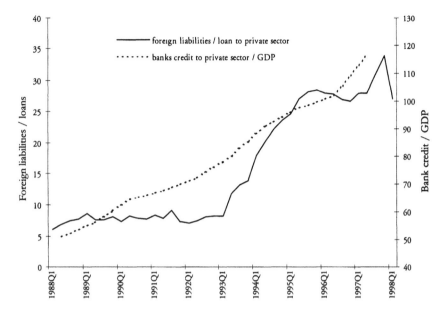

Source: Author's calculations using quarterly data from the Bank of Thailand and quarterly GDP data from National Economic and Social Development Board, Bangkok.

The export slowdown of 1996 did not cause the crisis; it was merely a trigger. In normal circumstances a temporary slowdown in exports would be met by an increased current account deficit, financed by a combination of reduced reserves and temporary borrowing from abroad. This slowdown coincided with an already high current account deficit, equivalent to around 8 per cent of GDP, which, combined with the high level of vulnerability to a crisis which had developed by 1996, affected confidence sufficiently to trigger the expectation of a devaluation, producing a self-reinforcing capital outflow.

The export slowdown of 1996 has attracted many attempts at explanation from observers of the Thai economy. Arranged in what would seem to be increasing order of importance, the causes of the export slowdown given include

- the political events of the previous two years
- monetary policy
- Thailand's trade liberalisation
- the congestion of industrial infrastructure
- falsification of export data to receive value-added tax rebates
- increasing competition in international markets from China since the latter's devaluation in 1994
- a slowdown in demand in importing countries
- and effective appreciation of the baht through pegging to the US dollar while the latter appreciated relative to the yen from late 1995 through 1997.

Each of the above probably played some role in 1996, especially the last, but two other factors appear to have been more important. These were the long-term real appreciation within Thailand resulting from the demand effects of foreign capital inflow, and a closely related phenomenon, a large increase in real wages.

Data on real wages provide a powerful explanation for Thailand's export slowdown and its concentration in labour-intensive industries. Research at the Thailand Development Research Institute has recently produced a reliable series of wage data for Thailand's manufacturing sectors. When these data on average nominal wages in manufacturing are deflated by the consumer price index they indicate that over the fifteen years 1982–96, real wages roughly doubled, but this increase was heavily concentrated in the years since 1990. Over the years 1982–90 the increase was from an index of 100 to 117, an average compound rate of increase of 2 per cent. But over the following six years to 1996 the same real wage index increased to 202, an average annual rate of increase of real wages of 9 per cent.

Both supply and demand-side forces played a role in the real wage increases. During the early stages of Thai economic growth the rising industrial and services sector demand for labour could be satisfied from a very large pool of rural labour with relatively low productivity. The potential supply of unskilled rural labour was so large and so elastic that as workers moved from agriculture to more productive jobs in the manufacturing and services sectors, it was possible for these sectors to expand their levels of employment without significantly bidding up real wages. Thailand at this time was a classic Lewis surplus labour economy. As this process continued that pool of cheap rural labour was largely exhausted, so that by the early 1990s labour shortages were becoming evident. Labour supply was no longer as elastic as it had been. Agricultural industries were themselves experiencing serious problems with seasonal labour shortages. Further increases in the demand for labour outside agriculture then led to rising wages.

Changes in the demand for labour as a consequence of the real appreciation also played a role. Non-tradables are on average more labour-intensive in their production than tradables. As non-tradables prices rose relative to tradables, wages were bid up relative to both tradables and non-tradables prices (the Stolper-Samuelson effect) and wages therefore rose relative to the consumer price index.

With the end of the era of cheap labour, the competitiveness of Thailand's labour-intensive export industries declined. The importance of this point is confirmed by the fact that the export slowdown was concentrated in labour-intensive industries such as garments, footwear and textiles. Thailand's export industries are especially vulnerable to increases in real wages for two basic reasons. First, many of Thailand's most successful export industries are highly labour-intensive, implying that a given increase in real wages has a large effect on their costs. Second, these export industries face highly competitive international markets for their products, where they act as price takers. This means that cost increases cannot be passed on in the form of increases in product prices, whereas producers for the domestic market may have greater scope for doing so.

THE CRISIS AND AFTER

Through late 1996 and the first half of 1997 the Bank of Thailand struggled to maintain the stability of the baht/US dollar exchange rate against speculative attacks. The speculation was fueled by expectations of a devaluation. Despite the insistence of the government and the Bank of Thailand that the exchange rate could be defended, market participants, correctly, did not believe them. The level of official foreign exchange reserves declined from US$40 billion in January 1997 to well under US$30 billion six months later. On 2 July, the Bank of Thailand announced a float of the currency. The rate moved immediately from 25 to 30 baht per US dollar. By January 1998 it was 55 baht/US$, subsequently moderating by February to 45 baht/US$. Late in 1997 IMF assistance was requested, and a stringent package of financial measures was required by the Fund.

The crisis had political casualties. In November 1997, a year after it came into government, the administration of Prime Minister Chavalit Yongchaiyudh was forced to surrender office as its coalition of political parties unraveled. It was replaced by a new coalition government led by Democrat Party leader and former prime minister, Chuan Leekpai, who had led the parliamentary opposition to the Chavalit government. The Chavalit government had lost public confidence, appearing unable to cope with the developing crisis.

The change of government gave Thailand a major political advantage in responding to the crisis that some of its neighbours lacked. The new government did not need to defend itself against blame for the crisis itself. Notwithstanding the parliamentary efforts of the new Opposition, now led by General Chavalit, there seemed little political necessity for debate as to whether foreigners, domestic businessmen or the domestic government were ultimately responsible for the nation's problems. Full attention could be given to instituting the reform package that might resolve the emergency.

There was considerable debate as to what the most appropriate reform package was. The government felt constrained to implement the IMF package and to announce public commitment to it. The package was widely criticised within Thailand, however, and behind the scenes the government was lobbying to have the package modified. The economic crisis produced a contraction of domestic demand much larger than expected by most observers, including the IMF. Private consumption and investment spending declined significantly. Inflation remained low, in spite of the mid-year depreciation of the baht.

The IMF program seemed a copy of packages the Fund had previously devised for Latin American countries burdened with external imbalances associated with massive public sector debt, hyperinflation and low rates of private saving. The external imbalance in Thailand, like most of its neighbours, lacked all of these features. Inflation was relatively low, debt was primarily a private sector problem (US$72 billion out of US$99 billion total external debt) and saving rates remained high. The crisis produced a massive contraction in private spending. The IMF package added a public sector contraction by initially requiring a budget surplus equivalent to 1 per cent of GDP, subsequently relaxed. Moreover, at a time when confidence in the financial sector was essential, the IMF required that problem institutions be closed. Given the circumstances of the time, this requirement seemed to many observers to be ill advised.

While the IMF rescue package was handled poorly, this was not the main failure— the developing crisis had apparently not been foreseen in time and was thus not averted. Some IMF officials have subsequently stated that the Thai government was properly warned during 1996 about the impending danger. If so, the warnings were not made public and cannot be verified. They were also inconsistent with published IMF commentary on Thailand during the immediate pre-crisis period, including Kochhar *et al.* (1996) and the Fund's *Annual Reports*.

The economic boom since the late 1980s had encouraged the Bank of Thailand to remove almost all of its earlier restrictions on movement of financial capital into and out of Thailand. What surprised all observers was the rate at which funds could flow out of the country in response to what seemed small changes in market sentiment, putting irresistible pressure on the Bank of Thailand's foreign exchange reserves. The crucial point was the very large volume of short-term capital that had entered Thailand during the boom. To attract this capital Thailand had removed most of the capital controls that had made maintenance of its fixed exchange rate policy consistent with a degree of monetary independence. The liberalisation meant that speculative attacks on the baht were now much easier. To attract large volumes of financial capital into Thailand it had been necessary to demonstrate not only that entry was open, but that the exit was unobstructed as well. When market expectations moved in favour of a devaluation, the rate of financial outflow was so great that the expected depreciation became inevitable. In January 1998 the influential *Bangkok Post Year-end Economic Review* commented that 'liberalised capital flows but a fixed exchange rate proved to be the undoing of the Thai economy' (*Bangkok Post Year-end Economic Review*:18).

WOULD CAPITAL CONTROLS HAVE MADE A DIFFERENCE?

Thailand had capital controls in place for several decades until they were largely dismantled from 1990 onwards. The controls were justified by the need to regulate speculative and destabilising capital movements. The paradox is that during most of the period when the controls were operative large capital movements were not occurring. Large capital inflows did not begin until around 1987. But during this brief period before they were abolished the controls were indeed inhibiting capital movements and this was a major reason for their removal. The controls were dismissed as anachronistic and unnecessary. Moreover, the forthcoming restoration of Chinese authority in Hong Kong led many to believe that if Thailand's capital markets were liberalised, Bangkok could become a major regional financial centre.

Given the current controversy over the efficacy of capital controls, the question arises as to whether the dismantling of Thailand's capital controls played a significant role in causing the crisis. We shall first review the capital controls Thailand had in place prior to 1990. Over the two decades ending in 1990, four reasons for lack of capital market openness were important: interest rate ceilings, direct capital controls, controls on the foreign exchange positions of commercial banks and the withholding tax on foreign borrowing.

Regulatory ceilings on both domestic lending and borrowing rates prevented the domestic interest rate increases that would otherwise have induced capital inflows when the domestic money supply was contracted. These interest rate ceilings were adjusted only slightly during shocks. Their impact on domestic interest rates seems clear. For example, from 1970 to 1981, commercial banks' deposits rates were equal to the ceiling rates and from 1982 to 1985, the actual time deposit rates of interest paid by commercial banks remained 0.5 per cent below the ceiling.

Bank of Thailand permission was required to move capital out of Thailand and this policy was policed vigorously. During periods of monetary expansion this arm of policy enabled the monetary authorities to prevent the outward flow of capital which would otherwise have deprived them of the capacity to expand the domestic money supply when desired. All outgoing payments were subject to approval. Until 1990, exporters were required to submit foreign exchange currency to banks within seven days after receiving payments from abroad.

Until 1990 holdings of foreign exchange deposits by Thai citizens were not permitted. Thais could not purchase foreign currencies for investment overseas and were thus greatly restricted in taking advantage of differentials between domestic and foreign rates of interest. Individuals were not permitted to take out of Thailand domestic currency exceeding 500 baht (equivalent to around US$20) or foreign currency exceeding US$1,000. In 1993 these limits were 50,000 baht (equivalent to around US$2,000) and US$10,000 of foreign currency. The degree of substitution between domestic and foreign assets was far from perfect; similarly, foreign liabilities were imperfect substitutes for loans obtained from domestic banks, since domestic deficit units could not access foreign capital markets. The government also imposed a limit on the volume of foreign debt of public enterprises.

In addition to the above instruments, the net foreign exchange positions of commercial banks were subject to regulation from 1984. Following the 1984 devaluation, the net future and current position of each commercial bank, whether positive or negative, could not exceed US$5 million or 20 per cent of the net worth of the bank, whichever was smaller. In April 1990, the ceiling on the net position of commercial banks was raised to 25 per cent of capital funds.

A withholding tax was applied to foreign borrowing at rates which were varied by the Minister of Finance either to encourage or discourage foreign capital inflows. This instrument created a tax wedge between the domestic and foreign costs of capital. The withholding tax rate was usually imposed at 10 per cent of the interest payments when the government wanted to reduce the capital inflows, and was exempted when the government considered that the domestic money market was too tight. Exemption was sometimes granted for loans with long maturity periods to attract long-term capital funds. The withholding tax rate was varied significantly from time to time. The adjustments were directed at influencing capital flows for stabilisation purposes.

Did the controls work? Their effectiveness in controlling short-term capital may be assessed by the behaviour of Thai interest rates. Over the period 1970–90, during periods in which the Bank of Thailand had pre-announced its intention to induce a monetary contraction, Thai interest rates rose and the spread between Thai interest rates and LIBOR interest rates increased. The reverse occurred during periods of monetary relaxation (Warr and Nidhiprabha 1996). The point is that this occurred in spite of Thailand's fixed exchange rate. If capital mobility were unrestrained, such an outcome would be impossible because short-term capital flows into or out of the country would defeat the efforts of the Bank of Thailand to influence domestic interest rates.

The impact was small, however, and short-lived. Regulated bank interest rates were clearly affected by the controls (Figure 13.9). However, the medium-term elasticity of short-term capital flows with respect to domestic interest was large (Warr and Nidhiprabha 1996) and although short-run deviations of domestic interest rates from international rates were made possible by the controls, over longer time periods Thai interest rates followed international rates very closely (Figure 13.10). The evidence suggests that capital controls were effective in slowing down the capital flows that lead to interest rate convergence, but that they did not prevent these flows. Considering

Figure 13.9 Thailand and the United States: lending and deposit rates, 1970–90

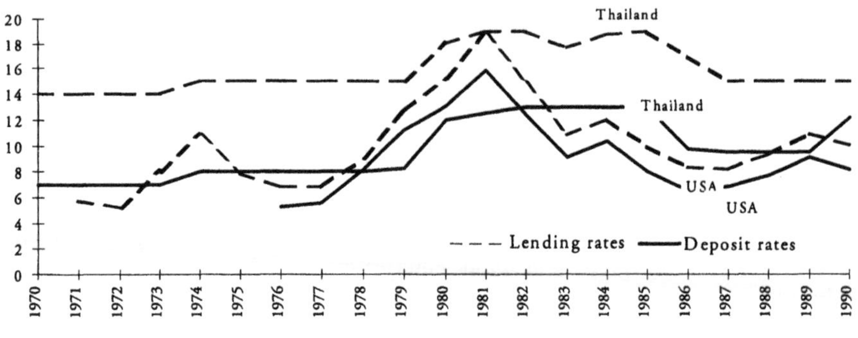

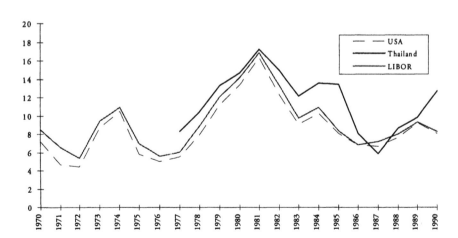

Source: International Monetary Fund, *International Financial Statistics*, various issues.

Figure 13.10 Thailand and international money market interest rates, 1970–90

Source: International Monetary Fund, *International Financial Statistics*, various issues.

the ease with which funds can now be moved internationally, it would seem likely that if the controls had been retained, or were reintroduced today, they would be even less effective than before in regulating capital flows.

The economic debate on the efficacy of capital controls continues and dogmatic positions on either side of this discussion are surely unwarranted by the limited evidence available. Nevertheless, capital controls would not seem to be the answer to preventing the development of vulnerability. If Thailand's capital controls had been left in place in the early 1990s, capital inflows might have been slower, but this alone would not have prevented the development of vulnerability. Still lacking were the properly enforced prudential banking regulations required to prevent overexposure of domestic banks. This was surely a more important matter than whether capital controls remained in place. Thailand would have been better served by the abandonment of the Bank of Thailand's obsession with pegged exchange rates and the attendant danger of exchange rate misalignment. If the exchange rate had been floated, or even devalued significantly, in mid 1996 the crisis might have been averted.

SUMMARY AND CONCLUSIONS

Thailand's crisis must be understood as the collapse of a boom. It was not caused by evil speculators or by corrupt politicians. It was caused by errors of macroeconomic policy, themselves an outcome of complacency arising from a decade of unprecedented economic growth. Central among these policy mistakes was the insistence on retaining a fixed exchange rate when circumstances no longer suited it. The boom produced a euphoria that also led business decision makers to take risks they would not ordinarily have accepted.

The prolonged boom which preceded the crisis was fueled by high levels of foreign direct investment. As the boom developed, these high levels of capital inflow, combined with Thailand's fixed exchange rate policy, set in train a Dutch disease real appreciation under which real wages increased unsustainably, undermining the competitiveness of the traded goods sector. In 1996 this produced a dramatic slowdown in export growth which provoked the expectation of a devaluation.

Over the same pre-crisis period, the vulnerability of the country's foreign exchange reserves to a financial panic had increased substantially. The vulnerability derived from a greatly increased stock of volatile capital which could be presented for conversion into foreign exchange at short notice. The growth of this stock of volatile capital relative to reserves was itself the outcome of macroeconomic policies. First, the attempt to sterilise capital inflows raised domestic interest rates and induced very large inflows of short-term foreign capital. Second, controls on capital movements were largely eliminated in the early 1990s. Third, the Bangkok International Banking Facility, established by the government in 1993, encouraged domestic banks to borrow abroad, short-term. Finally, non-bank financial institutions were encouraged to borrow abroad as well, in the hope of qualifying for highly profitable domestic banking licenses.

Thailand had had capital controls for several decades when they were dismantled from 1990 onwards. The controls were justified by the need to regulate speculative and destabilising capital movements. But during most of the period prior to 1990 large capital movements were not occurring. Large capital inflows did not begin until around 1987, but during this brief period before they were abolished the controls were indeed inhibiting capital movements and that was a major reason for their removal. If Thailand had retained its capital controls, short-term capital flows would have slowed. This may have reduced the rate of growth during the period of economic boom, but would also have restrained the development of vulnerability arising from the build up of stocks of short-term capital. Removal of the capital controls while still retaining a fixed exchange rate was a mistake. Nevertheless, evidence from the period in which these controls were in place suggests that if they had been retained the effect would have been small. Capital controls are not a substitute for effective prudential regulation of the banking sector or for a sensible exchange rate policy.

14 The financial crisis in Korea and its aftermath

A political economic perspective[*]

Hak K. Pyo

The East Asian financial crisis first developed in Thailand in July 1997, quickly spread to Malaysia and Indonesia, and ultimately landed in the Republic of Korea (hereafter Korea). After two years, the crisis-inflicted economies have been somewhat stabilised as a result of IMF rescue plans and restructuring efforts. But the contagion has had a devastating social and economic impact in the region. It has also affected domestic politics and regional security. After two years in painful economic debacle, we are still left with fundamental questions. Why were only certain countries hit by the contagion while others escaped? What was the ultimate cause of the financial crisis? How can we assess the various restructuring programs pursued by the crisis-inflicted governments?

The purpose of this chapter is to provide retrospective answers to these questions by specifically analysing the Korean situation. An in-depth, country-specific analysis of Korea seems warranted because we can learn as much from its failure to avoid the contagion as we can from its economic success story. We need to understand why the economy collapsed, even while the Korean government and international organisations such as the IMF and World Bank insisted that the country's macroeconomic fundamentals remained sound.

Typical interpretations of the 1997 financial crisis in Korea can be summarised as follows. First, the pre-crisis macroeconomic fundamentals were sound, and the collapse did not fit the typical balance of payments crisis model. Foreign debt was fairly low, the fiscal position was strong and the exchange rate was not overvalued. Moreover, notwithstanding the large terms of trade deterioration of 1996–7, the current account deficit remained modest and export growth continued at a remarkable pace (Borensztein and Lee 1998). Second, Korea's crisis was a financial sector crisis, rather than real sector or currency crisis, as a result of cumulated weak loan portfolios and large maturity mismatches in foreign currency operations due to a built-in system of moral hazard (Radelet and Sachs 1998).

Contrary to these interpretations, this chapter advances the following propositions. First, the ultimate cause of the 1997 financial crisis lies in the industrial sector, which could not maintain a regulatory equilibrium due to dramatic changes in both the domestic and international political economy (Pyo 2000). Second, the pre-crisis economic fundamentals were far from sound and stable. There had been continuing decline in the rates of return to capital and the exchange rate regime had been operated out of political motivation by policy authorities and rent-seeking by beneficiaries of foreign capital.

THE POLITICAL ECONOMY OF THE 1997 FINANCIAL CRISIS

The 1997 financial crisis in Korea originated from the failure of macroeconomic stabilisation policy, mainly due to political instability during democratic transition. According to an earlier estimate (Pyo 1994), the optimal growth rate of real GDP for the Korean economy in the mid 1990s was 7.4 per cent. But the actual growth rates of real GDP in 1994 and 1995 were 8.3 per cent and 8.9 per cent. Such high growth was not sustainable. Even though the domestic gross savings ratio hit a record high level of 36.2 per cent in 1993, it was exceeded by even higher domestic investment ratios during the subsequent four years (Table 14.1).

Overinvestment under regulatory equilibrium

Using a simple model of moral hazard, Krugman (1998) has pointedly explained why there was widespread overinvestment in East Asia prior to the region's financial crisis. As outlined further in Pyo (2000), this overinvestment is an oligopolistic regulatory equilibrium as a consequence of industrial development based on the excess competition. Okuno-Fujiwara *et al.* (1980) and Suzumura and Kiyono (1987) have shown that measures taken to stimulate competition can result in an inefficient equilibrium. Assuming that each firm in the industry behaves in a Cournot-Nash fashion and that government can regulate entry into the industry but cannot enforce marginal cost pricing for each firm, the above two studies have shown that, in the long run, the number of firms established in the Cournot-Nash equilibrium with free entry and exit exceeds the so-called second-best number of firms established as a result of maximising total social surplus (the sum of consumers' and producers' surpluses). (Excess competition is distinguished from excessive competition, which refers to a competitive (not oligopolistic) industry with free entry, but where exit does not rapidly occur when excess capacity arises and labour mobility is low). In other words, a regulatory equilibrium with entry restrictions could be welfare-improving and could be used to justify Japan's post-war industrial policy.

This model explains why we observe a larger number of automobile manufacturers, shipbuilders, airlines, oil refineries, semiconductor manufacturers, telecommunication equipment providers, mobile phone companies and so forth in Korea than normally observed in developing or smaller advanced countries. A regulatory equilibrium would be optimal if and only if the following two conditions are met. First, there should be no policy failure on the part of government—the government must know exactly how many firms should exist in each industry. Second, there must be a perfect capital market without moral hazard so that those allowed to enter have almost unlimited access to loans. Thus, the phenomenon of 'too-big-to-fail' sets in—entered firms tend to overinvest in order to survive in the industry, expecting they will be bailed out if they run into trouble.

Table 14.1 Korea: principal economic indicators, 1991–9

	1991	1992	1993	1994	1995	1996	1997	1998	1999*
Per capita income (US$)	6,745.0	6,988.0	7,811.0	8,998.0	10,823.0	11,380.0	10,307.0	6,742.0	8,581.0
Real GDP growth (%)	9.2	5.4	5.5	8.3	8.9	6.8	5.0	-6.9	10.7
Consumption	7.9	5.6	5.4	7.1	8.2	7.2	3.2	-9.8	8.5
Investment	13.3	-0.7	6.3	10.7	11.9	7.3	-2.2	-21.1	4.1
Investment and savings ratio									
Domestic investment ratio	39.1	36.8	35.4	36.5	37.3	38.1	34.4	21.3	27.0
Gross savings ratio	36.1	34.9	36.2	35.5	35.5	33.8	33.4	34.0	33.7
Current account (US$bil.)	-8.3	-3.9	1.0	-3.9	-8.5	-23.0	-8.2	40.0	25.0
Trade account	-6.8	-1.8	2.3	-2.9	-4.4	-15.0	-3.2	41.6	28.7
Exports	70.5	76.2	82.1	95.0	124.6	130.0	138.6	132.3	143.6
(growth rate, %)	(10.5)	(6.6)	(7.3)	(16.8)	(30.3)	(3.7)	(5.0)	(-2.8)	(8.6)
Imports	77.3	78.0	79.8	97.8	129.1	144.9	141.8	93.2	119.7
(growth rate, %)	(16.7)	(0.3)	(2.5)	(22.1)	(32.0)	(11.3)	(-3.8)	(-35.5)	(-28.4)
Nominal wage rate (%)	17.5	15.2	12.2	12.7	11.2	11.9	7.0	-2.5	12.1
CPI (%)	9.2	4.6	5.8	5.6	4.7	4.9	4.4	7.5	0.8
Unemployment rate (%)	2.3	2.4	2.8	2.4	2.0	2.0	2.6	6.8	6.3
Fiscal balance (bil. won)	-1,706.7	-688.5	234.9	1,729.7	1,712.1	108.4	-69.6	-13,219.0	-15,510.0
Money and banking									
Reserve money	18.2	10.9	27.5	9.2	16.3	-12.2	-12.5	-8.1	37.6
(growth rate, %)									
Loans of DMB	20.8	15.0	12.0	18.0	12.2	16.2	13.1	-0.1	24.9
(growth rate, %)									
Yield of corporate bonds	18.9	16.2	12.6	12.9	13.8	11.9	13.4	15.1	8.8
Stock price index	657.1	587.2	728.2	965.7	934.9	833.4	654.5	406.1	806.8
(4 January 1980=100)									
Won/US$ exchange rate	760.8	788.4	808.1	788.7	774.7	844.2	1415.2	1207.8	1,148.4
Foreign debt and investment (US$bil.)									
Gross foreign debt	39.1	42.8	43.9	96.9	127.2	164.3	158.1	149.4	1,364.0
Net foreign debt	11.9	11.1	7.9	23.7	34.9	52.9	52.7	19.6	-9.2
Foreign exchange reserve	13.7	17.2	20.3	25.7	32.7	33.2	20.4	52.0	74.3
Foreign direct investment	1.2	0.7	0.6	0.8	1.8	2.3	2.8	5.4	9.3
Foreign portfolio investment	2.3	5.0	10.6	8.1	13.9	21.2	12.3	-0.3	6.9

Sources: The Bank of Korea, Monthly Bulletin, July 2000; The Ministry of Finance and Economy, Monthly Economy, July 2000.

The consequence of unchecked overinvestment is a rapid decline in the rates of return to capital. According to Pyo and Nam (1999), the economy-wide real rate of return to gross capital stock declined from 25 per cent in the 1970s to 9 per cent in the mid 1990s. The latter was lower than Japan's 12 per cent rate of return. Kwack (1994) reported that the rates of return on net capital stock in Korean manufacturing industries fell very rapidly from 25 per cent in 1972 to 10 per cent in 1990, a rate lower than that in the United States. The profit rate in manufacturing in Korea declined from 7.9 per cent to 0.9 per cent in 1996 (Borensztein and Lee 1998).

Chaebol and *zaibatsu*

The business groups called *chaebol* in Korea may look quite similar to the Japanese *zaibatsu* but they are different in many respects. First, Korean *chaebols* had to rely more extensively on developing export markets than Japanese firms, because Korea's domestic market size was less than 5 per cent of the Japanese domestic market in 1975 (US$20.9 billion compared to US$499 billion in terms of GNP) and less than 9 per cent in 1995 (US$453 billion compared to US$5,156 billion in terms of GNP). As a result, two types of *zaibatsu* could coexist in Japan: one, a highly specialised technology leader in multinational markets (for example, Toyota, Sony and Toshiba), and the other, a business group of horizontally diversified firms (such as the Mitsubishi group, Mitsui group, Sumitomo group and Fuji group). But in Korea only the latter type (including Samsung, Hyundai and Lucky-Goldstar) could be established since specialisation was riskier than diversification under the oligopolistic setting of government regulation on entry and exit in each industry. In addition, diversification through cross-shareholding could generate higher economies of scale in a limited domestic market.

Second, business groups in Korea are governed quite differently from those in Japan. As a result of the dissolution of *zaibatsu* under the MacArthur administration, only a few dominant family groups could own and manage *zaibatsu*. The corporate ownership structure in Japan is thus more diversified than in Korea, and the role of institutional investors is much more important. Consequently, the decision making process and corporate governance in Japan are much more consensus-based than in Korea. Such a difference to ownership structure and governing pattern can make a substantial difference in the outcome of excess competition, because a more consensus-based system can survive better than an authoritarian owner-management system at a time of policy failure and can better protect itself from overextension through a built-in system of checks and balances (Pyo 2000).

CAPITAL MARKET LIBERALISATION BY WEAK GOVERNMENT

Established in the transition from a military-backed authoritarian regime to a seemingly democratic one, the government led by President Kim Young-sam was destined to be weak. As revealed in a series of highly controversial public hearings on political contributions to two ex-presidents, the major forms of political contribution by *chaebols* were an entry fee to the regulated industries or an access fee to government-controlled banks. This system demanded an almost absolute authoritarian power which could command not only a unified window of political contribution but also a unified system of honouring favours in the form of explicit or implicit government directives to ministries and banks. The changed Korean political economy could no longer sustain such a regulatory equilibrium as it became extremely difficult for a non-authoritarian regime to coordinate and monitor political contributions and an effective incentive-distributing system.

A second development in Korea's political economy was the rapid undersupervised opening of the capital market at the time of joining the WTO and accession to the OECD. As the productivity of capital declined and the rate of profit shrank, Korean business groups lobbied for more access to loans at cheaper interest rates, rather than cutting back their pre-emptive or speculative investment demands, because they expected that domestic industries would increasingly be subject to foreign competition. As the gross domestic investment ratio started to exceed the gross domestic savings ratio, business groups looked for foreign sources of funds. These demands were matched by the unchecked inflow of emerging market funds from Japan, the United States and Europe.

Foreign portfolio investment in equity and bonds increased drastically from US$2.3 billion in 1991 to US$21.2 billion in 1996 (Table 14.1). Most direct borrowings by *chaebols* were on an approval basis. Indirect borrowings through banks or finance companies were also subject to government control, generating an environment for rent-seeking. Korean *chaebols* formed a strong alliance for lowering domestic interest rates, liberalising borrowing from abroad and keeping exchange rates fixed. The timing for capital market liberalisation coincided with Korea's accession to the OECD and the inauguration of the WTO. Thus there was momentum from both inside and outside the country for rapid capital market liberalisation.

Most foreign lenders required loan guarantees by domestic banks, which in turn looked for explicit or implicit guarantees from the Bank of Korea. Moral hazard is defined as actions of economic agents in maximising their own utility (to the detriment of others) in situations where they do not bear the full consequences. A system of moral hazard in Korea was created as a result of lack of coordination by an absolute power. For example, in mid 1997 before the impending financial crisis, the Bank of Korea was fighting the Ministry of Finance and Economy over the issue of banking supervision. One of the most damaging developments during the two-month period preceding the December 1997 crisis was domestic political instability, which paralysed the management of the economic system.

The end of the Kim presidency came early in the last year of his term in 1997 as his son was indicted in the highly controversial political scandal involving the bankruptcy of Hanbo Steel Co. By mid October 1997, the ruling party was split into two factions, and the party actually put up two presidential candidates for the December elections. It was apparent that the opposition party led by Kim Dae-jung would have a good chance of winning the election. International investors and foreign banks and firms in Korea felt uneasy because they were not sure of the platform of the opposition party. By late October, Japanese banks, the largest creditors to Korean banks and firms and usually better informed of the political situation in Korea than any other foreign entity in Seoul, started to call in existing loans to Korean banks and declined to extend them. From early November, Korean banks and general trading companies in Tokyo started complaining about the unwillingness of Japanese banks to extend usual credit lines and export–import credits. It was also unfortunate timing for the Japanese banks, because they were being hit hard by the East Asian financial crisis and a series of troubles in domestic financial institutions such as Hokkaido Bank, Yamaichi Securities and the Japan Long-term Credit Bank.

The Bank of Korea and the Ministry of Finance and Economy miscalculated the situation by assuming that most of the short-term foreign loans would be renewed. In a series of massive interventions, they started depleting foreign exchange reserves to defend the won. If they had allowed the complete floating of the won and kept foreign exchange reserves at their end of October level, they could have avoided the massive exodus of foreign capital, as Taiwan had done. At the time, the economic management system as a whole was in fault under a weak presidency. By mid November, most foreign investors realised that economic fundamentals in Korea were not as strong as they had thought and that political uncertainty was greater than initially assessed. They started pulling out funds, leaving most financial institutions in Korea insolvent with short-term debts. The policy authorities realised this after depleting the country's foreign exchange reserves, and had no alternative but to ask help from the IMF. In short, the Korean financial crisis in December 1997 provides yet another example of economic policy failure in the middle of distributive politics.

Park and Song (1998) argue that international investors were mainly responsible for spreading the East Asian contagion and that while macroeconomic similarities may have contributed to the spreading of the Thai crisis to Southeast Asian countries, this did not necessarily apply to Taiwan and Korea. But, considering the magnitude of the IMF bail-out package, it is difficult to place the sole blame for the triggering of financial crisis on foreign investors.

In conclusion, even though there had been a long-term decline in capital productivity and profit rates in Korean industries, the financial crisis of December 1997 could have been avoided by a reasonable economic management system with appropriate checks and balances between the Ministry of Finance and Economy and the Bank of Korea. The political power vacuum near the end of the Kim Young-sam presidency not only invited the outright exodus of foreign capital but also resulted in a devastating failure of policy coordination. In this regard, the immediate cause of the crisis was more political than economic.

IMF-LED AUSTERITY MEASURES: AN ASSESSMENT

The core of the IMF-mandated restructuring programs carried out by the newly elected government were a replica of past IMF programs—a high interest rate policy and tight fiscal policy to restore stability in the foreign exchange market and financial restructuring. They were also combined with World Bank mandates for corporate restructuring. While credit must be given to the IMF-mandated programs for restoring investor confidence and achieving macroeconomic targets, there is much room for improvement in designing a set of policy targets after such crises. As the IMF (1999) itself admitted later, their initial prediction that there would be relatively mild recession and currency depreciation turned out to be wrong, forcing the IMF to allow crisis-inflicted East Asian governments to implement expansionary fiscal programs. To put the initial IMF-led policy response in perspective, pre-crisis compared to post-crisis movements in the areas of monetary policy, fiscal policy and capital flows are examined.

Monetary and fiscal policy

The immediate cause of the crisis was not a lack of domestic savings or reckless fiscal deficits but rather a temporary lack of liquidity in foreign exchange reserves due to cumulated overinvestment, which was accelerated by the political crisis. The fiscal balance showed continuous surpluses during 1993–6 (Table 14.1). The current account deficit was manageable, even though in 1996 it reached 4.4 per cent of GDP. Therefore, as Corden (1999) suggests, fiscal policy should have been modestly expansionary rather than drastically contractionary.

Monetary policy should also have been shock-absorbing rather than shock-creating. The growth rate of reserve money was already negative (-12.2 per cent) in 1996, reflecting the slowdown in business investment well before the financial crisis (Table 14.1 and Figure 14.1). Due to the sharp reduction in reserve money before the crisis, the meager increase during the first half of 1998, and the further reduction in the second half of 1998, there was a massive credit crunch (Table 14.2 and Figure 14.1). Loans of deposit monetary banks decreased (rather than increased) during the second half of 1998. Policy authorities overreacted to achieve unrealistic monetary policy goals at a time of liquidity crisis and almost non-existent inflationary pressure due to a drastic drop in aggregate demand.

Financial restructuring should have been viewed as a medium-term goal rather than a short-run response to the crisis. The drastic reduction in reserve money reflects closures of several banks and finance companies during 1998. To compensate for these closures, there should have been a more flexible reserve money policy so that usual business operations, including export and import loans, could be financed routinely. During the first six months or so after the break out of the Korean financial crisis in December 1997, even companies with good credit standing could not finance some routine activities notwithstanding new investment. Considering the fact that high debt-equity ratios cannot be reduced overnight, the sudden imposition of the Bank for International Settlements' standard to banks and finance companies was too ambitious. Such drastic measures can hardly be justified at a time of abnormal liquidity shortage.

Foreign capital inflow: composition and volatility

Since the financial crisis in Korea erupted with the sudden exodus of foreign capital and non-renewal of short-term loans, it is important to examine the movement of foreign capital in both the pre-crisis and post-crisis periods. Foreign debt status and the exchange rate are closely related, so these statistics need to be considered simultaneously.

The decomposition of foreign investment into foreign direct investment and foreign portfolio (stocks and bonds) investment indicates that there was a large inflow of foreign bonds investment before the financial crisis in December 1997 (Tables 14.1 and 14.2 and Figure 14.2). After the crisis, investment in stocks increased steadily while investment in bonds was volatile, decreasing again from the third quarter of 1998. The magnitude of foreign direct investment has occupied a minor portion of overall foreign investment and remained quite stable in both the pre-crisis and post-crisis periods. Therefore, we can conclude that the large inflow of mutual funds and hedge funds into Korea's bond market, which had just begun to open before the crisis, and its sudden exodus was another immediate cause of the financial crisis in 1997.

Table 14.2 Korea: economic indicators before and after the currency crisis of December 1997

	1997				1998				1999	
	I	II	III	IV	I	II	III	IV	I	II
Interest rates (%) (end of period)										
CD (91 days)	13.23	11.79	13.39	18.55	22.60	16.93	10.37	7.70	6.92	6.20
Corporate bond (3 years)	12.69	11.65	12.36	24.31	18.94	16.64	12.51	8.30	8.55	8.06
Call rate (overnight)	12.91	11.17	13.17	21.29	23.48	15.71	8.21	6.72	4.98	4.79
Money and banking (end of period) (growth rate, %)										
Reserve Money	-24.7	-12.4	-21.8	-12.5	7.7	0.3	-1.1	-8.1	1.7	3.1
Loans of DMB	20.8	18.8	13.9	13.1	12.2	6.3	-2.4	-0.1	-1.8	6.7
Unemployment										
Rate (%)	3.1	2.5	2.2	3.1	6.5	7.0	7.3	7.9	8.0	6.2
1,000 persons	646	550	470	561	1,182	1,485	1,600	1,586	1,750	1,435
Production and investment (growth rate, %)										
Industrial production	4.4	6.2	7.2	3.6	-6.2	-12.2	-9.5	-1.6	12.5	22.7
Machinery orders	19.0	16.1	22.7	6.3	-18.8	-25.4	-15.4	-11.4	8.4	31.8
Balance of payments (US$bil.)										
Current account	-7.4	-2.7	-2.1	4.0	10.8	10.9	9.6	8.7	6.2	6.5
Trade account	-5.4	-0.8	-0.03	3.1	9.7	11.3	10.4	9.8	6.6	7.7
Exports (growth rate, %)	-5.6	7.1	15.6	3.6	8.4	-1.8	-10.8	-5.5	-5.9	3.1
Imports (growth rate, %)	3.9	0.8	-3.8	-14.8	-36.1	-37.0	-39.9	-28.7	8.1	22.3
Exchange rate (end of period)										
Won/US$	897.1	888.1	914.8	1,415.2	1,378.8	1,385.2	1,373.6	1,207.8	1,224.7	1,155.9
Average stock price index (end of period)	656.7	765.2	676.5	390.3	523.0	313.3	312.2	524.7	586.2	841.4
Foreign investment (US$mil.)										
FDI	-507	-226	-661	-212	-335	346	491	114	619	1,272
Portfolio investment	2,595	5,829	5,444	428	3,806	568	-3,877	-2,374	953	4,365
Other investment	2,128	1,124	-4,021	-9,999	-5,131	1,102	438	1,428	-480	-6,550
National accounts (growth rate, %)										
GDP	4.9	6.2	5.5	3.6	-3.6	-7.2	-7.1	-5.3	4.6	8.9
Consumption	4.1	4.1	4.9	-0.1	-8.4	-9.7	-8.9	-5.8	5.0	6.6
(Private)	4.5	4.4	5.3	-0.1	-9.9	-11.2	-10.4	-6.9	6.3	8.3
Investment	0.8	2.2	-3.6	-7.2	-20.6	-23.7	-22.2	-17.9	-4.3	4.9
(Equipment)	4.2	1.3	-12.6	-25.9	-38.3	-46.1	-39.3	-27.4	12.9	37.2
(Structure)	-1.9	2.9	2.7	4.5	-5.9	-7.8	-12.0	-13.7	-13.7	-8.5

Sources: The Bank of Korea, *Monthly Bulletin*, September 1999; Ministry of Finance and Economy, *Monthly Economy*, September 1999.

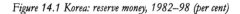

Figure 14.1 Korea: reserve money, 1982–98 (per cent)

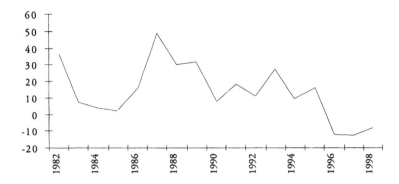

Source: The Bank of Korea, 1999. *Monthly Bulletin*, April, Seoul.

Figure 14.2 Korea: foreign investment by type, 1987–98 (US$million)

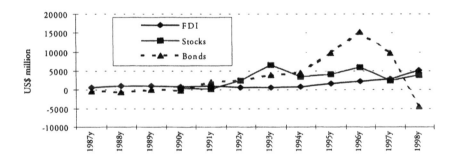

Source: The Ministry of Finance and Economy, 1999. *Monthly Bulletin*, May, Seoul.

One of the most significant determinants for foreign investment is the movement and outlook for exchange rates. The exchange rate was kept almost fixed at around 800 won per US dollar during 1992–6 and started depreciating during the first half of 1997 (Tables 14.1 and 14.2 and Figure 14.3). But the magnitude of change was too timid and the speed of adjustment too slow due to the market intervention by the Bank of Korea. Since the fourth quarter of 1998, the exchange rate has been stable at around the 1,200 won per US dollar. Thus, we may conclude that the won was kept overvalued by about 33 per cent during the pre-crisis period. The overvaluation of the won was another major factor contributing to the sudden exodus of foreign capital when investors realised that economic fundamentals in Korea were not strong enough to warrant further investments.

Even though the net foreign debt in 1996 (US$52.9 billion) was only 10.2 per cent of Korea's nominal GDP for the year (US$520 billion), gross foreign debt in 1996 (US$164.3 billion) reached 31.6 per cent of the year's nominal GDP (Figure 14.4).

Figure 14.3 Korea: exchange rate (versus US$), 1984–98

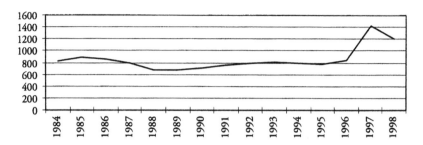

Source: Bank of Korea, 1999. *Economic Statistics Yearbook*, Seoul.

Figure 14.4 Korea: foreign debt, 1982–98 (US$million)

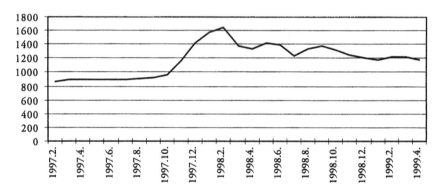

Source: The Ministry of Finance and Economy, 1999. *Monthly Bulletin*, May, Seoul.

The gross debt increased almost four-fold between 1993 and 1996. As of 29 December 1997, Korea's gross debt was US$153 billion, of which 52.4 per cent (US$80.2 billion) was short-term debt with maturity of less than a year (Pyo 1999:153). The relevant magnitude during financial crises is gross debt rather than net debt (defined as gross debt minus the country's foreign assets) because most foreign assets cannot be readily liquidated due to heavy transaction costs and lack of time and information. In addition, some foreign assets can be almost useless bad loans or accounts receivable. Therefore, the ratio of usable foreign reserves to total amount of short-term debt serves as a better indicator than that of foreign reserves to net debt outstanding. As outlined in Pyo (1999), there were two issues at hand after the IMF-led South Korea bail out. One was the imminent issue of following up the debt restructuring plan concluded between the Korean government and creditor banks. Since there were not enough official resources available from IMF, World Bank and G7 countries combined that could replace all the loans maturing, private creditor banks had to accept a new arrangement. Even though banks from different countries had different interests at stake, it was doubtful any bank would pull the plug on the eleventh largest country in the world. The East Asian crisis needed to be stopped in Korea. Otherwise, there was no guarantee it would not spill over to Japan, China, and ultimately to Europe and the United States.

Unlike the bail out of Latin debts in the 1980s, in which banks were required to reduce interest charges, none of the banks owed money from Korea was expected to incur such losses because they would receive higher interest rates on the loans being rolled over to compensate for their high risk. In addition, South Korea had a good track record in paying off loans from the IMF, World Bank and commercial banks in the 1980s.

In the end, the Korean government managed to agree with major creditor banks to restructure outstanding loans by the end of April 1998. Such an agreement sent a strong signal for market stability so that the won/US$ exchange rate started to stabilise significantly during the second quarter of 1998. The IMF-led bail out was necessary but not sufficient to solve the liquidity problem. The bilateral agreement between the Korean government and creditor banks played a crucial role in putting the economy back on the recovery track.

WELFARE LOSS AND RESTRUCTURING PROGRAMS

It is still too early to assess fully the entire social and economic impact on Korean society of the 1997 financial crisis. But it appears certain that almost every segment of social life has been devastatingly affected by the crisis; its impact will no doubt be felt over a much longer period of time than anticipated initially. With the break out of crisis by the announcement of the record (US$57 billion) IMF-led bail-out package on 5 December 1997, the won/US$ exchange rate soared from the pre-crisis level of 900 won per US dollar to 1,950 won per US dollar. The call rate reached 30 per cent at one time during the month. The magnitude of the credit crunch was so severe that many exporters could not even negotiate letters of credit. The growth rate of reserve money declined by 12.5 per cent and 8.1 per cent by the end of 1997 and 1998 respectively (Table 14.2). The growth rate of total loans of deposit monetary banks dropped from 13.1 per cent to -0.1 per cent during the same period.

Welfare loss and widening income inequality

As the IMF-mandated austerity measures continued during 1998, both the growth rate of industrial production and machine orders fell dramatically, by 7.3 per cent and 17.9 per cent respectively (Table 14.2). Within one year of the crisis, the unemployment rate had increased from 2.2 per cent to 7.4 per cent, leaving 1.6 million people unemployed by the end of 1998. The growth rate of real GDP plummeted from 5.0 per cent in 1997 to -5.8 per cent in 1998. During 1998, real consumption and investment fell by 8.2 per cent and 21.1 per cent (Table 14.1). After the exchange rate realignment, per capita income fell from US$10,037 to US$6,823.

According to a report by the Bank of Korea (1999), the amount of net outflow of real gross national income (GNI) to foreign nationals in 1998 reached 27.4 trillion won (6.9 per cent of real GDP) due to the fast deterioration of terms of trade, which continued to decline from a base of 100 in 1995 to 85.7 by 1998. As a result, the growth rate of real GNI, which accounts for the deteriorating terms of trade, was a lot slower than that of real GDP, which explains the terrible loss of economic welfare from the crisis.

A more troubling aspect of social disintegration is found in widening income and wealth inequality. The rich, who held financial assets when the crisis broke out, earned interest income at an annual interest rate of above 20 per cent as a result of the credit crunch. Then, as interest rates started to lower from the end of 1998, they quickly moved to the stock and bonds market—the average stock price index more than doubled from 400 to above 800 between December 1998 and June 1999. But the poor and the unemployed did not have such leverage to adjust to the turbulent economic conditions.

According to the 1998 Annual Report on the Family Income and Expenditure Survey by the National Statistical Office (1999), the labour and capital income of the highest 10 per cent in 1998 increased by 8 per cent, while that of the other 90 per cent of income earners decreased sharply. In particular, the income of the bottom 20 per cent declined by 17.2 per cent, while the average rate of income reduction in the entire sample was 9.9 per cent. The ratio of absolute poverty among wage and salary earners increased from 3.0 per cent in 1997 to 6.8 per cent in 1998 (Moon and Yoo 1999).

Government-led restructuring programs

The new government led by President Kim Dae-jung aimed at restoring foreign investors' confidence as the first priority, because in the short run it would be difficult to recover from the crisis without injecting foreign capital again. The government also pursued an almost simultaneous restructuring of the banking and corporate sectors. The core of the financial restructuring was the injection of public funds into troubled banks and the sale of two banks and other bank stocks to foreign capital (Table 14.3).

The main thrust of the plan was the initiative taken by the newly established Financial Supervisory Commission. Between November 1997 and December 1998, a total of 40.9 trillion won was injected to restructure the financial sector—19.9 trillion won for the purchase of non-performing loans, 13.2 trillion won for recapitalisation and loss coverage of failing banks and 7.8 trillion won for deposit payment.

Table 14.3 Outline of financial sector restructuring in Korea since the financial crisis (trillion won)

Category	Amount injected Nov. 1997–Dec. 1999	Amount to be injected by 1999	Total
Purchase of non-performing loans	19.9	12.6	32.5
Recapitalisation and loss coverage	13.2	4.3	17.5
Deposit payment	7.8	6.2	14.0
Total	40.9	23.1	64.0

Source: Ministry of Finance and Economy press release, 29 December 1998.

While the injection of massive public funds in such extraordinary circumstances is understandable, it is not clear why the burden of restructuring should have fallen on taxpayers—why not on management, labour unions and stockholders? The validity and the efficiency of the Financial Supervisory Commission's direct involvement from the exchange of letter of intent to the final signing of the sales contract of the banks to the private foreign investors is also questionable. A responsible body representing stockholders, management, labour and creditors should have been appointed; and this body should have negotiated deals with foreign counterparts. It is not clear why stocks of failing banks were sold to foreigners rather than domestic residents. Still more troubling is why the IMF and World Bank either condoned such plans or remained silent about the legitimacy of using public funds in such an arbitrary way. If there were precedents for this in times of economic crisis, they should have clarified their positions in public.

The corporate restructuring programs have been handled in an even more heavy-handed way. Virtually all the implementation plans involve only the top five *chaebols* (called the Top 5) (Table 14.4). While no one doubts that their economic power is enormous and that they must be held responsible for overinvestment and reckless diversification, they alone cannot be held accountable for everything that went wrong. As pointed out in Pyo (1999), the Korean *chaebols* could not develop like their Japanese *zaibatsu* counterparts. Since the domestic market size of Korea is less than 5 per cent the size of Japan, *chaebols* could not specialise in one industry like Sony, Toyota and Toshiba—since each industry was regulated explicitly or implicitly by the government, it was too risky for the *chaebol* to specialise in a single business line.

The direct involvement of the government in so-called big deals will exercise a far-reaching negative impact on the relationship between government and business. The government should have reformed the banking sector sequentially by first inviting foreign capital and appointing foreign directors as board members of banks. Then, it should have allowed the new bank management to assess each *chaebol's* financial situation and recommend a set of corporate restructurings, possibly including big deals. One of the most damaging aspects of the current big deals is that they will encourage another round of moral hazard among the Top 5 rather than eliminate it. Now each *chaebol* can blame the government for forced deals, claiming it was a loser rather than a beneficiary of such deals.

Moreover, the government's concentration on the Top 5 in its efforts at corporate restructuring sent an incorrect but strong signal to the market that only the Top 5 would be safe in periods of financial turmoil. In other words, government policy created economy-wide moral hazard by making the power of the Top 5 even greater than before. According to the Security Exchange Commission, the Top 5 are lagging far behind in restructuring efforts. While their assets occupy more than 40 per cent of the total assets held by listed firms, their asset restructuring since November 1997 occupies only 3.2 per cent (3.5 trillion won) of total asset restructuring by all listed firms (111.9 trillion won). After the restriction on the top thirty *chaebols* total investment was abolished in February 1998, total investment by the top thirty *chaebols* in their subsidiaries fell by 44 billion won as of September 1998, but investment by the Top 5 increased by 3.4 trillion won. According to the Financial Supervisory Commission,

Table 14.4 Outline of corporate restructuring in Korea after the financial crisis

Business restructuring for core competence includes
* exit of non-viable affiliates
* creditor bank limits on loans to non-viable affiliates
* top 5 *chaebols'* sell-off, M&A and recapitalisation
* ensuring Top 5 *chaebols'* independent management systems are based on transparency and responsibility
* big deal restructuring among Top 5 *chaebols* with creditor banks under the Corporate Structure Improvement Plan in the areas of petrochemicals, aircraft and railroad vehicles; power generation facilities and ship engines; semiconductors; oil refining; and automobiles and electronics. This is to be concluded by December 1998 and co-signed by five government ministers to ensure implementation according to schedule.

Elimination of cross guarantees. Top 5 *chaebols* will eliminate cross-guarantees among its subsidiaries with different business lines by 31 December 1998 and all cross-guarantees by 31 March 2000.

Substantial improvement of capital structure. Top 5 *chaebols* and their creditor banks will revise arrangements under the Capital Structural Improvement Plan by 15 December 1998, including implementation plans of debt-equity swap and sell-off of non-core affiliates. Enhancement of transparency of corporate management. Top 5 *chaebols* are to prepare a combined financial statement starting from financial year 1999, be run by a board of directors with independent auditors and are not to subsidise their affiliates through inappropriate internal transactions.

Source: The Ministry of Finance and Economy.

while the Top 5 *chaebols* reduced their bank loans by 22 trillion won, they have almost monopolised corporate bonds and the CP market by raising a new 38.3 trillion won. Even in the middle of the financial crunch, the Top 5 have been entering deregulated markets such as life insurance and telecommunication services.

One of the remarkable features of industrial development in Korea was the high degree of competition among the top thirty or more *chaebols* (Pyo 1999). The Top 5 had to compete not only among themselves but also with other smaller, more specialised *chaebols*. But big deals are creating still wider gaps between the two groups of *chaebols*. The silence of the IMF and World Bank on the legitimacy or the efficiency of the direct involvement by the Korean government in corporate restructuring and big deals is very troubling. Some local newspapers claim that the IMF and World Bank primarily represent the interests of industrial nations and that they are condoning big deals to weaken the power of *chaebols*, which are their potential competitors. In fact, the IMF and World Bank are being blamed for the wrong reason. The industrial nations have made concerted efforts to help arrange IMF rescue packages for Korea, but the IMF and the World Bank have condoned the reinvigorated oligopolistic policies of the Korean government.

The major big deal between Samsung and Daewoo, which envisioned the swap of Samsung's ailing automobile company with Daewoo Electronics Company, failed. Samsung automobile company has been put into court-ordered receivership, and the

Daewoo group itself has been put into a de facto work-out program. Again, by government initiative, Daewoo's creditor banks and financial companies have decided to inject a record amount of new loans (6.5 trillion won, or approximately US$5.4 billion) to keep the group afloat. Despite incurring a tremendous social cost, the government-led big deals have not produced positive results but rather have created another round of moral hazard and the postponement of corporate restructuring by the troubled companies.

CONCLUDING REMARKS

The Korean economy started to stabilise from the second half of 1998 (Table 14.2). By mid 1999, the won/US$ exchange rate had stabilised at 1,200 won per US dollar. The growth rate of real GDP was -5.8 per cent for the entire year of 1998, but started to recover from the first quarter of 1999, recording an increase of 4.6 per cent. The stock price index had recovered from the lowest point of 312.2 at the end of the third quarter in 1998 to its pre-crisis level of 676.5 (at the end of the third quarter of 1997) by the end of the first quarter in 1999. By the end of the second quarter, it had reached 900, considerably surpassing the pre-crisis level. Usable foreign exchange reserves increased from US$12.4 billion at the end of January 1998 to US$54.5 billion at the end of March 1999 and to over US$60 billion by the end of June 1999. This is a rather impressive rebound from the deep recession caused by the financial crisis. However, as the failure of the government-led big deals illustrates, it will be difficult to sustain growth momentum given Korea's huge outstanding debt and the political uncertainty inherent in the process of democratisation unless Korea succeeds in continuing its reforms in both financial and industrial sectors.

The Korean financial crisis should be seen as a combination of market failure and policy failure. It is important to realise that a volatile capital market in a developing economy can create a combination of moral hazard and weak banking supervision, particularly in times of political crisis, and that financial crisis is usually preceded by a long period of decline in rates of return and profitability in the real sector.

The timely IMF-led intervention was necessary but not sufficient to restore the crisis-inflicted economy to financial stability. The concerted action by G7 countries to endorse the IMF programs and to provide indirect guarantees for the IMF loans was inevitable. More importantly, the agreement between the local government and its creditor banks was the sufficient condition to fully restore market confidence.

It is important for economic institutions in Korea to learn from past mistakes. Korea has to learn how to institutionalise systems of conflict management. While the government is succeeding in restoring investor confidence and stabilising exchange rates, it is repeating the mistake of resorting to non-market means to solve what is essentially market failure. The creation of two widening gaps after the crisis—income disparity between the rich and the poor and an industrial disparity between the Top 5 *chaebols* and the other *chaebols*—is a most disturbing phenomenon because smaller disparities were the main engine of growth in the Korean economy.

NOTE

* An earlier version of this paper was written while the author was visiting professor at the Faculty of Economics, University of Tokyo during September 1998–August 1999. It was presented at the Asia-Pacific Security Policy Seminar on 10 June 1999, organised by the Southeast Asia Studies Program, the Paul H. Nitze School of Advanced International Studies (SAIS), Johns Hopkins University, Washington, DC. I am indebted to Karl Jackson and participants at the SAIS seminar for their helpful comments.

Part 6

East Asian experiences with capital controls

15 Capital mobility, crisis and adjustment

Evidence and insights from Malaysia

Prema-Chandra Athukorala

Every major economic crisis stimulates rethinking of the fundamental economic paradigms. A key focus of the brainstorming triggered by the East Asian crisis of 1997–9 has been the role of international capital mobility in making countries susceptible to crises and the rationale behind the use of capital controls as a crisis management tool. This chapter contributes to this debate by examining the Malaysian experience through the crisis. Malaysia provides an interesting case study given its significant capital market liberalisation prior to the onset of the crisis, and its bold move to break with the ideological consensus in crisis management that has governed international financial relations over much of the post-war period. A key theme running through the chapter is the role of domestic macroeconomic policy in determining the developmental gains that a country can reap from international capital mobility, while maintaining domestic economic stability.

THE PRE-CRISIS CAPITAL ACCOUNT REGIME

Malaysia's development success is widely attributed to its long-standing commitment to maintaining a pro-market and outward-oriented policy stance. Despite the early emphasis on import substitution and aborted attempts in the 1970s to promote heavy industries via public sector participation, Malaysian policy makers have, by and large, stayed clear of quantitative import restrictions as a policy tool. Tariff rates were relatively high in the 1960s, but were reduced progressively across the board in the ensuing 20 years. Although exporters were required to repatriate foreign currency sales proceeds within six months, this was not a binding constraint on production for export as the import trade regime remained highly liberal. Despite mandatory approval procedures, the exchange rules relating to all current account transactions remained liberal. With this policy orientation, Malaysia achieved Article VIII status (for current account convertibility) under the IMF Articles of Agreement on 11 November 1968, becoming the fourth Asian country to enter this country league after Hong Kong (15 February 1961), Japan (1 April 1964) and Singapore (9 November 1968).

A natural companion to outward-oriented trade policy was a firm commitment to foreign direct investment promotion. Foreign direct investment approval procedures and restriction on foreign equity ownership were very liberal by the developing country standards even in the 1950s and 1960s, when hostility towards multinationals was common in the developing world. This emphasis on foreign direct investment promotion received added impetus with a notable shift in development policy towards export-oriented industrialisation in the early 1970s. In 1970 legislation provided for the establishment of special export processing zones, which allowed 100 per cent foreign ownership and exemption from general labour legislation (including employment quotas for *bumiputras* (ethnic Malays)) for export-oriented investors.

The policy regime relating to non-foreign direct investment capital inflows and outflow of capital was liberal throughout the post-war period compared to most other developing countries (Williamson and Mahar 1998). However, liberalisation in this sphere was generally more cautious by Malaysia's own record of trade liberalisation. Even so, the 1970s saw removal of most restrictions. By the end of the decade, the few remaining controls included ceilings of RM1 million on foreign currency borrowing by residents and RM10 million on domestic borrowing by non-resident controlled companies. While the limit on foreign currency borrowing was flexible as far as productive purposes were concerned, in general, Bank Negara Malaysia continued to apply the borrowing limit for prudential supervision of the country's external assets and liabilities (Yusof *et al.* 1994; BNM 1994). Residents were free to place deposits abroad, lend to non-residents, purchase immobile properties or invest in foreign equity, provided such investments were not financed by borrowing in Malaysia.

Further liberalisation of capital controls was an important element in policy reforms initiated in the late 1980s. As part of the government's objective of promoting the Kuala Lumpur Stock Exchange, foreign share holdings of local brokerage firms was increased from 30 per cent to 49 per cent. Tax rates for both foreign and local fund managers were reduced from 30 per cent to 10 per cent. In October 1990, the Malaysian government launched a program to develop Labuan Island as an international offshore financial centre. It was envisaged that, with the Asia Pacific region emerging as the fastest growing region in the world, Labuan would play a key role in enhancing the attractiveness of Malaysia as a world investment centre (BNM 1994:45–7). Licensed offshore banks, offshore insurance entities and other offshore companies operating in Labuan were declared non-residents for exchange control purposes. This initiative enabled these institutions to freely operate foreign currency accounts and move funds into and out of Malaysia without being subject to any exchange control monitoring. Licensed offshore banks were also permitted to accept deposits and grant loans in foreign currency. Investment guidelines were liberalised to allow Malaysian fund management companies to form joint ventures with foreign fund management companies. Management companies of unit trust funds located in Labuan were permitted to invest in Malaysian securities. A generous tax exemption was granted on 65 per cent of income from Labuan-based firms and expatriates in Labuan have to pay tax on only 50 per cent of income.

In late 1993 the ringgit came under strong buying pressure as the booming economy created expectations about the currency's increasing strength. Speculators brought ringgit in large amounts, increasing short-term deposits and forward transactions. In order to avoid an adverse effect on export competitiveness from a sharp exchange rate appreciation, the central bank imposed a number of restrictions on capital inflow during January–February 1994. These restrictions included ceilings on external liabilities of commercial banks, a ban on sales of short-term debt instruments to foreigners, restricting ringgit deposits of foreign institutions to non-interest-bearing accounts, prohibiting non-trade-related currency swaps and a new maintenance charge on non-interest-bearing foreign deposits. Once speculative pressure subsided and the exchange rate returned to its late 1993 level, the central bank gradually removed the controls and freed capital flows, completely lifting all restrictions by August 1994 (World Bank 1996:67–8). These capital controls appeared drastic and, like in the case of the recent capital control episode, led to considerable speculation about capital flight from Malaysia (and from other East Asian countries). In particular, there was a widespread concern about a possible future contraction in foreign investment flows to Malaysia, both portfolio investment and foreign direct investment (*Asian Wall Street Journal*, 17 February 1994). Against these predictions, capital inflows to the country continued to expand at an increasing rate during the ensuing three years.

CAPITAL FLOWS AND SIGNS OF VULNERABILITY

Foreign capital inflows to Malaysia have historically been dominated by foreign direct investment. Even in the first half of 1990s, foreign direct investment accounted for almost 70 per cent of total net capital flows (Table 15.1). From the mid 1980s, there was a boom in the amount of foreign direct investment coming into the country—between 1987 and 1991 foreign direct investment inflows increased almost ten-fold. From 1991 until the onset of the recent financial crisis, the volume of foreign direct investment flowing to Malaysia remained higher than to any of the other ASEAN countries.

As foreign direct investment inflows were more than sufficient to finance the current account deficit and to generate a surplus in the basic balance, there was no need for Malaysia to resort to large-scale external borrowing. At the same time, the Malaysian

Table 15.1 Malaysia: net capital inflow, 1990–7

	1990	1991	1992	1993	1994	1995	1996	1997	1990–6
Total (US$ million)	1,789	5,584	6,607	10,799	1,235	7,612	9,416	2,729	6,149ᵇ
(% GDP)	4.2	11.9	11.3	16.8	1.7	8.7	9.5	2.8	13.9
Composition (% of total)									
Official long term	-58.7	3.5	-0.9	-3.6	11.8	-1.1	-1.1	60.6	-3.1
Private	158.7	96.5	100.9	103.6	88.2	101.1	101.1	39.4	103.1
Foreign direct investment	130.6	71.5	78.1	46.4	335.2	55.2	53.7	187.3	69.5
Portfolio investment	-10.6	-12.6	46.8	92.4	433.6	28.2	37.1	-370.8	53.8
Bank credit	38.7	37.6	7.5	-34.7	-680.5	19.0	10.3	222.9	-15.0

Notes: ᵃ Net capital flows comprise net direct foreign investment, net portfolio investment (equity and bond flows) and official and private bank borrowings. Changes in national foreign exchange reserves are not included. For each country, the difference between total and private flows represents net official flows. ᵇ Annual average.
Source: Bank Negara Malaysia, *Monthly Statistical Bulletin*, Kuala Lumpur (various issues).

central bank, unlike its counterparts in Indonesia, Thailand and Korea, continued to maintain prudential regulations on foreign borrowing by the corporate sector. Consequently there was no significant accumulation of foreign currency borrowing in the lead up to the crisis in Malaysia (Table 15.1). Malaysia's foreign debt remained between 25–30 per cent of GNP while the debt-service ratio (the ratio of debt payments and interest payments to export earnings) varied in the range 6.3–8.5 per cent during 1989–96, both remarkably low by developing country standards (Table 15.2). There was, however, an explosion in foreign capital flows to the Malaysian sharemarket from the early 1990s. This new form of reliance on foreign financing combined with weaknesses in corporate governance quickly overwhelmed prudential bank borrowing practices to generate financial fragility.

Capital market liberalisation initiatives in Malaysia in the early 1990s coincided with the growing enthusiasm of hedge funds and other institutional investors for investing in emerging-market economies (World Bank 1996). Thus, there was a significant increase in the net inflow of portfolio investment. These capital inflows, driven primarily by the boom in the Malaysian sharemarket, accounted for 45 per cent of total annual capital inflow in 1996 compared to 13 per cent in the previous year. Thus, the volume of volatile capital, defined to cover both short-term borrowings and portfolio capital, had increased to sizable levels by the mid 1990s, resulting in an erosion in the country's ability to defend against a speculative attack on the domestic currency (Table 15.3 and Figure 15.1). The degree of reserve cover provided for mobile capital declined from over 150 per cent in the early 1990s to 63 per cent by mid 1997.

Table 15.2 Malaysia: external debt, 1990–8

	1990	1991	1992	1993	1994	1995	1996	1997	1998	1990–6
Total (US$ billion)	17.0	18.5	21.9	26.9	28.1	34.0	39.0	60.8	40.8	26.3[a]
(% of GDP)	39.6	39.3	37.7	41.9	38.7	38.9	39.2	62.2	91.8	39.3
Composition	100	100	100	100	100	100	100	100	100	100
Medium and long-term debt[b]	90.4	85.9	76.5	75.0	80.7	80.9	74.3	74.7	82.2	79.6
Federal govt	53.9	49.9	37.4	28.0	20.1	15.7	10.7	7.6	9.3	27.0
NFPEs[c]	25.7	22.9	20.4	24.6	27.7	32.2	29.9	30.7	33.3	26.9
Private sector	10.8	13.2	18.7	22.4	32.9	33.0	33.7	36.4	39.5	25.7
Short-term debt[d]	9.6	14.1	23.5	25.0	19.3	19.1	25.7	25.3	17.8	20.4
Banking sector	9.6	14.1	23.5	25.0	13.4	13.3	17.4	18.9	12.3	16.8
Non-bank private sector	0.0	0.0	0.0	0.0	6.0	5.8	8.3	6.4	5.5	3.6
External debt service ratio[e]										
Total	8.3	6.9	9.3	6.4	5.5	6.6	6.9	5.5	6.7	7.1
Federal govt	-	2.7	4.2	2.8	1.4	1.4	1.1	0.7	1.0	2.3

Notes: [a] Annual average; [b] Debt with a tenure of more than one year; [c] Includes both government guaranteed and non-guaranteed debt of non-financial public enterprises; [d] Debt with a tenure of one year and below. [e] Repayment and interest payment of external debt as a percentage of gross exports of goods and service. - data not available.
Source: Compiled from Bank Negara Malaysia, *Monthly Statistical Bulletin*, March 1999, Kuala Lumpur.

Table 15.3 *Malaysia: end-of-year stock of mobile capital and foreign exchange reserves, 1990–8*

	1990	1991	1992	1993	1994	1995	1996	1997	1998
Mobile capital[a] (US$ billion)	6.3	6.5	12.4	23.9	27.7	31.9	38.9	31.0	18.0
Mobile capital composition (%)									
Short-term debt[b]	26	40	41	28	20	20	26	50	40
Banking sector	26	40	41	28	14	14	17	37	28
Non-bank private	0	0	0	0	6	6	8	13	13
Portfolio investment	74	60	59	72	80	80	74	50	60
Foreign exchange reserves (US$ billion)	10.0	11.1	18.5	29.7	26.0	25.5	27.9	21.4	25.4
Reserve adequacy ratio[c] (%)	158.7	170.5	148.7	124.2	94.0	79.9	71.8	67.8	141.2

Notes: [a] Short-term debt + portfolio investment; [b] Debt with a tenure of one year and less;
[c] Stock of mobile capital as a percentage of foreign exchange reserves. This ratio had declined to 55.8 per cent by end June 1997. The increase in the annual figure for 1997 compared to 1996 simply reflects the depletion of the stock of portfolio investment, which occurred more rapidly than the decline in foreign reserves following the speculative attack on the ringgit in July.
Source: Compiled from Bank Negara Malaysia, *Monthly Statistical Bulletin*, Kuala Lumpur (various issues).

Figure 15.1 *Malaysia: reserve adequacy, 1990–8 (foreign exchange reserves as a percentage of the stock of mobile capital)*

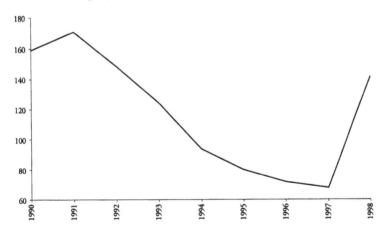

Note: Mobile capital is defined as the sum of short-term borrowing and portfolio investment.
Source: Compiled from Bank Negara Malaysia, *Monthly Statistical Bulletin*, Kuala Lumpur (various issues).

Increased foreign equity investment fueled a sharemarket boom in Malaysia from the late 1980s. By the mid 1990s, with a market capitalisation of around US$200 billion, the Kuala Lumpur Stock Exchange was the third largest in the Asia Pacific after Tokyo and Hong Kong. There were days when the turnover on the Kuala Lumpur Stock Exchange was higher than that in New York. By the mid 1990s, the sharemarket capitalisation in Malaysia of over 300 per cent of GDP was substantially higher than in any country in the world. At the onset of the crisis, foreign investors accounted for only 30–40 per cent of market activity. However, the actual influence of foreign participation on the expansion and operation of the sharemarket was probably much greater than suggested by this figure because local investors always followed the market-leading foreign investors. The sharemarket expansion was also inexorably linked with the domestic banking system. Lending for sharemarket activities turned out to be a major source of bank credit expansion.

In sum, by the mid 1990s, the Malaysian economy was experiencing a sharemarket bubble in which both foreign investors and domestic banks played a pivotal role. This had set the stage for a speculative attack on the currency. However this itself would not have translated into a financial crisis had it not been for some serious pitfalls on the domestic policy front.

The expansion of the sharemarket was not accompanied by initiatives to redress underlying weaknesses of corporate governance (Searle 1999). Most of the listed companies in Malaysia are tightly controlled by a handful of powerful families. These families often retain majority stakes even in public companies. Moreover, in many cases, the interests of company bosses and politicians are closely interwoven. Manipulation of intercompany share transactions in order to augment profit in privately owned companies (at the expense of listed companies) has been a common occurrence in the Malaysian corporate world. Such malpractice made share trading vulnerable to financial panic because unconnected (minority) shareholders had every reason to worry about how they would be treated in the event of a market downturn. When foreign participants started pulling out to avoid currency risk following the onset of the currency crisis in mid 1997, local players panicked. Given past experiences, the minority shareholders were naturally concerned that they might be hardest hit in troubled times (*The Economist* 20 December 1997:111). Foreign investors were providing funds to Malaysian firms with high debt ratios and long-term alliance relationships, which would not have been acceptable in the West. The extent of portfolio capital outflows owed much to the realisation that much of the capital should not have been committed in the first place.

The Malaysian banking system has historically been sturdier than its counterparts in the region. Capital adequacy ratios maintained by the Malaysian banks were the highest in Southeast Asia excepting Singapore. By the mid 1990s the average capital adequacy ratio for all banks had reached over 10 per cent. Some banks boasted ratios of 14 per cent, compared with the 8 per cent ratio recommended by the Bank for International Settlements. There was also a requirement that all banks set aside 1 per cent of total outstanding loans as a general provision, in addition to specific provisions made for problem loans (1.5 per cent). Non-performing loans in the banking system fell from 5.5 per cent in 1995 to 3.9 per cent in 1996. Foreign currency exposure of the banking system remained low thanks to the central bank policy of specifying stringent net open positions on foreign borrowing. By mid 1997, the aggregate net open position of the banking system was less than 5 per cent of total bank liabilities (BIS 1998).

Despite this apparent soundness, the banking system had made the economy increasingly vulnerable to a crisis because of a massive accumulation of outstanding domestic credit with heavy exposure to the property sector (broadly defined to include share trading and the real estate sector) (Soros 1998). The rate of growth of bank credit to the private sector rose from 12 per cent per annum during 1990–4 to over 26 per cent during 1994–6. The ratio of outstanding credit to GDP increased from an average level of 85 per cent during 1985–9 to 120 per cent in 1994 and then to over 160 per cent when the financial crisis broke in mid 1997. This was the highest credit build up (increase in private sector leverage) among the countries in East Asia (Athukorala and Warr 1999). Speculators consider a massive credit build up of this nature as an indicator of policy makers' reluctance to use the interest rate as a policy tool in the event of a speculative attack on the currency.

Total credit to the property sector accounted for around 40 per cent of total outstanding bank credit. It is believed that this share could have been much higher (around 55 per cent) if unclassified loans to conglomerates which are normally used to finance property were appropriately taken into account. The increased exposure to the property sector further weakened the financial position of the banks as this lending led to a property glut. By the end of 1997, more than 5.8 million square feet of new office space was under construction in the Kuala Lumpur metropolis, on top of 5.6 million square feet of space available at the time (*Far Eastern Economic Review*, 10 April 1998:60).

The sharemarket bubble and the credit boom had their roots in the rapid erosion in the quality of macroeconomic management. Over many years (except during the period 1981–6 when Malaysia experienced a major macroeconomic crisis triggered by a public investment boom), the government maintained a reputation for sound fiscal policies. However, the big push towards the year 2020 from the early 1990s was characterised by fiscal excesses, the intensity of which has increased over the years. Public investment expenditure surged, pushing the total investment to GDP ratio to 46 per cent in 1996, the highest in the region at the time. Much of this expenditure went to massive infrastructure development projects contracted to private companies in the patronage network that provided support for the political regime. These companies soon became the dominant players in the sharemarket. The construction boom also contributed to the credit boom as providing easy credit to the construction companies from politically linked banks and other 'captive' financial institutions was an implicit condition built into the contractual arrangements. Another source of credit growth was an aggressive government campaign to promote Malaysian overseas investment, implemented with the direct involvement of Prime Minister Mahathir as part of the desire to promote the image of Malaysia as an economic leader amongst developing economies. With a modest start in the early 1990s, annual overseas investment (mostly in construction and real estate development) by Malaysian companies increased to US$3 billion (amounting to almost 50 per cent of total foreign direct investment inflows) by 1996. Off-budget financial support, mostly in the form of government-sponsored bank loans, was a key element of the incentive package offered to these investors.

Rapid growth of government-sponsored bank lending contributed to weakening the policy autonomy of the central bank. Historically Bank Negara Malaysia had maintained a reputation among the central banks in newly independent countries in the British Commonwealth for strict pursuance of conservative monetary policy and banking regulation (Bruton 1993). However, in the context of a credit boom that had government backing at the highest political level, its role diminished to that of a bystander. The Bank Negara Malaysia Annual Reports of 1994, 1995 and 1996 repeatedly pointed to the risk of the rapid credit built up with a heavy concentration in property and share trading loans. However it failed to take any action to redress the problem other than some limits on lending to the property sector and sharemarket dealings introduced in March 1997. Perhaps the most vivid evidence of a policy conflict between the central bank and the Prime Minister's Department emerged from the policy dialogue within the ruling party in the lead up to the announcement of an IMF-style crisis management package by the then Finance Minster Anwar Ibrahim on 5 December 1997. The following quotation from a commentary in the *Far Eastern Economic Review* on the cabinet meeting of 3 December that approved the policy package makes interesting reading.

> [At the meeting] Anwar presented position papers dating back to 1995 that revealed that both the Finance Minister and the Central Bank had warned of potential economic problems ahead. These included an overheating economy, megaprojects that could strain the country's resources, and unproductive Malaysian investment abroad. Having set the stage, the Finance Minister then asked the cabinet to sanction his tough medicine (Jayasankaran 1997:14–5).

Quite apart from the massive credit accumulation, the ability of the Malaysian banking system to face a crisis had been weakened over the years because of the growing dominance of local banks (and the diminishing role of foreign banks) in the banking system. Despite significant initiatives in financial liberalisation, controls on the entry of foreign banks into the economy remained intact. In the early 1980s, the central bank ruled that only local banks could open new branches. There was also a 60/40 borrowing guideline for foreign firms operating in Malaysia, stipulating that these firms raise at least 60 per cent of their finances with local banks. With activities of foreign banks artificially frozen, new deposits gravitated towards local banks. By the mid 1990s foreign banks held about 30 per cent of total bank deposits in the country, down from over 70 per cent in the early 1980s. A greater role for foreign ownership would have provided the banking system with new capital, better management practices and access to foreign lenders of last resort.

CRISIS AND POLICY RESPONSE: FROM MUDDLING THROUGH TO CAPITAL CONTROLS

When the Thai baht came under heavy speculative attack in mid May, the ringgit also experienced heavy selling pressure. The central bank responded with a massive foreign exchange market intervention—it sold close to US$1.5 billion to prop up the ringgit. The ringgit was held steady through continued market intervention for another week and then relinquished to market forces on 14 July 1997. Between the first week of July

1997 and 7 January 1998 when the slide hit the bottom (with US$1 buying RM4.88), the ringgit depreciated by almost 50 per cent against the US dollar. In tandem with ringgit collapse the sharemarket tumbled. Between July 1997 and mid January 1998, the All Ordinaries Index of the Kuala Lumpur Stock Exchange fell by over 65 per cent, whipping almost US$225 billion off share values, the biggest stockmarket plunge among the five crisis countries in East Asia. The currency and stockmarket turmoil that began in July 1997 quickly translated into economic collapse (Athukorala 1998).

Unlike Thailand, Indonesia and Korea, Malaysia succumbed to the crisis with only a little foreign debt exposure in its banking system. For this reason, it was able to muddle through without an IMF-sponsored rescue package. The initial response of the Malaysian government to the outbreak of the currency crisis was one of denial. Given the perceived soundness of economic fundamentals, Prime Minister Mahathir's immediate reaction was to pounce on currency speculators and punish them through several initiatives involving direct government intervention in the sharemarket. After five months of policy indifference, a major policy package was announced by the then Finance Minister Anwar on 5 December 1997. According to many commentators this amounted to an IMF policy without the IMF. However, the government quickly backtracked from this policy stance in favour of *ad hoc* counter-cyclical measures with a view to 'avoid a recession-deflation spiral' (BNM 1999:4). Given the heavy domestic credit built up in the economy, increases in interest rates (market-determined rather than policy-driven) coupled with a rapid contraction in economic activity quickly reflected in a massive accumulation of non-performing loans and corporate failures. On 5 May 1998, Prime Minister Mahathir made it clear that he disagreed with the IMF on the need to raise the interest rate further. A National Economic Recovery Plan designed to manage the crisis without IMF involvement and primarily through domestic demand expansion was announce in mid July (NEAC 1998).

In the absence of a clear policy anchor, such policy tinkering was ineffective in avoiding further economic collapse, let alone generating recovery. By August 1998, the economy was in recession and there were no signs of achieving currency and share price stability. According to national account estimates released in the last week of August, the economy had contracted by 6.8 per cent in the first quarter of 1998, compared to a 2.8 per cent contraction in the previous quarter. The net non-performing loan ratio of the banking system had risen from 4.1 per cent of total outstanding loans at the end of 1997 to 9 per cent at the end of 1998, and international credit rating agencies placed the figure as high as 40 per cent (Soros 1998:144). To make matters worse, the much hoped for export-led recovery was not on the horizon despite the massive improvement in competitiveness achieved through currency depreciation. Business confidence as measured by the business confidence index of the Malaysian Institute of Economic Research had dipped sharply for three consecutive quarters. The Institute's consumer confidence index was also at an all-time low.

Reflecting falling business confidence, there was a large outflow of short-term capital in the first quarter of 1998. Net private short-term capital registered a deficit of US$2.3 billion, a reversal from the net inflow of US$1 billion in the previous quarter (Table 15.4). Due to this massive capital flight, the recession-induced current account surplus did not provide an improvement in foreign reserves.

Table 15.4 Malaysia: balance of payments, 1997–9 (US$million)

	97Q1	97Q2	97Q3	97Q4	98Q1	98Q2	98Q3	98Q4	99Q1	99Q2
Exports	19,367	19,407	20,339	18,801	17,330	17,422	19,135	19,531	18,237	-
Imports	17,708	20,177	18,840	17,368	14,446	13,689	13,756	13,602	14,079	-
Trade balance	1,659	-770	1,499	1,433	2,883	3,733	5,379	5,929	4,158	-
Services and transfers (net)	-2,649	-2,663	-1,966	-1,983	-1,240	-1,536	-2,079	-2,851	-	-
Current account	-990	-3,033	-780	-550	1,643	2,197	3,300	3,078	-	-
Long-term capital (net)	2,361	3,302	-190	1,542	372	785	-667	1,202	-	-
Basic balance	1,371	270	-970	993	2,015	2,982	3,109	4,723	-	-
Private short-term capital (net)	1,827	-1,728	-5,167	794	-2,317	-1,185	-1,207	-589	-	-
Error and omissions	-2,339	878	2,960	-2,583	-162	-1,560	4,226	1,032	-	-
Overall balance =										
Change in reserves	859	-580	-3,177	-797	-464	237	6,128	4,723	1,537	1,105

Note: - data not available.
Source: Compiled from Bank Negara Malaysia, *Monthly Statistical Bulletin*, Kuala Lumpur (various issues).

A striking feature of capital outflows was that they largely took the form of ringgit (rather than foreign currency) flowing into Singapore. These flows were triggered by very attractive money market rates of between 20 and 40 per cent in Singapore, which provided a hefty premium over a domestic rate of about 11 per cent coupled with a weakening exchange rate for the ringgit. As much as RM35 billion (US$8.2 billion) had ended up in Singapore at the height of the crisis in mid 1998. This amounted to over 150 per cent of the total domestic supply of currency (M1) and 70 per cent of M2 in Malaysia. Policy makers became increasingly concerned about the internationalisation of the national currency, which carried a potential threat to economic stability and monetary policy autonomy. The strong demand for offshore ringgit and the consequent build up of offshore ringgit deposits increased the vulnerability of the ringgit, undermining the effectiveness of monetary policy (BNM 1999:10).

These developments propelled a serious rethinking of policy directions. Choices available to the Malaysian government had become severely limited, however. Aggressively easing monetary conditions to boost aggregate demand and to provide the highly leveraged domestic firms with breathing space would have intensified capital flight, weakening the ringgit further and precipitating the sharemarket collapse. To make matters worse, a planned attempt to issue sovereign bonds in the United States and Europe to raise US$2 billion for implementing the banking sector restructuring program had to be shelved in late August because of an unanticipated downgrading of Malaysia's credit rating by international rating agencies.

The root cause of the worsening economic situation was the market perception that Malaysia would be less committed to structural reforms as it was not under an IMF program (BNM 1999:5). However, entering into an IMF program was not politically acceptable to the Malaysian leadership. Given the intimate link between business and government forged under the New Economic Policy over the previous two-and-a-half decades, the positive stabilising impact of such a move had to be weighed against its negative effect on politically connected business groups and the sociopolitical stability of the country (Crouch 1998). Macroeconomic policy that aimed to adjust the economy through market-determined interest rates was bound to have a severe effect on the debt-ridden private sector firms and the viability of banks. These were already suffering from the burst of the real estate bubble and the sharemarket crash. Prime Minister Mahathir summed up his position on this issue as follows.

> If we do not lower interest rates, not only will companies, but also banks and the government will encounter financial difficulties. When our financial position becomes very serious, we will have no option but to seek IMF assistance. We will then be subject to IMF's dictates (Government of Malaysia 1998:13).

In this context, Mahathir opted to abandon policy tinkering along conventional lines in order to stimulate the economy through fiscal and monetary expansion, while insulating the domestic interest rate from short-term capital mobility through capital controls. While Mahathir's expression of interest in capital controls dates back to early in the crisis (Athukorala 1998), the new policy has received a measure of legitimacy from recent developments in the international economic policy debate on crisis management. In particular Krugman's (1998) controversial piece in *Fortune* that argued for using capital controls as a crisis management tool received wide attention in the

Malaysian policy debate and news media. There was also growing attention in the financial press to the fact that China and Taiwan, the two economies in the East Asian growth league with controls on short-term capital movements, fared much better than the rest of the region during the crisis. The recent experiences of countries like Chile and Slovenia in using capital controls to manage shorter-term capital inflows also received wide attention. Another related factor is Malaysia's prior experience in using temporary capital controls to successfully avert a speculative attack on the ringgit in 1994.

As a first step, on 31 August 1998 Malaysia made the offshore trading of Malaysian company shares illegal in a move to control speculative trading in the over-the-counter sharemarket in Singapore, where short-selling of Malaysian shares continued despite illegal prohibition of such activities in Malaysia. This was followed by the imposition of stringent controls over short-term capital flows (1 September) and fixing the exchange rate at RM3.80 per US$ (effective 2 September).

The new capital controls banned trading in ringgit instruments among offshore banks and stopped Malaysian financial institutions offering domestic credit facilities to non-resident banks and stockbrokers. With a view to stopping speculative trading in ringgit in overseas markets (predominantly in Singapore), the use of ringgit as an invoicing currency in foreign trade was banned with immediate effect and legal tender on all ringgit deposits held outside the country was abolished with effect from 30 September. A twelve-month withholding period was imposed on repatriation of proceeds (principal and profit) from the sale of securities. There were also stringent limits on the approval of foreign exchange for overseas travel and investment (Table 15.5).

The capital control element of the new policy package was modified in February 1999. The twelve-month withholding period was replaced with a graduated tax on capital and profit repatriation (Table 15.6). Unlike the original controls, the new revision was implemented after consulting investors (Merrill Lynch 1999). Although some commentators have treated it as backsliding, the new capital tax is a pragmatic move towards greater flexibility with a view to bringing fresh capital into the country. It is designed to avoid any pressure associated with the resumption of capital inflows on the exchange rate. The new graduated levy scheme is obviously more market-conforming than the original twelve-month outright withholding provision and it also appears to be less restrictive than the Chilean capital controls of the early 1990s (De Gregorio *et al.* 1998; von Furstenberg and Ulan 1998:65–7).

With the policy autonomy gained through capital controls, the government swiftly embarked on a macroeconomic package to stimulate the economy. The central bank reduced its three-month intervention rate (on which interest rates are based) from 10 per cent to 9.5 per cent and cut the statutory reserve ratio to 6 per cent from 8 per cent a week before the introduction of capital controls in order to inject liquidity into the debt-ridden banking system. The three-month intervention rate stood at 6.0 per cent by early July 1999. The statutory reserve ratio by that time was a mere 4.5 per cent, compared to a pre-crisis level of 10 per cent. On 9 September the central bank advised banks to expand their loans at a rate of 8 per cent a year. This was accompanied by a revision to the formula used in computing the base lending rate so that reductions in the intervention rate are better reflected in cost of bank credit. Several other measures were introduced to encourage credit expansion. These included relaxation of credit limits on commercial bank and financial company lending for the purchase of property and shares, easy financing for purchase of cars, special loan schemes for assisting smaller industries and low income groups and relaxing credit limits on credit cards (Yap 1999).

The 1999 budget presented by Mahathir on 23 October proposed a stimulus package that called for a deficit of 6.1 per cent of GNP, compared to a 1.9 per cent deficit in 1998. It proposed no major spending proposals beyond RM4 (US$1) billion earmarked for road and rail projects. The major economic stimulus took the form of tax reductions, including a total waiver of income tax for 1999. There were also tax breaks for industries of national and strategic importance and import duty reductions on machinery and equipment imports.

The government aims to finance the bulk of the deficit by issuing Malaysian government securities which will be absorbed largely by provident, pension and insurance funds. Only about one-third of the required amount is to be raised externally, mainly from bilateral and multilateral sources. In 1998 gross foreign borrowing amounted to RM4 (US$ 1.1) billion, including RM1.2 billion from the World Bank to finance projects reviewing the economy and as assistance to vulnerable groups, and RM2.4 billion from the Japanese government. A syndicate foreign currency loan of RM5.1 billion was obtained from twelve locally incorporated foreign banks.

Speedy implementation of the programs (initiated in early 1998) for dealing with non-performing loans, recapitalisation of debt-ridden banks and corporate restructuring were the other points emphasised in the reform package. The financial requirement for acquiring non-performing loans by the Pengurusan Danaharta Nasional Berhad (the National Asset Management Company) was estimated at RM15 billion. As at 31 March 1999, Danaharta had acquired a total of RM23.1 billion non-performing loans, amounting to 31.8 per cent of the total non-performing loans in the banking system. Recapitalisation of banks under Danamodal Nasional Berhad (the Bank Restructuring Company) had to be completed before the end of 1999. As at 31 March 1999, Danamodal had injected RM6.4 billion into ten banking institutions. As at 31 May 1999, the Corporate Debt Restructuring Committee had received sixty applications involving corporate debts amounting to RM32.5 billion. Of these, six cases were withdrawn or rejected as non-viable, eleven cases involving RM10.9 billion were completed, and the balance, involving debts totaling RM3.3 billion, had to be settled by the end of June 1999.

A noteworthy feature of the reform process so far is the relatively high weight assigned to monetary policy compared to fiscal policy. One consideration behind this policy choice is the need to avoid crowding out private sector investment, which had been adversely affected by interest rate hikes and the credit squeeze. Another, and perhaps the more important, consideration was institutional bottlenecks impinging on speedy implementation of new government projects. The greater emphasis placed on monetary policy relative to fiscal policy was presumably a major factor in the choice of capital controls as a pivotal element of the reform package. To use monetary policy for internal balance (in violation of the Muldell assignment of using fiscal policy for internal balance and monetary policy for external balance) essentially requires capital controls to insulate the economy from international capital movements (Branson 1993:34).

Table 15.5 Malaysia: exchange control measures prior to and after 1 September 1998

Transaction	Prior to 1 September 1998	New
Transfers based on external accounts	Transfer between external account holders freely allowed	Transfer of any amount between external accounts requires prior approval Sources of funding external accounts are limited to: (a) proceeds from sale of ringgit instruments, securities registered in Malaysia or other assets in Malaysia; (b) salaries, wages, commissions, interests or dividends; (c) sales of foreign currency. Use of funds in accounts is limited to purchase of ringgit assets in Malaysia.
General payments	Residents were freely allowed to make payments to non-residents for any purpose. Amounts of RM100,000 and above were permitted provided the resident did not have any domestic borrowing (if the payment was for investment abroad), or the payment was made in foreign currency (for non-trade purposes)	Residents are freely allowed to make payments to non-residents for any purpose up to RM10,000 in ringgit or foreign currency, except for imports of goods and services. Amounts exceeding RM10,000 require approval and are allowed in foreign currency only
Export of goods	Payments were to be received in foreign currency or ringgit from an external account	Payments are to be received from an external account in foreign currency only
Credit facilities to non-residents	Non-resident correspondent banks and non-resident stock-brokering companies were permitted to obtain credit facilities up to RM5 million from banking institutions to fund mismatch of receipts and payments through their external accounts	Domestic credit facilities to non-resident corresponding banks and non-resident stock-brokering companies are no longer allowed
Investment abroad	Residents with no domestic borrowing were allowed to make payment to non-residents for purposes of investing abroad	Corporate residents with domestic borrowing were allowed to invest abroad up to the equivalent of RM10 million per calendar year on a corporate group basis. Residents with no domestic borrowing are allowed to make payment to non-residents for investment abroad up to an amount of RM10,000 or its equivalent in foreign currency per transaction. All residents require prior approval to make payments to non-residents for investing abroad of an amount exceeding RM1,000 equivalent in foreign currency

Credit facilities from non-residents	Residents were allowed to obtain ringgit credit facilities of below RM100,000 in aggregate from non-resident individuals	Residents are not allowed to obtain ringgit credit facilities from any non-resident individual
Trading in securities	There were no restrictions on secondary trading of securities registered in Malaysia between residents and non-residents and among non-residents. For transfer of securities registered outside Malaysia from a non-resident to a resident, the resident was subject to the rules on investment abroad an authorised depositor	Ringgit securities held by non-residents must be transacted through an authorised depositor. All payments by non-residents for any security registered in Malaysia must be made from an external account (in foreign currency or in ringgit) All proceeds in ringgit received by a non-resident from the sale of any Malaysian security must be retained in an external account at least for one year before converting to foreign currency. All payments to residents for any security registered outside Malaysia from non-residents must be made in foreign currency
Import and export of currency notes, bills of exchange, insurance policies, etc.	A resident or non-resident traveller was free to import or export any amount of ringgit notes or foreign currency notes in person. Export of foreign currencies required approval. Authorised currency dealers were allowed to import any amount of ringgit notes, subject to reporting to Bank Negara Malaysia on a monthly basis. A resident traveller is permitted to bring ringgit notes up to RM1,000 only and any amount of foreign currencies	A resident traveller is permitted to export ringgit notes only up to RM1,000 and foreign currencies up to the equivalent of RM10,000 A non-resident traveller is permitted to import ringgit notes up to RM1,000 only and any amount of foreign currencies. A non-resident traveller is permitted to export ringgit notes up to RM1,000 only and foreign currencies up to the amount brought into the country
Transaction in the Labuan International Offshore Financial Centre	Licensed offshore banks were allowed to trade in ringgit instruments up to permitted limits	Licensed offshore banks are no longer allowed to trade in ringgit instruments

Note: The new controls were confined to short-term capital flows and aimed at making it harder for short-term portfolio investors to sell shares and keep the proceeds, and for offshore hedge funds to drive down the currency. With the exception of limits on foreign exchange for foreign travel by Malaysian citizens, there was no retreat from the country's long-standing commitment to an open trade and investment policy. No new direct controls have been imposed on import and export trade. Foreign investors in Malaysia are free to repatriate dividends and equity related to their direct investment in the country. Immediately following the imposition of capital controls, the central bank introduced new regulatory procedures to monitor repatriation of profits and capital by foreign companies operating in Malaysia. These were swiftly removed in response to protest by these firms (Zefferys 1999). A questionnaire conducted by the Malaysian Institute of Economic Research in late 1998 failed to detect any significant impact of new capital controls on operational and investment decisions of both local and foreign firms (MIER 1998). The majority (about 60 per cent) indicated political stability, rather than capital controls, as the most important criterion for investing in Malaysia. Over 85 per cent of firms (90 per cent of firms with foreign direct investment) disclosed plans to maintain investment levels in the next few years.
Source: Compiled from Bank Negara Malaysia, *Quarterly Bulletin*, Second Quarter 1998, Kuala Lumpur and IMF, 1997, *Exchange Arrangements and Exchange Restrictions Annual Report 1997*, IMF, Washington, DC.

Table 15.6 Malaysia: capital repatriation introduced on 15 February 1999

Repatriation period	Tax on the principal (%)	Tax on profit (%)
For funds brought in before 15 February 1999		
Between 4 February and 31 March 1999	30	0
Between 1 April and 30 May 1999	20	0
Between 1 June and 31 August 1999	10	0
On or after 1 September 1999	0	10
For funds brought in after 15 February 1999		
Up to 12 months after profits are made	0	30
More than 12 months after profits are made	0	10

Source: Compiled from Bank Negara Malaysia Press Release, 15 February 1998.

HOW CAPITAL CONTROLS WORK

A major doubt about the effectiveness of capital controls as a crisis management tool relates to the ample scope for avoidance and evasion (Hale 1998; Edwards 1999). The general argument is that the more extensive are trade and investment links, the more difficult and costly it is to control capital account transactions because of the multiplication in the number of arbitrage possibilities that arise in the course of normal business. The problem with this argument is that it is based on a misleading mixing of placing funds abroad retail and exporting capital wholesale (Williamson 1993:36). The mere fact that it is always possible for owners of capital to transfer their funds abroad through a parallel market does not necessarily imply that capital controls that specifically focus on moving capital wholesale have no effect. There is ample evidence from both developed and developing countries that capital controls are in fact effective in substantially reducing, if not preventing, capital flows of the latter type, in particular placement abroad of institutional savings (Eichengreen 1998; De Gregorio *et al.* 1998; Radelet and Sachs 1998).

Evidence from capital controls in Malaysia is consistent with these findings. The indications are that controls helped the government to lower interest rates and encourage a revival of domestic consumption and investment without precipitating capital flights. Following the imposition of capital control measures, the net international reserve position increased from US$20.2 billion in August 1998 to US$29.8 billion in May 1999. Short-term capital flows stabilised in the first quarter of 1998. Thus the foreign reserve position began to move in tandem with the surplus in the current account. As foreign exchange controls were targeted only at short-term investment flows, and trade and foreign direct investment-related transactions continued to remain liberal, the policy shift did not result in the emergence of a black market for foreign exchange.

The easing of monetary policy seems to have improved liquidity conditions and lowered cost of credit in the economy. Reductions in nominal domestic deposit rates, combined with the marginally higher domestic inflation rate, were reflected in a significant narrowing of real interest rate differentials with other countries. In December

1997, the real interest rate differential with the United States was 1.85 per cent and with Singapore, 0.61 per cent. These differentials further increased to 2.56 per cent and 1.69 per cent in February 1998. This pattern has been reversed under the new policy regime. The real differential with the United States turned negative in September 1998 and stood at -2.31 per cent by early 1999. Against Singapore, the differential turned negative earlier, around late June 1998, when Singapore raised its interest rates. This differential widened to -2.57 per cent in October and then moderated to -1.97 per cent by early 1999 (BNM 1999).

Investors have responded favourably to the change in capital control measures introduced in February 1999. During the period from 15 February to 9 June 1999, the net cumulative portfolio capital inflow to Malaysia amounted to nearly US$3 billion. A total of about 6,000 new accounts were opened for the inflow of new capital after 15 February 1999. The new levy, unlike the original twelve-month withholding period, permits investors to take investment decisions in line with recovery prospects, while factoring the levy into their estimates of the potential return on investment in Malaysia. Increases in capital flows under the graduated levy imply that the term structure of inflows would have changed in favour of investments with longer maturity period. This has been the experience of countries like Chile and Colombia under capital inflow tax regimes (De Gregorio *et al.* 1998; Cardeas and Barrera 1998; von Furstenberg and Ulan 1998).

Following the imposition of capital controls on 1 September 1998, Malaysia was dropped from the country coverage of Morgan Stanley Capital International and International Finance Corporation capital market indexes. Lack of transparency at the time controls were imposed was as much an issue as the controls themselves. It is pertinent to mention here that the imposition in the early 1990s of capital controls on repatriation of existing capital that involved a lock up of five years did not lead to an exclusion of the Chilean market from these indexes. Presumably this was because transparency was not an issue in Chile. When Malaysia introduced market-friendly changes to capital controls in February 1999, market analysts anticipated that Malaysia would soon be reinstated in these indexes (Merrill Lynch 1999). In line with these expectations, on 13 August 1999 Morgan Stanley Capital International announced that it would reinstate Malaysia in its All Country Far-East Ex-Japan Index and Emerging Market Free Index with effect from February 2000. This decision, coupled with the ending of uncertainty about the possible outcome of the lifting of the one-year moratorium on portfolio investment, is likely to boost the recent pick up in fresh portfolio capital inflows to Malaysia.

When the capital controls were first introduced (and even after the new levy was introduced on February 15) many observers were concerned about the potentially massive outflow of short-term foreign debt and portfolio investment after 1 September 1999. However, the ending of the one-year moratorium turned out to be a non-event. According to Bank Negara Malaysia data, total portfolio capital outflow in the first three days of September amounted to only US$456 million, compared to a total stock of US$4–5 billion potentially movable foreign portfolio investment. This suggests that investors do not find it difficult to factor in the new profit tax on portfolio investment, as ground rules are now transparent and signs of economic recovery are clearly visible.

The fixing of the exchange rate at 3.80 ringgit per US dollar was originally considered by many observers as a risky strategy (Athukorala 1999). The new fixed rate was implemented as part of a policy package whose prime aim was to artificially inflate the economy through pump priming. Under this strategy, there exists the possibility that domestic inflation could result in real exchange rate appreciation, shifting the cost of adjustment disproportionately to the tradable sector, hindering an export-led recovery.

As yet there are no indications of this pessimistic scenario unfolding. Domestic inflation pressures have continued to moderate. The rate of CPI inflation (year-on-year) declined from 5.3 per cent in January 1999 to 2.9 per cent in May, raising the prospects of an average inflation rate of about 2.5 per cent for the whole year. Meanwhile the PPI showed a declining trend from February onwards. From a growth rate of 1.2 per cent (year-on-year) in January, it recorded a negative rate of 4.2 per cent in April, with the domestic component of the PPI declining faster (-5.2 per cent) than import component (-3.2 per cent). Under these circumstances, the fixed exchange rate has so far assisted Malaysian exporters by making their products more competitive than those of other crisis-affected countries in East Asia (Figure 15.2). In Thailand and Korea, while domestic price trends have been similar to that in Malaysia, appreciation of the nominal exchange rate propelled by the resurgence of short-term capital flows has begun to be reflected in an appreciation of the real exchange rate.

Many commentators expressed fear that capital controls would hamper the economic recovery by adversely affecting foreign direct investment in Malaysia ('The road less traveled', *The Economist*, 1 May 1999:79; Hale 1998). Any policy measure that constitutes a significant departure from the long-standing commitment to economic openness could certainly have an adverse impact on the general investment climate of the country. Moreover, in Malaysia, the decision to impose controls appeared so sudden and arbitrary that it called into question the general credibility of the government's whole framework for foreign investment. However, whether this would translate into a significant reduction in foreign direct investment flows remained debatable at the time. The pessimistic view was based on a false aggregation of foreign direct investment with portfolio investment and short-term bank credits. Foreign direct investment flows are however determined by long-term considerations governing the international production decisions of multinational enterprises, not by financial panic and related short-term economic changes. What is primarily important for attracting foreign direct investment is a firm commitment to the maintenance of an open current account (Bhagwati 1998b).

There are no data on realised (actual) investment to systematically examine this issue. However, the available data on the value of investment applications and approvals do not point to a major reversal in investment flows (Table 15.7). Based on data for the first five months, there was a strong likelihood that foreign direct investment approvals in 1999 would reach about the same level as in 1998. The total value of proposed new investment, a better indicator of investor response to more recent policy changes, has however declined from 1997 at a faster rate than the total value of approved investment. Perhaps investors are worried about future policy directions.

There are two factors other than capital controls which may have adversely affected investment trends. First, given excess capacity in domestic manufacturing, it is unlikely that domestic market-oriented foreign direct investment will increase in the recovery

Figure 15.2 Malaysia, Korea and Thailand: J.P. Morgan real exchange rate index, 1996–9

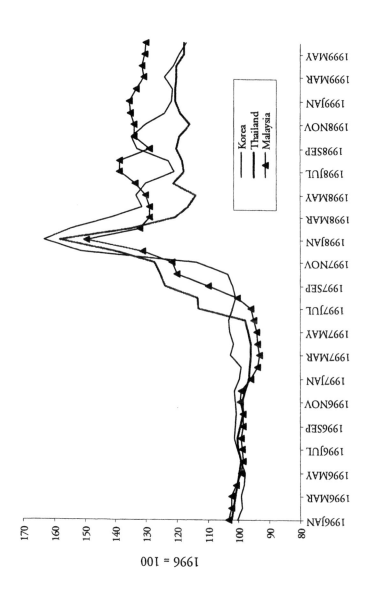

Note: Producer price of the given country relative to that of its trading partners are both expressed in a common currency. Producer price is measured net of food. The original index had been inverted here so that an increase in the index indicates an increase in relative competitiveness (real depreciation).

Source: J.P. Morgan website http://www.jpmorgan.com

process. This view is consistent with the trends in investment by local investors. From 1997 domestic private investment (which is overwhelmingly domestic market-oriented) has grown at a much slower rate than foreign direct investment (Table 15.7). Second, investment flows from Japan and Taiwan, which together accounted for nearly one-half of total investment flows to Malaysia, have slowed down, probably due to domestic economic troubles. During January–May 1999, approval of investment from these two countries fell by 64 per cent and 70 per cent respectively compared with the same period in the previous year.

According to foreign direct investment data based on balance of payments records, in recent months foreign direct investment inflows to Thailand and Korea have increased at a faster rate than those to Malaysia. However these figures need to be taken cautiously because in the two former countries acquisition by foreign companies of assets or equity of domestic companies has been a major component of foreign capital inflows. For instance during the period 1 January–15 April 1999 capital inflows relating to these activities amounted to US$27 billion in Korea and US$20 billion in Thailand, compared to US$2 billion in Malaysia (*Far Eastern Economic Review*, 17 June 1999:38).

RECOVERY

In the first quarter of 1999 the year-on-year rate of contraction of the Malaysian economy moderated to -1.2 per cent from -10.3 per cent in the previous quarter. The economy recorded 4.1 per cent year-on-year growth in the second quarter of 1999, ending the year-long recession. Many independent analysts predict an average annual growth rate of 9 per cent or more in the next two quarters, leading to a growth rate of 5–6 per cent for 1999, compared to 6.5 per cent contraction in 1998.

Signs of recovery first emerged in the first quarter of 1999 in the services sectors (particularly in financial services) and domestic market-oriented industries. By the second quarter recovery had become broader, with export-oriented manufacturing showing impressive output growth. In that quarter total manufacturing output expanded by 12 per cent year-on-year, contributing nearly one-half of total GDP growth. Export-oriented production contributed 35 per cent of this growth. The significant pick up in export-oriented manufacturing is in sharp contrast to the experience of Thailand, perhaps reflecting the competitive edge gained through the currency peg.

Table 15.7 Malaysia: investment applications and approvals in manufacturing (US$billion)

	1996	1977	1998	1999 (January–May)
Applications	16.7	12.2	5.1	1.4
Foreign direct investment	7.0	5.1	3.2	0.8
Local	9.7	7.1	2.9	1.4
Approvals	13.6	9.2	6.7	2.0
Foreign direct investment	6.8	4.1	3.3	1.7
Private domestic	6.8	5.1	3.4	0.3

Note: Original values in ringgit were converted into US dollars using the period-average exchange rate (line *rf* in IMF, *International Financial Statistics*, March 1999).
Source: Malaysia Industrial Development Authority (MIDA) press releases.

On the expenditure side, private consumption stabilised in the first half of the year and was expected to pick up strongly in the second half of the year. The consumer sentiment index compiled by the Malaysian Institute of Economic Research exhibited a clear upward movement in the first quarter of 1999. Other private consumption indicators such as sales and production of passenger cars, sales tax and import of consumer goods have also recorded an improvement in the first quarter of 1999.

As yet there is no clear sign of recovery in private investment. So far only public investment has begun to increase, reflecting the new investment drive. The Malaysian Institute of Economic Research's business confidence index, which declined steeply for three consecutive quarters starting from the second quarter of 1997, recorded a turnaround in the fourth quarter of 1998 and improved further in the first quarter of 1999, suggesting that private investment would pick up in the second half of the year. The delayed recovery of private investment is consistent with the existing excess capacity and stock in the economy. According to the Malaysian Institute of Economic Research's survey of business sentiment, capacity utilisation in the first quarter of 1999 was 75 per cent, compared with an average of 85 per cent for the boom years of 1987–96. While there is no satisfactory indicator, excess capacity in the building and construction sector is presumably much greater.

According to the survey of retrenchments (conducted by the Department of Labour) there has been a significant decline in worker layoffs in recent months. Weekly worker layoffs occurred at a rate of over 500 a week in 1998, reached a peak of 2,637 in the third week of March 1999 and then declined to 274 in the last week of June (*Business Times*, 1 July 1999).

Growth in the CPI declined to below 3 per cent in April and May from a high of 5.85 per cent in July 1998, despite the heavy emphasis on fiscal and monetary expansion as part of the recovery strategy. Rapid expansion in domestic output propelled by the ample availability of cheap bank credit, still sizable excess capacity production in the economy and the effective nominal anchor provided by the fixed exchange rate seems to explain the favourable inflationary experience. An added factor appears to be government policy toward migrant workers. Despite initial moves to repatriate a large number of foreign workers, mostly from the construction sector, the authorities have continued to allow the importation of foreign workers in large numbers for employment in the traded goods sectors, export-oriented manufacturing in particular. This policy has been instrumental in keeping a lid on wage growth.

Merchandise imports, which continuously declined for over a year from the onset of the crisis, have begun to pick up in recent months. Total imports in the first half of 1999 were 11.5 per cent higher than the corresponding period in the previous year. This was however overwhelmed by export growth (16 per cent) to generate an increase in the trade balance of 5.5 per cent. There was no significant change in the net services balance. The net capital account balance indicated a minor improvement in the second quarter thanks to an increase in portfolio capital inflows following the relaxation of capital controls in March. Total net foreign reserves increased by 15 per cent between the end of 1998 and mid 1999 (from US$20 billion to US$27 billion), the largest percentage increase among the five crisis countries.

With these signs of recovery, foreign analysts have begun to acknowledge that the Malaysian economy is doing better than expected. Major credit rating agencies, which downgraded Malaysia's international credit rating immediately following the imposition of capital controls, have now revised their assessments of Malaysia's prospects. A US$2 billion global bond issue by the Malaysian government in May 1999 was three times oversubscribed, reflecting renewed confidence by global investors in the economy. Malaysian crisis management strategy was recently commended by Stanley Fischer as being 'very well thought out' (*The Star* 12 June 1999). He in particular noted that exchange controls had assisted Malaysia regaining control over monetary policy.

CONCLUDING REMARKS

The Malaysian experience has been interpreted by some observers to imply that a country can succumb to an international financial crisis even if it has faithfully followed the conventional policy advocacy on the sequencing of current and capital account liberalisation and macro management (Bhagwati 1998b; Furman and Stiglitz 1998; Radelet and Sachs 1998). Our analysis of the policy trends and economic performance in the pre-crisis Malaysian economy does not support this view. It is true that capital account opening followed current account opening. But by the time these reforms were implemented there had been a clear departure from conventional macroeconomic prudence. The opening of domestic capital markets to equity investors was not appropriately combined with initiatives to improve corporate governance. Massive bank lending fueled by the public investment boom and the dramatic expansion in share trading created a highly leveraged economy. This, coupled with a sharemarket bubble in which foreign institutional investors played a big role, set the stage for a speculative attack on the currency and the subsequent economic collapse. Closer regulation and monitoring of private sector foreign currency borrowing by the central bank prevented accumulation of excessive foreign borrowing in Malaysia, unlike in Thailand, Korea and Indonesia. However, this favourable feature of the policy environment was overwhelmed by haphazard capital account liberalisation, along with a significant departure from fiscal and monetary prudence. The erosion of policy autonomy historically enjoyed by the central bank was reflected in a massive credit build up in the economy and significant deterioration in the quality of banks' asset portfolios.

Malaysia has certainly survived the dire predictions made by many observers at the time it embarked on its radical policy path in October 1998. Once the authorities decided to follow the conventional Keynesian recipe (or depression economics, to use Krugman's (1999) terminology), capital controls seem to have provided a conducive setting for the effective pursuance of such policies. The new policy has prevented massive capital outflow and permitted sustaining a significant interest rate differential with the rest of the world. The subsequent shift in the capital control regime from a one-year withholding period to a market-friendly graduated tax seems to have helped regain the confidence of portfolio investors while influencing the term structure of such inflows.

News commentaries note that not only Malaysia but other crisis-affected countries have started to show signs of recovery (Hiebert 1999; Lim 1999). But this grouping of countries ignores that these economies are vastly different in terms of sources of vulnerability to crisis and economic structure, which determine flexibility of adjustment to a crisis. If the degree of recovery is measured by conventional indicators, only

South Korea has thus far recorded a faster recovery rate than Malaysia. But Korea is a major industrial power with a diversified manufacturing base and national companies, which have their own international marketing networks. It is also alleged that, unlike Thailand, Korea and Indonesia, Malaysia really did not have a serious crisis to begin with (Jomo 1998). This observation is based on Malaysia's low foreign debt level and other general economic indicators such as a higher growth and domestic saving rates, which are not relevant in analysing the vulnerability of country to a currency crisis. It ignores the explosive mix of sharemarket bubble and domestic credit boom that developed in Malaysia in the lead up to the crisis.

The inference that capital controls have helped crisis management in Malaysia by no means implies that these controls should be retained after the economy recovers. Despite its underlying logic in a crisis context, the new strategy is costly in terms of long-term growth. The rationale behind the imposition of capital controls is to avert a painful economic collapse and to provide a conducive setting for the implementation of the required adjustment policies, in particular banking sector restructuring. The danger is that the complaisance induced by possible temporary recovery through expansionary policies may lead to postponement of long-term structural reforms, and thus to long-term economic deterioration. Moreover, any form of market intervention of this nature involves economic costs associated with bureaucratic controls and related rent-seeking activities. And prolonged use of controls is likely to compounds these costs. The greatest challenge for the Malaysian policy makers is to strengthen the domestic financial system and to regain macroeconomic prudence, which sadly dissipated during the period of growth euphoria in the early 1990s, in order to set the stage for the removal of costly capital controls.

16 Why was China different?

Yiping Huang and Ligang Song

China has come to the international spotlight in the wake of the East Asian financial crisis for at least two reasons. First, the post-reform Chinese economy resembles remarkably the other East Asian economies. Like Indonesia, Malaysia, Korea, Thailand and Japan, China experienced export-led growth, with a significant expansion in labour-intensive exports in the early stage of development. Rapid growth was accompanied by a rapid increase in domestic savings and massive inflow of foreign capital (Perkins 1986; Garnaut 1989). The banking sector dominated financial intermediation and the ratio of non-performing loans was astonishingly high. A natural question to ask is whether will China be the next victim of the crisis (Lardy 1998a; Rudi Dornbusch, 'Is China next?', *Financial Times*, 4 August 1998). Second, China's economic performance has become the key to the current economic stability of East Asia. During 1997–8, China was the only major economy in the region that managed to sustain significant growth. In particular, maintaining the stability of the renminbi was seen as the last hope in achieving a new equilibrium in the regional currency system and facilitating an early recovery (Garnaut 1998). The Chinese government took up the challenge and made a firm commitment not to devalue the renminbi in the short term. Concerns, however, were frequently expressed about how long China would be able to defend its overvalued currency (Song 1998).

Most economists predicted that a currency crisis was unlikely to eventuate in China. Relative to its crisis-affected neighbours, China's macroeconomic fundamentals were healthy. It also has the extra insurance of capital account controls. But being surrounded by crisis-affected economies (which also form important economic partners), China could not be totally immune to the crisis. The predicted effects of the exchange rate commitment were to be transmitted into the economy through the following two real sector variables

- falling foreign direct investment inflow because of difficulties in source countries and doubts about the short-term prospects for the East Asian market
- stagnation or decline of exports because of reduced demand from the crisis-affected economies and tougher competition in the third markets.

While fully recognising these adverse effects, the Chinese government was optimistic about short-term prospects (Huang 1999). Immediately after taking office in early 1998, Premier Zhu Rongji (*People's Daily*, 19 March 1998) predicted that the impact of the East Asian crisis on China would be minimal and announced a new set of ambitious policies including

- improving the efficiency of the large state-owned enterprises within three years
- reforming the banking sector, including restructuring the central bank system
- maintaining the stability of the renminbi to contribute to the recovery of the region
- downsizing government organisations by half
- introducing a fiscal stimulation package and carrying out residential housing reform.

Although Premier Zhu expected possible 'landmines and abysses' when announcing this comprehensive policy program, he was confident that, with careful macroeconomic management and progress on reforms, China would be able to surmount the East Asian crisis relatively easily. Exports only account for about 20 per cent of China's total GDP, even according to the official statistics (SSB 1998). In addition, China is a large country and much of inland China is yet to experience economic take off. There is great potential for inward-oriented growth based on regional collaboration. Even for exports, the negative impact might be minimised through special measures such as tax rebates and productivity growth.

This chapter assesses the performance of the Chinese economy since the onset of financial crisis in Thailand in July 1997 and explores the factors that made China different from the other crisis-affected East Asian economies. It analyses the potential risks facing the Chinese economy. The central focus is the consequences of and prospects for China's capital account control and foreign exchange policy.

HOW HAS CHINA WEATHERED THE CRISIS?

China's GDP grew at 8.8 per cent in 1997 and 7.8 per cent in 1998. Strong growth momentum was sustained in 1999—with a GDP growth rate of 7.1 per cent (Table 16.1). Industrial sector growth in China, though slowing, was strong in 1998, with light industry growing slightly faster than heavy industry. (This gap, however, was reversed after 1998.) Decomposed by ownership, joint-stock and foreign-funded industrial firms experienced the most rapid expansion, growing at 11.9 and 12.7 per cent respectively in 1998. Collective industrial firms only managed average growth, while state-owned enterprises grew at a below average rate of 4.9 per cent. Such high economic growth rates are not extraordinary compared to China's own performance during the reform period. They are nonetheless remarkable considering the negative growth rates experienced by most of China's neighbours.

Investment by the state sector, boosted by the infrastructure construction programs initiated by the government in 1998, has been the prime force behind the impressive economic growth since 1998. The state sector's investment growth reached 19.6 per cent in 1998 and peaked in the first two months of 1999 at 28.3 per cent. As a number of projects were completed, growth began to decline from March. During the first five months of 1999, the growth of fixed asset investment by the state-owned sector slowed to 17.5 per cent, a decline from 22.7 per cent for the first quarter and 18.1 per cent for the first four months. Growth of industrial value-added has exhibited a clear

Table 16.1 China: macroeconomic indicators, 1995–9

	1995	1996	1997	1998	1999ᵃ
Real GDP (% real change)	10.5	9.5	8.8	7.8	7.1
Gross industrial output (% real change)	20.3	16.6	13.1	8.9	9.6
Inflation (CPI % change)	17.1	8.3	2.8	-0.8	-1.4
Growth of M2 broad money supply (%)	29.5	25.3	19.6	14.8	14.7
Exchange rate (RMB/US$)	8.32	8.30	8.28	8.28	8.28
Fixed asset investment (% nominal change)	13.3	10.6	9.0	14.1	8.9
Retail sales (% nominal change)	26.8	20.1	10.2	6.8	6.7
Exports (% changes in US$)	23.0	1.5	21.0	0.5	6.1
Imports (% change in US$)	14.2	5.1	2.5	-1.5	18.2
Merchandise trade balance (US$ billion)	16.7	12.2	40.3	43.6	29.2

Sources: State Statistics Bureau, *Chinese Statistical Yearbook 1998* and CEIC Data Company Limited, Hong Kong.

downward trend, falling from 10.1 per cent for the first quarter to 9.7 per cent for the first four months and 9.5 per cent for the first five months. In May 1999, the growth rate rose 8.9 per cent on a year-on-year basis (Song Quan, 'Industry growth slowing down', *China Daily*, 10 June 1999). These figures demonstrate the critical contribution of state investment to real growth (Xu Binglan, 'Investment growth rate falls', *China Daily*, 16 June 1999).

The monetary environment, measured by the growth rate of money supply (M2), was relatively tight in 1998 and early 1999 (Table 16.1). The central bank has introduced continuous cuts in interest rates over the past two years, reducing the one-year loan rate from 10.1 per cent in 1996 to 3.25 per cent in June 1999, to encourage spending by both households and enterprises. Prices, however, have continued to fall. Deflation began in October 1997 when the retail price index first slipped into negative territory and the index has continued to fall. Figures at mid 1999 showed that the RPI dropped 3.5 per cent and CPI fell 2.2 per cent year-on-year in May 1999 (Christine Chan, 'Deflation points to failure of stimulus,' *South China Morning Post*, Internet Edition, 16 June 1999). From January to May, CPI fell 1.7 per cent, while RPI dropped 3.2 per cent, compared with the same period in 1998. While prices fell, retail sales continued to grow. Retail sales of consumer goods rose 6.7 per cent in 1999.

As expected, China's export sector has encountered difficulties. The government has introduced policy measures to stimulate exports, including increasing the rebate rate of value-added taxes for exports (regarded by some economists as a hidden form of currency devaluation) to offset the adverse effects of overvaluation of the renminbi. In 1998, exports grew by 0.5 per cent and imports fell by 1.5 per cent. In the first five months of 1999, exports decreased by 5.3 per cent but imports jumped by 15.3 per cent. These changes were directly related to exchange rate policy—Chinese exports became less competitive against exports from the crisis-affected economies and imports became much cheaper. Decomposition of export growth data by destination markets indicates that growth of exports to East Asian markets declined quickly and was negative during most of 1998, while exports to the United States and European Union markets continued to experience rapid growth (Figure 16.1). This is the income effect (Huang and Yang 1998). At the end of 1998, as the crisis-affected economies started the process of recovery, their demand for imports increased and the falling growth rates of China's exports to these markets bottomed out. Competition in the United States and European Union markets also intensified because of the crisis-affected economies' newly gained competitiveness through sharp currency devaluation. Growth rates of China's exports to these markets dropped significantly from mid 1998. For instance, China has reportedly lost large iron and steel contracts to Korean manufacturers—the price effect in action (Huang and Yang 1998). During the first five months of 1999 this trend continued. Exports to Hong Kong, Taiwan and Russia dropped, while exports to the United States, Japan, Korea, Australia, Canada and the European Union increased. Agricultural, machinery and electronic exports increased, while iron and steel, chemicals, textile, garment, shoes and toy exports all decreased.

In 1998, the current account surplus maintained its 1997 level, as did realised foreign direct investment (but contracted foreign direct investment declined significantly). In the first quarter of 1999, however, the current account surplus started to decline. While contracted foreign direct investment was steady at US$8.7 billion, realised foreign direct investment was only US$7.3 billion, a 15 per cent decrease. As about 80 per cent of China's foreign direct investment was from East Asian economies, a significant fall in of foreign direct investment from these economies was expected, given their liquidity problems at home. McKibbin (1998) also predicted that there would be capital

Figure 16.1 China: export growth by destination, 1997–8 (per cent)

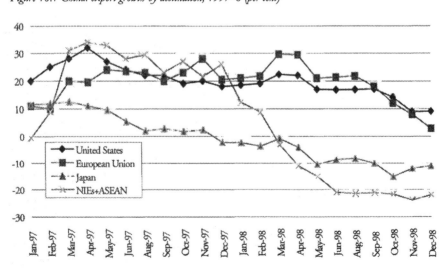

Source: Customs Statistics, China Customs.

flight out of East Asia, mainly to the United States market, because of the relative changes in risk premia. The exchange rate in the regulated market was stable, appreciating very slowly after 1994. The black market rate fluctuated, partly depending on the tightness of government controls, but was mostly below 10 RMB/US$ (as compared to the official rate of 8.28 RMB/US$). At the end of 1998, foreign exchange reserves increased slightly to US$145 billion, up from US$140 billion a year before. Given the large current account surplus, the small increase in foreign exchange reserves may have reflected the public's (households and enterprises) preference for holding foreign exchange given exchange rate policy.

In short, the Chinese economy is sound. It did not experience the financial meltdown suffered by other East Asian economies. Impacts of the regional crises, however, are being strongly felt through transmissions of the real variables.

THE IMPORTANCE OF CAPITAL ACCOUNT CONTROLS

When the crisis first erupted in East Asia, many economists warned about risks in the Chinese economy that could potentially lead to great instability (Lardy 1998a; Huang and Yang 1998; Song 1998)

- a currency crisis, caused by balance of payment problems or heavy capital outflows
- a banking crisis, caused by bank runs due to loss of depositor confidence and bank insolvency.

In retrospect, China's performance in averting a currency crisis was smooth. It even made a positive contribution to regional economic stability by maintaining the value of the renminbi. There are many reasons why China, almost alone, was able to ride out of the currency crisis storm. Although China followed the East Asian growth model, it is distinct in a number of respects. First, since the early 1990s, China had maintained significant current account surpluses, with 1993 as the only exception. In 1997, when the crisis broke, China had a current account surplus of nearly US$30 billion and this was maintained in 1998 (Table 16.2). This is in sharp contrast to the persistent current account deficits in Thailand and Indonesia before the crisis began.

Second, while China was the largest capital importer in East Asia, more than 60 per cent of the capital inflow was in the form of foreign direct investment and more than 80 per cent of the international borrowing was in the form of long-term debts from international organisations and foreign governments. The debt-service ratio stayed at

Table 16.2 China: economic indicators for the external economy, 1995–8

	1995	1996	1997	1998	1999
Current account balance (US$ billion)	1.6	7.3	29.7	29.3	13.4
Growth of foreign direct investment inflow (%)	5.9	12.3	7.0	0.0	-6.7
Foreign exchange reserves (US$ billion)	73.6	105.0	139.9	145.0	154.7
External debt (US$ billion)	94.6	104.6	118.6	146.0	130.0
External debt service ratio (% of exports)	9.1	9.9	11.8	14.3	12.6

Sources: State Statistics Bureau, *Chinese Statistical Yearbook 1998* and CEIC Data Company Limited, Hong Kong.

low levels. In comparison, the large volumes of short-term portfolio investment in other East Asian economies presented a destabilising factor once confidence in their currencies manifested as a problem.

Third, China rapidly built up large foreign exchange reserves in the years prior to the crisis. From 1996, the size of foreign exchange reserves was roughly the same as total external debts and far greater than short-term external debts. In 1997, for instance, foreign exchange reserves were US$140 billion while total external debts were US$119 billion. The world's second largest foreign exchange reserves provided a first line of defence against any instability induced by a lack of confidence.

Finally, China still exercised strict controls over its capital account, although it realised free convertibility of the renminbi on the current account in compliance with the IMF's Article VIII provisions. While it is controversial as to how effective controls were in stopping capital flight (Huang and Yang 1998), they served as an important layer of insulation from the instability in the international capital market. Since the crisis began in East Asia, China has substantially tightened its controls over capital movements.

In summary, the factors that distinguish China from the other crisis-affected East Asian economies fall into two categories: those related to China's healthy macroeconomy and those associated with capital account controls.

The continued rapid growth of income, deeper integration into the world commodity markets, increasing flexibility in structural adjustment and significant current account surpluses were important factors in China's ability to weather the crisis. But these conditions would not have been sufficient to avert the crisis. In our assessment, capital accounts control played a dominant role. Controls prevented attacks on the Chinese currency by international speculators in overseas capital markets. Significant capital flight was stopped by further tightening controls. More importantly, controls were responsible for some of the advantageous factors mentioned above. Foreign direct investment's dominance in capital inflow, for instance, is directly attributable to the controls on the capital account. Likewise, the large foreign exchange reserves were built in part as a strategic measure to fight any disturbance to the regulated exchange rate.

Control of capital flows imposes severe costs on the Chinese economy by restricting Chinese households and enterprises' access to international capital markets (borrowing or lending). But currently the benefits of having the controls as a buffer against external uncertainties outweigh the costs, especially because inflow of foreign direct investment to China is already very strong. This is made clear in later discussion about the fragility of the domestic financial system.

China will eventually introduce a floating exchange rate regime. This decisive reform will critically depend on a number of other conditions. One important precondition is a substantial improvement in the business practices of the banking sector. The ratio of non-performing loans to total bank assets was about 25 per cent before the crisis began, much higher than those in the crisis-affected economies, and some state-owned banks were technically insolvent (Lardy 1998b:5). These banks could fall into deep trouble should bank runs, triggered by a loss of depositor confidence, occur. Given the dominant role of the state-owned banks, such problems would cause widespread instability in the economy (Lardy 1998b).

Unfortunately, the banking sector cannot be reformed in isolation. It is now locked into a unique triangular relationship with the state-owned enterprises and public finance policy. First, the state-owned enterprises, though continuously undergoing reform, remain very inefficient. The findings on total factor productivity performance have been mixed. Some studies have found evidence of significant positive total factor productivity growth (Jefferson *et al.* 1992 and 1996), while others have reported stagnant or even negative productivity change (Woo *et al.* 1994). There is, nonetheless, no disagreement among China watchers about the worsening financial performance of the state-owned enterprises. In 1996, the state-owned enterprises as a whole made a net loss of 38 billion yuan, and these dire results have continued (SSB 1997). The estimated 30 per cent of redundant workers in the state sector also pose potential employment pressure on the rest of the economy.

Second, the financial system has become increasingly fragile (Lardy 1998a; Huang and Yang 1998). The average ratio of non-performing loans for the four large state-owned banks in 1997 was much higher than the ratios in Thailand, Korea, Malaysia and Indonesia before the financial crisis began (McLeod and Garnaut 1998). Meanwhile, real estate bubbles and excess production capacity are widespread, especially in the coastal region.

Third, the central government fiscal position has weakened during the reform period. The ratio of the formal budget revenue to GNP fell from 35 per cent in 1978 to 11.5 per cent in 1997 (SSB, various years). Although many local governments were compensated by the raising of extra-budgetary revenues, the economic power of the government, especially the central government, declined significantly. The major proportion of fiscal resources is spent on personnel and administrative activities. Important issues such as social security, infrastructure development and regional disparity are hardly addressed. The budget deficit rose sharply from RMB14 billion in the 1984–6 period to RMB167 billion in the 1995–6 period. In 1999 the fiscal balance was -2.1 per cent of GDP, compared to -1.2 per cent in 1998 and -0.8 per cent in 1997.

The problems of this banking sector/state-owned enterprise/public finance policy relationship are mutually induced. The inefficient state-owned enterprises, for instance, demand budget subsidies and contribute to non-performing loans. This exacerbates the already poor financial and fiscal conditions. Due to the shortage of fiscal revenues, the government has often had to shift its fiscal responsibilities to the state-owned banks in the form of policy loans. Policy loans are often set at low interest rates and are rarely paid back. The complexity of the relationship suggests that the previous sector-by-sector or incremental approach to reform may no longer be applicable. China's own experiences have proven that, among these three, reform of any one sector cannot succeed without having successfully transformed the other two. While the state-owned enterprises continue to be inefficient, for instance, it is not possible to reform the state-owned banks or the fiscal system. Furthermore, these problems are also responsible, at least partly, for the other difficulties facing China, such as unemployment pressures and regional disparity.

Over the past two years, the situation has worsened. The financial performance of all types of enterprises deteriorated after the crisis began. A national work conference estimated that about half of China's collective enterprises were on the brink of bankruptcy (*China Economic Times*, 24 June 1999). Not only has the relative contribution by the collective sector to industrial output declined, but the number of employees has also decreased. In 1998, the asset-liability ratio of 313,000 urban industrial and commercial enterprises averaged 78.2 per cent. About 55,000 enterprises, or 17.6 per cent of the total, are insolvent, and around 50 per cent of these enterprises are on the brink of bankruptcy. The 47,000 collective financial enterprises suffered RMB9.15 billion in net losses. Their bad debts reached RMB308.59 billion, accounting for 33.3 per cent of the total loans. Rural credit cooperatives were in a particularly grim situation, with their rate of bad debts reaching as high as 37 per cent. Overall industrial performance has deteriorated. In 1998 total realised industrial profit was 147.3 billion yuan, a fall of 17 per cent relative to 1997; total industrial losses amounted to 155.8 billion yuan, an increase of 22.1 per cent over 1997 (net industrial losses reached 8.5 billion yuan in 1998). Of this, total losses incurred by state-owned enterprises reached 102.3 billion yuan, 21.9 per cent higher than 1997. By the end of 1998, the total industrial inventory had reached 609.4 billion yuan, a 5.5 per cent increase over the level in 1997 (SSB 1999). One study indicates that the state-owned enterprise debt-asset ratio was 60.79 per cent and bad debts accounted for 25 per cent of their total assets by the end of 1996. State-owned enterprise non-performing loans accounted for 77.8 per cent of the total (Furen Dong, 'Carefully nurturing security markets,' *People's Daily* (Overseas Edition), 3 July 1999).

The financial difficulties in the enterprise sectors exacerbate the situation in the banking system. In 1998, China introduced a number of new reform policies for the financial sector, including granting more autonomy to the state-owned banks to make lending decisions (both on projects and interest rates), introducing a new accounting system consistent with international practice, and reorganising the central bank system by replacing provincial branches with regional headquarters. The financial performance of the banking sector, however, did not improve, mainly because of huge public spending and continued extension of loans to the loss-making state-owned enterprises. In 1997, the reported ratio of non-performing loans was 24 per cent and about 6 per cent of total loans were bad debts (Huang and Yang 1998). China has not disclosed any information about non-performing loans since then, but some estimates of this ratio are as high as 30–50 per cent (Chang 1998; John Pomfret, 'China set to tackle economic woes', *Washington Post Foreign Service*, Saturday 16 January 1999:A21). Recognising this difficulty, Chinese authorities have accelerated the reform process. The Guangdong International Trust and Investment Corporation, with an outstanding debt of about US$4 billion, was pronounced bankrupt at the end of 1998, sending a shocking signal to the international capital market. Four asset management companies, in association with the four large state-owned banks, were set up to deal with RMB1.3 trillion bad debts (equivalent to 19 per cent of China's GDP).

Will there be bank runs in China? Locally, this is possible, but nation-wide bank runs remain unlikely. The government is the guarantor of bank deposits. If bank runs occur, the central government has the capacity, using both financial and fiscal resources, to settle anxiety. This does not rule out the possibility of a bank crisis. One such scenario under which this could occur is if the government were to abruptly open up the domestic financial sector and liberalise the capital account. The vulnerable state-owned banks would then face immediate competition from foreign banks both inside and outside China. The current interest rate gap between renminbi and US dollar-denominated deposits could trigger a large-scale conversion from the renminbi to US dollars. The state-owned banks would lose good customers and the balance sheet would start to deteriorate quickly. Another such scenario is related to slow growth. When economic growth slows down, growth of household deposits falls sharply. Banks may face a liquidity constraint, since currently about 70 per cent of deposits are made by households. Compounding this, when the growth rate falls, enterprises are more likely to run into financial difficulties (especially when slow growth is accompanied by price deflation which further reduces the profit margin) and thus non-performing loans could accumulate rapidly.

EXCHANGE RATE POLICY AND DEFLATION

The other side of capital account controls is control over the exchange rate. At the beginning of 1994, the Chinese government unified its two exchange rates, the official rate and the secondary market rate, and the new rate was set at 8.7 RMB/US$. Later, to comply with IMF Article VIII, the government realised free convertibility of the renminbi on the current account. It was originally planned that in 2000, the renminbi would become freely convertible (that is, capital account controls would be abandoned). While free convertibility of the renminbi is still on the government's policy agenda, it will now occur at a later date.

After the East Asian financial crises began, the renminbi became the only currency experiencing nominal appreciation in the region. China was strongly urged by the international community not to devalue its currency in order to avoid further rounds of competitive devaluation. The Chinese government agreed to this, although it was somewhat contradictory to the general principle of market-oriented reform. The exchange rate in the official market has been remarkably stable since then (Table 16.1). By late 1998–early 1999, most crisis-affected economies were on their way to recovery.

The expected consequences of the East Asian financial crises and China's own foreign exchange rate policy were slower growth of exports and slower inflows of foreign direct investment. The unexpected effects included continuous price deflation and a slowdown of the domestic economy. The Chinese economy is experiencing a serious price deflation, with signs of potential recession throughout the economy (Figure 16.2). China's commodity retail price index increased by only 0.8 per cent in 1997 and decreased by -2.6 per cent in 1998. The two-year cumulative figure for the agricultural purchase price index dropped 12 per cent and the factor price index for industrial products fell by 4.4 per cent. Fixed asset investment price movements turned negative in 1998, but prices for service products (such as telecommunications and medical services) increased by substantial amounts. In the short term, price deflation benefits household consumption, particularly low income earners (rural households or laid-off workers from state-owned enterprises), and therefore contributes to the social stability. It increases competitive pressures among producers, including foreign firms. Falling domestic prices also help exporters enhance the competitiveness of their products on the world market. However, falling prices have negatively affected

Figure 16.2 China: deflation, 1997–9

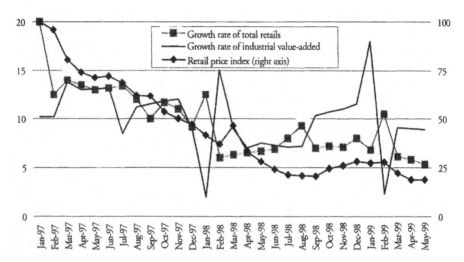

Source: Statistical Yearbook of China, 1999.

the economy by reducing the profits for enterprises, lowering incomes for employees and weakening both producer (including foreign investors) and consumer confidence. The decline in the price indexes of production materials began even earlier than the CPI decline.

Economists have suggested three factors as the causes of price deflation in China. The first factor is insufficient demand. High savings in East Asian economies have been regarded by many as a key factor behind the rapid economic growth in the region. However, high savings without spending have become a big concern for the Chinese government. Why do people not spend? On the one hand, there are uncertainties among ordinary people associated with reform to pensions, housing, insurance, medical care and education. Faced with these uncertainties, the majority of the households insist on depositing their money in banks despite the low interest rate. A related reason is the expectation of slower income growth and greater expenditure on consumer durables, automobiles and houses. On the other hand, the rising real interest rates discourage spending by both households and enterprises. From 1995 to June 1999, the nominal interest rate for one-year loans was reduced from 12.1 per cent to 3.25 per cent. The real interest rate, however, jumped from -2.7 per cent to 6.45 per cent. Thanks to the non-convertibility of the renminbi and capital controls, individuals and enterprises' savings have been kept in Chinese banks even though their deposit rates are lower than the US dollar rate.

The second factor is excess supply. China has been facing excess capacity problems for several years. According to the 1995 industrial census, the average ratios of capacity utilisation ranged between 60 and 70 per cent. Domestic excess supply was further exacerbated by changes in the external sector: difficulties in the export sector and cheaper imports.

The third factor is changes in monetary policy. Some economists attribute the weak domestic demand at least partly to the 'soft-landing' package (a tight monetary policy) (Institute of Economics 1998; Dong 1998; Huang 1999). While successful in cooling the economy, the package excessively drove down domestic demand. As early as the end of 1997, many economists warned of weak domestic demand as a result of tight monetary policy (CCER 1998; Dong 1999b).

Though all these factors have contributed to deflation and the weak domestic economy in one way or another, they nevertheless missed the most important cause— China's exchange rate policy in the face of financial crises in the region. The transmission from a fixed exchange rate policy to deflation is as follows

- the collapse of East Asian currencies coupled with China's commitment to maintain the value of the renminbi suddenly rendered Chinese exports relatively more expensive

- demand shifted from Chinese exports toward exports from elsewhere— equivalent to an inward shift of the demand curve for Chinese exports

- this changed the relative returns to production for the domestic and export markets, and so more products were supplied to the domestic market

- the renminbi prices of Chinese products fell.

Two outcomes were possible. Under rigid wages and prices, exports would fall substantially, domestic output prices would decline somewhat and production would contract significantly. Under flexible wages and prices, domestic wages and intermediate prices would be forced down. Domestic output prices would decline accordingly, but the reduction in exports would be less dramatic. This latter scenario was what we observed in the Chinese economy. This was why the pressure for devaluation was not particularly strong.

Price deflation was a natural response to the exchange rate policy. Under a fixed exchange rate with flexible prices, overvaluation is resolved through downward pressure on domestic prices. Without this, we would not be able to explain why deflation occurred at this particular time while all the other demand and supply-side factors had been present for many years.

The reasons for the Chinese government's reluctance to devalue the renminbi are understandable. Apart from the political importance of maintaining the commitment, the implications of devaluation for the large number of fragile international trust and investment corporations is also a major concern. Given their substantial borrowing from the international capital markets, most international trust and investment corporations are shaky financially. Even a mild devaluation could easily push the majority of them over the edge. This is another reason to clean up the domestic financial system before introducing any further substantial reforms.

CONCLUDING REMARKS

The post-reform Chinese economy has much in common with the other East Asian economies, yet China did not join most of its neighbours in the recent financial meltdown. China differs from most of the other East Asian economies in some important areas—the current account balance, continued growth momentum and the diversity of the domestic economy.

The main difference, however, lay in the degree of financial liberalisation. Immediately prior to the financial crises, the Chinese financial system was no healthier than those of its neighbouring economies, reflected in poor profitability, low capital adequacy ratios and high levels of non-performing loans. But importantly, China maintained its capital account controls: the renminbi was freely convertible on the current but not the capital account. Capital account controls have efficiency costs, but helped to protect China's vulnerable financial sector from instabilities in the international capital market. Furthermore, capital account controls were an important contributor to other advantageous conditions, such as the large foreign exchange reserves and the dominance of foreign direct investment in total capital inflows that helped China to avert a currency crisis.

Non-convertibility also enabled China to make a no-devaluation commitment in order to help the recovery of the regional economy. This was extremely important in preventing competitive devaluations and China's integration into the regional political system. It has also brought some adverse side effects. Price deflation was a natural response to the no devaluation policy in a world where other currencies collapsed overnight. To achieve a new equilibrium in export and domestic markets, domestic prices had to fall. Because of the adjustments in domestic prices and introduction of the tax rebate policy, overvaluation of the Chinese currency in real terms is limited.

The real economy was affected by rigid nominal exchange rate and price deflation, deceleration of GDP growth and stagnation of exports. This was particularly undesired as the Chinese government was about to push through critical reforms to state-owned enterprises and state banks. It is for this reason that at the height of the East Asian financial crisis, many analysts predicted that it was inevitable that China devalue the currency. On several occasions even the authors of this paper were of this view.

While the devaluation argument appeared logical, in retrospect the critical test is whether the stimulation program (including fiscal expansion, tax rebates and salary rises) can carry through until corporations and households are ready to take over the main driver of growth of production and consumption. Although the Chinese government was successful in lifting GDP growth in 1998 and 1999, it is clear that fiscal spending can support growth for a very long period. Fortunately, by the end of 1999, most of the crisis-affected economies were well on the path to recovery. This helped boost China's exports (by 38 per cent in the first half of 2000) and to reduce pressure on the exchange rate. Within China, the corporate sector's profit margin increased again as consumer spending began to pick up slowly. By mid 2000, CPI deflation was long gone. Today the possibility of devaluation is almost zero. In fact, if the government really expands the band of exchange rate fluctuation as is widely speculated, the RMB will appreciate rather than depreciate.

The next policy question concerns liberalisation of the capital account, particularly in light of comprehensive reforms committed in association with WTO membership. Capital account liberalisation is on the agenda but no detailed timetable is set. In the short term we believe that the benefits of liberalisation are limited as long as FDI inflow is strong. Learning from the experiences of other East Asian economies, China needs first to build a strong domestic financial sector before it takes any measures to liberalise the capital account.

Part 7

Looking to the future

17 The private sector and the framework for international capital flows

George Vojta

Crisis conditions in emerging market countries have abated. The turmoil of 1997–8 has receded—exchange rates and financial markets in crisis-affected countries have recovered, interest rates have declined and positive growth rates (notably in some East Asian countries) emerged in the second quarter of 1999. The improvement in macro fundamentals is encouraging. On the other hand, the pace of reform remains slow—comprehensive corporate and financial sector restructuring has yet to be undertaken. The fact that market recovery has occurred ahead of structural reform should not obscure the fact that many of the problems which contributed to the recent crisis have yet to be addressed.

The international community has recently given serious attention to the global financial architecture and addressed questions of appropriate change in the light of recent crisis experience. One of the most complex issues is the role of the private sector in both crisis prevention and crisis management. Although there is a general understanding that the private sector is the only sufficient source of the capital, technology and skill necessary to re-establish and maintain global growth, the role of the private sector in crisis situations remains controversial. The issue merits continuing attention—private sector activity prior to, during and after crises has been crucial to outcomes.

The 1997–8 crisis demonstrated, once again, that the public sector and multilateral institutions do not and will never have adequate resources to resolve crises on their own. At best the official sector can promote a supportive policy and regulatory climate to encourage global growth, stability and private sector activity. The controversial nature of the direct official and multilateral institutional programs in Mexico, Korea, Thailand and Indonesia reinforces the view that private sector support must be the principal solution to both financial crises and long-term global growth. This analysis focuses on emerging market economies, but the principles advanced apply to all countries in which the private sector is active.

PRIVATE SECTOR PARTICIPATION IN THE GLOBAL ECONOMY

The private sector's role in the global economy cannot be addressed in a general manner. It is necessary to consider specific segments of private sector participation, in terms of the resources each segment commands and the motivation and accountabilities that guide decisionmaking. Statistical profiles of private sector activity in countries under stress show a variety of patterns of behaviour. Over time, however, the factors that command private sector support for a particular country are reasonably constant. Understanding these factors is the best perspective from which to consider the private sector's role in crises.

The main private sector players in financial contexts include proprietary market participants; short and long-term commercial bank and trade credit providers; securitised debt, equity and derivative underwriters; secondary market fixed income/equity investors; foreign direct investors; and local public and private investors.

These players will support and participate in the economic and financial affairs of host countries if ongoing conditions in the country positively correlate with their motivation and accountabilities. Further, if such positive correlation occurs over time, the prospects for private sector support through a crisis are materially improved. The specific issues relative to each participant class need to be understood clearly.

PROPRIETARY MARKET PARTICIPANTS

The major global commercial and investment banks and some insurance companies and hedge funds commit their own capital (often leveraged with bank debt) to assume principal risk positions in global market currencies, interest rates, fixed income and equity instruments, utilising both cash and derivative markets. Three basic trading risks are taken: proprietary risk (outright long or short positions for the institutions' own account); arbitrage risk (relative value trades involving the same instrument in different markets, different instruments in the same market and different instruments in different markets); and convergence risk trades (which take a point of view on the relative value ratios between different instrument, currencies, interest rates or markets). Principal market activity attracts criticism as speculation, with destabilising consequences; in reality this activity makes markets more efficient by trading out price anomalies. Proprietary market activity also is a prime source of market discipline, as it reacts to macro and micro trends. In the simplest terms, proprietary activity takes long (favourable) or short (unfavourable) positions in the fields in which it is acting. In many emerging markets it is difficult or impossible to take short positions (or to hedge long risks); in these circumstances, risk profiles are confined to long positions or no position at all. Proprietary activity must take a long or short position to earn a profit.

Proprietary activity in emerging markets is vulnerable to abrupt changes in market volatility, liquidity risk and contagion risk. The risks associated with proprietary activity have been steadily magnified by the spread of information technology throughout the world. In stressful market conditions, reactions are instantaneous and often one-sided (all participants take similar actions at roughly the same time based on availability of the same information).

Principal market participants are motivated by the need to earn a profit, avoid loss and to achieve substantial positive returns on risk capital employed. Typically, results are measured on a current mark-to-market valuation basis. Proprietary professionals are compensated in a highly incentivised manner relative to their profit/loss experience, usually over a one-year time frame. Market participants assume, maintain and often increase long risk positions if they view macro and micro conditions favourably over the near term; if country conditions deteriorate, risk positions are rapidly adjusted to neutral or, where possible, short. Significant changes in long, neutral or short positions can cause abrupt changes in the short-term capital account of affected countries. Countries in which market participants are active are under continuous scrutiny by proprietary traders.

PROVIDERS OF SHORT AND LONG-TERM BANK AND TRADE CREDITS

Bank and corporate enterprises provide credit to counterparties (public and private) in global markets if they deem debtors able to service and repay the credit extended on the contractual terms agreed. In making credit decisions, lenders assess country risk, industry risk, business cycle risk and individual counterparty risk. Lenders are motivated to extend loans to make a financial profit, to advance commercial objectives and to avoid loss (of both interest and principal). Accountability for professionals responsible for credit activities is based on the realisation of net credit income (after costs of funding, other costs and credit losses) and return on credit capital employed to support the lending activity.

When conditions in a country turn negative, lenders rapidly contract credit to reduce exposure and avoid loss. Loans are collected as they mature, with short-term loans and the current maturities of term loans collected first. As the East Asian crises of 1997–8 demonstrated, short-term credit for trade and other purposes can be withdrawn rapidly, contributing significantly to capital flight and foreign exchange reserve loss in many countries during that period.

Institutions which have credit (or investment) exposures to local institutions resort to managing leads and lags in payment obligations when countries become troubled to mitigate risk and avoid loss. Dividends, royalties, collection of receivables and repatriation of capital are accelerated where possible; obligations owed, both short and long-term, in foreign or local currencies, are deferred, and if possible increased to reduce long credit exposures (which often are coupled with currency exposures). Accelerated lead and lag flows are as destabilising to the short-term capital account as credit contraction.

UNDERWRITERS OF SECURITISED DEBT, EQUITY AND DERIVATIVE TRANSACTIONS

The globally active investment and commercial banks dominate underwriting and derivative transactions. Incidental to this activity is the carrying of securities and derivative risks on the underwriter's books, while transactions are in distribution to investors or to make orderly secondary markets in these instruments. Most financing is international and in currencies other than the local currency of issuers; local underwriting has been confined to the developed and more developed emerging economies.

After the emerging market debt crisis of the 1980s, which was principally a bank debt crisis, most emerging market countries switched to securitised financing, mostly fixed income but including some equity. This recourse to capital markets diversified the investor base in emerging markets. Investment fund and fiduciary investors, as opposed to bank and corporate lenders, became prominent in the early 1990s. The emergence of the derivative market, permitting issuers to hedge or take points of view on interest rates, currencies, commodity and securities prices, occurred consequent to the deregulation and liberalisation of financial markets.

Underwriters of securities and derivatives transactions are diligent in assessing risk. If the underwriter believes that the issuer can service the obligation and that favourable returns can be expected, he or she commits capital and warrants to third party investors to whom the issue will be distributed that the risks are acceptable for the rewards offered.

Underwriters are motivated by the desire to earn profits from underwriting and market making and to avoid loss. If country conditions deteriorate, underwriting first diminishes, then ceases, cutting off the country from international capital markets. Underwriters also seek to limit market-making commitments. In these circumstances, local capital markets often collapse.

An extended period of deteriorating country conditions usually calls into question the ability (and sometimes the willingness) of local issuers to service debt and equity obligations. The crises of the 1990s demonstrated that the diversification of financing sources to include securities, equities and derivatives in addition to the traditional bank and commercial debt made financial restructuring more complex as a wider array of institutions and instruments was involved. Issuing countries tended to be more hesitant to assume responsibility for securitised debt, equity and derivatives obligations relative to bank and commercial debt, complicating matters even further. A decrease in country ratings by rating agencies in these circumstances raised the cost of finance, and in some instances, eliminated access to the international capital markets. Regaining access to international financial markets depends on the establishment of a credible macro turn-around program and successful renegotiation and restructuring of impaired debt and derivative obligations. If crises produce defaults, even temporarily, regaining market access becomes more difficult.

INVESTMENT FUNDS

Investment funds, typically mutual funds, and portfolio investment by institutional fiduciaries (and high net worth individuals) have played a prominent role in many countries. In recent years the flow of such investment into emerging market countries has accelerated, attendant to liberalisation of capital and currency controls and favourable growth prospects.

In assessing the performance of fiduciary managers, investment results are measured on a current mark-to-market basis—investors accept a high risk/reward trade-off and expect returns in excess of the index benchmarks in the major financial markets. Failure to achieve this results in a loss of funds under management. Success, on the other hand, is handsomely rewarded.

If conditions deteriorate and local financial and securities market prices decline, fund managers usually hedge or liquidate investment positions and repatriate funds out of the country, rather than take short risks, which they often cannot do, even if allowed. Investments can take time to exit because fund managers may view the market disturbances as temporary and choose to maintain (or even increase at favourable prices) their long investment profile. However, if negative conditions persist, fiduciary investment managers will eventually exit the market, even if losses must be sustained in so doing.

There is an important point regarding the behaviour of proprietary market participants, bank and commercial credit providers and fiduciary investors. In crisis conditions, in which governments and multilateral institutions are providing direct financial assistance (for example, in Mexico, Korea, Thailand and Indonesia), the public sector has shown increasing unwillingness to extend direct assistance, which would have the effect of financing the exit of proprietary market participants, lenders and private fund investors. Such action is deemed politically unacceptable by the governments and multilateral institutions involved. In these circumstances, the private sector often has been criticised for excessive, foolish risk decisions by the public sector. Governments and multilateral institutions strongly encourage private sector participants to provide relief to countries by stopping destabilising exit behaviour, providing additional credit and investment support in the form of restructuring, extension, forgiveness and new financial assistance. This is the basis for the call for the private sector to bear more of the burden of adjustment and to be bailed in to participate directly with the public sector in crafting and executing solutions.

FOREIGN DIRECT INVESTMENT

Corporations, financial institutions and private equity funds make foreign direct investments for both strategic and financial reasons. Strategic investors invest to advance their business franchise in the global marketplace, with the expectation of earning absolute profits and acceptable returns on the capital invested over the long term. Strategic investment options are taken up for two reasons: if the country market represents a favourable opportunity for establishing the investor's core business franchise or if direct investment would fill a strategic role in the corporation's global business system (for example, a low cost production facility for component parts to be shipped to the company's production centres). The decision to invest requires a favourable assessment of the host country's growth prospects, political stability and business conditions such as investment, trade and foreign exchange regimes and the tax and legal context. Macro wealth creation will, of course, add value to the investment.

In most cases, if conditions in a country deteriorate, the strategic investor cannot take immediate defensive action because of the intrinsic illiquidity of the investment but will act decisively to protect existing investments from being written down or written off. Direct private investment is not as volatile in the short run and strategic investment behaviour is not a factor in short-term crises, except for defensive lead and lag management and defensive hedging activity by strategic investors which can magnify crises. If negative conditions persist the strategic investor will try to hedge the investment and eventually execute options for an exit. If negative conditions persist further, strategic investors will eliminate the affected country from any investment consideration at all. Countries affected by the absence of direct strategic investment flows must rely on domestic savings for such investment, but often these are not adequate and cannot be effectively mobilised. The country will cease to benefit from the inward flows of technology and skill.

A financial buyer is a provider of medium-term capital, often private equity, to overseas countries motivated solely by the desire to realise investment gains through a profitable exit from their investment (via a sale to a third party or a public offering). Such investors typically are prepared to invest over a three–five-year timeframe for this purpose. Financial investors seek to avoid loss but accept that financial investing is a portfolio exercise in which losses are expected to be more than offset by significant realised gains. Financial investors require a favourable assessment of a country's prospects, in the same way as a strategic investor does, to justify capital commitments. Both strategic and financial investors utilise their own capital or capital they manage for their clients. Debt leverage also is utilised.

There is currently an enormous pool of investable capital in the global economy controlled by strategic and financial buyers actively looking for attractive investments in distressed situations. Distressed asset investors are prepared to invest if they believe both country and industry conditions have reached rockbottom and hence see prospects for an upward trend in the medium term. Distressed asset investors require realistic market valuations, always substantially lower than the historic carrying values of assets on the books of current owners, which means the current owners must bear a substantial loss. A third requirement is that the local climate for a reorganisation and restructuring of the distressed investment must be favourable.

The East Asian crisis in particular created distressed investment opportunities. In several countries, special purpose government agencies have been established to buy troubled assets from current local owners for ultimate sale to third parties at discounted prices, with the government agencies bearing the loss. To date, relatively few transactions have been consummated; the most important reason for this is an unwillingness or inability of current owners to mark asset values down far enough to attract investment capital.

LOCAL INVESTORS

Domestic investors in the debt and equity of local counterparties are also motivated by profit seeking/loss avoidance behaviour. The crisis experience has shown that local investors will exit long risk positions in the local economy as macro conditions deteriorate and currencies become vulnerable to devaluation.

In crises, local investors export capital out of their countries and liquidate assets or liabilities subject to currency devaluation risk (local currency investments or foreign currency liabilities serviced from local currency cash flows). In a number of countries the initial crisis of confidence involved foreign investors, but exit actions by local citizens magnified the crisis considerably.

SOME CONCLUSIONS

Although public sector participants in the debate about the role of the private sector in the global financial system tend to gloss over the specifics, private sector behaviour controls the decisionmaking that commits or withdraws resources and initiates transfers of technology and skill. This behaviour must be recognised, acknowledged and respected if meaningful private sector assistance in crises and in support of ongoing growth is to be achieved.

The basic accountabilities of all classes of participants in the private sector are ultimately the same. They are obligated to invest resources, capital, technology and skill to earn profit and satisfactory returns on capital. The mission is to create wealth for shareholders and clients. They are required to avoid loss. The professional people that manage private sector activities are measured by their profit/loss results and return on capital and are compensated in a highly incentivised manner. Some activities have different time frames for measuring accountable performance, but the fundamental mission is common to all.

From the point of view of host countries, support from the private sector requires creating favourable country conditions to encourage the private sector to take a net positive risk in their markets. The regime must allow private investors to retain and repatriate profits and capital invested in orderly fashion, without a prohibitive sacrifice of value. If these conditions do not exist, private sector support will be weak.

Government actions that forcibly require the private sector to behave against its intrinsic accountabilities and value system will cause a loss of private sector support. The bail-in crisis logic applied to the private sector is an example of this type of action; other examples are unilateral abrogation or default of contracts and property rights and arbitrary changes in the rules of the game (for example, the sudden imposition of capital or exchange controls).

THE PRE-CRISIS INVESTMENT PERSPECTIVE

Prior to the two periods of crisis in the 1990s, the private sector point of view on assuming risk in the global economy was well known. The crisis periods damaged this point of view and highlighted the issues involved in the new standards-based approach by the international community to restore stable conditions and solid growth prospects for the global economy.

Preconditions for risk commitments by the private sector in specific countries include reasonable political stability and continuity of development policy, macroeconomic and financial policies sufficient to produce reasonable prospects for sustained growth, orderly foreign exchange, interest rate and price trends and reasonable liquidity conditions. This general framework justified a conclusion that positive returns could be expected for trading, credit and investment commitments and that the country's general condition allowed for orderly exits from risk assumed.

Foreign investors assumed that host governments desired their involvement in their economies and accepted the obligation to service debt, equity and contractual obligations and the need for foreign investors to earn a profit and acceptable returns on capital. It was also assumed that foreign governments would confine corruption to levels that did not impair or complicate private sector activity.

Foreign investors demonstrated a liberal tolerance for policy ranges involving the foreign exchange, tax, trade and investment regimes. They also were tolerant of the fact that in most countries effective legal recourse to protect contract and property rights and facilitate corporate reorganisation did not exist. There was also tolerance for a significant lack of transparency in the public and private sectors. Foreign investors made the assumption that these shortcomings would be overcome by direct approaches to local government and local institutions with the expectation that these entities would work willingly and positively to support acceptable solutions to problems. Positive weight was given to host country willingness to provide explicit or implicit state guarantees to compensate for deficiencies in transparency relative to local risks. So long as the host country was viewed as positively inclined toward foreign investment and committed to conducting its affairs in an orderly, rational fashion, it was felt that the government could be relied upon to assist foreign investors when needed. The private sector also assumed that risks across countries and regions were diversified, thus giving further protection from portfolios effects. Countries that fell within the range of these parameters were reasonably supported by foreign investment, access to external finance and were of continuing interest to the private sector. Countries that fell outside these parameters often had a negative or neutral attitude toward attracting private foreign investment as well. In these cases, the private sector dealt with these countries on a limited, conservative (often collateral) basis or not at all. Countries abandoned by the private sector were left as wards of the international community, having to make do with grants and subsidies to maintain standards of living.

The first sign that this pre-crisis private sector view was lacking occurred with the emerging market debt crisis of the 1980s. The experience of debt default and the abrogation of financial contracts from a combination of inability and unwillingness to pay shocked the private sector. The resulting losses incurred by financial institutions and corporations, coupled with a period of severe macro instability, compounded this negative experience. Many countries, particularly in Latin America, experienced zero or declining growth throughout the 1980s. Nonetheless, by the end of the decade a reasonable period of global recovery was established and international trade, foreign investment and other resource flows, particularly to emerging markets countries, resumed and accelerated.

The dual financial crises of 1994–5 and 1997–8 shattered the positive global business climate once again. Macroeconomic and political instability recurred in several countries, many times in an unexpected fashion. The private sector's view of investment and other risk prospects turned negative. Most troublesome was the experience of the inability or unwillingness of the government to defend the debt and responsibly deal with other exposures to the private sector. Consequently, the costs to foreign investors as a result of the absence of viable legal protection and the consequences of a lack of transparency concerning risks were exposed in dramatic fashion. In some countries, corruption and an unhealthy collusion between government, local corporations and financial institutions were exposed. The resources of countries affected by the crises were rapidly depleted. More losses were incurred by the private sector and across the board exit behaviour by all classes resulted.

As the private sector withdrew support, and where possible exited from the countries caught up in crises, affected countries went through severe adjustments. Major currency devaluations, skyrocketing local interest rates, tight money, severe contractions of imports, the collapse of local financial markets, declines in GNP growth, and a deterioration of the financial sector as a result of a massive increase in problem assets, corporate and financial institution debt defaults occurred. Market contagion across East Asia and other emerging market countries was widespread, overwhelming the protection of portfolio diversification.

TOWARD THE FUTURE

Although crisis conditions have abated, markets have recovered and growth has been re-established in some countries, progress on structural reform has been slow. In the immediate post-crisis period, starting in mid 1998, the international community focused on remedies for the global financial system and its crisis management capabilities. After considering, but then rejecting ideas for radical change, the world community, led by the G7 countries, with support from multilateral institutions, opted for a more pragmatic, step-by-step approach to systemic reform. The consensus view among G7 countries is that the most appropriate approach is to elaborate for key areas global best practices standards, which when fully implemented in emerging market and other countries would improve the global financial system and its capacity to manage and withstand crises. Presently, standards are being articulated for fiscal policy, monetary policy, national income and balance of payments accounting transparency, cross-border insolvency, corporate governance, securities and insurance regulation, core principles of banking supervision, accounting standards and auditing standards, payments systems, and money laundering.

There is a general consensus that weaknesses in the financial sectors of crisis-affected countries compounded the problems and caused recovery to be more prolonged and difficult. Consequently, there is an effort to establish programs to upgrade the financial sector, particularly in emerging market countries. The project to upgrade and harmonise financial regulation under the auspices of the Bank for International Settlements and its newly established Financial Stability Forum, the banking sector reviews initiated by the IMF and the comprehensive development framework put forward by the World Bank represent major initiatives.

The approach to reform is sensible but emerging market and many other countries are far from being able to comply with the global standards being elaborated. Non-G7 countries have not been meaningfully involved in the discussion of standards. To date there has been only sporadic, announced acceptance of some of these standards and to the writer's knowledge, no country has articulated a general plan to achieve compliance with new standards. The initiatives for financial sector reform are new and have yet to have a meaningful, general impact. Given the current conditions in emerging market economies in particular, what can be done to achieve a significant commitment by the private sector to assist in crisis prevention and management directly and to support ongoing emerging market growth? Fortunately, there are positive answers to these questions.

Attracting private sector support is almost exclusively in the hands of host countries themselves. Countries have the option to choose to attract the private sector to support growth and to assist in difficult periods. If countries choose to have recourse to the private sector (many chose not to), the first step is to visibly announce this decision and a willingness to do what is necessary to win and maintain such support. Historical experience, ideological bias and nationalistic extremism must be put aside and economic progress adopted as a national priority. An indispensable part of this decision is to respect the motivation and values that govern private sector behaviour. If possible, this affirmation should be on the agenda of all important political groups (whether in power or not) to assure continuity of commitment over time.

Almost all countries, especially emerging market countries, are a long way from implementing global best practices, but countries have the option to commit to implementation of these standards (in a modified form if necessary) within a definite period of time and to announce an effort to achieve compliance, including important milestones and periodic progress reports to the international community.

In the interim period, during which global standards are being implemented, countries have the option to

- adopt and maintain fiscal and monetary discipline
- achieve political stabilisation and a national commitment to stable growth, utilising the international and national private sector as the main engines of implementation
- publish rules and regulations by which domestic financial and commercial markets will operate, including the role of foreign participation, without arbitrary government interference
- make explicit commitments to maintain a competitive exchange rate policy, liberalised tariff and trade rules, a positive foreign investment regime with respect to contract and property rights, a fair tax regime and to pledge government support to deal with bankruptcy and institutional reorganisation, respecting the rights of all creditors evenly, even though institutional reforms have not yet taken place
- commit to the elimination of corruption that impairs the private sector's ability to conduct business
- implement a communication policy explicitly directed at the private sector that achieves transparency, appropriate disclosures about both progress and problems on a timely, ongoing basis and reaffirms the continuity of the rules of the game for doing business in the country
- express a commitment to financial sector and corporate reform, including debt restructuring, which treats all creditors fairly
- acceptance of market discipline as a positive source of necessary feedback concerning economic performance
- maintenance of accessibility of government officials to the private sector so that mutually beneficial constructive dialogue is maintained.

The foregoing amounts to an enhanced country posture that resembles, but goes beyond, the favourable pre-crisis private sector perspective but which puts the role of the private sector positively and centre stage as an indispensable long-term partner in a country's development. Fortunately, all of the above steps can be achieved in current circumstances. Given the state of the world, this is the only feasible path to achieve growth and prosperity and the most favourable possibilities for support during crises. Failure to embrace this path is a decision to forego national growth.

If a country credibly commits to and executes an enhanced interim program and adopts a realistic path toward achieving global standards, it is certain that the private sector will take the country seriously and examine positively opportunities to get directly involved. Local investors will do the same. In due course tangible private sector commitments to the country will be made. Net risk will be taken with the expectation that profit and acceptable returns on capital deployed will occur. As positive returns occur, the private sector will increase commitments to the country and a virtuous cycle of wealth creation will be established.

If a crisis occurs in a country that is on a positive track, the private sector will participate in constructive resolution. What is often overlooked is that private sector activity anticipates the possibility that loss-threatening problems will occur when making initial decisions to commence or increase activity in a given country. If the probability of such problems occurring is deemed to be high, private sector participants will ask for higher rewards and in many instances some form of security as conditions for their proposed involvement. If such conditions are accepted by counterparties in the country, business is done.

The private sector strongly prefers to know of problems in the early stages, well before a full-blown crisis erupts. The private sector has a basic self-interest to prevent problems from getting worse and to resolve crises, because it is the best available option to prevent loss on the risk portfolio that has been assumed.

Given a positive willingness by country counterparties to work proactively, constructively and fairly with private investors and lenders, the private sector will always opt for cooperation and support to resolve problems because it is the surest way to defend against major loss in their portfolios. The private sector value system endorses working for solutions so as to avoid major write downs and write offs of risk exposure. The private sector will restructure exposures and provide additional support if credible solutions to problems are developed with their involvement and the constructive cooperation of their country counterparties. Above all, the private sector desires problems to be resolved before serious losses must be recognised (particularly as mandated by accounting rules) and to re-establish the viability and favourable prospects for their investments and risk exposures. The earlier the private sector is invited into problem situations, the more likely constructive involvement will occur.

Not all losses can be avoided; that is the nature of private business (mistakes are made, risk environments change unexpectedly); but losses can be mitigated and more than offset by gains in the total portfolio of risk if host countries stay on course with their development strategy. In this context, losses are a cost of doing business to the private sector, not a cause for total exit from the market. The argument has come full circle—host countries can control the extent of private sector involvement and support in their development by establishing a favourable environment for private sector activity, committing to implementation of global best practices and executing these commitments visibly and faithfully. Initially the private sector is reactive, waiting to see if positive conditions will be created. If the private sector concludes that this has occurred, specific opportunities to take risk with the expectations of earning profit and good returns on capital will be sought. Meaningful private sector involvement occurs or it does not occur—there is no real in-betweens—depending on country conditions. If the private sector is involved, help and support is voluntarily forthcoming to prevent and solve problems and crises. Efforts to compel private sector support are counter-productive. If the private sector is coerced, voluntary future involvement in the country will be minimal.

All countries have sufficient access to the necessary fora to communicate with the private sector as to plans, programs and problems. In any country's affairs, the leading financial and corporate private sector participants are readily identifiable and can be formally and informally organised. Allegations that communications outlets are insufficient are not correct; they are available to host countries, but countries must choose to use them actively.

It is ironic that obtaining direct private support and access to the resources they control is at the discretion of countries which need these resources to grow. A realistic analysis of the state of the global economy yields this conclusion; there is no other effective option available. Major, formal overhaul of the global financial system is not needed; the successful path to future progress has been established and is practically implementable. There are grounds for optimism that emerging market and other economies can re-establish and sustain stable growth.

18 Post-communist transition and the post-Washington consensus

Grzegorz W. Kolodko

The centrally planned economy has ceased to exist. Even in countries still considered socialist, such as China and Vietnam, the mechanism of economic coordination has shifted to a great extent from state intervention to market allocation. During the 1990s the process of post-socialist transformation has advanced significantly. About thirty countries in Eastern Europe, the former Soviet Union and Asia are involved in vast systemic changes. Undoubtedly, these changes are leading to full-fledged market economies, though the precise outcome of transformation will vary across countries. Some, leaders in transition and well placed geopolitically, are set to join the European Union in the foreseeable future; others, lagging behind in systemic changes, will remain hybrid systems with the remnants of central planning alongside elements of market regulation and a growing private sector. Some will expand quickly and catch up with their developed neighbours within a generation, others will experience sluggish economic growth and a relatively low standard of living.

Transition to a market economy is a lengthy process involving many spheres of economic activity. New institutional arrangements are of key importance for successful transformation. A market economy requires not only liberal regulation and private ownership but also adequate institutions. Transition can only be executed in a gradual manner since institution building is a gradual process based on new organisations, new laws and new behaviour. The belief that a market economy can be introduced by shock therapy is wrong, and when attempted, has caused more problems than it has solved. Liberalisation and stabilisation measures can be introduced in a radical manner, although this is not always necessary, and indeed, is only possible under certain political conditions.

The main argument in favour of transition was a desire to put the countries in question on the path of sustainable growth. It was assumed that shifting property rights from state to private hands and the allocation mechanism from state to free market would soon enhance saving rates and capital formation, as well as allocative efficiency. Thus it ought also to have contributed to high quality growth. Unfortunately, for a number of reasons this has not occurred. In all transition economies, before any growth has occurred (and in some countries there has been no growth yet) there has been a severe contraction, ranging from 20 per cent over three years in Poland to over 60 per cent in nine years in Ukraine (Table 18.1). These unfavourable results are the consequence of both the legacy of the previous system and the policies exercised during transition.

Table 18.1 Recession and growth in transition economies, 1990–7

Country	Years of GDP decline	Did GDP fall?	GDP growth (average % pa) 1990–3	GDP growth (average % pa) 1994–7	GDP growth (average % pa) 1990–7	1997 GDP index (1989 = 100)	Rank
Poland	2	no	-3.1	6.3	1.6	111.8	1
Slovenia	3	no	-3.9	4.0	0.0	99.3	2
Czech Republic	3	yes[a]	-4.3	3.6	-0.4	95.8	3
Slovakia	4	no	-6.8	6.3	-0.3	95.6	4
Hungary	4	no	-4.8	2.5	-1.1	90.4	5
Uzbekistan	5	no	-3.1	-0.3	-1.7	86.7	6
Romania	4	yes	-6.4	2.1	-2.2	82.4	7
Albania	4	yes	-8.8	4.9	-2.0	79.1	8
Estonia	5	no	-9.7	4.1	-2.8	77.9	9
Croatia	4	no	-9.9	3.0	-3.4	73.3	10
Belarus	6	no	-5.4	-2.6	-4.0	70.8	11
Bulgaria	6	yes	-7.4	-3.6	-5.5	62.8	12
Kyrgyzstan	5	no	-9.3	-2.4	-5.8	58.7	13
Kazakhstan	6	no	-6.7	-6.0	-6.3	58.1	14
Latvia	4	yes	-13.8	2.2	-5.8	56.8	15
Macedonia	6	no	-12.9	-0.8	-6.9	55.3	16
Russia	7	yes[a]	-10.1	-5.3	-7.7	52.2	17
Turkmenistan	7	no	-4.5	-12.5	-8.5	48.3	18
Lithuania	5	no	-18.3	0.5	-8.9	42.8	19
Armenia	4	no	-21.4	5.4	-8.0	41.1	20
Azerbaijan	6	no	-14.5	-5.7	-10.1	40.5	21
Tajikistan	7	no	-12.2	-8.4	-10.3	40.0	22
Ukraine	8	no recovery	-10.1	-12.1	-11.1	38.3	23
Moldova	7	yes[a]	-12.6	-10.2	-11.4	35.1	24
Georgia	5	no	-24.1	2.9	-10.6	34.3	25

Note: [a]GDP contracted again in 1998.
Source: National statistics, international organisations and author's own calculations.

These policies were based to a large extent on the so-called Washington consensus. This set of policies stresses the importance of liberalisation, privatisation and opening of post-socialist economies as well as financial discipline. However, being developed for another set of conditions, crucial elements necessary for systemic overhaul, stabilisation and growth in transition economies were missing. These elements included institution building, improvement of corporate governance of the state sector prior to privatisation and the redesign of the role of the state, instead of its urgent withdrawal from economic activities. The incorrect assumption that emerging market forces can substitute for the government in setting up new institutions, investing in human capital and developing infrastructure has caused severe contractions and growing social stress.

The need to manage the institutional aspects of transition has only been recognised and addressed in the later stages of transition. The technical assistance of the International Monetary Fund and the World Bank dealing with these issues may have an even more important positive influence on the course of transition and growth than their financial involvement. Lending by these organisations is often called assistance despite the fact that these loans are commercial credits with tough accompanying terms enforcing far-reaching structural reforms and policies thought to bring durable growth.

There is a need to search for a new consensus about policy reforms necessary for sustained growth. The East Asian contagion, East European transition and Brazilian crisis suggest that healthy financial fundamentals and liberal, transparent deregulation are not the only decisive factors. Sound institutional arrangements, re-regulation of financial markets and wise government policy are also essential. Against the recent experience of crises in several emerging markets (including the ones in transition countries) the outline of a new consensus—a post-Washington consensus—can be drawn. It points not only to the need for liberal markets and open economies, but stresses the new role of the state, the fundamental meaning of market organisations and the institutional links between them and the need for more equitable growth.

After losing over a quarter of GDP between 1990–8, growth in the majority of the post-socialist transition economies is gaining momentum. Although not yet the case in the two most sizable, Russia and Ukraine, they too have the chance to become growing economies (Kolodko 1998). In the coming years, the post-socialist emerging markets will become not only rapidly growing economies, but—owing to the East Asian turmoil—will form the fastest growing region in the world. How fast this growth will occur depends on policy reform. The direction of these reforms will also depend on cooperation with international organisations and their technical advice and financial support, which are conditionally linked to execution of market-friendly policies and implementation of sound structural reforms. Thus these organisations' influence on the course of reform is much stronger than their actual financial engagement and undertaken risk.

POLICY WITHOUT GROWTH: MISSING ELEMENTS

From the beginning of this decade the Washington consensus has been the accepted path from stabilisation to growth. It was assumed that tough financial policy accompanied by deregulation and trade liberalisation would be sufficient to conquer stagnation and launch economic growth, especially in the developing countries toward which the Washington consensus was addressed. Despite the fact that the policy reforms advised by this line of thought were at that time mostly relevant to the Latin American experience, they were applied to structural crisis issues in other regions, including transition economies.

A summary of the 1989 Washington consensus given by John Williamson (1997:60–1) follows in ten points that at the time seemed to be agreed upon by influential financial organisations, political bodies, and professional economists.

- Fiscal discipline. Budget deficit should be small enough to be financed without recourse to the inflation tax.
- Public expenditure priorities. Expenditure should be redirected from politically sensitive areas toward neglected fields with high economic returns and the potential to improve income distribution.

- Tax reform. Tax reform involves broadening the tax base and cutting marginal tax rates. The aim is to sharpen incentives and improve horizontal equity without lowering realized progressivity.

- Financial liberalisation. The ultimate objective of financial liberalisation is market-determined interest rates, but experience has shown that, under conditions of a chronic lack of confidence, market-determined rates can be so high as to threaten the financial solvency of productive enterprise and government.

- Exchange rates. Countries need a unified (at least for trade transactions) exchange rate set at a level sufficiently competitive to induce a rapid growth in nontraditional exports and managed so as to ensure exporters that this competitiveness will be maintained in the future.

- Trade liberalisation. Quantitative trade restrictions should be rapidly replaced by tariffs, and these should be progressively reduced until a uniform low tariff in the range of 10 percent (or at most around 20 percent) is achieved.

- Foreign direct investment. Barriers impeding the entry of foreign firms should be abolished; foreign and domestic firms should be allowed to compete on equal terms.

- Privatisation. State enterprises should be privatised.

- Deregulation. Governments should abolish regulations that impede the entry of new firms or that restrict competition, and then should ensure that all regulations are justified by such criteria as safety, environmental protection, or prudential supervision of financial institutions.

- Property rights. The legal system should provide secure property rights without excessive costs and should make such rights available to the informal sector.

With the experience gained overhauling the Latin American economies over the first half of the 1990s and the lessons learned from Eastern Europe and the former Soviet Union, a new agenda was presented. While it includes obvious points from earlier thoughts, there are certain new concerns and accents. Again, ten points were raised (Williamson 1997:58).

- Increase saving by (*inter alia*) maintaining fiscal discipline.

- Reorient public expenditure toward (*inter alia*) well-directed social expenditure.

- Reform the tax system by (*inter alia*) introducing an eco-sensitive land tax.

- Strengthen banking supervision.

- Maintain a competitive exchange rate, abounding both floating and the use of the exchange rate as a nominal anchor.

- Pursue intra-regional trade liberalisation.

- Build a competitive market economy by (*inter alia*) privatising and deregulating (including the labour market).

- Make well-defined property rights available to all.

- Build key institutions such as independent central banks, strong budget offices, independent and incorruptible judiciaries, and agencies to sponsor productivity missions.

- Increase educational spending and redirect it toward primary and secondary school.

The new items on this agenda correctly address the issues of institution building, environmental protection and investment in education, yet they are still missing some points of great importance which are especially pertinent to transition economies. First, dealing with corporate governance reform in the state sector before privatisation is not mentioned, nor is the behavioural aspect of institution building. Also the necessity of equitable growth is still overlooked. The shortest point on the agenda of the early Washington consensus, that concerning privatisation, is in reality a long-term policy challenge. Even if there is a sound commitment to privatise quickly and extensively—which is not always the case—it is not feasible, for both technical and political reasons. There are also the issues of sequencing, pace, distribution of costs and benefits and the efficient exercise of corporate governance.

As for the institutional aspect of reform, in post-socialist transition economies, unlike in distorted developing market economies, it is not enough merely to establish organisations, for instance, an independent central bank or comprehensive tax administration. Cultural changes are also necessary to facilitate efficiency and growth, changes in behaviour within organisations and changes in the interactions between them.

The early Washington consensus was actually aimed at countries that had already market economies, not those in transition. Joseph Stiglitz (1998a), while stressing the importance of governments as a complement to markets, points out that the consensus achieved in the late 1980s and early 1990s between the United States treasury, the IMF and the World Bank, as well as some influential think tanks, was catalysed by the experience of Latin America in the 1980s. He claims that for this reason countries facing different challenges have never found satisfactory answers to their most pressing questions in the Washington consensus.

There has always been a question as to the actual existence of a Washington consensus. Was a consensus achieved, or was the effort just an intention and well-motivated attempt? According to Stiglitz, the latter is the case.

> There is no standard terminology for these sets of doctrines, and various practitioners advocated these doctrines with varying degrees of subtlety and emphasis. The set of views is often summarized as the 'Washington consensus', though to be sure, there never was a consensus even in Washington (let alone outside of Washington) on the appropriateness of these policies (Stiglitz 1998b:58).

The partial failure of the Washington consensus with regard to transition economies must be linked with the neglect of the significance of institution building for the beginning of growth, even if economic fundamentals are by and large in order. Such oversight explains why so many Western scholars initially did not understand the real problem. Institutions change very slowly, but they have a strong influence on economic performance. As the 1993 Nobel Laureate in economics states, since

> …Western neo-classical economic theory is devoid of institutions, it is of little help in analyzing the underlying sources of economic performance. It would be little exaggeration to say that, while neo-classical theory is focused on the operation of efficient factor and product markets, few Western economists understand the institutional requirements essential to the creation of such

markets since they simply take them for granted. A set of political and economic institutions that provides low-cost transacting and credible commitment makes possible the efficient factor and product markets underlying economic growth (North 1997:2).

Expectations of growth were based on the assumption that market institutions, if they had not yet appeared automatically, would somehow come into existence soon after liberalisation and stabilisation measures were executed. It was believed that if policies were put in place to secure the progress of stabilisation and enhance sound fundamentals, the economy should regain momentum and start to develop quickly. What actually happened was much more depressing. Because of a vacuum with neither plan nor market system, productive capacity was utilised even less than previously, savings and investment began to decline, and instead of fast growth, there was deep recession. A lack of institutional development turned out to be the missing element in transition policies based on the Washington consensus. Instead of sustained growth, liberalisation and privatisation without a well organised market structure led to an extended contraction. This was not only the legacy of a socialist past, but also the result of current policies.

In some cases, the Washington consensus may be relevant to the challenges faced by distorted less developed market economies, as certain market organisations have always been in place. In post-socialist countries, however, organisations essential to a market economy were either distorted or did not exist, so the economy could not expand. Some institutions had to be developed from scratch. Hence, even with progress in liberalisation and radical privatisation, there was still no positive supply response. Misallocation of resources has continued, although this time for different reasons.

At the outset of transition the only relatively developed market infrastructure was a commodities trading network, but even this was operating under chronic shortages. Capital market structures were non-existent. The lack of financial intermediaries discouraged accumulation and worsened allocation of savings. Thus, immediately after the collapse of socialism, the lack of proper regulation of the emerging capital market and the dearth of such key organisations as investment banks, mutual funds, stock exchanges and security control commissions caused distortions that could not be offset by liberalisation and privatisation.

Organisations and institutional links must be developed gradually. Professionals must be retrained to enable them to work in the market environment. This takes years—it would be much wiser to manage the processes of liberalisation and privatisation at a pace compatible with the speed of human capital development. Otherwise, market forces will not be able to shape economic structures and increase competitiveness and growth potential. A dissonance between liberalisation measures and institution building has occurred in a number of countries that took a bit more of a radical approach toward transition. In these cases creative destruction, popular in Poland at the beginning of 1990s, failed to deliver, because there was too much destruction and not enough creation.

Socialist countries were full or over full-employment economies. A social security system protecting against unemployment did not exist, because it was not needed. All countries in this region have had to develop a safety net from scratch. Before such systems could be implemented, in addition to the misallocation of capital, there has been a misallocation of labour.

Since the mid 1990s, the Bretton Woods organisations have started to pay more attention to market structures and behaviour. Developing and transition economies learned quickly that there is no sustained growth without sound fundamentals. Later, it was learned that the market and growth need both liberalisation and organisation. More recently contractions in transitional economies and the East Asian crisis have shown that even with sound fundamentals—a balanced budget and current account, low inflation, a stable currency, liberalised trade and a vast private sector—there will not be sustained growth if these favourable features are not supported by an appropriate institutional set up. In fact, without such a set up, the fundamentals themselves will deteriorate, as has happened in the Czech Republic or more recently in Brazil.

There seems to be a growing agreement that the early Washington consensus must be revised and adjusted toward actual challenges and new circumstances. If it is going to work, elements concerning institutional arrangements must be included. The specifics will vary depending on the context—overhauling the Latin American debt crisis, counteracting East Asia's contagion or fighting the Eastern European transitional depression. In the latter, eight elements regarding institutional framework are of key importance

- the lack of organisational infrastructure for a liberal market economy
- weak financial intermediaries unable to allocate efficiently privatised assets
- a lack of commercialisation of state enterprises prior to privatisation
- unqualified management unable to execute sound corporate governance in a deregulated economy
- a lack of institutional infrastructure for competition policy
- a weak legal framework and judicial system, and a consequent inability to enforce tax code and business contracts
- poor local government unprepared to tackle the issues of regional development
- a lack of non-governmental organisations supporting the functioning of the emerging market economy and civil society.

Hence, policies that under other conditions may have worked were not effective in overcoming the crisis in the post-socialist economies. Even if the targets and instruments as such were well defined, they could not be reached and used as envisaged, since they were put into use within a systemic vacuum.

TOWARD A NEW CONSENSUS

Rather than a permanent agreement between principal partners, the process of developing a new consensus must involve a constant search for better understanding and new partners. These features are indispensable for its ultimate success. As situations change and knowledge evolves, new documents and programs, accentuating additional points of concern and examining old points in a different light, come to the fore. A good example of such progress is the World Bank's *Annual Development Report 1996*, devoted entirely to the transition from plan to market (World Bank 1996), and the September 1996 IMF Interim Committee Declaration on a *Partnership for Sustainable Global Growth* (IMF 1996).

The latter statement may be seen as a modified version of the early Washington consensus. Among eleven points, six are of special relevance to transition economies. The first stresses that monetary, fiscal and structural policies are complementary and reinforce each other. The third claims that there is a need to create a favourable environment for private savings. The seventh emphasises that budgetary policies have to aim at medium-term balance and a reduction in public debt, while the ninth says that structural reforms must be supplemented with special attention to the labour markets. The tenth point stresses the importance of good corporate governance, and the eleventh cautions against corruption in the public sector and money laundering in the banks, warning that monitoring and supervision must be strengthened. Other points, also important for sustainable development, address the issues of exchange rate stability, disinflation, resisting protectionist pressure, progress toward increased freedom of capital movement and fiscal adjustment by reducing unproductive spending while ensuring adequate investment in infrastructure.

The Washington consensus is not an official position taken by any particular organisation or institution. It is rather a gathering of policy options being agreed upon by important partners to such an extent that the agreement may be considered a consensus. Yet there is still a search for agreement between the organisations as well as among the policy makers, policy-oriented researchers and advisors. Being personally involved in research, advice giving and policymaking, it was quite interesting for me to receive a reaction to the outcome of my involvement from the author of the Washington consensus. In a personal communication, John Williamson wrote

> I was particularly pleased that you have tried to define an alternative to big bangery in terms of a more careful design of individual policy components rather than generalized go slow ('gradualism'). On just about all the individual items you identify, certainly including protection and privatisation, I agree with you in retrospect, and indeed I would have agreed with you at the time…But in all honesty I have to confess that I still worry that had I been in the place of Balcerowicz (who was the minister of finance in Poland in 1989–91) I might not have put together the decisive package that I think in retrospect Poland needed at the time, and that laid the foundation for your successful period in office. Perhaps one needed a little bit of overkill to make it emotionally possible for your allies to accept that the world had changed, and even to give you the opportunity of correcting their excesses and in the process winning their acceptance of the new model? It reminds me of the situation in my home country: I am much more comfortable with Tony Blair than with Mrs. Thatcher, but I am not sure that we could have had him without her.

In this case, psychological and political rather than economic and financial arguments are given as factors favouring the radical set of policies undertaken at the beginning of the 1990s. Nonetheless, it seems that we still differ as to the evaluation of the scope and costs of that overkill. Was it only 'a little bit of overkill' of otherwise necessary measures, or was it a serious excess of unnecessary radicalism, as seems to be proved elsewhere (Kolodko 1991; Nuti 1992; Rosati 1994; Poznanski 1996; Hausner 1997)?

When ideas and strategies involving more gradual change and the active involvement of the state in institutional redesign in post-socialist transition economies were first expounded (Kolodko 1989 and 1992; Laski 1990; Nuti 1990; Poznanski 1993), and when they were later implemented in Poland (Kolodko 1993, 1996 and 1999), they were unorthodox and controversial. In fact, these new ideas did not argue for more gradual change *per se*, but recognised that the necessary changes would be time-consuming by their very nature. In 1997 and 1998, however, even in official international circles, there have been widespread signs that a new consensus is emerging, and that it is, to a certain extent, based on the ideas implemented in Poland in 1994–7 (Kolodko and Nuti 1997). Thanks to its multi-track approach, Poland is now recognised as having avoided the adverse experiences of other transition economies. The new ideas and policies, developed under 'Strategy for Poland', were to some extent elaborated against the mainstream of the early Washington consensus and now have contributed importantly to its revision.

In the aftermath of the East Asian crisis, thoughts regarding the Washington consensus have also begun to change among the most influential opinion leaders in the international financial community. This has been accompanied by a much belated beginning of doubt raising regarding the accuracy of the recipe proposed for post-socialist emerging markets, especially for the most important, Russia. A consensus has not yet been agreed on, but lessons are gradually being learned.

> The benefits brought by short-term international lenders are questionable: they do not provide new technology, they do not improve the management of domestic institutions; and they do not offer reliable finance of current account deficit. In countries with high savings rates, they also increase already excessive investment rates. To manage the inflows, borrowers may have to accumulate huge reserves…The Asian saga proves, once again, that liberalisation of inadequately regulated and capitalized financial system is a recipe for disaster (Wolf, M., 1998. 'Ins and outs of capital flows', *Financial Times*, 16 June).

The Bretton Woods organisations base their financial involvement on tough fiscal and monetary policy. Whether it was a period of 10 per cent GDP decline, or a period of 10 per cent expansion, there was always pressure to bring the fiscal gap down and keep the real interest rate up. Even when the budget deficit was smaller than that of industrial countries and the real interest rate was so high that it was not possible to contain the deficit further due to soaring costs of servicing the public debt, there was a permanent requirement to continue fiscal and monetary tightness. High real interest rates are agreeable to portfolio investors, but impose costs on both taxpayers and the business sector owing to the crowding-out effect.

The importance of a change in corporate governance—as opposed to a sheer transfer of property titles—is now being recognised even by early keen supporters of rapid, mass privatisation. There is no clear evidence that the privatised enterprises perform better than state enterprises. Nicholas Stern (1996:8) points to the process of restructuring, which '...itself will be a major and fundamental task involving investment, hard decisions and dislocation. It will be much less painful if economic growth, effective corporate governance and well-functioning safety nets are established'. Thus good corporate governance of public enterprises and sound competition policy are at least as essential for recovery as privatisation and liberalisation.

After the *laissez-faire* of the early transition, values of cooperation and solidarity are being rediscovered. Even billionaire financier George Soros has not hesitated to admit that

> Although I have made a fortune in the financial markets, I now fear that the untrammeled intensification of laissez-faire capitalism and the spread of market values into all areas of life is endangering our open and democratic society...Too much competition and too little cooperation can cause intolerable inequities and instability (Soros 1997).

While it should be obvious that transition based on *laissez-faire* must bring 'intolerable inequities and instability' (Kolodko 1999), it is still not acknowledged widely enough and, indeed, is still challenged.

Yet the World Bank (1996) *World Development Report* emphasises very strongly the need for social consensus, though difficult to attain, considering falling output and growing inequality in transition economies.

> Establishing a social consensus will be crucial for the long-term success of transition—cross-country analyses suggest that societies that are very unequal in terms of income, or assets tend to be politically and socially less stable and to have lower rates of investment and growth (World Bank 1996).

It is now rather accepted that in economies still affected by structural rigidities, such as formal and informal indexation and sluggish supply response, once inflation has fallen well below a threshold of about 20 per cent, attempts at speeding up disinflation have significant, perhaps intolerable costs—as for instance in Romania in 1998–9—certainly higher than the moderate, but steady falling inflation actually experienced by some countries leading in transition and those recently following Poland's path. What counts is that inflation should continue to fall steadily and noticeably, without ever accelerating again. Such a process of disinflation contributes not only to increasing the credibility of the government and monetary authorities, but secures the predictability of economic developments and creates a better business environment and more international confidence.

The prerequisites for enhancing the savings ratio are real income growth, stabilisation and optimistic expectations. Only against such background can the propensity to save steadily increase. The EBRD (1996) *Transition Report*, which is devoted to infrastructure and savings, stresses the equal roles of increasing government savings—especially through the overhaul of social security and pension systems, and more broadly based taxation at lower rates—and the development of contractual savings and life insurance. From this perspective, the pressure for high real interest rates has been grossly misplaced. The fiscal and quasi-fiscal activities of central banks, notably in the emerging economies and especially in post-socialist countries, have attracted considerable attention (Fry 1993). In particular, the costs of sterilisation policies, which are the result of excessive interest rate differentials and/or of undervalued currencies, have come to the fore (see the OECD (1996) country study of the Czech Republic). It turns out that for a considerable time, the central banks of both the Czech Republic and Poland have wasted about 1 per cent of GDP in their unfortunate sterilisation policies (Nuti 1996).

There is yet one more key feature of the emerging consensus. Along with the continuous leading role of the Washington-based organisations, especially the IMF and the World Bank, the consensus must encompass more partners. Other international organisations, such as the United Nations, OECD, WTO, International Labour Organisation and European Bank for Reconstruction and Development, should play a bigger role than they have thus far. Regional organisations, like ASEAN in Asia, CEFTA in central Europe, or the CIS in the former Soviet Union, should be better prepared to present their purpose in the global forum and try to influence the process of changing the international financial and economic order. Some international non-government organisations ought to be more influential too.

Thus the search for the new consensus must rely not only on the quest for new policies agreed on in Washington, but also on the policies agreed on between Washington and other regions of the global economy. There are many hints that such a process is underway, but there is much more yet to be accomplished.

THE MEANS AND ENDS OF ECONOMIC POLICY

The lack of success of policies based on the early Washington consensus is also due to the confusion of the means of the policies with their ends. A sound fiscal stance, low inflation, stable exchange rate and overall financial stabilisation are only the means of economic policy, while sustained growth and a healthier standard of living are its ends. Yet after several years of exercising these policies, neither growth nor a higher standard of living has been achieved in transition countries. Important changes like privatisation and liberalisation are merely instruments, not targets. It is strange that so often these processes are presented as a core of economic policy, if not as its ultimate end. Too much attention is focused on the means that hypothetically should lead to an improvement of efficiency and competitiveness, instead of concentrating on the outcome. Such bias leads to policy distortion—the tools become the goals themselves, without sufficient concern about their impact on the real economy.

In economic policy it is sometimes assumed that as, at some stage, things should run themselves, there is no need to think about how to manage them. An extreme example of such thought is the supposition that the best policy is no policy. It should be obvious to all those involved in economic research, advice and policy that such confusion cannot be explained merely by the naiveté and laziness of economists and politicians. Actually, they do work hard. The intellectual misunderstandings result from political antagonism, and the difference is more about conflicts of interests than about alternative theoretical concepts and scientific explanations.

Policy mistakes do occur due to a lack of experience and proper knowledge, but more often from obedience to a particular interest group or theoretical schools, that happen to be ideological and political lobbies too. This is why there are no leftist or rightist doctors or engineers, but there are leftist and rightist economists and policy makers. John Williamson (1990) distinguishes the political from the technocratic Washington, stressing their different priorities and policy options. However, there are important divisions not only between the political and technocratic parts of Washington, but also within them.

What makes the picture still more complex is the fact that some technocrats do play, even if unintentionally, political roles as well. This is also true with regard to the Bretton Wood organisations, especially the IMF. Their influence and the consequences of their policies have such serious implications for particular countries and regions, if not the entire global economy, that sometimes they have much more to decide than what may be seen as purely technocratic concerns. The position of the IMF towards such big countries in transition as Russia and Ukraine are the best points in case here.

But the issue is even more complex than that, because—aside from intellectual controversies and different normative values—there are also different political, economic and financial interests involved. Otherwise it would be impossible to interpret why erroneous policies continued, in many cases, even after it was obvious that they were wrong. This was the case, for instance, with early liberalisation and stabilisation policy in Poland in 1989–92, the neglect of corporate governance in the Czech Republic in 1993–6, the Russian privatisation of 1994–8, executed with the active involvement of politically connected informal institutions, and with fraudulent Albanian financial intermediaries in 1995–7, which were tolerated until the whole economy eventually collapsed.

Such events serve as examples of the confusion of economic policy targets with instruments. Economic policy is not to be judged by the pace of privatisation, but by its efficiency, measured first by the increase of competitiveness and budgetary proceeds, and then by the increase in national income. The strong insistence to accelerate privatisation coming from some lobbies and their political allies is merely aimed at selling the assets cheaper. Thus there are entities that are able to buy these assets not faster, as is publicly suggested through political connections and dependent news media, but to acquire them cheaper than under a more reasonably paced procedure. Assets that sell fast, sell cheap. And those who buy fast, buy cheap.

There have been warnings, criticisms and intellectual and political opposition against these unwise policies, but they have still been followed. Why? Not due to a lack of good economic ideas or sound policy programs, but because of pressure from strong lobbies and interest groups. In designing good policy, it is important not only to be right but also to be able to enforce the preferred policies. Often it happens that the strongest lobby is not with truth and logic, but with power and money.

True reform, that which lifts the welfare of many as opposed to a particular few, must always be thought of as a means to long-term targets. Otherwise, there will be fictitious progress reflected in an artificial improvement. Policies that increase private sector share, trade liberalisation or the deregulation of capital transfers at the expense of economic growth and the standard of living represent a deterioration not an improvement. Yet, often, economic status is judged from the perspective of a particular group of interests and this perspective is presented as a picture of the general economic situation.

When evaluating the standing of an economy or a policy, one must consider not only what is being examined, and by what means it is scrutinised, but also who is carrying out such an evaluation. With this in mind, it is obvious that, for instance, the evaluations of Moody's rating agency and the Russian trade unions must be as different as the interests of the Morgan Stanley investment bank and the Siberian miners.

The aims of development policy are now more comprehensive and the attitudes of those who subscribed to the Washington consensus are changing, primarily the World Bank. Policy should be concerned with not only a balanced economy and sustained growth, but also with improvements in the standard of living, distribution of income, the environment, and, last but not least, democracy itself. 'Our understanding of the instruments to promote well-functioning markets has also improved, and we have broadened the objectives of development to include other goals, such as sustainable development, egalitarian development, and democratic development' (Stiglitz 1998a:1). The World Bank always has always been more inclined toward social issues and human capital development than other international financial institutions. Usually banks look to profits rather than the human development index as an indicator of success. It must be acknowledged that the World Bank has been involved in a number of projects, not only in transition economies, that serve to increase standards of living and decrease poverty.

Now even the IMF claims that it too would like to aim at a more fair distribution of the fruits of growth, if only the advised policies would deliver some. Stanley Fischer, the IMF First Deputy Managing Director, himself concerned about equitable growth for a long time, has raised the question of why equity considerations matter for the Fund.

> First, as a matter of social justice, all members of society should share in the benefits of economic growth. And although there are many important arguments about precisely what constitutes a fair distribution of income, we accept the view that poverty in the midst of plenty is not socially acceptable. But, second, there is also an instrumental argument for equity: adjustment programs that are equitable and growth that is equitable are more likely to be sustainable. These are good enough reasons for the IMF to be concerned about equity considerations—whether it be poverty reduction or concerns about income distribution in the programs the IMF support (Fischer 1998:1).

Undoubtedly, the experience of transformation has contributed significantly to these changes. We still have to deal with the difficult road from contraction to growth in post-socialist economies, but we have also experienced fast growth in the reformed socialist economies of East Asia, which—unlike the Eastern European and the former Soviet Union transition economies—did not follow many early Washington consensus suggestions. Now these experiences, together with the aftermath of the East Asian crisis, are working as a catalyst for the emergence of a post-Washington consensus in the same way that the Latin American debt crisis of the 1980s ignited the formation of its predecessor. However, there is still a long distance to travel from the emerging intellectual consensus to a real political agreement about appropriate policy reforms and actions. And, of course, even if intellectual consensus is closer than before, controversies regarding different normative values and contradictory interests do remain.

TRANSITION AS A PROCESS OF SYSTEMIC REDESIGN

The only chance for the ultimate success of transformation is to design suitable institutions. This design is more difficult in post-Soviet republics than in Eastern Europe, because in the former there was a lack of even such basic institutions as a sovereign central bank, and private ownership of the means of production was virtually non-existent. In the reformed socialist economies of East Asia the process is proceeding at a much slower pace and yet it also is directed at further liberalisation and opening up.

Some post-socialist countries have taken a course of gradual, perhaps even too gradual, liberalisation and privatisation. Though generally followed by milder contraction, the slow pace has been associated with a delay of crucial structural reforms as well. If the time were used for appropriate institution building, it would pay off. If, however, it is wasted, the chances for long-term expansion are indeed weak.

Other countries have followed a path of rapid change. Although under these circumstances contraction was more severe in early stages, later, institution building is often more advanced. In the long run, after learning the bitter lesson that market economies do not expand without a wise government-led development policy and well designed institutions, both the Eastern European and former Soviet economies in transition as well as the reformed economies of China and Vietnam, have a chance to succeed in their market endeavours.

The government involvement in the process of comprehensive institution building is of vital importance. This, as much as liberalisation, is the essence of transition. Without adequate institutional arrangements, liberalisation and privatisation are unable to deliver what nations expect from their economies. If the state fails to design a proper institutional set up, market failures prevail and informal institutionalisation takes over. Instead of a sound market, in the words of the chief economists of the World Bank and the European Bank for Reconstruction and Development, a bandit capitalism emerges.

> It is easy to identify institutional arrangements that work well: each partner does what it is supposed to do, there is good coordination, little conflict and the economy grows smoothly and rapidly. We can also recognise ill-functioning institutional arrangements: change is inhibited by bureaucratic requirements or there is 'bandit capitalism' with pervasive corruption and deceit (Stern and Stiglitz 1997:20).

Such institutional pathologies could arise as a result of transition-by-chance, as opposed to transition-by-design. In several cases inaccurate transition policy has led to such adversity. An economy in which only the stupid pay taxes, contracts are not executed as agreed and payments are not made on time is hardly a market economy. It is chaos stemming from institutional disintegration.

Without the knowledge of how a new system works, and without a vision of how to get to that system, there is no way to accomplish the target on time and in good shape. Transition becomes protracted: costs are higher than necessary, results are not as good as they could be and the whole process lasts longer than would otherwise be necessary. And, as was stressed by the advocates of transition-by-design contrary to the supporters of transition-by-chance, the recession lasts longer, recovery comes later and output expands more slowly (Poznanski 1996). Thus institutional design is a paramount task during the time of transition. At the same time, its accomplishment is more difficult because of institutional discontinuity. The old set up, for instance, central price regulation or investment allocation by Gosplan and branch ministries, does not work anymore, yet the new one, for instance, investment banking or a stock exchange, is not yet in place. Thus there is a systemic vacuum.

Market capitalism requires private property rights, but also a competitive enterprise sector, functioning markets and respect for the rules of market allocation. Well performing financial intermediaries are necessary to facilitate trade transactions and investment deals, as well as to promote savings. But the market, its introduction notwithstanding, also needs a proper legal environment, one that is able to support execution of market rules, enforcement of contracts and the correct behaviour of economic agents (firms, households, organisations and the government). For these reasons, transition calls not for a dismissal of government, but for its streamlining and adjustment to the new circumstances. The World Bank, unlike the advocates of market fundamentalism, admits this.

> The state makes a vital contribution to economic development when its role matches its institutional capability. But capability is not destiny. It can and must be improved if governments are to promote further improvements in economic and social welfare (...) Three interrelated sets of institutional mechanisms can help create incentives that will strengthen the state's capability. These mechanisms aim to:
> Enforce rules and restraints in society as well as within the state
> Promote competitive pressures from outside and from within the state, and
> Facilitate voice and partnership both outside and within the state (World Bank 1997).

This is true for all economic systems, regardless of economic structure, GDP level or institutional advancement, and is particularly true for transition economies. In countries where the rules were previously fundamentally different from current post-socialist regulations, the introduction of new behaviours and the enforcement of new regulations for economic entities calls for even harder and more determined state effort than elsewhere.

Unfortunately, the state's ability to attack the issue of law enforcement is much weaker during transition than it was under state socialism. It is also weaker than under the governments of traditional market economies, with mature civil societies and well functioning institutions. Post-socialist states have been deliberately weakened by neoliberal policies, often led with the official support of the governments of leading industrial countries and international organisations. For example, the Russian government is weak and unable to collect taxes not because of any legacy from the communist period, but owing to ill advised deregulation and privatisation. It is difficult to bring matters under the sovereignty of the new state, because they have been allowed to get out of control of the old state, mainly because of mismanaged liberalisation and the manner in which institutional redesign occurred.

As for new partnerships between market players, that is precisely what gradual institution building is about. In the long term, such partnerships enhance the environment for growth, but at the initial stages ongoing changes can destabilise existing links between partners involved in economic activities. The old relationships cease to exist, while the new ones are only in *statu nascendi*. Thus active state participation is needed, since market relations are often associated with inappropriate events owing to activities of various lobbies and informal organisations, including organised crime.

TRANSITION AS AN INSTRUMENT OF DEVELOPMENT STRATEGY

New institutional set ups must be founded on the basis of organisations that did not exist—since they were not needed—under centrally planned economies. Transition calls not only for a new legal system, but also for learning a new type of behaviour. Enterprises, banks, the civil service and state bureaucracy, even households must all quickly learn how to perform under the circumstances of their new reality—the emerging market system. Political leaders in post-socialist countries do not have, as Moses did, forty years to turn their people around. To accelerate this process and cut the costs of institutional and cultural adjustment requires special training and education efforts by political and intellectual elites, and non-governmental organisations. The Bretton Woods institutions are contributing to this acceleration. After acknowledging that providing new skills and knowledge can be more important than just lending money, they have started to pay much more attention to technical assistance and professional training.

In countries that enjoyed a relatively liberal system under socialism, the process of learning has been much faster. If there was already a private sector and decentralised management of state companies, the learning of new methods of corporate governance is smoother. If there was already a two-tier banking system, learning sound commercial banking is easier. If there was already an anti-trust body, this previously relatively useless organisation (because of the shortages) now must regulate well supplied markets to make them truly competitive.

In countries which had traditional centrally planned regimes until the late 1980s, learning is slower. This factor explains the differences in the economic performance of such neighbours as Hungary and Romania. The faster is the process of institution building, the better is the environment for business activity and hence for growth. Government guidance and intervention can hasten the whole process, as was the case in Poland in the 1990s, but if mismanaged, as it was over the same period in Russia, can spoil it too. Nonetheless, such a risk cannot be an excuse for state withdrawal. The risk calls for wise guidance and rational intervention.

In the very long term, transition should be seen as a major instrument of development policy. Systemic changes that do not lead toward durable growth and sustainable development do not make sense. However, some reforms are ideologically motivated, expounded without deep concern about their pragmatic implications for society. This must not be neglected since it can be very strong, especially during periods of revolutionary change. And the post-socialist transformations are revolutionary, regardless of their pace.

The situation is more complex, because behind these political motivations there are always some particular interest groups. To counterbalance these interests with lobbies oriented toward long-range progress and development is not easy, since such a group would need to resist strong pressures coming from interest groups. Interest groups fight with any and all means for their own present interests, but there are no lobbies fighting with such determination and force in favour of long-term development and remote policy targets. The only visible and somewhat effective lobby is the environmental lobby.

However apparent it is that systemic transition is not the target but merely the path to a more important goal, there is still some confusion on this point. This confusion is primarily about the interdependence of institutional changes and real economy expansion. Should a system be praised when economic growth is not satisfactory and the potential to expand is weak? Of course not, yet strangely enough, it often is. It is apparent in professional discourse that reforms are appreciated for their own sake, without paying enough attention to their real outcomes.

The enormous contraction in Eastern Europe and the former Soviet Union has been a result of, on one hand, deficiencies of development policy and exaggeration of the significance of transition per se and, on the other, a confusion of transition with liberalisation and privatisation. Policies have focused mainly on stabilisation measures, trade liberalisation and privatisation, without paying enough attention to events in the real economy such as output, consumption, investment and unemployment. This approach changed the initial conditions (though not always for better) and caused contraction instead of growth.

In the long run, the design of an economic system plays an instrumental role in expansion and development. When one set of solutions has ceased to serve its purpose, another must replace it. Hence, the system ought to be flexible enough to meet the challenge of changing circumstances. The current transformation should be seen only as an historical episode, albeit a very important one, which may serve development needs well, if policies are managed in an appropriate way.

Attention to development policy and treatment of market-oriented reforms as the means for successful development have contributed significantly to the high rate of growth in China and Vietnam (Montes 1997). This is indeed interesting, because there has not yet been any such example of durable growth in post-socialist economies of Eastern Europe and the former Soviet Union. The reform of the socialist system that failed in Europe worked in Asia. China and Vietnam have adjusted their systems as required for the sake of further growth. Reform has been seen as a means of expansion, not as a target.

Within each political system there is room for some variation, for distinct policies and exercises. The system itself cannot serve as a substitute for good policy. Frequently it is sufficient to improve the current framework rather than overhaul an entire system. Of course, during transition there is also room for varying qualities of economic policy, government action and for various forms of involvement of the international community.

INSTITUTION BUILDING

We speak of building institutions, but in reality, they must be learned. After the failure of shock therapy, the process of post-socialist change has been managed in a more reasonable way, by deliberate measures carried out at a slower pace. By the very nature of this long and complex process, it can not be carried forward in a radical way. It takes time and is costly in both financial and economic terms. It is risky and can expose the country to social and political tensions. Only part of the multi-layer transition process, namely liberalisation linked with stabilisation, can be executed—if political conditions permit—in a radical manner. Even this is not an imperative, but a policy choice depending on the extent of monetary and fiscal disequilibria and the range of social tolerance.

Structural adjustment, institutional reform and behavioural changes require a long time. For example, in Eastern Europe it is estimated that about 77 per cent of computer software is pirated, while in the United States such malpractice stands at about 20 per cent. While the United States figure is not insignificant, it is four times less than in transition economies. Such a difference cannot be explained solely on the basis of more efficient law enforcement and better marketing. The more important difference is that between a weak market culture and a mature one. Yet even in mature markets the process of behavioural change must continue if, despite the sophistication of market institutions and established market culture, as much as one-fifth of computer software is still stolen.

From the viewpoint of the societies concerned and their political elites, it must seem that this will be a very lengthy process, but in reality it should be seen as a very short historical incident, considering the mighty and comprehensive changes that are taking place. Establishing the traditional market economies, although accomplished under different circumstances, took longer than the current transformations in socialist and post-socialist countries. Ten years is really a very short period in which to turn an economy around. Post-socialist transition, despite the hardship it has brought, should be seen as relatively rapid process of complex changes in structures, institutions and behaviours.

The difficulties have not derived from a lack of knowledge of how the market works, but from not knowing how to make the transition from the late socialist economies to a market system. The most challenging problem is not finding a target design for new organisations and institutions but the process of transition leading toward those targets. The most difficult question to be answered, therefore, is not how it should look and work at the very end, but how to get from here to there.

Simultaneously, a process of learning-by-doing is taking place. Both in the East and the West previous theoretical explanations and pragmatic approaches have evolved significantly. Professionals from transition countries have gained knowledge of market performance. Great political and intellectual debates, training at home and abroad and simple experience of the process, have brought tremendous progress *vis-à-vis* the qualifications of researchers, entrepreneurs and political elites. Professionals from developed countries, including government representatives dealing with transition, experts in international organisations and the business community has learned about the specific circumstances of transition. They have been able to absorb knowledge on various features of post-socialist realities, and have understood that one should attack the challenges in a somehow different, rather unorthodox way. Major lessons about the significance of institution building for durable growth have been learned at last, and the proper policy conclusions seem to have been drawn.

Unfortunately, the process of learning-by-doing has been very costly for the eastern European and former Soviet nations. Future growth should not be counted as compensation for the past slump. It was forecast that the production of the whole region would grow, yet in several cases this has not been a reality. Worse, there are post-socialist economies in which output is shrinking and further contraction is expected (Table 18.2). In the first ten years of transition, GDP in post-socialist economies contracted more than during the great depression in 1929–33. This was not necessary and could have been diminished, if existing knowledge about the possible alternative methods of transformation had not been neglected and the adjustment of Western economic thought and policy advice to actual challenges had been quicker.

Later, there were better orchestrated attempts aimed at gradual, but steady institution building. By institutions we mean not only the organisations and the links between them, but also the behaviour of economic agents. With much better coordinated international assistance, transition policies have shifted in the right direction in a number of countries. Market organisations have been created, new laws have been drafted and adopted and new skills have been taught. Indeed in the late 1990s Eastern Europe, and to a lesser degree the former Soviet Union, looked different than in the early 1990s. Yet there is still a long road to travel.

POLICY CONCLUSIONS

Events in post-socialist economies have been greatly influenced by policies based on the Washington consensus. In turn, the experience gained in applying these policies has had a significant impact on the revision of these policies. The range of issues on which there is consensus among the major partners in the global financial, economic and political scene has expanded over the years.

The post-socialist transformation has contributed to this evolution of attitudes. New issues and problems have emerged together with the emerging post-socialist markets, and hence there are new concerns, toward which views differ and are far from being agreed on. Nevertheless, there are numerous symptoms of an urgent need for a new consensus. Additionally several new elements must be emphasised in what has been agreed on in the past.

The main policy conclusion, and the key implication of the post-Washington consensus, is that institutional arrangements are paramount for progress toward durable growth. An institutional set up sufficient for far reaching liberalisation and free market performance, must be created in countries moving away from statist, centrally planned economies. If there is a choice between developing these institutional arrangements spontaneously (by chance) or in a way directed by the government (by design), then the latter option is more suitable in the case of post-socialist countries. The governments of industrial countries and international organisations must assist some governments in these attempts. Those countries which, due to strong government commitments, have designed and developed the necessary institutions are doing much better. Recovery has come sooner, growth is robust and there is the prospect of sustainable development. Those which have chosen to trust that a major institutional overhaul will occur by itself or have not been able to lead this complex process adequately are lagging behind in both transition advancement and pace of growth.

Table 18.2 Forecast of economic growth in transition economies, 1998–2002

Country	1997 GDP index (1989=100)	Rate of growth					Average 1998–2002	Ranking[a]	GDP index 2002	
		1998[b]	1999	2000	2001	2002			1997=100	1989=100
Poland	111.8	4.8	4.5	5.0	5.4	5.7	5.6	9	128.4	143.2
Slovenia	99.3	4.3	3.7	4.3	4.4	4.8	4.7	15	123.4	122.6
Slovakia	95.6	5.3	2.2	4.0	5.6	6.9	5.3	10	126.3	120.8
Hungary	90.4	5.2	4.3	4.1	4.0	4.1	4.7	13	123.7	111.8
Albania	79.1	4.3	6.2	8.9	8.0	4.4	7.2	4	136.0	107.6
Uzbekistan	86.7	4.5	4.5	4.3	3.8	4.2	4.6	16	123.2	106.8
Czech Republic	95.8	-2.5	0.5	3.3	3.9	5.2	2.1	23	110.6	106.0
Estonia	77.9	6.4	6.1	5.9	6.9	5.9	7.1	5	135.3	105.4
Romania	82.4	-4.7	2.2	4.9	4.8	5.1	2.5	22	121.5	92.7
Croatia	73.3	4.2	2.9	4.3	4.1	4.3	4.3	19	121.4	89.0
Bulgaria	62.8	3.5	2.7	4.6	5.2	5.2	4.6	17	123.0	77.3
Yugoslavia	62.7	5.4	1.3	3.9	4.7	5.5	4.5	18	122.5	76.8
Latvia	56.8	6.6	5.4	4.4	3.9	5.4	5.7	8	128.5	73.0
Kyrgyzstan	58.7	3.0	3.0	4.7	5.2	5.7	4.7	14	123.5	72.5
Turkmenistan	48.3	4.7	12.1	16.0	3.5	4.2	9.4	2	146.8	70.9
Kazakhstan	58.1	1.4	0.6	3.0	5.5	8.3	4.0	20	120.0	69.7
FYR Macedonia	55.3	5.3	4.7	4.6	4.1	4.1	5.0	12	125.0	69.1
Belarus	70.8	4.2	-9.3	-5.8	1.5	2.9	-1.4	26	93.0	65.8
Azerbaijan	40.5	7.9	7.9	9.0	9.9	10.7	10.9	1	154.4	62.5
Lithuania	42.8	7.4	4.5	3.7	3.8	4.1	5.2	11	125.8	53.8
Armenia	41.1	5.7	4.4	5.0	5.7	6.1	6.0	6	129.9	53.4
Tajikistan	40.0	4.3	4.3	5.8	5.5	5.9	5.7	7	128.6	51.4
Russia	52.2	-4.7	-5.3	-2.6	3.9	4.1	-1.0	25	95.1	49.6
Georgia	34.3	7.2	5.1	7.9	9.4	8.0	8.7	3	143.6	49.3
Moldova	35.1	-2.2	0.7	4.1	5.2	6.2	2.9	21	114.5	40.2
Ukraine	38.3	-2.0	-5.2	-1.1	4.0	4.6	0.0	24	100.0	38.3

Notes: [a] Ranking is according to the 2002 GDP index (1997=100) and 1998–2002 average rate of growth.
[b] Preliminary evaluation.

Source: PlanEcon, 1998a. Review and Outlook for the Former Soviet Union, PlanEcon Inc, Washington, DC; PlanEcon, 1998b. Review and Outlook for Eastern Europe, PlanEcon Inc, Washington, DC; author's calculations based on Table 18.1.

The size of the government is less important than the quality of its policies and the manner in which changes to government have been implemented. In transition economies the issue is not just downsizing the government, but a deep restructuring of the public finance system and changes to policy targets and means. Fiscal transfers should be redirected from non-competitive sectors toward institution building (including those dealing with behavioural and cultural changes), investment in human capital and hard infrastructure. Attempts to downsize the government through cuts to expenditure can cause more harm than good for launching recovery and growth. Even if a small government is sometimes better than a large one, often governments can not be downsized without causing an economic contraction. Downsizing should occur only when the economy is on the rise, though most often it is attempted in periods of deep contraction. Thus, the general problem lies in restructuring expenditures rather than cutting them to create an illusion of concurrent, albeit unsustainable fiscal prudence.

Unlike certain liberalisation measures, institution building, by its nature, must be a gradual process. Feedback between specific inputs to this process and its output must be monitored constantly and policies adjusted. The post-socialist transition is uncharted waters—one should not rely on misguided analogies with experiences from distorted market economies. Institution building must be innovative, particularly regarding privatisation and development of capital markets.

If institution building is neglected, an informal institutionalisation will fill the vacuum. Extreme cases are vast corruption and organised crime—the two main maladies in countries after liberalisation and privatisation under weak governments. Sometimes governments are weak because they were too large and were forced to downsize before the infant market was able to substitute for the state. Prematurely or too extensively downsized governments are not strong enough to control the market, which expands in the informal sector (shadow economy) while difficulties mount in the official economy. Profits accrue to the informal sector, while revenues fall in the official sector, with all the negative consequences for the budget and social policy. Thus the market works in a way where profits are privatised, but the losses are socialised in a politically unsustainable way.

In transition economies, policies must transform and streamline the judicial system to serve the needs of the market economy. This is a great challenge, since the old system of contract execution under planned allocation has ceased to exist, but a new system of contract implementation under market rules and culture has not yet matured. The establishment and development of new laws, for example, trade and tax codes, capital market regulations, property rights protections, competition and anti-trust rules, banking supervision, consumer protection and environmental protection, are even more important and ought to be addressed before privatisation of state assets. Creation and advancement of a legal framework for the market economy should be much higher on the agenda of international financial organisations. It must be placed ahead of liberalisation and privatisation, since the latter can contribute to sound growth only if the former is secured.

A shift of competence and power from the central government to local governments is necessary for the deregulation of the post-socialist economy. Such a shift means moving the public finance system toward decentralisation and streamlining local governments by giving them more fiscal autonomy. Otherwise the process of weakening the central government is not balanced by enhancing the power of local governments. The joint position of both levels of government must be seen as an integrated entity needed for the sake of gradual institution building. If local governments have not been strengthened when the central government diminishes, and market forces are not yet supported by new institutional arrangements, then liberalisation and privatisation will not necessarily improve capital allocation and raise efficiency.

There is an urgent necessity to accelerate the development of non-government organisations. Next to the private sector and the state, this is the third indispensable pillar of a contemporary market economy and civic society. Without a range of non-government organisations, there is a continued tension between the state and society, and the expanding private sector does not provide a satisfactory solution to this matter. There are spheres within the public domain that must depend neither on the state nor on the profit-oriented private sector. A growing part of international technical, financial and political assistance must be channeled into enhancing non-government organisations. Otherwise the infant market economy and democracy in post-socialist countries will not evolve fast enough and the transition will be incomplete. The delay of institutional infrastructure provided by the non-government organisations becomes a growing hurdle for successful systemic changes and high quality growth.

During transition income policy and government concern for equitable growth has great meaning. Whereas increasing inequity is unavoidable during the initial years of transition, the state must play an active role, through fiscal and social policies, in controlling income dispersion. There is a limit of disparity beyond which further expansion of overall economic activity becomes constrained and growth starts to slow or recovery is delayed. If disparity growth is tolerated for a number of years during an economic contraction, so that the standard of living is improving for a few and declining for many, then political support for necessary reforms will evaporate. Hence, large inequities turn against crucial institutional and structural reforms.

Post-socialist transition is taking place at a time of worldwide globalisation, hence opening and integration with the world economy is an indispensable part of the endeavour. Yet these processes must be managed carefully with special attention to short-term capital flow liberalisation. It must be monitored and controlled by the countries' fiscal and monetary authorities with the support of international financial institutions, such as the IMF and Bank for International Settlements. It is better to liberalise capital markets later than sooner. Institution building must be advanced enough and stabilisation ought to be consolidated into stability. Only then should financial markets be liberalised, and then in a gradual manner. Otherwise the societies of young emerging markets and democracies are not going to be supportive of the introduction of the market mechanism or integration with the world economy, and they may even become hostile toward such changes.

International organisations should not only support, but also insist on further regional integration and cooperation. If growth is expected to be durable and fast, it requires export expansion, which will depend on strong regional links. This calls for institutional support, such as export–import banks, commodity exchanges and credit insurance agencies. This should be the main institution building concern of the European Bank for Reconstruction and Development, and supported by directed lending and technical assistance from this bank. This type of market infrastructure is still underdeveloped in transition economies, thus regional trade and cross-country foreign direct investment are lagging behind overall changes. What should be one of the driving forces of sustainable growth is actually one of its main obstacles.

The Bretton Woods organisations should reconsider their policies toward transition economies. If the IMF primarily deals with financial liquidity, currency convertibility, fiscal prudence and monetary stabilisation, the World Bank should focus its attention mainly on conditions for equitable growth and sustainable development. For obvious reasons these two kinds of economic policy aims—or rather the means in the former case and the ends in the latter—are often contradictory. There is an inclination to confuse the ends with the means of policy, to subordinate long-term development policy to short-term stabilisation policy. Yet the record of transition so far has clearly proved that there has been neither much development nor stability. Hence, the future fiscal and monetary policies must be subordinated to development policy, not the other way around. There is a need for the World Bank performance criteria describing socioeconomic development as much as there is such a need for the traditional IMF fiscal and monetary criteria. The new set of criteria should always stress the implications of advised financial policies for growth, capital allocation, income distribution and the social safety net. The World Bank should not accept and support policy reforms and actions that, while aiming at financial stabilisation, may lead to social destabilisation resulting from lack of growth, spreading poverty, increasing inequality and divestment in human capital.

These interactive processes of learning-by-monitoring and learning-by-doing will continue for several years. Even if there is, as indeed there seems to be, a growing chance for some kind of the post-Washington consensus, this must be seen as a process, and not as a one-off event. Such an emerging consensus must be accomplished among many more partners than just the important Washington-based organisations. Otherwise, the policies agreed on in Washington will not be able to deliver what they promise. This is also an important policy conclusion that should be obvious in the era of globalisation. Furthermore, what may be agreed on currently must be revised often if conditions and challenges change. The quest for a comprehensive and implementable consensus on policies facilitating sustainable growth must continue.

Part 8

Conclusions

19 Reflections on capital mobility and domestic stability

Ross Garnaut

The East Asian financial crisis of 1997–8 arrived suddenly in the consciousness of the international community. It cut deeply into economic activity in many East Asian countries and sent shock waves through the international economy. It then departed as swiftly as it had come, leaving important but different legacies in various economies.

The financial crisis in a couple of countries, and most particularly in the world's fourth most populous country, Indonesia, left in its wake economic and political wreckage that will take many years to clear. In many countries, it left a legacy of increased commitment to building and strengthening policies and institutions that are helpful to sustaining economic stability and growth. Everywhere it left many questions about the extent to and the conditions under which deep integration into global capital markets and the associated international capital mobility are consistent with domestic economic stability.

The earlier chapters in this book describe and interpret the impact of the crisis on economies in three regions: East Asia itself; Latin America; and the transitional economies in Eastern Europe.

The experiences of economies in the three regions covered by the book are markedly different. The central story in East Asia was the collapse of a long boom that in its later stages was associated with the excesses of a 'bubble economy'. Some of the excesses were encouraged by a new era of open capital accounts and large-scale short-term international capital movements. The central story in Latin America concerned the effects of imperfect policy responses to more conventional macroeconomic imbalances. The central story in Eastern Europe was of the incapacity of weak institutions to cope with shocks from abroad, with especially damaging consequences when combined with exchange rate misalignment, and with markedly more favourable outcomes in countries in which a longer experience of managing an open market economy had strengthened institutions through learning by doing.

The stories of individual economies damaged by the crisis within each of the three regions also differ greatly from each other. This is partly a product of the way different authors emphasise different issues and events, but it also has a basis in different realities. Amongst the economies that were damaged less by the shocks from the international economy in 1997 and 1998, there seems to be less variation in experience.

This concluding chapter reflects on the general wisdom that can be distilled from the experience of many countries in three regions, through the most widespread and challenging episode in international financial instability in modern monetary history.

THE DIFFERENT PATHS TO POOR PERFORMANCE

The countries that avoided recession and major economic dislocation in the late 1990s shared a number of characteristics. Or rather, they had one or another of two sets of shared characteristics, with some qualities common to the two groups. They shared reasonably strong macroeconomic fundamentals: budget deficits and public debt within reasonable limits, and a more or less realistic exchange rate. This was a necessary though not a sufficient condition for reasonably stable performance through the shocks of the crisis period. They tended to have moderate current account deficits, funded with a high proportion of direct foreign investment rather than portfolio capital flows. And they had either a competitive and well-managed and well-regulated domestic financial system, or they restricted short-term capital movements with exchange controls. In most cases of strong domestic financial systems, the strength had emerged from a number of years of operating within a competitive and reasonably open framework, in all cases with major episodes of financial instability along the way to the building of a strong system. For the cases of reliance on exchange controls, awareness that financial liberalisation elsewhere had generally been associated with a period of expensive learning-by-doing and sometimes by financial crisis became a major consideration in planning for reform of banking and finance.

There were more varied ways of performing badly through the crisis. Severe macroeconomic imbalances of a conventional kind and in particular badly misaligned exchange rates were a sufficient condition for major disruption when the cold winds blew from the international monetary economy. An open capital account and a recent history of high levels of short-term capital inflow went a long way towards the precipitation of recession and sometimes of crisis, needing in addition one only of a weak and poorly regulated banking system or misjudgment in macroeconomic policy responses. The securing of domestic economic stability through a major episode of external financial stability depended on high quality domestic policy responses and on domestic and international confidence in policy. As a result, domestic political instability was a separate cause of disruption, and in Indonesia turned what would have been a period of economic difficulty and recession into catastrophe.

A straightforward reading of the case studies in this book suggests that the responses to external instability were different in the three regions of East Asia, Latin America and Eastern Europe and Russia. The causes of instability in Eastern Europe that are identified in the case studies give prominence to weaknesses in banking and financial institutions including regulatory systems. These were most acute in Russia, where they interacted with severe exchange rate misalignment. Other Eastern European economies, notably Poland, had stronger institutions, partly as a result of learning-by-doing in earlier financial crises.

On closer examination, there is a question about whether the apparently distinctive differences across the three regions are the consequence not of variations in objective reality, but in the questions that came to be asked most frequently in the three regions. This is a question that readers can usefully keep in mind as they assess the lessons from the country studies.

The East Asian case studies place more emphasis than the others on the role of macroeconomic imbalances. The central story is of a long boom from the mid 1980s to the mid 1990s encouraging an expectation of continuing economic expansion which, in turn, dulled awareness of risk in investment and supported the overvaluation of assets and exchange rates. An exceptional feature of East Asian macroeconomic imbalances in the period leading into the crisis is the extent to which they derived not from public deficits, but from private expenditure and short-term foreign borrowing. The exchange rate misalignment was greatly exacerbated by the hybrid exchange rate systems that were being applied during the 1990s, neither institutionally fixed (as in the special case of the Hong Kong currency board) nor freely floating, but more or less fixed to the US dollar or to baskets dominated by the dollar. This took East Asian developing economies' effective exchange rates much higher when the United States dollar appreciated strongly against the yen and most other currencies in 1996 and 1997, at a time when strong demand at home and weakening export demand was in any case tending to generate exchange rate overvaluation. The high capacity to sustain rapid economic growth in East Asia was no protection against recession and crisis, although it was an important support for recovery once macroeconomic imbalances had been corrected, through exchange rate depreciation and other adjustments.

Latin America generally did not perform as badly as East Asia during the crisis. For those Latin American economies that were damaged most in the crisis, conventional macroeconomic imbalances generated principally within the public sector were the major source of vulnerability to external financial instability.

STABLE NEIGHBOURS AND CONTAGION

Looking across the three regions, what appeared in 1997 and early 1998 as an East Asian crisis, and for a while in the second half of 1998 looked as if it were a global emerging markets crisis, after the event again looks mainly like an East Asian crisis—albeit an East Asian crisis that sent shock waves everywhere and precipitated major problems in a limited number of other economies.

The different experience of the three regions draws attention to the importance of having stable neighbours, and illuminates the phenomenon of 'contagion' in the spread of financial crisis. The Latin American economies are deeply integrated into the North American and especially the US economy. This is particularly important for Mexico. The continued strong growth of the United States through the East Asian crisis—indeed, the sustenance of growth in the United States through capital flight from East Asia to a safe haven—was strongly supportive of continued export expansion and economic growth in Latin America. This helped to stabilise economic activity in East Asia against the shocks from East Asia: the small loss of exports through decline in activity and a lower exchange rate in East Asian trading partners was balanced by the maintenance of import demand in the United States, and by the effects on exports of heightened competitiveness as a result of exchange rate depreciation. It was feared during the crisis that the enhanced competitiveness of East Asian suppliers following their own large exchange rate depreciation would diminish Latin American countries' export opportunities in third markets, including the United States. As it turned out, the disruption to normal economic activity and to the financing of production and exports in East Asia during the crisis prevented the reflection of enhanced East Asian price competitiveness in expanded exports prior to the restoration of economic stability, by which time a substantial part of the East Asian depreciations had been reversed. Increased competition from East Asia in third countries is more intense in the recovery, when it is less dangerous to stability in Latin America.

Eastern Europe's main external trading relationships are with Western Europe, which was growing at moderate rates through the East Asian crisis. This provided some insulation from diminished export opportunity to East Asia, although rather less than the North American orientation of Latin America.

The story was very different in East Asia, where intra-regional trade amongst economies deeply affected by the financial crisis was much more important than in either Latin America or Eastern Europe. In the long boom from the mid 1980s to the mid 1990s, a majority of the real growth in East Asian economies was to other East Asian markets. The rapidly growing economies of East Asia were joined by a virtuous circle of economic growth, trade liberalisation and import expansion. Import growth in each economy supported the exports and therefore the environment for economic expansion and trade liberalisation in others. The virtuous circle went into reverse in 1997, with currency depreciation and economic contraction in one economy leading to a fall in imports and a decline in the export opportunities of neighbours. The power of the regional transmission of contractionary pressures across East Asia during the crisis was greatly underestimated, contributing to the general tendency to misjudge the extent of the recession and therefore the appropriate settings of macroeconomic policies.

The directions of the influence on economic activity of the regional transmission mechanisms reversed again with the stabilisation and then the return to growth in one after another East Asian economy from the September quarter of 1998. Again, a failure to take into account the strength of the trade links amongst East Asian economies led to an underestimation of growth in the recovery phase.

The international transmission of recessionary tendencies through trade contraction was recognised as having been of large importance during the Great Depression of the 1930s. The amelioration of the international transmission of recession was an important motive for the establishment of the International Monetary Fund in the immediate aftermath of the Second World War. The high intensity and large and increasing role of intra-East Asian trade in the 1990s made these international transmission mechanisms important on a regional basis. The International Monetary Fund's misjudgment of the extent of the contraction and therefore of the appropriate setting of macroeconomic policy resulted to a considerable extent from underestimation of the power of these influences.

While the buoyant US economy was less effective as a brake on contraction in East Asia than in Latin America, the maintenance of strong import growth across the Pacific was one element in the early and strong East Asian recovery. The avoidance of recession (and in the case of China a fixed exchange rate against the US dollar) in China, Taiwan and Australia, economies that played significant roles in the intense intra-regional trade of East Asia, also contributed to early and strong East Asian recovery.

Trade was certainly the most regionally concentrated of the channels for the international transmission of contractionary pressures during the crisis, distinguishing East Asia from other regions of emerging market economies. But there were other channels as well. A general increase in risk premia on investment in emerging markets was another important source of contagion, contributing to contagion in East Asia, and providing as well the main link into Latin America and Eastern Europe.

ECONOMIC POLICY AND FINANCIAL CRISIS

Earlier chapters in this book have suggested a range of conclusions about the policies that contributed to crisis and its avoidance, to the depth of recession in economies in crisis, and to the process of recovery. Inevitably there has been a focus on the experience of particular countries. This final chapter provides an opportunity to examine whether there are general conclusions to be drawn, and whether generalisations from this large sample of countries are representative of the experience of some important cases that are not covered in the book.

The most fundamental issue raised by the crisis is whether the benefits of an open capital account are worth the associated risk to stability from international capital mobility. Grenville (Chapter 2) and Miller and Zhang (Chapter 3) draw attention to the International Monetary Fund's advice prior to the crisis favouring capital account liberalisation generally, reflected in September 1997 in proposals to introduce a new commitment to open capital accounts at the IMF's Annual Meeting in Hong Kong.

The book's focus on the crisis draws attention to the costs of free capital flows. In general, the benefits take the form of enhanced long-term growth prospects, which are not closely related to short-term stability. There is therefore a bias against open capital accounts in the focus of this study. Is there anything that we can say about whether the costs of instability outweigh the longer-term growth benefits?

Grenville alone in the earlier chapters addresses this issue directly. He concludes that the costs of crisis, and the contribution of volatile capital movements to the risk of crisis, are so large, that the modest growth benefits of free short-term capital movements cannot be presumed to exceed them. Huang and Song (Chapter 16) come down quite firmly against capital account liberalisation in China until financial reform has been taken much further. Prema-Chandra (Chapter 15) provides a favourable review of Malaysia's modest experiments with new exchange controls. Vojta (Chapter 17), on the role of the private sector, presumes net gains from free capital flows, but does not argue the case closely.

Direct foreign investment gets unambiguously good reviews here and in the recent international discussion generally. Direct foreign investment introduces new technology and approaches to management, as well as expanded international market access. Direct foreign investment may or may not significantly augment domestic capital resources, but this is not its most important contribution to growth. Direct foreign investment is not subject to sudden and precipitous reversal with the ebb and flow of market sentiment. Countries which received a high proportion of capital inflow in the form of direct foreign investment were much less affected by the international monetary instability of 1997–8.

The long-term gains from keeping the capital account open to short as well as long-term capital flows are of three kinds.

First, short-term flows provide some augmentation of domestic capital resources that can, in principle, contribute to increased output. If it were not for the periodic reversals, this might be a worthwhile source of gain.

Second, and potentially more significantly, it is sometimes argued that, with smoothly operating financial markets, short-term capital flows can be stabilising. Markets can see through short-term weakness in the current account of the balance of payments, resulting for example from a short-term deterioration in the terms of trade, and compensate for them with short-term capital flows. This is a means of financing the maintenance of activity through what would otherwise be a period of costly and unnecessary adjustment. Perhaps short-term capital movements do indeed play this role, in economies with a sufficiently long history of openness and efficient regulation for all relevant market players to have become deeply experienced in their operation. Dadush and Dasgupta (Chapter 1) provide a list of arguments why fluctuations in capital movements are much less likely to be stabilising in developing than developed countries. The evidence of continued overshooting of the floating exchange rates, presented for the Australian case by Grenville, and the large losses of major international financial enterprises taking positions on macroeconomic parameters in recent years, suggest that even in developed countries, the lags in the learning process are long.

The strongest case for an open capital account in the wake of the financial crisis is a highly practical one: short-term capital flows are not easily deterred over long periods without inhibiting trade and other investment flows that are much more important for growth. A country that is deeply integrated into the international economy through trade flows is unable to exclude substantial short-term capital flows through leads and lags in trade-related payments. The larger the trade share of domestic economic activity, the greater the potential for destabilising trade-related capital movements. Similarly, the presence of high levels of direct investment creates opportunities for related short-term movements of capital. An attempt to control the related opportunities for short-term capital flows will increase the transactions costs of genuinely growth-enhancing trade and investment. It follows that the costs of capital controls rise with deepening integration into the international economy. Firms become more effective in evading controls over time, so there is an inexorable tendency to rising transactions costs of capital controls with the passing of time.

The main lesson from the crisis is that the risks of volatility of short-term capital flows in an economy with a weak financial system are very large. The risks are so large that great care should be taken that the ground is laid for capital account liberalisation by improvements in regulatory systems and the competitive environment for domestic banking and finance, so that liberalisation proceeds in step with the strengthening of financial systems. Even then there will be risks, as the experience of operating in an open, competitive financial system is a final and necessary part of the building of a strong financial institution.

This is one area where the crisis has changed the received wisdom on economic policy. It is no longer widely presumed that early opening of the capital account is desirable. The IMF is now much more careful with its advice and pressure on capital account opening. Some countries that were on a path to early capital account opening, most importantly China, have delayed the next steps into the indefinite future. And a couple of countries, most significantly Malaysia , now see limited controls on short-term capital movements as a normal part of their repertoire of economic management instruments.

These developments in policy in relation to the capital account are broadly consistent with the lessons of recent experience. They need to be tempered, however, with realisation that the achievement of the full potential gains from integration into the international economy over the longer term will require the strengthening of domestic regulatory systems, and more generally the reform and strengthening of financial systems, to reduce the risks and costs of the short-term capital flows that are an inevitable accompaniment of the gains from international integration.

The earlier chapters make a strong case for freely floating exchange rates, at least in economies which have chosen to open themselves to the potential gains from open capital accounts. Exchange rate overvaluation, of a kind that has no parallel in economies with freely floating rates, played a significant part in the onset of crisis in East Asia and Russia. Countries with some history of freely floating rates generally did better, with Australia one outstanding example. This would seem to make a case for the floating exchange rate system.

The qualifications come from the experiences of currency board systems, no cases of which have been covered in this book. In the depths of the crisis, the currency board systems, for example of Hong Kong and Argentina, came under great stress. The monetary contraction that was associated with large-scale capital outflow forced substantial reductions in economic activity. But the systems held, avoiding the extreme economic dislocation as a result of unanticipated massive exchange rate depreciation experienced in many other countries. Recovery from recession came quickly and strongly, as domestic costs and prices fell. The strong recovery depended on price and structural flexibility in domestic economies. The experience of the Hong Kong currency board at least suggests that this option is worth considering as an alternative to freely floating rates in economies with high degrees of flexibility in domestic prices and economic structure.

There are a number of clear lessons from the crisis on settings of fiscal and monetary policy. One is to confirm the old wisdom on cautious settings of demand policies. Sound budgets and the moderation in monetary growth are not sufficient conditions for the avoidance of crisis, but they help. Their absence is certainly a sufficient condition for crisis.

A second lesson emerges, from the East Asian evidence in particular, that excessive fiscal and monetary contraction during the crisis can be counterproductive to the stabilisation objectives to which it is directed, and can deepen recession and delay recovery. Vines and Irwin (Chapter 5), Warr on Thailand (Chapter 13), McLeod on Indonesia (Chapter 12), Prema-Chandra on Malaysia (Chapter 15) and Pyo on Korea (Chapter 14) all point to the costs of excessive fiscal and monetary contraction in the first year of the crisis, in all cases consistently with advice at the time from the IMF.

The common error was underestimation of the extent of the contraction that was already in process. The misjudgment needs to be explained. As previously discussed, it was to a considerable extent the consequence of underestimation of the effect of the regional transmission of recession through contraction of intra-regional trade.

There is an associated lesson arising out of large increases in interest rates during the first year of crisis. The objective of this tightening of monetary policy was to limit the depreciation of the domestic currency, with its domestic inflationary and international contractionary consequences. Not only did the monetary contraction go too far in exacerbating recession, in some economies, including in the important Indonesian case, the increases in interest rates seem to have been counterproductive to the objective of holding up the exchange rate. Monetary contraction at the height of the crisis contributed to an acceleration in the decline of domestic businesses, damaging confidence in stabilisation and recovery, and reducing incentives to hold domestic assets. The resulting encouragement of net capital outflow outweighed the contribution that higher interest rates made to increasing incentives for capital inflow.

The general lesson is that there is no presumption that policies to induce severe contraction of demand will be helpful to stabilisation and recovery once financial crisis has taken hold, at least in countries that did not have large macroeconomic imbalances resulting from excessive fiscal expansion prior to the instability.

LEARNING AND THE STRENGTH OF THE FINANCIAL SYSTEM

The crisis of the late 1990s left a legacy of awareness of the importance to economic stability of a strong financial system, with effective prudential supervision and regulation, and sound internal governance processes.

The call for better regulation and corporate governance became a mantra, and a sound basis. However, it sometimes came to be something of a mantra without operationally meaningful content.

There has been a tendency in the discussion of governance and prudential supervision since the onset of crisis to compile long lists of elements of good regulation and governance, with the length of the list detracting from coherence and a sense of priority. It would be more productive to focus on a small set of central issues.

First on the list for effective prudential supervision of financial institutions, especially banks, is the enforcement of high minimum ratios of capital to assets at risk. The capital adequacy ratios that are necessary to secure stability in the banking system are higher for developing than for developed countries, reflecting the greater vulnerability to instability.

The capital adequacy ratios have no meaning unless there is transparent accounting on a consistent basis, so reform of the system of financial reporting is the second central issue in prudential supervision. Transparent accounting is also of central importance for effective corporate governance more generally.

The third central prudential issue is the supervision of related party transactions. This is a matter for corporate governance and regulation generally, but its operation in the financial sector is particularly important for economic stability in modern conditions of international capital mobility.

Several of the country studies have emphasised the value of a central bank operating independently of Government in the setting of monetary policy. The problems deriving from central bank dependence were greatest in Indonesia (Soedradjad, Chapter 4), but were prominent in the financial crisis in several countries. The difficulty is that the prescription is more difficult than the production of a response, a reality underlined in Russia (Popov, Chapter 9).The building of the professional strengths necessary for a central bank to be effective, alongside the development of a culture of independence inside and beyond the bank, takes time as well as political will, since much of the institutional strengthening requires experience and learning by doing.

Learning by doing over time and from earlier errors seem to be unavoidable parts of the process of building an effective financial system in an open, competitive financial environment. The editors noted in Chapter 1 that 'All 31 emerging markets' have experienced at least one liquidity crisis. Grenville (Chapter 2) observes that the strength of the Australian financial system through the East Asian financial crisis derived to a considerable extent from earlier domestic financial and external payments and exchange rate liberalisation, and from the lessons learned by the regulatory authorities and market participants in episodes of banking and exchange rate instability following deregulation. Australia was fortunate in being able to do its learning under less intense external pressures than those experienced by East Asian countries through the crisis. The resistance of Poland to recessionary pressures in 1998 owes much to learning from the crisis of the early 1990s (Wagner, Chapter 7). Czechoslovakia benefited from earlier experience of managing financial instability (Abel and Darvas, Chapter 8).

The learning proceeds more quickly and thoroughly in a competitive and internationally open financial environment. But there is risk of financial instability in domestic and external financial deregulation, much more so if an episode of international instability follows closely on reform. Hence there is a dilemma. The costs and difficulties of remaining closed to international transactions increase over time. But some macroeconomic problems are a likely, and severe problems a possible, consequence of reform, before learning and institution-building more generally have reduced the risks of reform. To initiate far-reaching reform, the authorities in an economy with a closed and structurally weak financial system have to be prepared to accept some short-term risks for long-term national economic gains.

Huang and Song (Chapter 16) point to a way to improve the trade-off between short-term risks of loss and long term gains from the international financial reform in an economy with a closed capital account: delay external financial liberalisation until domestic reform has gone a long way. Their suggestion for China is consistent with wisdom from earlier Latin American experience.

LEARNING IN THE INTERNATIONAL SYSTEM

International players, and not only domestic authorities in the countries affected by the crisis, learned a great deal from the experience of 1997–9. Standard IMF prescriptions for macroeconomic policy during a financial crisis were tested. They were found wanting in a crisis that had its origins in private rather than public sector imbalances and capital flows. The lessons suggested a more cautious approach to fiscal and monetary policy during the crisis. These lessons had been embodied in macroeconomic policy prescriptions by the middle of 1998. This was a factor in and perhaps a precondition for the stabilisation and recovery of exchange rates and activity in East Asia in the second half of 1998.

As already noted, a number of economies in East Asia and the IMF drew valid lessons about the value of a more measured and conditional approach to capital account liberalisation. There are few signs yet, however, of the IMF or others appreciating the extent to which failure to take into account the intra-regional transmission of contraction contributed to the misjudgment of macroeconomic policy in East Asia during the first year of the crisis.

The private sector, too, learned much from the crisis. The sad reality is that the most important lessons for the private sector, about the risks associated with asset inflation in a long boom, have been learned many times before. After the crisis, these particular lessons will not need to be absorbed again until the experience of the late 1990s has receded in personal and corporate memories.

Other private sector lessons were specific to the recent global diversification of portfolio investment from advanced economies, especially the United States. Mutual funds experienced large losses as a result of their naivety, and these were exacerbated by the herd reactions to setbacks in emerging markets. The greater caution and knowledge that will follow the disaster of the late 1990s will provide some antidote against repetition of recent mistakes.

Nowhere was learning more necessary or more powerful than in the operations of the new highly leveraged and weakly regulated investment vehicles, the so-called hedge funds, mostly from the United States, through the crisis. Grenville decries the fact that highly leveraged hedge funds did not act in stabilising ways, as reflected in the losses that they took on speculative positions against some regional currencies. He argues for greater disclosure requirements and transparency for the hedge funds.

The problem of destabilising movements of capital by the hedge funds is unlikely to be as important for a considerable time as it was through the East Asian crisis. The large losses forced the pace on learning, and for that reason will not be repeated in the extreme form of 1997–2000. And the experience of recent years has weakened the more speculative participants in the market, and enhanced the relative position of funds that have been more effective in hedging out poorly understood risks, and retaining exposure only to well understood sources of possible loss.

The recent experience has focussed the attention of regulatory authorities, especially in the United States, to the dangers that unhedged exposures by highly leveraged institutions pose for financial instability in the developed countries, whose credit to the hedge funds is at risk. With the new awareness of the potential problem, this would seem to be amenable to normal prudential supervision in the home economies of the funds and their bankers.

In addition to his suggestions for supervision of hedge funds, he suggests greater requirements of disclosure for these institutions, as well as 'stand-still' and 'bail-in' procedures for private, international financial institutions in the process of moving from crisis.

The 'bailing in' proposal does not have unanimous support in the book. Vojta argues that it would diminish international investors' willingness to provide capital. He urges instead attention to improving, including through rendering more transparent, the governance of domestic financial institutions. There is no argument against this prescription, the importance of which is a theme that runs through the book. But following the recent crisis, not all governments in the countries covered by this book will accept the view that opportunities to diminish the risks of financial crisis should be forgone simply to maintain the highest possible level of capital inflow. The lessons of 1997–9 support their caution.

References

Alexashenko, S., 1999. *The Battle for the Ruble*, Alma Mater, Moscow (in Russian).

Andrew, R. and Broadbent, J., 1994. *Reserve Bank Operations in the Foreign Exchange Market: effectiveness and profitability*, Reserve Bank of Australia Research Discussion Paper No. 9406, Sydney.

Arndt, H. and Hill, H., 1999. *Southeast Asia's Economic Crisis: Origins, Lessons, and the Way Forward*, Institute of South East Asian Studies, Singapore.

Árvai, Zs. and Vincze, J., 1997–8. *Vulnerability of Currencies: financial crises in the 1990s*, Acta Oeconomica, 49(3–4):243–69.

Athukorala, P.-C., 1998. 'Malaysia', in R.H. McLeod and R. Garnaut (eds), *East Asia in Crisis: from being a miracle to needing one?*, Routledge, London:85–101.

——, 1999. 'Swimming against the tide: crisis management in Malaysia', *ASEAN Economic Bulletin*, 15(3):281–9.

—— and Warr, P., 1999. *Vulnerability to a Currency Crisis: lessons from the Asian Experience*, Working Papers in Trade and Development No. 99/6, Division of Economics, Research School of Pacific and Asian Studies, Asia Pacific School of Economics and Management, The Australian National University, Canberra.

—— and Menon, J., 1999. 'Outward orientation and economic performance: the Malaysian experience', *World Economy*, 22(8):1119–39.

Asian Development Bank, 1997. *Asian Development Outlook 1997 and 1998*, Manila.

—— and World Bank, 1998. *Managing Global Financial Integration: emerging lessons and prospective challenges*, Asian Development Bank, Manila (mimeo).

Åslund, A., 1994. 'The case for radical reform', *Journal of Democracy*, 5(4):63–74.

——, 1999a. Why has Russia's economic transformation been so arduous?, Paper presented to the World Bank's Annual Bank Conference on Development Economics, Washington DC, 28–30 April 1999.

——, 1999b. 'Russia's collapse', *Foreign Affairs*, September/October:64–77.

Aspe, P., 1995. *The Mexican Way of Economic Transformation*, Series of Lectures at the London School of Economics, MIT Press, Cambridge.

Associacao Nacional das Instituicoes do Mercado Aberto, *Retrospectiva 1995*, Table 3.6.

Bank of Korea, 1999. Recent Trends in Real Gross National Income (GNI), Internet press release, April 23, Seoul.

Bank of Mexico, 1994. *Annual Report 1993*, Bank of Mexico, Mexico City.

Begg, D., 1998. *Pegging Out: lessons from the Czech exchange rate crisis*, CEPR Discussion Paper No. 1956, CEPR, London.

—— and Wyplosz, C., 1999. Why untied hands are fundamentally better, paper presented at the Fifth Dubrovnik Conference on Transition Economies, Dubrovnik, 23–25 June 1999.

Bhagwati, J., 1998a. 'The capital myth: the difference between trade in widgets and dollars', *Foreign Affairs*, 77(3):7–12.

——, 1998b. Asian financial crisis debate: why? how severe?, paper presented at the conference on Managing the Asian Financial Crisis: Lessons and Changes, organised by the Asian Strategic Leadership Institute and Rating Agency Malaysia, Kuala Lumpur, 2–3 November.

BIS (Bank for International Settlements), 1997. *Compendium of documents produced by the Basle Committee on Banking Supervision*, BIS, Basle.

——, 1998. *International Banking and Financial Market Development*, BIS, Basle.

——, 1999. *Capital Requirements and Bank Behaviour: the impact of the Basle Accord*, Basle Committee on Banking Supervision Working Papers No. 1, BIS, Basle.

Blinder, A.S., 1998. *Central Banking in Theory and Practice*, MIT Press, Cambridge.

BNM (Bank Negara Malaysia), 1994. *Money and Banking in Malaysia*, BNM, Kuala Lumpur.

——, 1999. *Annual Report of the Board of Directors for the Year Ended 31 December 1998*, BNM, Kuala Lumpur.

Bofinger, P., Flassbeck, H. and Hoffmann, L., 1997. 'Orthodox money-based stabilisation (OMBS) versus heterodox exchange rate-based stabilisation (HERBS): the case of Russia, the Ukraine and Kazakhstan', *Economic Systems*, 21(1):1–33.

Bond, T.J. and Miller, M., 1998. *Financial Bailouts and Financial Crises*, International Monetary Fund, Washington DC (mimeo).

Borensztein, E. and Lee, J-W., 1998. Financial distortions and the crisis in Korea, unpublished paper, International Monetary Fund, Washington, DC.

——, Berg, A., Milesi-Ferretti, G.M. and Pattillo, C., (forthcoming), *Anticipating Balance of Payments Crises: the role of early warning systems*, IMF Occasional Paper, Washington DC.

Borio, C.E.V., Kennedy, N. and Prowse, S.D., 1994. 'Exploring aggregate asset price fluctuations across countries', *BIS Economic Papers*, No. 40 (April):100.

Branson, W.H., 1993. 'A comment on John Williamson's paper', in M. Reisen and B. Fischer (eds), *Financial Opening: policy issues and experiences in developing countries*, OECD, Paris:35–7.

Bruno, M., 1995. 'Does inflation really lower growth?', *Finance & Development*, 32(3):35–8.

—— and Easterly, W., 1995. Inflation crisis and long-run growth, unpublished paper, World Bank, Washington DC.

Bruton, H.J., 1993. *The Political Economy of Poverty, Equity and Growth: Sri Lanka and Malaysia*, Oxford University Press, New York.

Buira, A., 1995. 'Reflections on the Mexican crisis of 1994', in G. Calvo, M. Goldstein and E. Hochreiter (eds), *Private Capital Flows to Emerging Markets After the Mexican Crisis*, Institute for International Economics, Washington, DC and Austrian National Central Bank, Vienna:315–19.

Bussière, M. and Mulder, C., 1999. *External Vulnerability in Emerging Market Economies: how high liquidity can offset weak fundamentals and the effects of contagion*, IMF Working Paper WP/99/88, International Monetary Fund, Washington DC.

Caprio, D. and Klingebiel, D., 1996. *Bank Insolvencies: cross-country experience*, Policy Research Working Paper 1620, World Bank, Washington DC.

Calvo, G., Leiderman, L. and Reinhart, C., 1993. 'Capital inflows and real exchange rate appreciation in Latin America: the role of external factors', *IMF Staff Papers*, 40(1):108–51.

Calvo, G., Goldstein, M. and Hochreiter, E. (eds), 1996. *Private Capital Flows to Emerging Markets after the Mexican Crisis*, Institute for International Economics, Washington, DC and Austrian National Central Bank, Vienna.

Campelo, A., Jr., 1997. 'Por que os juros não caem', *Conjuntura Econômica*, 51(7):35–6.

Cardenas, M. and Barrera, F., 1997. 'On the effectiveness of capital controls: the experience of Colombia during the 1990s', *Journal of Development Economics*, 54(1):27–57.

Cardoso, E., 1998. 'Virtual deficits and the Patinkin effect', *IMF Staff Papers*, 45(4):619–46.

—— and Fishlow, A., 1990. 'The macroeconomics of Brazilian external debt', in J. Sachs (ed.), *Developing Country Debt and Economic Performance*, University of Chicago Press, Chicago:269–392.

—— and Goldfajn, I., 1998. 'Capital flows to Brazil: the endogeneity of capital controls', *IMF Staff Papers*, 45(1):161–202.

—— and Leiderman, D., 1999. Brazil, the World Bank, and the International Monetary Fund: short stories of a ménage à trois, World Bank, Washington, DC (mimeo).

Cargill, T.F. and Elliott, P., 1999. Financial liberalization and crisis in Japan and Korea: lessons for China, Paper presented at the 1999 ASSA Meetings, New York, 3–5 January.

CCER (China Center for Economic Research, Peking University), 1998. 'Seeking effective policy combination under multi economic objectives: analyses of China's macroeconomic situation in 1998 and some recommendations', *Economic Research Journal [Jingji Yanjiu]*, 4(April):1–10.

Central Bank of Russia. *Economic and Financial Situation*, Central Bank of Russian Federation, Department of Research and Information, Moscow.

Central European, 1998. 'Nowhere left to run', October:38–9.

Central European, 1998. 'Investors search for redemption', November:38–9.

Chang, G.H., 1998. *The Chinese Economy in the Asian Financial Crisis: the prospect of the stability of RMB*, HIID Development Discussion Papers No. 669, Harvard Institute for International Development, Cambridge.

Chang, R. and Velasco, A., 1997. *Financial Fragility and the Exchange Rate Regime*, Federal Reserve Bank of Atlanta Working Paper No 97–16.

Chapple, S., 1991. *Financial Liberalisation in New Zealand, 1984–90*, UNCTAD Discussion Paper 35, UNCTAD, New York.

Claessens, S., Dooley, M. and Warner, A., 1995. 'Portfolio capital flows: hot or cold?', *World Bank Economic Review*, 9(1):153–74.

Claessens, S. *et al.* 1999. *Financial Restructuring in East Asia: halfway there?*, Financial Sector Discussion Paper No. 3, World Bank, Washington DC.

Claessens, S., Oks, D. and Polastri, R., 1998. Capital flows to central and eastern Europe and former Soviet Union, Paper prepared for a NBER study, NBER, Cambridge.

Cole, D.C. and Slade, B.F., 1996. *Building a Modern Financial System: the Indonesian experience*, Cambridge University Press, Cambridge.

Cooper, R., 1999. *Should Capital Controls Be Banned?*, Brookings Papers on Economic Activity 99/1, Brookings Institution, Washington, DC.

Corbo, V. and Hernandez, L., 1996. 'Macroeconomic adjustment to capital inflows: lessons from recent Latin American and East Asian experience', *The World Bank Research Observer*, 11(1):61–85.

Corbett, J. and Vines, D., 1999. 'Asian currency and financial crises: lessons from vulnerability, crisis and collapse', *World Economy*, March.

Corden, W.M., 1984. 'Booming sector and Dutch disease economics: survey and consolidation', *Oxford Economic Papers*, 36(3):359–80.

——, 1997. Is there a way out? Are the IMF prescriptions right?, notes from a lecture given in Singapore, 5 August 1998, mimeo.

——, 1999. *The Asian Crisis: is there a way out?*, Institute of Southeast Asian Studies, Singapore.

Cox, H., 1999, 'The market as God', *The Atlantic Monthly*, 1999(March):18–23.

Cukierman, A., Neyapti, B. and Webb, S.B., 1992. 'Measuring the independence of central banks and its effect on policy outcomes', *The World Bank Economic Review*, 6(3):353–98.

Crafts, N., 1998. East Asian growth before and after the crisis, London School of Economics, London (mimeo).

Crouch, H., 1998. 'The Asian economic crisis and democracy', *Public Policy*, 11(3):39–62.

Dadush, U. and Dhareshwar, A.M., 1993. *External Shocks and Financing in Developing and Industrial Countries*, Development Economics, World Bank, Washington DC.

Danaharta (National Asset Management Company, Malaysia), 1999. *Operations Report, 20 June–21 December 1998*, Kuala Lumpur.

De Gregorio, J., Guidotti, P. and Vegh, C., 1994. *Inflation Stabilisation and the Consumption of Durable Goods*, International Monetary Fund, Washington DC.

——, Edwards, S. and Valdes, R.O., 1998. Capital controls in Chile: an assessment, Paper presented to the 1998 IASE-NBER Conference, Center for Applied Economics, Department of Industrial Engineering, Universidad de Chile, Santiago, 3–4 June.

Demirguc-Kunt, A. and Detradiache, E., 1997. *The Determinants of Banking Crises: evidence from industrial and developing countries*, World Bank Policy Research Working Paper 1828, World Bank, Washington DC.

Desai, P., 1998. 'Macroeconomic fragility and exchange rate vulnerability: a cautionary record of transition economies', *Journal of Comparative Economics*, 26(4):621–41.

Dewatripont, M. and Tirole, J., 1994. *The Prudential Regulation of Banks*, MIT Press, Cambridge.

Diamond, D. and Dybvig, P., 1983. 'Bank runs, deposit insurance, and liquidity', *Journal of Political Economy*, 91(3):401–19.

Diaz-Alejandro, C.F., 1985. 'Goodbye financial repression, hello financial crash', *Journal of Development Economics*, 19(September/October):1–24.

Djiwandono, J.S., 2000. 'Bank Indonesia and the recent crisis', *Bulletin of Indonesian Economic Studies*, 36(1):47–72.

Dooley, M.P., 1997. *A Model of Crises in Emerging Markets*, NBER Working Paper No. 6300, NBER, Cambridge.

——, 1998. 'Are capital inflows to developing countries a vote for or against economic policy reforms?', in R. Agenor *et al.* (eds), *The Asian Financial Crisis: causes, contagion and consequences*, Cambridge University Press, Cambridge.

——, 1999. Responses to volatile capital flows: controls, asset liability management, and architecture, University of California, Santa Cruz (mimeo).

Dong, Furen, 1999. Keynote speech, 11th Association for Chinese Economic Studies Annual Conference, University of Melbourne, Melbourne, 15–16 July.

Dornbusch, R., 1997. 'A Thai-Mexico primer', *The International Economy*, September/October:20–3, 55.

—— and Givazzi, F., 1999. Heading off China's financial crisis, unpublished paper, Department of Economics, Massachusetts Institute of Technology, Cambridge.

Durjasz, P. and Kokoszczynski, R., 1998. 'Financial inflows to Poland, 1990–96', *Empirica* 25:217–42.

EBRD (European Bank for Reconstruction and Development), 1995. *Transition Report 1995*, EBRD, London.

——, 1996. *Transition Report 1996*, EBRD, London.

——, 1997. *Transition Report Update 1997*, EBRD, London.

——, 1998. *Transition Report 1998: financial sector in transition*, EBRD, London.

Edwards, S., 1998. 'The Mexican peso crisis: how much did we know? When did we know it?', *The World Economy*, 21(1):1–30.

——, 1999. 'A capital idea? Reconsidering a financial quick fix', *Foreign Affairs*, 78(3):18–22.

Eichengreen, B., 1998a. *Globalizing Capital: a history of the international monetary system*, Princeton University Press, Princeton, New Jersey.

——, 1998b. Exiting from a peg without precipitating a crisis, Alexandre Kafka Lecture, Rio de Janiero, December.

——, 1999a. *Towards a New International Financial Architecture: a practical post-Asia agenda*, Institute for International Economics, Washington DC.

——, 1999b. 'One economy, ready or not', *Foreign Affairs*, 78(3):118–22.

——, Masson, P., Savastano, M. and Sharma, S., 1999. 'Transition strategies and nominal anchors on the road to greater exchange-rate flexibility', *Princeton Essay in International Finance No. 213*, Department of Economics, International Finance Section, Princeton, March.

—— and Mody, A., 1999. *Lending Booms, Reserves and the Sustainability of Short-Term Debt: inferences from the pricing of syndicated bank loans*, NBER Working Paper 7113, NBER, Cambridge.

—— and Rose, A.K., 1999. 'Contagious currency crises: channels of conveyance', in T. Ito and A. Krueger (eds), *Changes in Exchange Rates in Rapidly Developing Countries: theory, practice, and policy issues*, NBER–East Asia Seminar on Economices, Vol. 7, University of Chicago Press, Chicago and London.

—— and Wyplosz, C., 1996. *Contagious Currency Crises*, NBER Working Paper 5681, NBER, Cambridge.

EIU (Economist Intelligence Unit), 1998. *Country Economic Report: Malaysia and Brunei, 3rd Quarter 1998*, EIU, London.

England, P., 1999. The Swedish banking and financial crisis, Paper presented at Oxford Review of Economic Policy Seminar on Financial Crises, Oxford, 9–10 July.

Enoch, C. and Green, J.H. (eds), 1997. *Banking Soundness and Monetary Policy: issues and experiences in the global economy*, International Monetary Fund, Washington DC.

Euromoney, 1996. 'Asia's economies start to slip', 1996(September).

Furman, J. and Stiglitz, J., 1998. Economic crises: evidence and insights from East Asia, Paper prepared for the Brookings Panel on Economic Activity, Washington, DC, November.

Fane, G., 1998. 'Financial regulation', in R. McLeod and R. Garnaut, *East Asia in Crisis*, Routledge, London:Chapter 17.

Faria, L.V., 1997, 'Lições esquecidas', *Conjuntura Econômica*, Fundação Getúlio Vargas, Rio de Janeiro, July 1997, 51(7):24–32.

Feldstein, M., 1998. 'Refocusing the IMF', *Foreign Affairs*, March/April:20–33.

Feridhanusetyawan, T., 1997. 'Survey of recent developments', *Bulletin of Indonesian Economic Studies*, 33(2):3–39.

Fernald, J.G. and Babson, O.D., 1999. *Why Has China Survived the Asia Crisis So Well? What risks remain?*, International Finance Discussion Papers, Board of Governors of the Federal Reserve System, Washington DC.

Fischer, S., 1995. 'Modern central banking', in F. Capie, C. Goodhart and N. Schnadt (eds), *The Future of Central Banking: the tercentenery symposium of the Bank of England*, Cambridge University Press, Cambridge:Chapter 2.

——, 1998a. The Asian Crisis: a view from the IMF, address to the Midwinter Conference of the Bankers' Association for Foreign Trade, 22 January. Available online at http://www.imf.org/external/np/speeches/1998/012298.htm.

——, 1998b. Economic crises and the financial sector, speech to the Conference on Deposit Insurance, Washington, 10 September.

——, 1998c. Opening remarks, presented to the conference on Economic Policy and Equity, International Monetary Fund, Washington DC, June 8–9.

——, 1999. On the need for an international lender of last resort, paper presented to the annual meeting of the American Economic Association. Available online at http://www.imf.org/external/np/speeches/1999/010399.htm.

Folkerts-Landau, D. and Garber, P.M., 1999. 'The new architecture in official doctrine', *Global Markets Monthly*, 2(2), April 1999, (a publication of Global Markets Research, Deutsche Bank AG).

Frankel, J. and Rose, A.K., 1996. 'Currency crashes in emerging markets: an empirical treatment', *Journal of International Economics*, 41(3/4):351–66.

Freixas, X. and Rochet, J-C., 1997. *Microeconomics of Banking*, MIT, London.

Friedman, T.L., 1999. *The Lexus and the Olive Tree*, Farrar, Straus & Giroux, New York.

Fry, M., 1993. *The Fiscal Abuse of Central Banks*, IMF Working Paper 93/58, International Monetary Fund, Washington DC.

Furman, J. and Stiglitz, J., 1998. 'Economic crises: evidence and insights from East Asia', *Brookings Papers on Economic Activity*, 98(2):1–136.

Garber, P.M., 1990. 'Famous first bubbles', *Journal of Economic Perspectives*, 4(2):35–54.

Garnaut, R., 1989. *Australia and Northeast Asian Ascendancy*, Australian Government Publishing Service, Canberra.

——, 1998a. 'The East Asian crisis', in R. McLeod and R. Garnaut (eds), *East Asia in Crisis: from being a miracle to needing one?*, Routledge, London:Chapter 1.

——, 1998b. The way out of the Western Pacific Economic Crisis, address to the Australia-Japan Business Cooperation Committee, Melbourne, 19 October.

——, 1998c. 'The financial crisis', *Asian-Pacific Economic Literature*, 12(1):1–11.

——, 1999. 'Twenty years of economic reform and structural change in the Chinese economy,' in R. Garnaut and L. Song (eds), *China: 20 years' economic reform, achievements and prospects*, Asia Pacific Press, Canberra:1–26.

Garnaut, R. and Huang, Y., 1995. 'China's reform and transition: opportunities and challenges for OECD countries', Report prepared for the Trade Directorate, OECD, Paris.

Gavin, M., 1998. Fiscal policy in emerging market economies, Paper presented at Capital Flows Seminar, Economic Development Institute (World Bank) and University of Maryland, College Park, MD, May 1998.

—— and Hausmann, R., 1995. *Overcoming Volatility in Latin America*, Inter-American Development Bank, Washington DC.

Gilbert, C., Powell, A. and Vines, D., 1999. 'Repositioning the World Bank', *Economic Journal*, November.

Gomulka, S., 1998. 'Managing capital flows in Poland, 1995–98', *Economics of Transition*, 6(2):389–96.

Goskomstat, various years. *Narodnoye Khozyaistvo SSSR* (National Economy of the USSR), Moscow.

——, various years. *Rossiysky Statistichesky Yezhegodnik* (Russian Statistical Yearbook), Moscow.

Grafe, C. and Wyplosz, C., 1997. The real exchange rate in transition economies, Paper presented at the Third Dubrovnik Conference On Transition Economies, Dubrovnik, Croatia, 25–28 June.

Greenspan, A., 1999a. Currency reserves and debt, Remarks before the World Bank Conference on Recent Trends in Reserves Management, Washington DC, 29 April. Available online at www.bog.frb.fed.us.

——, 1999b. Efforts to improve the architecture of the international financial system, Testimony before the Committee on Banking and Financial Services, US House of Representatives, 20 May.

Griffith-Jones, S., 1997. *Causes and Lessons of the Mexican Peso Crisis*, Working Paper No. 132, WIDER/UNU, Helsinki.

Gruen, D., Gray, B. and Stevens, G., 1998. 'Australia', in R.H. McLeod and R. Garnaut (eds), *East Asia in Crisis: from being a miracle to needing one?*, Routledge, London and New York:207–23.

Gruen, D. and Kortian, T., 1996. *Why Does the Australian Dollar Move So Closely with the Terms of Trade?*, Reserve Bank of Australia Research Discussion Paper No. 9601, Sydney.

Guitian, M., 1997. 'Banking soundness: the other dimension of monetary policy', in C. Enoch and J.H. Green (eds), *Banking Soundness and Monetary Policy*, International Monetary Fund, Washington DC:41–62.

Goldfajn, I. and Valdes, R., 1996. *The Aftermath of Appreciations*, NBER Working Paper 5650, NBER, Cambridge.

Government of Malaysia, 1998. *The 1999 Budget Speech*, Ministry of Finance, Kuala Lumpur, 23 October.

Hale, D., 1998. 'The hot money debate', *The International Economy*, November/December:8–12, 66–9.

Halpern L. and Wyplosz, C., 1997. 'Equilibrium exchange rates in transition economies', *IMF Staff Papers*, 44(4):430–61.

Hanke, S., Jonung, L. and Schuler, K., 1993. *Russian Currency and Finance: a currency board approach to reform*, Routledge, New York.

Hausner, J., 1997. The political economy of the socialism's transformation, Paper presented to the UNU/WIDER Project Meeting Transition Strategies, Alternatives and Outcomes, Helsinki, 15–17 May.

Herrera, S., 1999. *Projecting Inflation in Brazil*, World Bank, Washington DC (mimeo).

Hiebert, M., 1999. 'Capital idea?', *Far Eastern Economic Review*, 162(26):55.

Hoenig, T.M., 1998. 'The international community's response to the Asian financial crisis', *Federal Reserve Bank of Kansas City Economic Review*, 83(2):5–7.

Hölscher, J., 1997. 'Economic dynamism in transition economies: lessons from Germany', *Communist Economies and Economic Transformation*, 9(2):173–81.

Huang, Y., 1999. *The Last Steps Crossing the River: Chinese reforms in the middle of the East Asian financial crisis*, Graduate School of Business, Columbia University, New York (mimeo).

—— and Yang, Y., 1998. 'China's financial fragility and policy responses', *Asian Pacific Economic Literature*, 12(2):1–9.

Illarionov, A., 1998. 'How the Russian financial crisis was organized', *Voprosy Ekonomiky*, 11:17–37 and 12:62–79 (in Russian).

Ingram, J.C., 1971. *Economic Change in Thailand: 1850–1970*, Stanford University Press, Stanford, California.

IMF (International Monetary Fund), 1996a. *Partnership for Sustainable Global Growth*, Interim Committee Declaration, IMF, Washington DC, 29 September.

——, 1996b. *International Financial Statistics*, IMF, Washington DC.

——, 1997a. *Exchange Arrangements and Exchange Restrictions Annual Report 1997*, IMF, Washington DC.

——, 1997b. *World Economic Outlook*, IMF, Washington DC.

——, 1999a. *IMF-Supported Programs in Indonesia, Korea and Thailand: a preliminary assessment*, IMF, Washington DC.

——, 1999b. *Communiqué of the Interim Committee of the Board of Governors of the International Monetary Fund*, Washington DC, 26 September (mimeo).

——, 1999c. External Evaluation of IMF Surveillance: Report by a Group of Independent Experts, IMF, Washington DC.

Institute of Economics, Chinese Academy of Social Sciences, 1998. 'Aggregate trend, financial risk and external shocks: analyses of the current Chinese macroeconomic situation', *Economic Research Journal [Jingji Yanjiu]*, 3(March 1998):3–14.

Instituto Brasileiro de Geografia e Estatística, 1997. *Sistema Financeiro, Uma Análise a Partir das Contas Nacionais, 1990–1995*, IBGE, Rio de Janeiro.

Irwin, G. and Vines, D., 1999. 'A Krugman-Dooley-Sachs third generation model of the Asian Financial Crisis', Oxford University, Oxford (mimeo).

——, 2000a. *Government Guarantees, Investment, and Vulnerability to Financial Crisis*, Centre for Economic Policy Research Discussion Paper.

——, 2000b. 'Lessons from Asia on avoiding financial crisis: the preconditions for capital account liberalisation', in C. Mayer (ed.), *Financial Instability*, Oxford University Press.

Jayasankaran, S., 1997. 'Malaysia: hit the breaks', *Far Eastern Economic Review*, 18(December): 14–15.

Jomo, K.S., 1998. 'Malaysia: from miracle to debacle', in S.K. Jomo (ed.), *Tigers in Trouble: financial governance, liberalisation and crises in East Asia*, Zed Books Ltd., New York:181–98.

Josephson, M., 1934. *The Robber Barons: the great American capitalists 1861–1901*, Harcourt, Brace and Company, New York.

Kaminski, B., 1997. 'The role of foreign direct investment and trade policies in Poland's accession to the European Union', in *Poland CEM: Strategies and Policy Options on the Road to European Union Membership*, World Bank, Washington DC.

Kaminsky, G.L. and Reinhart, C., 1997. *The Twin-Crises: the causes of banking and balance of payments problems*, Working Papers in International Economics 37, Center for International Economics, University of Maryland, College Park.

Kemmerer, E.W., 1910. *Seasonal variations in the relative demand for money and capital in the United States*, 61st Cong. 2d sess. S.Doc. 588.

Kenward, L.R., 1999a. 'Assessing vulnerability to financial crisis: evidence from Indonesia', *Bulletin of Indonesian Economic Studies*, 35(3):71–95.

——, 1999b. 'What has been happening at Bank Indonesia?', *Bulletin of Indonesian Economic Studies*, 35(1):121–7.

Khoman, S., 1993. 'Education', in P.G. Warr (ed.), *The Thai Economy in Transition*, Cambridge University Press, Cambridge.

Kim, D. and Santomero, A., 1988. 'Risk in banking and capital regulation', *Journal of Finance*, 43(5):1219–33.

Kochhar, K., Dicks-Mireaux, L., Horvath, B., Mecagni, M., Offerdal, E. and Zhou, J., 1996. *Thailand: the road to sustained growth*, Occasional Paper No. 146, IMF, Washington DC.

Kolodko, G.W., 1989. *Reform, Stabilisation Policies and Economic Adjustment in Poland*, WIDER Working Papers 51, WIDER/UNU, Helsinki.

——, 1991. 'Inflation stabilisation in Poland: a year after', *Rivista di Politica Economica*, 6(June):289–330.

——, 1992. *From Output Collapse to Sustainable Growth in Transition Economies: the fiscal implications*, IMF, Washington DC.

——, 1993. 'A strategy for economic transformation in eastern Europe', *Moct-Most*, 4(1):1–25.

——, 1996. *Poland 2000: the new economic strategy*, Poltext, Warsaw.

——, 1998. 'A plan for Russia', *The Harriman Review, Special Issue: the Russian economy in crisis*, December:24–7.

——, 1999a. *From Shock to Therapy: the political economy of post-socialist transformation*, Oxford University Press, Oxford.

——, 1999b. *Ten Years of Postsocialist Transition: the lessons for policy reforms*, Working Paper 2035, World Bank, Washington DC.

—— and Nuti, D.M., 1997. The Polish Alternative: old myths, hard facts and new strategies in the successful transformation of the Polish economy, WIDER Research for Action 33, WIDER/UNU, Helsinki.

Krugman, P., 1979. 'A model of balance of payments crises', *Journal of Money, Credit, and Banking*, 11(3):311–25.

——, 1997. Currency crises, Paper prepared for NBER conference, WHERE, October 1997. Available online at http://web.mit.edu/krugman/www/crises.html

——, 1998a. 'America the boastful', *Foreign Affairs*, 77(3):32–45.

——, 1998b. 'Saving Asia: it's time to get radical', *Fortune*, 138(5):74–80.

——, 1998c. What happened to Asia? Available online at http://web.mit.edu/krugman/www/DISINTER.html.

——, 1998d. The eternal triangle: explaining international financial perplexity, available online at http://web.mit.edu/krugman/www/triangle.html.

——, 1998e. The other bear market: the run on Russia. Available online at http://www.slate.com/Dismal/98-09-10/Dismal.asp.

——, 1999a. 'Balance sheets, the transfer problem, and financial crises'. Available online at http://web.mit.edu/krugman/www/.

——, 1999b. 'Analytical afterthoughts on the Asia Crisis'. Available online at http://web.mit.edu/krugman/www/.

——, 1999c. *The Return of Depression Economics*, Norton and Company, New York.

Kwack, S.Y., 1994. 'The rate of return on capital in the United States, Japan, and Korea, 1972–1990', in S.Y. Kwack (ed.), *Korea Economy at a Crossroad*, Praeger, Westport, Connecticut.

Lane, T., Ghosh, A., Hamann, J., Phillips, S., Schulze-Ghattas, M. and Tsikata, T., 1999. *IMF-Supported Programmes in Indonesia, Korea and Thailand: a preliminary assessment*, Occasional Paper No. 178, IMF, Washington DC.

Lardy, N.R., 1998a. 'China and the Asian contagion', *Foreign Affairs*, 77(4):78–88.

——, 1998b. *China's Unfinished Economic Revolution*, Brookings Institution and Institute for International Economics, Washington DC.

Lim, L., 1999. Malaysia's response to the Asian financial crisis, Statement before the Subcommittee on Asia and the Pacific Committee on International Relations, US House of Representatives. Available online at http://www.house.gov/international_relations.

Lindgren, C-J. *et al.*, 1996. *Bank Soundness and Macroeconomic Policy*, IMF, Washington DC.

Manorungsan, S., 1989. *Economic Development of Thailand, 1850–1950*, Institute of Asian Studies Monograph No. 42, Chulalongkorn University, Bangkok.

Mau, V., 1998. 'Political nature and lessons of financial crisis', *Voprosy Economiky*, 1998(11):45–64 (in Russian).

Mazumdar, S.C., 1997. 'Regulatory monitoring, closure costs and bank moral hazard behavior', *Journal of Regulatory Economics*, 12:267–89.

McCawley, P., 1976. 'Survey of recent developments', *Bulletin of Indonesian Economic Studies*, 12(1):1–43.

McKibbin, W., 1998. 'Internationally mobile capital and the global economy', in R. McLeod and R. Garnaut (eds), *East Asia in Crisis: from being a miracle to needing one?*, Routledge, London and New York:227–44.

—— and Martin, W., 1998. *The East Asian Crisis: investigating causes and policy responses*, Working Paper in Trade and Development No. 98/6, Economics Department, Research School of Pacific and Asian Studies, The Australian National University and Brookings Discussion Paper in International Economics No. 142, The Brookings Institution, Washington DC.

McLeod, R., 1997a. 'Some comments on the rupiah 'crisis'', in H. Hill and T.K. Wie (eds), *Indonesia's Technological Challenge*, Institute of Southeast Asian Studies, Singapore:96–103.

——, 1997b. 'Policy conflicts in Indonesia: the impact of the current account deficit target on growth, equity and stability', *ASEAN Economic Bulletin*, 14(1):32–45.

——, 1998a. 'Indonesia', in R. McLeod and R. Garnaut (eds), *East Asia in Crisis: from being a miracle to needing one?*, Routledge, London and New York:31–48.

——, 1998b. 'The new era of financial fragility', in R. McLeod and R. Garnaut (eds), *East Asia in Crisis: From being a miracle to needing one?*, Routledge, London and New York:333–51.

——, 1999a. 'Indonesia's crisis and future prospects', in K.D. Jackson (ed.), *Asian Contagion: the causes and consequences of a financial crisis*, Westview Press, Boulder:209–40.

——, 1999b. 'Crisis-driven changes to the banking laws and regulations', *Bulletin of Indonesian Economic Studies*, 35(2):147–54.

—— and Garnaut, R. (eds), 1998. *East Asia in Crisis: from being a miracle to needing one?*, Routledge, London and New York.

McKinnon, R.I., 1973. *Money and Capital in Economic Development*, Brookings Institution, Washington DC.

—— and Huw Pill, 1997. 'Credible economic liberalisations and overborrowing', *American Economic Review*, 87(2):189–93.

Merrill Lynch & Company, 1999. Malaysia: relaxation of capital controls, Kuala Lumpur, 5 and 9 February.

Merton, R., 1977. 'An analytic derivation of the cost of deposit insurance and loan guarantees', *Journal of Banking and Finance*, 1(1):3–11.

MIER (Malaysian Institute of Economic Research), 1999. *The Impact of Currency Control Measures on Business Operation*, MIER, Kuala Lumpur.

Milesi-Ferreti, G.M. and Razin, A., 1996. 'Current account sustainability', *International Journal of Finance and Economics*, 1(3).

Miller, M. and Zhang, L., 1999. 'Creditor panic, asset bubbles and sharks: three views of the Asian crisis', in D. Dasgupta, U. Dadush and M. Uzan (eds), *The Aftermath of the Asian Crisis*, Edward Elgar, London.

Miron, J.A., 1986. 'Financial panics, the seasonality of the nominal interest rate, and the founding of the Fed', *American Economic Review*, 76(1):125–40.

Montes, M., 1997. Vietnam: is there a socialist road to the market?, Paper presented to the UNU/WIDER Project Meeting Transition Strategies, Alternatives and Outcomes, Helsinki, 15–17 May.

——, 1998. *Currency Crisis in Southeast Asia* (updated edition), Institute of Southeast Asian Studies, Singapore.

—— and Popov, V., 1999. *The Asian Crisis Turns Global*, Institute of Southeast Asian Studies, Singapore.

Moody's Investor Service, 1998. Ratings and rating actions, sovereign ceilings for foreign-currency ratings, 18 February. Available online at www.moodys.com.

Moon, H.P. and Yoo, K.J., 1999. *Perspectives on Unemployment and Welfare Policy*, KDI Policy Forum, Korea Development Institute, Seoul (in Korean).

Naim, M., 1995. 'Mexico's larger story', *Foreign Policy*, (June).

Naughton, B., 1997. 'Economic reform in China: macroeconomic and overall performance', in D. Lee (ed.), *The System Transformation of the Transition Economies: Europe, Asia and North Korea*, Yonsei University Press, Seoul:27–64.

NEAC (National Economic Action Council), 1998. *National Economic Recovery Plan: agenda for action*, Prime Minister's Department, Kuala Lumpur.

——, 1999. Prof. Merton is wrong. Available online at http://neac.gov.my.

Nekipelov, A., 1998. 'The nature of Russia's economic catastrophe: an alternative diagnosis', *Transition: the newsletter about reforming economies*, October 1998.

Nellor, D.C., 1998. 'The role of the International Monetary Fund', in R. McLeod and R. Garnaut, *East Asia in Crisis: from being a miracle to needing one?*, Routledge, London:Chapter 15.

NERI (National Economy Research Institute), 1998. *China Macroeconomic Analysis 1998:3Q issue*, Beijing.

North, D.C., 1997. *The Contribution of the New Institutional Economics to an Understanding of the Transition Problem*, WIDER Annual Lectures 1, WIDER/UNU, Helsinki.

Nuti, D.M., 1990. 'Crisis, reform and stabilisation in central eastern Europe: prospects and

Western response', in *La Grande Europa, La Nuova Europa: Opportunita e Rischi*, Monti Dei Paschi Di Sienna, Sienna.

——, 1992. *Lessons from Stabilisation and Reform in Central Eastern Europe*, CEC Working Papers 92, Council of the European Community, Brussels.

——, 1996. Exchange rate and monetary policy in Poland 1994–96, or the case for privatising the National Bank of Poland, Paper presented to the UNU/WIDER Project Meeting, Transition Strategies, Alternatives and Outcomes, Helsinki, 15–17 May.

Obstfeld, M., 1995. 'International capital mobility in the 1990s', in P. Kenen (ed.), *Understanding Interdependence: the macroeconomics of the open economy*, Princeton University Press, Princeton, New Jersey.

OECD (Organisation for Economic Cooperation and Development), 1996. *Czechoslovakia 1996*, OECD Economic Surveys, OECD, Paris.

Okuno-Fujiwara, M., Postlewaite, A. and Roberts, J., 1980. 'Oligopoly and competition in large markets', *American Economic Review*, 70(1):22–31.

Orlowski, W.M. and Szczepanska-Maciejuk, O., 1998. *Determinants of Financial Flows in the EU and the Associated States of Central and Eastern Europe and the Implications for Enlargement: the case of Poland* (draft), Independent Center for Economic Studies, Lody.

Pardede, R., 1999. 'Survey of recent developments', *Bulletin of Indonesian Economic Studies*, 35(2):3–39.

Park, Y.C. and Song, C.Y., 1998. The East Asian financial crisis: a year later, Paper presented at the conference on Financial Crisis, Market Economy, and the Government, Center for International Research on the Japanese Economy, University of Tokyo, Tokyo, 7–8 September.

Patinkin, D., 1993. 'Israel's stabilisation program of 1985, or some simple truths of monetary theory', *Journal of Economic Perspectives*, 7(2):103–28.

Perkins, D., 1986. *China: the next giant?*, University of Washington Press, Seattle.

PlanEcon, 1998a. *Review and Outlook for the Former Soviet Union*, PlanEcon Inc., Washington DC.

——, 1998b. *Review and Outlook for Eastern Europe*, PlanEcon Inc., Washington DC.

——, *PlanEcon* (various issues), PlanEcon Inc., Washington DC.

Polanyi, K., 1944. *The Great Transformation*, Octagon Books, New York.

Popov, V., 1996a. 'Inflation during transition: is Russia's case special?', *Acta Slavica Iaponica*, Tomus XIV:59–75.

——, 1996b. *A Russian Puzzle: what makes Russian economic transformation a special case*, WIDER/ UNU RFA 29, Helsinki.

——, 1997. 'Lessons from currency crisis in South East Asia', *Voprosy Ekonomiky*, 1997(12):94–106 (in Russian).

——, 1998a. 'Investment in transition economies: factors of change and implications for performance', *Journal of East-West Business*, 4(1/2):47–98.

——, 1998b. 'Preparing Russian economy for the world market integration', in A. Fernandez Jilberto and A. Mommen (eds), *Regionalisation and Globalisation in the Modern World Economy*, Routledge, London:86–127.

——, 1998c. 'Economic outcomes of transformation: the impact of initial conditions and economic policy', *Voprosy Ekonomiky*, 1998(7):42–64 (in Russian).

——, 1998d. 'Institutional capacity is more important than the speed of reforms', *Voprosy Ekonomiky*, 1998(8):56–70 (in Russian).

——, 1998e. 'Will Russia achieve fast economic growth?', *Communist Economies and Economic Transformation*, 1998(4):421–49.

——, 1999a. 'The financial system in Russia as compared to other transition economies: the Anglo–American versus the German–Japanese model', *Comparative Economic Studies*, 41(1):1–42.

——, 1999b. 'Russia's financial collapse', *NIRA Review*, 6(1):3–7.

——, 1999c. 'Exchange rates in developing and transition economies', *EKO*, 1999(5):40–52 (in Russian).

——, 1999d. 'Lessons from the currency crises in Russia and in other countries', *Voprosy Ekonomiky*, 1999(6):100–22 (in Russian).

——, 2000. 'Shock therapy versus gradualism: the end of the debate (explaining the magnitude of the transformational recession)', *Comparative Economic Studies*, 42(1):1–57.

Portes, R. and Vines, D., 1997. *Coping with International Capital Flows*, Commonwealth Secretariat, London.

Poznanski, K., 1993. 'Poland's transition to capitalism: shock and therapy', in K. Poznanski (ed.), *Stabilisation and Privatisation in Poland*, Kluwer Academic Publishers, Boston.

——, 1996. *Poland's Protracted Transition: institutional change and economic growth*, Cambridge University Press, Cambridge.

Pu, Y., 1998. China's new challenge: deflation, Special to ChinaOnline. Available online at http://www.chinaonline.com/Csubs/econ_news/en_c81102Pu.asp.

Pyo, H.K., 1993. 'The transition in the political economy of South Korean development', *Journal of Northeast Asian Studies*, 12(4):74–87.

——, 1994. 'Optimal growth rate: theory and estimation', in H.K. Pyo (ed.), *Economic Development in Korea: assessments and prospects*, Seoul National University Press, Seoul:1–24 (in Korean).

——, 1996. Sustainability of export growth in East and Southeast Asia, paper presented at Asian Development Outlook conference, Asian Development Bank, Manila, November.

——, 1997. Is export-led growth in South Korea sustainable?, Paper presented at seminar on East Asia, East Asian Institute, Columbia University, New York and Asia Society, Washington DC, November.

——, 1999a. 'The financial crisis in Korea: anatomy and policy imperatives', in K.D. Jackson (ed.), *Asian Contagion: the causes and consequences of a financial crisis*, Westview, Boulder:151–69.

——, 1999b. The financial crisis in Korea and its aftermath: a political-economic perspective, paper presented at the International Capital Mobility and Domestic Economic Stability Conference hosted by the Reinventing Bretton Woods Committee, The World Bank and The Australian National University, Canberra, 13–16 July.

——, 2000. 'Excess competition, moral hazard, and industrial trauma in Korea (1997–1998)', in D. Dasgupta, U. Dadush and M. Uzan (eds), *The Aftermath of the Asian Crisis*, Edward Elgar, New York.

—— and Ahn, S., 1998. *The Differential Impacts of Exchange Rate Variations on Investment in Manufacturing by Industries: Korea (1985–1996)*, Seoul National University, Seoul.

——, Kim, K.H. and Cheong, I., 1996. 'Foreign import restrictions, WTO commitments, and welfare effects: the case of Republic of Korea', *Asian Development Review*, 14(2):21–43.

—— and Nam, K.H., 1999. *A Test of Convergence Hypothesis by Rates of Return: Evidence from OECD countries*, Discussion Paper Series CIRJE-F-51, Faculty of Economics, University of Tokyo, Tokyo.

Radelet, S. and Sachs, J., 1998a. *On the Onset of East Asian Financial Crisis*, Harvard Institute for International Development, Cambridge.

—— and Sachs, J., 1998b. 'The East Asian financial crisis: Diagnosis, remedies, prospects', *Brookings Papers on Economic Activity* 1:1–89.

Research Group for China's Financial System Reform, 1997. 'A tracking study of the Chinese financial system reform', *Reform [Gaige]*, 3:64–75 and 4:83–98.

Reserve Bank of Australia, 1999a. The impact of hedge funds on financial markets, paper submitted to House of Representatives Standing Committee on Economics, Finance and Public Administration's Inquiry into the International Financial Markets Effects on Government Policy, June. Available online at http://www.rba.gov.au.

——, 1999b. Hedge funds, financial stability and market integrity, Paper submitted to House of Representatives Standing Committee on Economics, Finance and Public Administration's Inquiry into the International Financial Markets Effects on Government Policy, June. Available online at http://www.rba.gov.au.

Robinson, D., Byeon, Y. and Teja, R., 1991. *Thailand: adjusting to success, current policy issues*, Occasional Paper No. 85, IMF, Washington DC.

Rochet, J.C., 1992. 'Capital requirements and the behaviour of the commercial banks', *European Economic Review*, 36(5):1137–70.

Rodrik, D., 1998. 'Who needs capital-account convertibility?', Symposium paper in Princeton Essays in International Finance, No. 207.

—— and Velasco, A., 1999. Short-term capital flows. Available online at http://www.ksg.harvard.edu/rodrik/papers.html.

Rosati, D., 1994. 'Output decline during transition from plan to market', *Economics of Transition*, 2(4):419–42.

Russian Economic Trends, various years. RECEP, Moscow, monthly issues.

Russian Economy in 1998, 1999. Trends and Prospects, Institute of Economics of Transition, 20(March) (in Russian).

Russian European Centre for Economic Policy (various years). *Russian Economic Trends*, Moscow.

Sachs, J., 1994. Russia's struggle with stabilisation: conceptual issues and evidence, Paper prepared for the World Bank's Annual Conference on Development Economics, Washington DC, April 28–29.

——, 1995a. *Why Russia Has Failed to Stabilise*, Working Paper No. 103, Stockholm Institute of East European Economics, Stockholm.

——, 1995b. 'Do we need a lender of last resort?', Frank D. Graham Lecture, Princeton University, Princeton, April.

——, Tornell, A. and Velasco, A., 1996. 'Financial crises in emerging markets: the lessons from 1995', *Brookings Papers in Economic Activity*, 1996(1):147–215.

Santiprabhob, V., 1997. *Bank Soundness and Currency Board Arrangements: issues and experience*, IMF Paper on Policy Analysis and Assessment, IMF, Washington DC.

Sargent, T. and Wallace, N., 1986. 'Some unpleasant monetarist arithmetic', in T. Sargent (ed.), *Rational Expectations and Inflation*, Harper and Row, New York.

Schadler, S., Carkovic, M., Bennett, A. and Kahn, R., 1993. *Recent Experiences with Surges in Capital Inflows*, IMF Occasional Paper 103, IMF, Washington DC.

Scherer, F.M., 1980. *Industrial Market Structure and Economic Performance* (2nd edition), Rand McNally, Chicago.

Searle, P., 1999. *The Riddle of Malaysian Capitalism: rent-seekers or real capitalists?*, Allen & Unwin, Sydney.

Shaw, E.S., 1973. *Financial Deepening in Economic Development*, Oxford University Press, New York.

Shmelev, N., 1998. 'The crisis inside the crisis', *Voprosy Ekonomiky*, 1998(10):4–17.

—— and Popov, V., 1989. *The Turning Point: revitalizing the Soviet economy*, Doubleday, New York.

Smith, H., 1998. 'Korea', in R. McLeod and R. Garnaut, *East Asia in Crisis: from being a miracle to needing one?*, Routledge, London:65–84.

Smorodinskaya, N., 1998. 'Capital flight in theory and in practice: the analysis of the Russian situation', *Banking Services*, 1998(9):5–20 (in Russian).

Sobol, D.M., 1996. *Central and Eastern Europe: financial markets and private capital flows*, Federal Reserve Bank of New York Working Paper No. 9626, Federal Reserve Bank of New York, New York.

Song, L., 1998. 'China', in R. McLeod and R. Garnaut (eds), *East Asia in Crisis: from being a miracle to needing one?*, Routledge, London and New York:105–19.

Soros, G., 1997. 'The capitalist threat', *The Atlantic Monthly*, February.

——, 1998. *The Crisis of Global Capitalism*, Little, Brown and Company, London.

State Statistical Bureau of China, 1999. *Statistical Report of National Economy and Social Development in 1998*, China Statistical Publishing House, Beijing.

Stern, N., 1996. The transition in Eastern Europe and the former Soviet Union: some strategic lessons from the experience of 25 countries over six years, Paper presented to the OECD/CCET Colloquium, Paris, 29–30 May.

—— and Stiglitz, J.E., 1997. A Framework for a Development Strategy in a Market Economy: objectives, scope, institutions and instruments, EBRD Working Paper 20, EBRD, London.

Stiglitz, J.E., 1981. 'Potential competition may reduce welfare', *American Economic Review*, 71(2):184–9.

——, 1998a. *More Instruments and Broader Goals: moving toward the post-Washington consensus*, WIDER Annual Lectures 2, WIDER/UNU, Helsinki, January.

——, 1998b. Economic science, economic policy, and economic advice, Paper presented to the Annual World Bank Conference on Development Economics, *Knowledge for Development*, The World Bank, Washington DC, 20–21 April.

——, 1998c. Macroeconomic Dimensions of the East Asian Crisis, in Centre for Economic Policy Research.

——, 1998d. Sound finance and sustainable development in Asia, Keynote address to the Asia Development Forum, Manila, 12 March. Available online at http://www.worldbank.org/html/extdr/extme/jssp031298.htm.

——, 1999a. 'Must currency crises be this frequent and this painful?', in P. Agenor *et al.* (eds), *The Asian Crises: causes, contagion and consequences*, Cambridge University Press, Cambridge.

——, 1999b. Whither reform? Ten years of transition, Paper presented to the Annual World Bank Conference on Development Economics, World Bank, Washington DC, 28–30 April.

Suzumura, K. and Kiyono, K., 1987. 'Entry barriers and economic welfare', *Review of Economic Studies*, 54(January):157–67.

Szapáry, G. and Jakab, Z., 1998. 'Exchange rate policy in transition economies: the case of Hungary', *Journal of Comparative Economics*, 26(4):691–717.

—— and Darvas, Z., 2000. 'Financial Contagion in Five Small Open Economies: does the exchange rate regime really matter?', *International Finance*, 3(1):25–51.

UNCTAD (United Nations Conference on Trade and Development), 1998. *World Investment Report: trends and determinants*, United Nations, New York and Geneva.

——, 1999. *World Economic Situation and Prospects for 1999*, United Nations, New York and Geneva.

Von Furstenberg, G.M. and Ulan, M.K., 1998. 'Courage and conviction: Chile's Governor Zahler', in G.M. Von Furstenberg and M.K. Ulan (eds), *Learning from the World's Best Central Bankers*, Kluwer Academic Publishers, Boston:39–74.

Walters, A., 1990. *Sterling in Danger: the economic consequences of pegged exchange rates*, Fontana/Collins, London.

Warr, P.G., 1986. 'Indonesia's other Dutch disease: economic effects of the petroleum boom', in J.P. Neary and S. van Wijnbergen (eds), *Natural Resources and the Macroeconomy*, Basil Blackwell, Oxford:288–320.

——, 1993. 'The Thai economy', in P.G. Warr (ed.), *The Thai Economy in Transition*, Cambridge University Press, Cambridge:1–80.

—— and Nidhiprabha, B., 1996. *Thailand's Macroeconomic Miracle: stable adjustment and sustained growth*, World Bank and Oxford University Press, Washington DC and Kuala Lumpur.

——, 1998. 'Thailand', in R. McLeod and R. Garnaut (eds), *East Asia in Crisis: from being a miracle to needing one?*, Routledge, London:49–65.

Williamson, J., 1990. 'What Washington means by policy reform', in J. Williamson (ed.), *Latin American Adjustment: how much has happened?*, Institute for International Economics, Washington DC.

——, 1993. 'A cost-benefit analysis of capital account liberalisation', in H. Reisen and B. Fischer (eds), *Financial Opening: policy issues and experiences in developing countries*, OECD, Paris:25–34.

——, 1994. 'In search for a manual for technopols', in J. Williamson (ed.), *The Political Economy of Policy Reform*, IIE, Washington DC.

——, 1997. 'The Washington consensus revisited', in L. Emmerij (ed.), *Economic and Social Development into the XXI Century*, Inter-American Development Bank, Washington, DC.

——, 2000. *Filling the Void: Viable Exchange Rate Regimes for East Asia*, Institute for International Economics, Washington DC.

—— and Mahar, M., 1998. *A Survey of Financial Liberalisation*, Essays in International Finance No. 211, International Finance Section, Princeton University, Princeton.

Woo, W.T., 1999. China's battle for stability amidst the regional crisis, Paper presented at the Davos Conference of World Economic Forum, January.

World Bank, 1993. *Global Economic Prospects and the Developing Countries 1993*, World Bank, Washington DC.

——, 1994. *Global Economic Prospects and the Developing Countries 1994*, World Bank, Washington DC.

——, 1996a. *Global Economic Prospects and the Developing Countries 1996*, World Bank, Washington DC.

——, 1996b. *Managing Capital Flows in East Asia*, World Bank, Washington DC.

——, 1996c. *World Development Report 1996: from plan to market*, World Bank, Washington DC.

——, 1997a. *World Development Report 1997: the state in a changing world*, World Bank, Washington DC.

——, 1997b. *World Development Indicators 1997*, World Bank, Washington DC.

——, 1997c. *Private Capital Flows to Developing Countries: the road to financial integration*, World Bank, Washington DC.

——, 1998a. *World Development Indicators 1998*, World Bank, Washington DC.

——, 1998b. *World Development Report 1998*, World Bank, Washington DC.

——, 1999a. *Global Economic Prospects and the Developing Countries 1998/99: beyond financial crises*, World Bank, Washington DC.

——, 1999b. *Global Development Finance 1999*, World Bank, Washington DC.

——, 1999c. *World Development Indicators*, World Bank, Washington DC.

——, 2000. *Global Development Finance 2000*, World Bank, Washington DC.

Yap, M.M-C., 1999. Financial crisis in Malaysia: adjustment through unorthodox policy, Paper presented in the Malaysia Forum, Department of Economics, Research School of Pacific and Asian Studies, The Australian National University, Canberra, 24 June.

Yasin, Y., 1999. Defeat or retreat? (Russian reforms and financial crisis), Report to the Economic Club, Moscow, January (in Russian).

Yusof, Z.A., Hussein, A.A., Alowi, I., Sing, L.C. and Singh, S., 1994. 'Financial reforms in Malaysia', in G. Caprio, I. Atias and J.A. Hanson (eds), *Financial Reform: theory and evidence*, Cambridge University Press, Cambridge:276–322.

Zefferys, N., 1999. Doing business in Malaysia: an American ground level perspective, Presentation to foreign journalists visiting Malaysia in his capacity as the President of the American Malaysian Chamber of Commerce. Available online at www.neac.gov.my.

Zettermeyer, J. and Citrin, D., 1995. Stabilisation: fixed versus flexible exchange rates, in *Policy Experiences and Issues in the Baltics, Russian and Other Countries of the Former Soviet Union*, IMF, Washington DC.

Zuckerman, M.B., 1998. 'A second American century', *Foreign Affairs*, 77(3):18–31.

Index

Page numbers in *italics* refer to figures or tables